A
DANGEROUS
WOMAN

A
DANGEROUS
WOMAN

American Beauty,
Noted Philanthropist,
Nazi Collaborator:
The Life of Florence Gould

SUSAN RONALD

ST. MARTIN'S PRESS  NEW YORK

www.stmartins.com

Designed by Meryl Sussman Levavi

The Library of Congress Cataloging-in-Publication Data is available upon request.

ISBN 978-1-250-09221-2 (hardcover)
ISBN 978-1-250-09222-9 (ebook)

Our books may be purchased in bulk for promotional, educational, or business use. Please contact your local bookseller or the Macmillan Corporate and Premium Sales Department at 1-800-221-7945, extension 5442, or by email at MacmillanSpecialMarkets@macmillan.com.

First Edition: February 2018

1 3 5 7 9 10 8 6 4 2

For Jonas, August, Isabeau, and Freya,

may you be alert to danger in its many guises.

CONTENTS

PART I · THE ASPIRING CHANTEUSE

1. San Francisco   3
2. From Fire to Flood and Death   14
3. *La Parisienne*   27
4. War and the Boy Next Door   37
5. Young Mrs. Heynemann   50
6. Home Again, War, and Folies   58
7. The Man They Call "Franck"   68

PART II · THE CRAZY YEARS

8. Taming All Those Monsters   87
9. Leaving the Perfumed Air of Bohemia   100
10. Careless People   106
11. An Amusing Intermezzo for Millionaires   118
12. Taking Stock   130
13. The Monégasque Feud Fit for a Prince   140
14. Hollywood Calling   152
15. The Phoenix Rises   159

16. Scandal, America, and Separate Lives   168

17. Dark Horizons   178

PART III · DARKNESS FALLS

18. Fifth Columnists and Fellow Travelers   191

19. Fall of France   202

20. Ludwig   213

21. The "Anything Goes" Occupation   219

22. In the Garden of Earthly Delights   230

23. The Occupation, 1942–1943   238

24. Florence the Banker   248

25. Liberation and Treason   261

PART IV · STILL A GOULD

26. No Safe Havens   279

27. Paper Clips and Friends Cast Long Shadows   284

28. A Fortune to Give Away   296

29. Queen of the Riviera   307

Epilogue   315

Author's Note and Acknowledgments   321

Cast of Characters   325

Glossary   337

Notes   339

Selected Bibliography   365

Index   371

PART ONE

THE ASPIRING CHANTEUSE

∽

An opera begins long before the curtain goes up
and ends long after it has come down. It starts in my
imagination, it becomes my life, and it stays part of
my life long after I've left the opera house.

—*Maria Callas*

I

◦◦◦

SAN FRANCISCO

Never let the facts get in the way of a good story.
—MARK TWAIN

"I RAN FOR MY LIFE," FLORENCE OFTEN RECALLED WITH A SHUD-
der, "through two great walls of flames toward the bay." She was only
ten years old at the time.

Years later, as she recoiled from the memory, her trembling voice
seemed to relive her absolute terror. Still, the actress in her had learned
over many decades that her oft-repeated tale required a meaningful
pause at this point. She had learned, too, that timing was essential to the
telling of any good story. So, here, Florence would stop and touch her elegant jeweled fingers to the perfect, outsized, three-tiered pearl necklace
caressing her throat. She held her audience, one by one, spellbound with
her fabulous green eyes. Florence understood instinctively that beauty,
as well as money, was power; and she had both in abundance.

The date she remembered was Wednesday, April 18, 1906. The place,
San Francisco. The time, 5:12 a.m. For those friends who hadn't heard
her story before, Florence willingly retold how she had survived the great
and terrifying San Francisco earthquake, embellishing the many death-
defying details they expected to hear. Her friends in France—and particularly in Paris—had never lived through such a seismic cataclysm. Oh, there

had been wars—cannonades heard across France's northern plains, death beyond imagining in the Great War—and of course the Nazi occupation. Florence had lived through these man-made upheavals in France, too, but the horror she described was the death of an entire city within minutes. Even the survivors of the Paris floods of 1910 could not comprehend such an instantaneous tear in the fabric of tens of thousands of lives. Only with the onset of the nuclear age could those who hadn't lived through a large earthquake begin to understand its swift devastation.

Florence's first great badge of courage *was* the San Francisco earthquake, not that she needed any medal in her long and wildly lived life. Perhaps it made her feel more American to tell tall tales no one else could imagine. It certainly set her apart, like her American-tinged accent that she cultivated, despite a lifetime lived in France speaking French. Being an American somehow made her grander, more significant—and Florence craved significance. That and her lust for phenomenal wealth and her need to be loved were the driving forces behind who she was, and what she did. During her eighty-seven years of life, she would achieve all three ambitions. So what if the truth was often bent to her will? At the end of the day, she had the means to bend it, and her entourage came to expect and desire whatever enchantment she devised for their pleasure.

So, who was Florence? Born Florence Juliette Antoinette Lacaze in San Francisco on July 1, 1895, she would die in Cannes, France, in 1983 as Florence Gould. In the intervening period, she was on the guest lists of Her Serene Highness Princess Grace of Monaco, French and American politicians, millionaires, and movie stars. She rubbed shoulders with the famous, artists, and seedy underworld characters who haunted every casino in Europe. Her life would become a rags-to-riches dream, if not a fairy tale, and she would host the glitterati, the literati, and those who preferred to live their lives in the shadows. Her story fires the imagination in a life writ large. From the time of the San Francisco earthquake, she seemed to be at the heart of some of the most chilling events of the twentieth century, and proved time and again that she was a born survivor. She wielded power in a way only the super-rich and beautiful can do: unrepentant for and unaware of the damage done to others. Nonetheless, once you were adopted as her friend, she became your generous benefactor. Her enemies soon discovered that she could be a formidable foe.

Florence lived her life through many mirrors of varying hues, with an unshakable belief in her beauty, wit, and charm. The truth, as for so many people with power, existed only as she chose to tell it; and the great San Francisco earthquake is a wonderful example of the artistry with which she crafted her tall tales. Her catlike green eyes flashed as she retold the horror of those three days of fire and brimstone to her French audiences. The beauty mark on her upper-left cheek was the only flaw on her alabaster skin, as if proof were needed that she was human, and not some goddess descended to earth. Her beautiful slender, long fingers grabbed at the pearls caressing her throat, while her mellifluous voice speaking in French, tinged with her ever-present American accent, rose and fell with each rise and fall of the quake.

Yet Florence never made any allusions to the roaring of the earthquake or its immediate destructive effects. Nor did she describe the nauseating sulphur smells after the first two shocks, nor the horrid aftertaste in her mouth. How could someone who was so observant be so oblivious? Hadn't she heard the family horses neighing and stomping in the stables, fearful of the seismic impending doom, as all the animals of the city were that morning? She omitted these details because, truthfully, Florence was in her bed, at home, presumably fast asleep when the terror struck.

How else could she omit recalling the quake's thundering northward into the city, lifting and rolling everything in its path, leaving utter destruction in its wake? She hadn't seen any buildings as they crumbled in an unstoppable, destructive domino wave of bricks and stones crashing back down to earth skewed, as if they were toys tossed carelessly from an infant's crib. The great commercial palaces of the American West's premier city were reduced to billowing clouds of rubble in seconds. Born in the Pacific beyond the Golden Gate, the earthquake sucked the waters from the bay, then rolled them back in with phenomenal force, spilling the ocean onto the streets of San Francisco. Enormous breakers far beyond a surfer's craziest conjuring pounded the city's thoroughfares.

Florence hadn't seen this, nor the total devastation of Chinatown, where she later claimed she was a constant visitor. From her home, north of San Francisco in Belvedere, in Marin County, she could not observe the frantic search and rescue of Chinese immigrants onto Angel Island in the bay. Only later would she hear about the metal cuvette known as the "Slot" for cable cars rising like a silk ribbon in the breeze before falling twisted and bent to the ground.*

There were, nonetheless, many eyewitnesses. Police constable Michael Grady had seen the Phelan Building lurch over Market Street, then be set back slanting onto its foundations, screeching and twisted. Constable Cook recalled the "deep and terrible rumbling" where "the earth seemed to rise under me, and at the same time both Davis and Washington streets opened up in several places and water came up out of these cracks."[1] The swaying of the Call Building, that of the Mutual Bank Building on Market, near Geary, and the twisting motion causing the windows to explode into millions of glass shards that showered the streets below remained a mystery to Florence in her retelling of that fateful morning.[2]

The great walls of flames Florence described occurred in the aftermath: the fire that engulfed San Francisco and raged for three days following the earthquake. The entire metropolitan area from Embarcadero North Street's Ferry Building west and south to Mission and Dolores streets was destroyed. Chinatown was burned to the ground, save one "solid brick wall, unshattered by the earthquake shock and unblackened by the breath of flame." Over its archway, the stone letters read "Occidental Board of Foreign Missions," proudly indicating that here stood a Protestant refuge for unfortunate Chinese foundlings.[3]

Landmarks like the Golden Gate Park were in flames for days. Libraries and brothels, art galleries and jails, homes and churches were reduced to pulverized masonry and smoldering, twisted iron. Everywhere was choked with unfathomable clouds of smoke and dust that made breathing the air outdoors a feat of heroism. As her parents and their friends described the carnage, the fire-ravaged, shoddily built, brick and wooden structures of the city became as real to Florence as the safety of her family home in Belvedere across the bay.

On Tuesday evening, less than ten hours before the quake, this bright

---

* The "Slot," or the tram tracks on Market Street, the widest thoroughfare in San Francisco at the time, became the social dividing line, a physical separation of blue-collar residents from the white-collar ones. Those who lived "south of the Slot" were generally considered blue-collar or new immigrants.

and beautiful fair-haired, beribboned child begged her mother and father to take her to the most celebrated event for San Francisco's glitterati: the opera. It was only the second time that the Metropolitan Opera of New York was performing in San Francisco, and its tenor, the magnificent Enrico Caruso—one of the most admired tenors of all time—was to sing the role of Don José in *Carmen*. At thirty-three, Caruso was at the height of his fame. Significantly for Florence, who believed that she, too, would be a famous opera singer one day, the desire to see and hear the great Caruso became an all-consuming passion.

For his part, Caruso was not impressed with San Franciscans, whom he described as "hobbledehoys"—nondescript mongrels who lacked the sophistication of the East Coast's audiences. When he read the reviews of his previous night's performance in *The Queen of Sheba*, Caruso called his western spectators "provincial arrivistes" and "artless rabble."[4]

Since Florence's father was in the newspaper business, such goings-on were known to her and made her gasp for the refined air of the East Coast and its preferred elegance. Devastated at the thought that she was among the "artless rabble," as the days passed and newspapers resumed their printing on makeshift presses in unsuitable premises, Florence poured over the society columns searching for something to redeem her and the rest of Caruso's western audience. Relief came only from Charles Aiken of *Sunset* magazine, who wrote, "All society—with a big S—was out in force. Beautiful women gorgeously gowned, with opera cloaks trimmed with ermine, and diamonds on hands and hair; men with pop hats and the conventional cast-iron sort of clothes that mean joyous discomfort; here were wondrous bunches of orchids and roses; the singing and acting that charmed and the deafening applause."[5] Florence, like so many other westerners, felt slyly happy when she heard what a coward Caruso had been during the quake—how he held on to his mattress for grim life, and how he wandered the streets of San Francisco in a reported hysterical state afterward.

∽

Florence's father was a French immigrant named Maximin Victoire Lacaze. He came to the great western city in California, as most of its 80,000 new arrivals did, with nothing in his pockets, a quick mind, and a burning desire to strike gold. Born in the southwest of France in the sleepy, rural village of Mont-de-Marrast in the *département* of Gers, Maximin began his adventure to San Francisco in the company of his sister Marianne's father-in-law in 1879. The California Gold Rush was long over, but the streets were still believed to be paved with golden opportunities. Despite many an illusion dashed, California—and its fair city of San Francisco—remained the mythical "land of milk and honey," or the *pays de cocagne,* in the European imagination, far removed from war, disease, pestilence, and famine.

Maximin soon learned that utopias, alas, exist only in our dreams. The Mexican-American War (1846–1848) had been officially settled by the Treaty of Guadelupe Hidalgo, signed between the two nations on February 2, 1848. Only nine days earlier, while building a sawmill for Captain John Sutter, John W. Marshall had noticed thousands of metallic flakes in the tailrace water, and knew instinctively it was gold. Although he vowed to keep his find a secret, it was the beginning of the California Gold Rush. If the Mexican government had known of California's sudden wealth, it might have fought on to retain the riches it so reluctantly ceded to its belligerent northern neighbor.[6] Thereafter, California became a magnet for opportunists and immigrants, scoundrels and churchmen, as well as those who simply wanted a better life.

By the time Maximin arrived in California, all gold claims had been staked. There were, however, other types of gold mines to plunder. An immigrant of eighteen, he was blond and handsome with beautiful bedroom blue eyes. Maximin's family often said that California-born Florence not only resembled her father with her long blonde tresses and her gorgeous, hypnotic green eyes, but that she also possessed her father's deadly brainpower. Unlike Florence, Maximin found life was a hard graft out of poverty into his modest riches. He began by sweating—literally— while learning English as a typesetter in a print shop on Montgomery Avenue in the city. Twelve- to fourteen-hour days, six days a week, were the norm for all workers at the beginning of the twentieth century. Yet Maximin drew great strength as part of the thriving French community of some 7,500 immigrants to San Francisco and slowly—by California standards—rose like cream to the top.

Florence's mother, Berthe Joséphine Rennesson Bazille Lacaze, was born in Paris on October 28, 1869, to a pretty little laundress, Florence Rennesson, nicknamed Florinte. The father's name on Berthe's birth certificate was inscribed as "unknown." While Florinte acknowledged her baby rather than give her up for adoption or put her into an orphanage, as was so frequently the case in the nineteenth century, she was hardly the maternal type. Berthe Rennesson grew up in a convent, with all the severity of an education associated with such an upbringing at the time. Florinte, meanwhile, headed off to America with her new man, Jean Bazille, in tow. It was not until many years later that she sent for Berthe, and Jean Bazille gave his stepdaughter his family name. He was the only father Berthe would ever know, and she was thankful for his many kindnesses. She vowed if she ever had children, they would never know the harsh realities of the convent, or life, or the shame of needing to dissemble their thoughts.[7] Berthe's vow helped make her daughter Florence the person she became.

Florence's only sibling, her younger brunette sister, Isabelle, would live in her shadow the whole of her life. Of the two girls, it seems that Florence was always the preferred child—the one on whom her parents focused their efforts. Perhaps Florence was the more charismatic, or even the more beautiful. Whatever the reasons, the girls remained in each other's company, frequently sniping at one another, for most of their lives.

Like many children at the age of ten, Florence was a follower of Mark Twain's adage "Never one to allow the facts to get in the way of a good story." With an eye for the dramatic, she reinvented herself in the image she wanted to portray to her world. "We had a golden youth, and could stroll the streets of San Francisco on our own," Florence recalled wistfully the illusory memory. She spoke of the fairy-tale life of her imagined youth roaming at will in the Presidio, Golden Gate Park, and Chinatown, either alone or with her sister. Her friends in Europe, listening to this fiction, could only sigh with envy at the independence Florence enjoyed as a child in an otherwise wasp-waisted world of corsets and suitable chaperones.[8]

And yet, given the Presidio's military role in the Spanish-American War and the Philippine-American conflict from 1898 until 1902 as one of an armed encampment, it is hardly likely that Florence's mother allowed her young daughter to wander there unattended. At the time of the earthquake, and the state of martial law imposed in its aftermath, the soldiers of the Presidio provided shelter, food, clothing, and protection from lawlessness and looting for the civilian population. Chinatown was marked in the *Annals of San Francisco* as a "no go area" for other immigrant communities, since the Chinese—or "celestials," as they were called then—were "aloof, infuriatingly haughty, separate, and stoically indifferent" to the Yankees of San Francisco. The *Annals* stated categorically that the Chinese immigrant could not be "materially modified." Nor could the Chinese, in this earlier age when differences in culture were frequently misunderstood and often expressed in blunt racial terms, be "closely assimilated to those of the civilizing and dominant race."[9] Given such bias, even the free-spirited Berthe Lacaze could hardly allow her treasured little blonde and brunette daughters to wander about in Chinatown on their own—day or night. After all, the term "shanghaied" originated in San Francisco's Chinatown in the late nineteenth century—a term born out of fears of being kidnapped into white slavery.[10]

Nevertheless, Florence's life was quite unlike a normal Yankee child's. No matter how hard the Lacaze family tried to assimilate, there was always an unhealthy prejudice in the city against foreigners. While Florence and Isabelle attended the local elementary school, they would remain outsiders. Not only was French spoken at home,* but the education of the girls remained a high priority for both their parents. At a time when most girls were brought up to become wives and mothers, Florence was encouraged to consider a profession that would grant her the freedom Berthe had been denied. What this "otherness" gave her was a perpetual alertness to opportunities as they arose, and the ability to develop new strategies to "belong."[11]

Her father found his own way of belonging through the newspaper community. By 1906, he was the city editor of the only French-language newspaper, *Le Franco-Californien*, which had a potential readership of 7,500 souls in a city of 400,000 inhabitants.

The founding owner of the paper, a dyed-in-the-wool reporter and

---

* Florence claimed later that she did not speak one word of French on her arrival in Paris. This was another of her "hero" stories that helped to explain away her cherished American accent when speaking French.

printer, Alfred Chaigneau, had immigrated to San Francisco back in 1849 at the height of the Gold Rush. Learning his trade on a French journal called *Le Phare*, Chaigneau launched his first title in 1886 in competition with pioneer journalist Edouard Debrec's *L'Echo du Pacifique*. A year later, the two French newspapers merged to form a daily and a weekly under the united title of *Le Franco-Californien* when Debrec lost the last of his several fortunes and became an inmate at the French Hospital of San Francisco. In 1898, Chaigneau sold out to a consortium of investors— while retaining a modest shareholding—headed by Auguste Goustiaux. It was Goustiaux who became the outspoken champion of the French colony in San Francisco.[12]

Goustiaux and by extension his city editor, Maximin Lacaze, were valued members of the press and San Francisco's thriving Bohemian Club. Bohemianism began, of course, as an international movement inspired by Henri Murger's *Scènes de la vie bohème* in 1845–49, in which the artist rejected the significance of money and suffocating social conventions of the day. Instead, bohemians embraced the life of a free spirit, something that suited many newcomers to San Francisco in their pursuit of gold.

Yet Yankee San Francisco adopted bohemianism with a significant western twist. Bret Harte, the author who so vividly depicted the miners, gamblers, and other rapscallions of the California Gold Rush, wrote that "Bohemia has never been located geographically . . . but any clear day when the sun is going down, if you mount Telegraph Hill, you shall see its pleasant valleys and cloud-capped hills glittering in the West. . . ."[13] Writers and journalists headed the roster of members at San Francisco's Bohemian Club, which was formed in the offices of the *San Francisco Chronicle*. Soon, it encompassed all important members of the chattering classes, including those from the twenty-odd foreign-language press corps. Their bohemian ideals would leave an indelible imprint on Florence's upbringing, too.

∽

Despite her tendency to exaggerate, some of Florence's truthful recollections of San Francisco shine through. The morning fire drills at school remain a common practice today. Unsurprisingly, the comic strip *Buster*

Brown, about the disturbingly pretty boy with a mischievous streak for practical jokes, was her favorite and she spent happy hours reading about his latest adventures. Then there was the abiding and fascinating memory of the family's Chinese manservant, who would spit on the freshly washed laundry as he ironed.[14] Still, why didn't she mention any childhood friends or family social engagements? Did she feel that these were not grand enough for her powerful adult image?

In truth, Florence frequently "summered" with her mother at private homes or hotels outside San Francisco. In September 1902, the social-climbing Berthe Lacaze placed a personal advertisement just below the society column in the *San Francisco Call*, announcing her week-long sojourn with "her little daughter Florence" at the home of Mr. and Mrs. Alfred Chaigneau at "Fern Grove, their beautiful home in Guerneville."[15]

The personal advertisement speaks volumes. A society column placement announcing the week-long stay of Mrs. Lacaze and her daughter at the Chaigneau home was, of course, placed in *Le Franco-Californien*. The *San Francisco Call*, however, did not deem either Mrs. Lacaze or the retired Alfred Chaigneau's social agenda of sufficient interest to the Yankee community to merit a society column's free placement. Yet, by 1904, the *San Francisco Call did* include the vacationing Berthe and Florence at Skaggs Springs in their society column, along with other glitterati of San Francisco, demonstrating Maximin's rise in significance in the city. That said, neither Mr. Lacaze nor little Isabelle accompanied them.[16]

Despite Florence's invented memories and embellishments, the San Francisco earthquake utterly changed the Lacaze family's future. Their wrangling over remaining or leaving the city would divide them forever. Maximin was a lone male voice amid a determined, terrified female chorus.* Later, Florence's rose-tinted memory imagined her father bundling her into a boat along with her sister, mother, and grandmother and escaping through the "two great walls of flames." Like so many of Florence's recollections, it was a colorful fiction.

Over 300,000 inhabitants of the city were evacuated by the Southern Pacific Railway free of charge; approximately 25,000 other inhabitants were evacuated by the navy from Fort Mason; and thousands more

---

* Florence's grandfather, Jean Bazille, had died in 1905.

escaped via the Union Ferry Building in San Francisco to Belvedere's near-neighbor, Oakland Pier. Given their position north of the city and proximity to the railway line, it is probable that Florence and her family were among the 300,000 evacuees aboard the Southern Pacific Railway. Interestingly, her future brother-in-law was one of its owners. The railroad was built by San Francisco's great entrepreneurs, Mark Hopkins, Charles Crocker, Collis P. Huntington, and Leland Stanford, back in the days of Jay Gould. Only later would Florence discover that one of the Goulds' bêtes noires, Edward H. Harriman, had muscled his way into the Southern Pacific's ownership and had squeezed millions away from Jay Gould's son, George.

Florence's memory might have been clouded by a simple, veiled, youthful wish. The bay became symbolic of her need to quench the family fire that raged at home, with her father arguing to stay, her mother and grandmother militating to leave. Within minutes, the quake had robbed Florence of her cherished childhood. *Le Franco-Californien*'s presses were destroyed. So, too, was the real estate Florinte had inherited from her husband on Montgomery Street, Spofford Alley, Clay Street, and Stockton Avenue. Literally, her vast wealth had crumbled to dust and ashes. Devastated at her losses, Florinte swatted aside any hint of her son-in-law's objections: her daughter and granddaughters would be brought to the safety and civilization of Paris.[17]

Like any good newspaperman at a time of peril, Maximin resolved to remain amid the chaos. He would rebuild his life and earning capacity, despite his mother-in-law's and wife's determination to go. He would oversee the rebuilding of Florinte's property holdings, in the hope that she would relent and bring the family back. As the women left San Francisco on the train to take them east, Florence etched the ruined city into her memory. Would they ever return? Would she ever see her father again? Maximin undoubtedly assured her that she would. For Berthe Lacaze and her mother, San Francisco was an experiment that had failed. In their opinion, it was no longer a fit place to bring up two little girls.

2

FROM FIRE TO FLOOD AND DEATH

So quietly flows the Seine that one hardly notices its presence.

—ARTHUR MILLER

LONG BEFORE THE LACAZE WOMEN DISEMBARKED AT LE HAVRE, San Francisco was a semi-functioning city once again. Within days, newspapers were printing, precarious buildings had been dynamited, and the rebuilding program begun. Even Maximin Lacaze's journal, *Le Franco-Californien,* shared a printing press and managed to run off a limited post-earthquake edition. Disaster aid and community spirit were lavish and quick back then.

Florence never mentioned her first trans-American journey by train, nor her first Atlantic crossing. It was her one and only adventure by train beyond the San Francisco Bay area, through the heart of the ever-changing early-twentieth-century landscape of America. More is the pity, too, as Florence was a keen observer and consummate storyteller when the mood struck her. Worse still, she never said if she regretted leaving San Francisco, or if she was looking forward to settling in France with her mother, sister, and grandmother. She would have been a hard-hearted child not to have held a tremendous sense of loss for what had been and would, more than likely, never be again. Florence knew that her mother, Berthe, by now nicknamed "Pompon" by the girls, and grandmother Florinte saw themselves as Parisians. Both women steadfastly believed that all culture and society worth knowing—and knowing about—emanated like a blinding sunbeam from the City of Light.

After the usual flurry of activity on arrival, Berthe, Florence, and Isabelle settled in a sumptuous apartment at 2 rue de Fleurus on the corner of rue de Luxembourg* in the Odéon quarter of the sixth arrondissement. Adjacent to the western edge of the Jardin de Luxembourg, the apartment was ideally located near the Seine River, and near the heart of the city's bohemian Left Bank. Their close neighbors were two fellow Americans, Leo Stein and his sister, Gertrude, who lived at number 27. Yet neither the Steins nor Florence ever alluded to meeting in their years living on the same street.

In the apartment block on rue de Fleurus, Florence met her lifelong friend, Cécile Tellier. Exact contemporaries, the two girls became instantly close. Florence's wonderful tales of her distant, sunny California oddly created a strong bond, since Cécile longed to travel. One day, while chattering in the way girls do, Florence told Cécile, "You'll see, one day I'll be a great singer. . . ." It was more than a pipe dream. Berthe was paying dearly for private tutoring for Florence with a musician known only as an "old professor of music," who lived on the aptly named avenue Mozart. He, too, believed that Florence's voice could be trained for the opera.

Naturally, the Lacaze girls were enrolled in school in the autumn of 1906. As Florence later claimed with charming embellishment, she had to attend accelerated French language classes.[1] More than likely, she trailed behind other French children at school due to her American studies and lack of Catholic teaching, and needed some private lessons to catch up. Then, as now, education in France was more rigorous than in America.

By the spring of 1907, when Florence and Cécile celebrated their Holy Communion together at Notre-Dame-des-Champs, the girls had

---

* Rue de Luxembourg was later renamed rue Guynemer after the World War I French flying ace Georges Guynemer, who died in 1917 in battle, age twenty-two. Florinte lived nearby in a comfortable apartment in the Montparnasse quarter of the city at 10 rue Léopold-Robert.

become inseparable. They attended the same private elementary and middle Catholic school, Dupanloup, and later, went on to the private Catholic Maintenon College together.[2] Cécile remained invisible, at times the wallflower languishing in Florence's shade by dint of the American's exuberant and, at times, outrageous personality. Yet nearly always, Cécile would be at Florence's beck and call, the beneficiary of her friend's legendary generosity.

Unlike Cécile, Florence was a bright student who, aside from music, loved history. Given Berthe's aversion to her own Catholic education, it seems astonishing that she should have sent her girls to private Catholic schools. Yet she wanted the best for her daughters. The stain of Berthe's illegitimacy and birth into poverty, so powerful in those days, could not be erased. But she knew she must try. If the girls were to mix and make proper matches with "good" families, the groundwork for the "right" connections could never be concocted by attending a public school—no matter how good. Berthe was quite aware that they lived in an era when women of quality did not work or forge their own way in the world, and she so wished for Florence to be that sort of woman.

Young Isabelle tried to shine as bright as her sister but was doomed to remain a poorer reflection in Florence's shadow. Apparently, Isabelle talked nineteen to the dozen every waking hour. Annoyed at her jabbering, Florence often claimed that in the time she said, "Isabelle, be quiet," her sister could tell two separate stories. Visitors from America thought that Isabelle was the more extravagant of the two sisters and had become more French, more coquettish, than Florence. She was proud of losing her American accent within weeks. Florence could have done so, too, if she wished, but being American and treasuring her accent were as critical to her living well as breathing. Florence was hardly a coquette, as the boy next door from Belvedere, California, later described his future sister-in-law, Isabelle. By her teens, Florence had honed her feline walk and vamp's ways to perfection and could ensnare any male victim she chose to achieve her ends. In these circumstances, the sibling rivalry between the Lacaze girls could only grow over the years. Florence was not about to relinquish center stage, then or ever.

By the end of 1907, Maximin was flourishing once more, and traveled to Paris to reclaim his family. Soon he realized that, already, he was too late. Not only did he meet with his wife's intransigence because she believed that the girls were better off and safer in Paris, but his little girls shrieked at the thought of being uprooted a second time.[3] Florence would argue that she could become a great opera singer only in Paris—after all, her "old professor" had told her so. Isabelle had quite forgotten San Francisco's attributes in the year since they'd left, and perhaps, too, felt that their father was alien to their new way of life. After spending the Christmas holidays *en famille*, Maximin returned alone to San Francisco early in 1908, arriving in New York aboard the ship *La Touraine* on February 23.[4] It was the last time Florence and Isabelle would see their father. On June 7 of that year, Maximin began his annual vacation in Santa Barbara at Villa El Verano in the company of a French widow, presumably resigned to his estrangement from Berthe and his daughters.[5]

∽

The Paris that Florence grew up in, and loved, was Haussmann's Paris. In 1853, to modernize the city—as well as to avoid the infamous barricades to which law and order had fallen victim previously—Napoléon III gave his prefect of the Seine, Georges-Eugène Haussmann, broad powers and authority to rebuild much of the city. Haussmann's Paris sported new grand parks open to everyone and an exquisite opera house with a copper dome and golden statues designed by Charles Garnier that Florence gawped at, dreaming of her future singing accomplishments.

There were wide boulevards, designed to consign the revolutionary barricades of the city to a distant memory. These grand avenues were, in turn, fringed with chic new apartment buildings topped with mansard roofs and beaux arts decorations that dotted the streets to beautify and encourage *les flâneurs*, those urban explorers of a literary penchant engaged in the opposite of nothing—a "gastronomy of the eye," in the words of Honoré de Balzac.

New sewers were dug to cope with a near doubling of the city's population, with nine new arrondissements and the corresponding civil administration to manage Haussmann's sweeping changes. Haussmann himself credited Napoléon III for bringing medieval Paris into the modern era: "The city is improved as no other ever was . . . by . . . the present Napoléon and he will thus . . . leave the grandest monument to his genius and power the world has seen. . . ."[6] Haussmann's Paris was also largely responsible for the next force of nature that Florence and all Parisians would miraculously survive.

New Year's Day 1910 was unseasonably warm, bathed in midwinter sunshine, and a stunning forty-three degrees Fahrenheit. Florence, like all Parisians, might have felt within her rights to think they were blessed. Though warm temperatures continued into the month, by the beginning of the second week of January, the sunshine was a mere memory. A low-pressure weather system churned slowly, gathering more and more moisture, off the coast of Brittany. For days on end, it hardly moved and relentlessly pitched its heavy rains onto northern France, the Netherlands, and England. By the third week in January, the water table in northern France had risen to near ground level and its rivers were swollen to bursting.

On January 21, only fifty miles southeast of Paris, the Loing River, one of many waterways feeding the Seine, was surging faster than anyone could remember. That morning, in the small coal mining town of Lorroy, miners loaded their coal, dug from the mines in the hillside on the edge of town, onto barges. These floated on the man-made canal that supplied Paris with its coal, the only means of warmth in the city during the winter. At midday, the miners trudged homeward through the congealed mud for their meal, as they had done every working day of their lives. Some never came back again. Suddenly, the entire village began to shake violently. Furniture and people were tossed like rag dolls in their kitchens with a force redolent of an earthquake. The unstable hillside—their very source of steady income for generations—collapsed in a terrifying avalanche of rock, mud, and trees, burying the miners and their families alive.[7]

That same afternoon, Parisians could see that the Seine was rising, too, but there was no panic. The river had flooded countless times since the city was first built—but only once, in 1896, subsequent to its redesign by Haussmann. The Seine's high walls were reinforced with sand and stone, nonetheless, as a precaution. By January 21, a portion of Quai de Valmy bordering Canal Saint-Martin on the Right Bank had sunk, collapsing a portion of the pavement. Still, the Lacaze family could not see the flooding from their rue de Fleurus apartment, and did not panic.

Water rose, too, through the basements of buildings. The number 12 Métro Line was flooding. Paris's prefect of police, Louis Lépine, became the man of the hour—the real-life, dogged Inspector Javert straight from the pages of Victor Hugo's *Les Misérables*. Like Javert, he felt the pulse of the city as a hands-on prefect with a zero tolerance for crime. Armed with little more than his thick mustache and goatee, he exuded a stoic calm that faced down gangsters and angry protesters alike. His single-mindedness to make Paris safe and a proper place to live—fighting the vices of pornography, panhandling, prostitution, vagrancy, and any other moral offense that irked his sense of duty—made him the darling of the bourgeoisie.[8]

Nonetheless, on January 21, Lépine was deprived of any information from the Hydrometric Service simply because the rivers flowed too quickly. Measuring stations along the Loing River could no longer report due to the raging floodwaters whipping away the telegraph lines. In the absence of real knowledge, Lépine simply looked at the seething waters and halted all river traffic immediately. Then he urgently ordered the civil engineers employed by the city to build a clay wall parallel to the Seine. It was too late.

The floodwaters short-circuited the power plants at Bercy and Saint-Denis just north of Paris, freezing the Métro to a standstill as water swamped the tunnels. Parisians began improvising: Women threw modesty to the winds and hiked their skirts up to their knees, some hitching a ride on passing river barges that replaced cars and horses. Temporary duckboards were erected on bricks to help people get about. Makeshift barricades were set up to close the underground station entrances, but the surging water was already cascading in great waterfalls down the stairs from the street above. Initially, Florence thought it was fun.

The head of the river Yonne, which feeds the Seine from the Massif Central mountain range in south-central France, had burst its banks, too. City after city fell victim to the unprecedented floodwaters. Still, the real crisis for Paris came when the Marne River, fed by its raging tributaries the Grand Morin and Petit Morin, spilled over into the Seine.[9]

By the evening of January 22, the only mode of transport on the streets of Paris was the rowboat. As dusk fell, the City of Light remained dark. The gas lamplighters had scrambled to find rowboats, but understandably, there was an insufficiency. The stench from the sewers and their detritus mingled with the roaring floodwaters, making the darkened, noisy city eerily threatening. Soldiers barricaded flooded areas at gunpoint, adding to Parisians' fears of insurrection. No one knew if the splash of oars would bring rescue or looters. It was a long, black night in the pouring rain.

∽

From their apartment on rue de Fleurus, Florence and her family could see the floodwaters approach. The Boulevard Saint-Germain, only a half dozen city blocks away, was inundated, and those who could no longer enter their homes had taken refuge in the Baroque church of Saint-Sulpice nearby. The much-admired author Guillaume Apollinaire would write, "Tonight, nearly 600 *misérables* are sleeping at Saint-Sulpice."[10] The church was only a few minutes' walk from the Lacaze home, and the river was still rising. On the Right Bank, the Seine was lapping at the streets in front of the Louvre. Again, barricades were hastily erected, in the hope of keeping the nation's treasures within safe.

As the Seine spread its tentacles throughout the length and breadth of the city, careless of its path through working-class neighborhoods and fashionable boulevards alike, fear spread. Debris, raw sewage, and formerly warehoused goods from the Bercy district were carried on the yellow floodwaters. Opportunistic treasure seekers braved the bridges of the city in search of liberated casks of wine or household furniture, rescuing their booty with huge hooked poles. Then there were the "sightseers" like American writer Helen Davenport Gibbons, who wrote that "the calamity was forgotten in the sport of watching huge barrels sucked one by one under an arch and jumping high in the air as they came out on the other side." She, like other Parisians, cheered on the flowing rubbish in a mock "Pooh Sticks" race, rooting for "their rubbish" to win as it emerged from the other side of the bridge.[11]

Volunteers and the Red Cross soon jumped into the breach to minister to the displaced and wounded. Churches and schools were coopted as improvised shelters, tended by the Union of French Women and the Catholic Sisters of Charity. Soldiers and police worked tirelessly to maintain public order, and everyone prayed at special Masses for the floodwaters to recede. Paris had pulled together. On January 28, one week after the state of emergency had begun, the Seine reached its peak.

The British journalist Laurence Jerrold, London's *Daily Telegraph* correspondent for Paris, was immediately reminded of a recent earthquake, while most journalists were comparing the City of Light to Venice. Jerrold reported that in December 1908, a devastating earthquake measuring 7.5 on the Richter scale hit in the Strait of Messina between Sicily and the mainland of Italy. A tsunami with forty-foot-high waves crashed onto cities and towns all along the Mediterranean. The sheer force and surprising speed of destruction was disastrous. The death toll was 60,000, with thousands more injured and homeless. Admittedly, Paris was flooded, but the waters' rise had taken a week, and no one had died.

The comparison to an earthquake and the devastation wrought would have also run through the minds of Florence and her family. Her father had been assured time and again that they were safe in Paris, that life was better. Florence may have seen the lighter side of this tragedy—as in playing "Pooh Sticks" on the bridges of Paris with the other children—since she had a keen sense of humor, yet it is difficult to believe that she would not have been shaken by this second natural disaster in her short life.

∽

Within a year of the malodorous floodwaters receding, another tragedy struck. Florinte died on February 18, 1911. No cause of death was recorded, but that was not unusual for an elderly patient. If Berthe had promised her husband that she would return to San Francisco after Florinte's passing, her words rang hollow as the months slid by, while she and the girls remained in Paris.

Sadly, just over nine months to the day, Maximin followed his mother-in-law to the grave on November 21, aged only fifty. His obituary, published in the *San Francisco Call*, stated simply that he was the husband of Berthe, father of Florence and Isabelle, and offered no cause of death. Arrangements for his funeral and burial in the Bay Area on November 24 were made by his Lacaze cousins in California. It was the family of prominent San Franciscan Louis Lacaze who informed Berthe and attended to all Maximin's funeral arrangements and interment at Holy Cross Cemetery just outside the city.[12]

In an age when appearances of normalcy in family relations mattered far more than the truth, Berthe must have sensed the unspoken danger, for she invented what seems like a ridiculous fiction today. Florence maintained that fiction, saying shortly before her own death as an elderly woman that they were a "happy family." She told everyone that her father's body arrived in Paris on January 6, 1912, and was buried in the Bazille crypt in the Montparnasse cemetery.[13] No one ever doubted the word of a woman noted for her phenomenal memory of people, places, and events.

There is no denying that Berthe was in an extremely awkward situation, both socially and financially. The fiction of Maximin being buried in a family crypt in Paris was designed to mitigate the facts from friends and prospective bridegrooms for her daughters, as well as to "big up" the family's status. If there was one glaring, but understandable, fault to lay at Berthe's door, it was that she considered any untruth that would strengthen Florence's chances of a good match worthwhile. The practice of the "untruth" was a trait that Florence would elevate to an art form.

Still, Berthe's primary concern was to reclaim the family "fortune" left by her mother and estranged husband in San Francisco. Fortunately, a very able American lawyer in Paris, Charles G. Loeb, the young partner in Valois & Loeb, was at hand.

Berthe's choice of Charles Gerson Loeb was both brave and inspired. Loeb was young, bright, hungry for business, and Jewish. That made him a controversial choice. Given that France was still reeling from the deep-seated anti-Semitic divisions released like the hellhounds of war by the Dreyfus Affair, Berthe had placed herself firmly in the active Dreyfusard camp, against the anti-Semites. It was a camp she gladly shared with other notable French thinkers like the future French prime minister Georges Clemenceau, Anatole France, and Marcel Proust.

"The *Affaire*," as the fate of Army Captain Alfred Dreyfus became known, divided France over twelve long years, deeply scarring French society and the French Third Republic. Dreyfus, the son of a wealthy Jewish textile merchant, was denounced by the real guilty party, and was convicted in 1894 for alleged acts of treason during the Franco-Prussian

War of 1870–71. The trial became a test of French republicanism, pitting the army, clerics, royalists, and anti-Semites—or "anti-Dreyfusards"—against the republicans and free thinkers.* Originally found guilty and transported to Devil's Island off the coast of French Guyana, Dreyfus was retried five years later in 1899, and found guilty again, despite revelations of the anti-Semitic plot between the French Ministry of War and Major Ferdinand Walsin-Esterhazy, the man who committed the treason. Author Émile Zola stood up for Dreyfus. His open letter to the president of the republic, printed in Georges Clemenceau's newspaper *Aurore* in 1898, entitled "*J'accuse,*" made Dreyfus's second trial possible.

Zola's attack accused the army colonels and generals of treachery, concealing documents that gave irrefutable proof of Dreyfus's innocence. The French press and citizenry, the anti-Dreyfusards, hardly came off any better: Zola wrote that they were all guilty of "social malfeasance" and poisoning the atmosphere of all France with their religious intolerance. Although found guilty again in 1899, Dreyfus was pardoned by the president of the Third Republic in the hope of stopping the unrelenting bitterness on both sides. In 1904, Dreyfus still sought to clear his name in a retrial, but it was only in 1906 that a civil court of appeal found him innocent of all charges, and reinstated him in the army.[†]

∽

Berthe was well aware of the divisions and anti-Semitic feeling in Paris. The *Affaire* tore at the weft and warp of society, and eventually gave rise to anticlericalism. It was not unusual to see dinner guests leave prematurely if anyone at the table held an opposing view regarding the *Affaire.* Former friends passed one another in silence in the street, or refused invitations from those who did not share their viewpoint. The tensions were mirrored among the intelligentsia, too, so that it became widely accepted that any words "would never have carried across the worlds that lay between them."[14]

Bravery aside, due to her five years residing in France, Berthe's right

---

* The *Affaire* became one of the four most seminal events in French history, along with the French Revolution, the occupation of France and the Vichy regime, and the May 1968 riots.

† Dreyfus served honorably in the French army during World War I. He died in 1935. The French army did not apologize until 1995.

to claim her mother's U.S. assets, as well as her dead husband's estate, required highly specialist knowledge, and Charles Gerson Loeb was her man, Jew or no. There is no evidence to point to an official separation between the Lacazes, or a prior relationship with another lawyer admitted to the California Bar. More than likely, Loeb was painstakingly selected from a list of practicing attorneys-at-law provided by the American Chamber of Commerce at the United States embassy in Paris. Berthe hadn't become part of the "American Colony," which resided in its moneyed splendor on the Right Bank. She hadn't socialized with the Left Bank bohemian Americans either, like her neighbors Gertrude Stein or Stein's soon-to-be life partner and fellow San Franciscan who also fled the earthquake, Alice B. Toklas. Nor had she hobnobbed with the author who analyzed the upper echelons of society and its reaction to social change, Edith Wharton. Without any personal touchstones to advise here, Berthe's knowledge of the right man for the job would have been limited.

Still, she chose well. The outcome of the legal battles ahead directly affected her daughters' future, and given Florence's as-yet-unproven flair for business, it is reasonable to assume that she, too, had a hand in selecting Loeb. He was ten years her senior, aged a mere twenty-five, sporting dark wavy hair and a thick mustache. His high forehead and rounded face with its aquiline nose were signs typically believed, at the turn of the twentieth century, to denote intelligence and good breeding. Born in New Orleans, Loeb was licensed to practice law in California, New York, and the U.S. federal ninth circuit courts.[15] From Berthe's potentially precarious financial perspective, Loeb's youth suggests an ambitious lawyer she thought could deliver a victory at bargain-basement prices. Undoubtedly, too, Florence's innocent youthful beauty, over and above an interesting test case of international law, proved an irresistible combination. Their friendship would continue until Loeb's death in 1944.

Armed with the facts, Loeb advised Berthe with due authority that she and her family had potentially lost their rights to automatically claim American citizenship, and therewith an American inheritance, due to the Expatriation Act of 1907. An extended residence abroad, as in the case of the Lacazes, presumed the loss of any American citizenship, *unless* it could be proven through satisfactory evidence to the U.S. gov-

ernment that it was never the person's intention to lose his or her American nationality. Satisfactory evidence was usually provided in the form of overseas permits for work in the consular, military, or other international business sectors. The intent of the law was to define which Americans had become permanent expatriates, and was directly aimed at women who had contracted an "international marriage." Berthe, Florence, and Isabelle fit the alien American profile perfectly.

Still, Loeb pondered, was Berthe's marriage to Maximin considered an international marriage by the terms confirmed in the new law? Both were born in France and had immigrated separately to California. Were Florence and Isabelle, both born Americans, now considered French through their residency in France for over five years? These were the tricky questions that Charles Loeb needed to consider quickly. Without steady income from Maximin's estate and Florinte's property, Berthe, Florence, and Isabelle would be penniless.

To complicate the situation further, Maximin's cousins and their families lived in San Francisco. Were these Lacaze cousins now American, and if so, would they contest any inheritance Berthe might claim from Maximin? A crucial unknown factor was whether they felt Berthe had deserted Maximin's home and their stricken city just when she was needed most at her husband's side. If they did resent her, and chose to contest the will, could Loeb counter their arguments successfully? Any kind feelings the family might have held were probably dashed by Berthe's 1908 refusal to return.

Then there were other unpalatable possibilities. Had the supposed last will survived the earthquake? Or had Maximin made a new will taking into consideration Berthe's 1908 rejection of his demands for her to return? Had he filed for a legal separation? Or had Maximin made a will at all? A legal battle looked likely, especially since the 1907 Expatriation Act had already been tested in numerous cases. Defending the interests of "foreign wives" against other "American" relations was, quite simply, futile. American courts, then as now, did not recognize the rights of aliens over Americans, and the American relative always won.[16]

The law was, of course, a travesty—but it was still the law. Florinte's estate alone was worth over $75,000. Her California testament declared Berthe her sole beneficiary. The estate comprised $56,000 in cash and

$20,000 in real estate and stocks, worth approximately $1.8 million in 2017.[17] Yet Maximin's will and estate remained a mystery. No will was published in the press. No probate announced. Could this mean that the Lacaze cousins intended to hold on to Maximin's assets?[18]

While Loeb fought for Berthe's and her daughters' inheritance, other arrangements needed to be made to make ends meet. In the time-honored tradition of the matronly mother and the beautiful daughter coming of age, Berthe turned to Florence as the sole solution to all their woes.

3

⚭

LA PARISIENNE

. . . all snobbery is about the problem of belonging.
—ALEXANDER THEROUX, American novelist

FLORENCE, AGED SIXTEEN, THOUGHT OF HERSELF AS *LA PARISIENNE*, that gigantic statue representing modernity, fashion, and glamour at the Exposition Universelle of 1900. The statue, sculpted by Paul Moreau-Vauthier, was the exhibition's focal point. All visitors walked into the Paris fairgrounds through the Porte Monumentale, where they were greeted by this female colossus, *La Parisienne*, in all her glory. She was modern, like Paris, stunningly beautiful, outfitted in Jeanne Paquin's haute-couture gown. She was quintessentially French. She was no Marianne, the allegorical, martial, patriotic symbol of France. *La Parisienne* invited all visitors, French and foreign, to enter and see a new, contemporary Paris, released from the shackles of tradition and the scandals of the Third Republic, to revel in the excitement that Paris represented to the world in culture, invention, and science.[1]

Florence saw herself as a living, breathing *La Parisienne*, modern, glamorous, sexy, a future Gaby Deslys, star of the Folies Bergère. Unlike Gaby, Florence wanted to find her feet in the rarefied world of opera. While she learned only about *La Parisienne* in school, Florence could easily relate to both *La Parisienne* and the designer of her haute couture,

Jeanne Paquin. The House of Paquin was the rising star in the fashion world, noted for wooing away clients from the aristocratic, traditional designs of Gaston Worth. Despite Paquin's short ascendency, she eclipsed the established, male House of Worth with her daring and innate feminine understanding of what women wanted to wear. Beautiful in her own right, Paquin had risen from humble origins to become first a model, then a designer, and finally the owner of her own fashion house. It was that kind of upward mobility that Florence admired and yearned to emulate, up to a point.[2] Where Paquin was happy for her fashions to shine in the limelight, Florence needed the oxygen of the limelight shining directly on her.

By 1900, money, or the lack of it, had become a gradually determining factor in social status. While land ownership still mattered, and marked an enviable noble heritage, the landed gentry throughout Europe were finding the new, raw capitalism of the early twentieth century hard to fathom, and harder still to adopt. The titled aristocracy were on the hunt for American heiresses born to wealthy robber barons of the ilk of the Vanderbilts, Morgans, and Goulds; or even, if the need absolutely dictated, daughters born to manufacturing giants like Isaac Merritt Singer, inventor of the first evenly stitching sewing machine.*

In Florence's Paris, it was a commonly known fact that all Americans were equally unacceptable in society, but their money was a necessary evil to be envied and plundered, so European aristocracy could plow on regardless. It was the American search and need for belonging in European society, coupled with the European requirement for new money, that changed many heiresses' and aristocrats' futures. Consuelo Vanderbilt was coerced into her marriage with the Duke of Marlborough by her mother, saving Blenheim Palace and the duke's other assets from oblivion. Marie Alice Heine, born in the French Quarter of New Orleans to a Jewish banking family, converted to Roman Catholicism to become the Duchess of Richelieu. When Alice was widowed as a young woman still of childbearing age, she remarried well, becoming Her Serene High-

---

* The first incarnation of the sewing machine was manufactured by Lerow and Blodgett some years before Singer's, but its stitching was so crude that it was never able to replace fine hand stitching as Singer's machine was later able to do in 1851.

ness of Monaco, Princess Alice.* Jennie Jerome, the first American-dollar "princess," and mother of Sir Winston Churchill, also gave her inherited fortune to underpin her husband's political career for the dubious pleasure of becoming Lady Randolph Churchill.

Florence ached to belong to the treasured circle of these elite society women, but despite her private school education, she lacked the money and connections to meet, much less marry into, such illustrious circles. While Charles Loeb toiled to obtain satisfaction through the California courts, Florence was, momentarily, relatively penniless. Dreams were one thing, reality quite another. Still, the sixteen-year-old was already a remarkable beauty, and knew it. Florence had also become a frightful snob—something everyone who met her remarked upon—and could not see herself living forever in obscurity, much less in poverty.

Certainly, Berthe instilled in her daughter an awareness that such beauty should provide Florence—and by extension her family—with an international passport to glamour, wealth, and happiness. As for the protagonist in the story *Gigi,* written by Florence's near contemporary, the French author Colette, it was Florence's duty to marry well and share her newfound wealth with the family. For Berthe, while it mattered if Florence's future was that of a demimondaine or an opera singer or the wife of a millionaire, she was a practical woman. If Florence could not marry well, then a world-famous opera singer would be her next choice for her daughter. Failing that, Florence would need to consider becoming a successful demimondaine.

The searing question was, could Florence marry well? Florence's world was changing rapidly. By 1913, the first self-made millionairess was a Polish Jew, Helena Rubinstein. Rubinstein had become rich from her mail-order business, which sold face cream to sun-ravaged Australian women in the Outback. Now Rubinstein owned beauty salons in Melbourne, London, and Paris and was searching for a salon in New York. "Beauty is power" was an early Rubinstein advertising slogan, and Florence decided that her beauty might provide her big break into the international high-society set of Paris.[3] While Florence thought she had

---

* She was a great-grandmother of Rainier III, Prince of Monaco, who married the American actress Grace Kelly.

the business sense to run an international company like Rubinstein's, it was not, yet, her passion, and it remained an unproven skill for some years to come.

Society and glamour, on the other hand, consumed her every waking hour. Back then, glamour was not about cosmetics and a slash of red lips for Florence. That was for later, when it became the fashion. It was about power, sexuality, and the unadulterated pleasure it could bring her. It was about luxury and excess. It was about living without the conventions or expectations of classical femininity. Above all, it was about heady sensuality and reveries beyond the ordinary, creating her own boldness, her own world of risk and self-assertion, and tipping the scales of an unequal male society in her favor. If her beauty could give her a leg up into that society so she could create her own world of glamour, so much the better. Certainly, her other great asset—her singing voice—gave another string to her bow, creating an aura of the exotic, the dangerously alluring.

Even at sixteen, Florence was a young woman on a mission. She combed the society columns, soaked in every bit of gossip and news about *le Tout-Paris*—the city's fashionable elite—and gleaned every crumb she could about the public and private lives of the *salonnières* (society hostesses) who might be susceptible to her charms. So, when she thought she was ready, Florence cajoled her old music professor into introducing her into the salon society. Alas, it seemed that the professor was found wanting in his connections to the salonnières whom Florence was determined to know. Perhaps, too, Berthe could no longer afford his lessons, and hence his failure to do as he was bid. But Florence would not be defeated. It seemed only natural that she should try to cultivate the American salonnières who had made Paris their home. Aside from her near neighbor Gertrude Stein, who was dowdy, masculine, and perhaps hideous to Florence's beautiful green eyes, there were, fortunately, others.

⁂

The American playwright, novelist, and poetess Natalie Clifford Barney held her court at 20 rue Jacob on the Left Bank within easy walking distance of Florence's home. Natalie was born in Dayton, Ohio, in 1876—nine years before Florence's birth in San Francisco. Natalie's father had become fabulously wealthy as the manufacturer of railway cars for most of the railroads that linked the east and west coasts of America. Her mother, Alice Pike Barney, had been encouraged to take her painting seriously by Oscar Wilde, and later studied art under the guidance of James McNeill Whistler.*

Having spent years in England and France, Natalie felt that puritanical America would never appreciate her artistic and lesbian leanings, and so she decamped from the USA and moved with her huge inheritance in tow to Paris. Her "Fridays," as her salons were called, positively dripped with panache and flair, exuding their influence on a carefully stage-managed setting. For sixty years, she influenced the literati of France, Britain, and America. Later, Truman Capote, who had become a regular after the Second World War, described Barney's Fridays as "a cross between a chapel and a bordello." [4] Favorites in the pre–Great War era included Oscar Wilde, Sinclair Lewis, Gertrude Stein, the influential Bohemian-Austrian poet and novelist Rainer Maria Rilke, T. S. Eliot, and Isadora Duncan, as well as Barney's Symbolist poetess lover Renée Vivien.

Barney's exquisite social mix of the intelligentsia with her outrageous and philosophical regulars was legend. Openly lesbian, she helped make lesbianism fashionable in 1900s cultured Paris. Even more extraordinary was that she was the first woman poet since Sappho to write openly about her love of other women. Barney loved the theater of her Fridays, and made those whom she liked share in her theatrical events. Once, she had herself delivered to her lover Renée Vivien in a box of lilies, alluringly attired for the boudoir. A headline-grabbing moment that Florence would have spotted in the papers, and probably rolled about laughing with her friend Cécile Tellier as they gasped and groaned for breath, was the reported entrance of the exotic dancer and courtesan Mata Hari, not yet infamous as a treacherous spy, to one of Barney's Fridays. The society column inches were flush with reports that Mata Hari daringly appeared in her birthday suit as Lady Godiva astride a white stallion as a prelude to her exotic performance.

---

* Many of Alice Pike Barney's paintings today hang in the Smithsonian Museum in Washington, D.C.

Florence might have been attracted to Barney's Fridays. They would certainly have given her an opportunity, as a salon chanteuse, to meet the rich, the powerful, and the famous. Still, was Florence willing to throw herself into the path of a notable lesbian who was then mourning the death of her British lover, Renée Vivien?* Always plucky, and still light-hearted, Florence may have had second thoughts. There were other salonnières, other Americans.

Perhaps Anna Gould? She was also an American railroad heiress, with a bit of a checkered past. By 1912, Anna was on her second French husband and was known as the Duchess de Sagan. In 1893, Anna had been engaged to Oliver Harriman, a cousin of the railroad magnate Edward Harriman, a close friend of Anna's brother George. In the spring of 1894, she went to Paris to buy her wedding trousseau at the House of Worth, and take up an introduction to Miss Anna Reed, who ran a Paris salon designed to "finish" American heiresses with élan. Reed introduced Anna to the Duc de Talleyrand-Périgord and his young cousin, the Count Marie Paul Ernest Boniface de Castellane, whom everyone called "Boni." By then, Anna had fallen in love with the *ésprit parisien* and mistook the counterfeit Boni for the genuine article. For Castellane, neither Anna's warts nor her clubfoot stood in the way of his pursuit of her eight-figure inheritance. In record time, Boni proposed marriage in anticipation of spending Anna's millions. Against the Gould family's wishes, Anna broke off her engagement to the young Harriman. After much family displeasure, she married the gambling, womanizing, at times bellicose Castellane. No wonder the marriage became Edith Wharton's inspiration for *The Buccaneers.*

Alas for Boni, shortly before the wedding day in New York, the Gould family sprang a trap and demanded his signature on a marriage contract. As distasteful as it was for the cash-strapped Castellane, he had no alternative than to obey. After all, his creditors, too, had already spent Anna's millions. But neither he nor his creditors realized whom they

---

* Vivien's life was short (1877–1909) and marred by drug abuse. Her birth name was Pauline Mary Tarn, and she inherited her British father's fortune at age twenty-one, moving to France permanently thereafter. Her mother became British upon her marriage, but had been born in Jackson, Michigan.

were dealing with: Anna maintained full control of her portion of the Gould family trust.[5]

By 1907, the Castellanes' internationally publicized divorce filled the society pages in France and the United States. Apparently, Boni had somehow managed to put Anna some $4.5 million in debt,* mostly in building their "pink palace" on avenue Malakoff. The family trust had to bail her out, but only on the proviso that her brother George become her official civil trustee in Paris, to prevent Boni from leeching more money from the estate.[6] Upon their divorce, Boni received a settlement of $250,000 and an annual income of $30,000—approximately a lump-sum payment of $6.11 million and annual income of $733,000 in today's money—from Anna's portion of the trust. Two years later, believing that she had secured a dispensation from Rome to marry Boni's cousin, the wealthy Hélie de Talleyrand-Périgord, Duc de Talleyrand and Prince de Sagan, Anna Gould of Tarrytown, New York, became a French duchess.

While Florence might have also read about Anna Gould's brother Frank Jay Gould, who was embroiled in his first divorce about the same time, it was Anna who attracted her eye. How could such an unattractive but wealthy woman, whose family had been shunned by the social set of New York for dozens of years, marry twice? Hadn't Anna recently been described by the Parisian Symbolist poet and aesthete Robert de Montesquiou as having "the eyes of a captured chimpanzee"?[7] No, Anna's salon, while hosting the aristocracy of Parisian society, would be too dull for Florence Lacaze. If there was one thing she was determined to have, it was excitement.

Unless or until the family's finances were on a sounder footing, Florence simply had to either marry her millions or sing for her living. Still, there was one American living in Paris who had the potential to offer Florence both. Winnaretta—"Winnie" to her friends—the Princesse de Polignac, held a salon dedicated to music and the arts in her home on avenue Henri-Martin on the Right Bank. Born in Yonkers, New York, Winnie embodied all that Florence hungered to be: wealthy, musical, and the throbbing heart of society.

---

* Approximately $109 million in 2017 dollars.

Winnie's inherited wealth came from her father, Isaac Merritt Singer, and his sewing machines. Her mother was the beautiful and musical Isabella Eugénie Boyer, thirty years her father's junior. Winnaretta was their second child, born at the end of the Civil War in 1865.* Her first memories, however, were of southern England. Just before the Franco-Prussian War of 1870–71, Isaac Singer emigrated from France to England, buying a home in London's Grosvenor Square and a sprawling estate in Paignton, Devon, which he ironically christened "The Wigwam."

When her father died, the ten-year-old Winnie returned to Paris to live with her mother and siblings. After a brief and incompatible marriage to Prince Louis de Scey-Montbéliard, at the age of twenty-two, which Winnie had agreed to merely to be released from her mother's overbearing guardianship, Winnie made it known that she would never again be dominated by another person.[8]

Newly divorced, Winnaretta—more frequently than not called "Madame Singer" by high society—established her own avant-garde music salon. She also began traveling widely throughout Europe, indulging herself in the luxury of escape. But eighteen months later, she unexpectedly agreed to marry Prince Edmond de Polignac. Why? He was a suspected homosexual and nearly thirty years her senior. True, his father was the son of Marie-Antoinette's beloved friend Yolande, Duchesse de Polignac. Still, French high society mocked the union in loud stage whispers. It was yet another unsuitable marriage. What le Tout-Paris hadn't known at the time was that Winnaretta was a confirmed lesbian. The marriage was a highly successful and affectionate one and may not have been a *marriage blanc* (unconsummated). While the role of women was changing rapidly, it was thought impossible for a divorced woman—no matter how much money she had—to become a successful salonnière. Winnaretta's all-too-short marriage to Edmond was a happy one, ending abruptly with Edmond's death in August 1901.

Unlike Natalie Barney's Fridays, Winnaretta, Princesse de Polignac, held her salon on the days that suited her performers. She had a lifelong

---

* Before marrying Isabella, Singer, a one-time traveling actor with his own troupe called the Merritt Players, had fathered sixteen children without the benefit of clergy. Winnaretta's siblings were brothers Mortimer, Washington, Paris, and Franklin, and sister Isabelle-Blanche, known as Belle-Blanche.

devotion to Wagner's music. Equally, she wanted to promote baroque music and the neglected genius of Handel and Bach. What especially interested Florence was that Winnaretta actively sought out living singers and composers who were still searching for their audiences. Today's international musical glitterati—Maurice Ravel, Claude Debussy, Serge Diaghilev, Frederick Delius, and Igor Stravinsky—owe their first successes to Winnaretta, Princesse de Polignac, and her salon. Yet, for Florence, it was the princess's interest in Marcel Proust's composer and singer lover, Reynaldo Hahn, that struck a chord. Winnaretta worked tirelessly to bring Hahn's music to public acclaim. Hahn had set poems written by Verlaine and Robert Louis Stevenson to his music in his *Études latines* and *Le ruban dénoué*, and he repeatedly performed at Winnaretta's salon as pianist and singer. Since Winnaretta took on neglected composers, perhaps she could also discover Florence and her voice?[9]

Florence saw further attractions to Winnaretta's salon, too. She promoted writers and artists. The young Jean Cocteau, later one of Florence's great friends, made early appearances at the salon, where he met the influential Marcel Proust. D. H. Lawrence was personally championed, too, in London for the Polignac Prize, awarded annually by the Royal Society of Literature.[*]

Florence, looking to establish herself in high society, might have reflected on the rumors that Winnaretta was a lesbian, but de Polignac seemed quite different from most who were increasingly uninhibited and set out to shock the world of high society. Hadn't the young novelist Colette[†] abandoned her unscrupulous reporter-satirist husband Henry Gauthier-Villars, known to all as "Willy," and taken to the stage at the Folies Bergère, performing with her lover, "Missy," the Marquise de Belbeuf? Didn't their lingering kisses in the middle of one of their numbers rock Paris? Colette, naturally, went further in her declaration of love for Missy by wearing bracelets engraved with the message "I belong to Missy."[10]

From everything Florence read, she knew that Winnaretta was sensitive to public opinion. She wanted no scandals. She was discreet and

---

* Lawrence was denied the prize by the jury.

† Born Sidonie-Gabrielle Colette (1873–1954), and nominated for the Nobel Prize for Literature in 1948.

took great pains to keep her private life private. Winnaretta used the coded mores of the nobility's world, and was protected by them: in one's private life, everything was permitted and possible so long as the unbroken veneer of public life was preserved.[11] So, if the price of fame and fortune meant that Florence had to cozy up to the Princesse de Polignac, perhaps it was worth the effort. First, though, Florence would need to find a way to be discovered by Winnaretta. The question remained: how? Failure was not an option she considered.

4

WAR AND THE BOY NEXT DOOR

I know only that what is moral is what you feel good after,
and what is immoral is what you feel bad after.

—ERNEST HEMINGWAY

WINNARETTA SINGER, PRINCESSE DE POLIGNAC, NEVER SPECIFICALLY mentioned engaging the aspiring chanteuse for her salon. Neither did Florence, for that matter. While the rest of the world watched Kaiser Wilhelm II rattle his saber at Europe, Florence was fully engaged in her homework, reading the society columns and attempting to get noticed among the American salonnières of Paris. Age nineteen, she remained unsuccessful in penetrating the rarefied echelons of the opera house, through either her breathtaking beauty or her voice. Her old professor had failed to introduce her into the world of the salonnières, and so Florence had become petulant, storming about, raging even, blaming everyone but herself or her singing voice for her signal failure to conquer Paris. A new obstacle had been placed in the way of her success. It seemed to her that all Paris had gone "Russian mad."

Serge Diaghilev, impresario of the Ballets Russes, had found favor with Winnaretta and other patrons while Florence was still a mere child. Winnaretta's stunning friend Élisabeth Greffulhe also used her position in society to promote modern music and musical artists—albeit without

Winnaretta's immense fortune. Presumably, Florence toyed with all sorts of possibilities for discovery, including abandoning the American-led salons in favor of others, like Élisabeth Greffulhe's, or more controversially, offering herself on the altar of one of the many high-society lesbian patrons of le Tout-Paris. Still, all things Russian prevailed in Florence's eyes. There were Nikolai Rimsky-Korsakov's exotic operas, ballet dancing by Anna Pavlova and the sensuous Tamara Karsavina, as well as the incomparable Vaslav Nijinsky. Even the androgynously beautiful Ida Rubinstein danced to packed houses. Diaghilev teamed up with Winnaretta's new friend, Igor Stravinsky, for their Russian ballet, *The Firebird*. It was simply maddening for the aspiring chanteuse—as if the voice had been squeezed from all musical interludes by these instrumentalist Russians to Florence's personal detriment.

The more Florence failed to enter the rarefied society of *le gratin*, or the upper crust, and rub shoulders with them, the more she ignored world-changing events surrounding her. Granted, Florence was very young. Yet she was also very clear-sighted when the need arose. It was no accident that she ignored suffragettes on her very doorstep and the drive to gain the right to vote entirely. The growth of the labor movement in Europe was a matter lingering on someone else's horizon. Social unrest in Paris, dozens of political scandals, and the deep scars left by the *Affaire* on the Third Republic appear to have affected her little. The isms of the early twentieth century simply held no meaning. The realpolitik of Germany's march to world dominance was equally ignored. Half the civilized world of Europe was trying to avert war, while the other half armed itself for the "great and joyous" conflagration ahead, according to the French press. The status quo was changing, with many salonnières like Winnaretta decamping to the relative safety of England or Switzerland. Yet Florence took notice only of herself, cocooned in the knowledge of her eye-catching beauty that must—*absolutely must*—lead to her fame and fortune. She was then, and would remain, no joiner of grand causes other than her own.

Nonetheless, the changes, even on a purely Parisian scale, were incredible. Florence never mentioned if she had been aware of the old Montmartre factory called the Bateau-Lavoir, the studio shared by Pablo Picasso and Georges Braque at the time—so christened because it creaked like the floating laundries moored along the Seine. Nor had the return of Leonardo da Vinci's painting of the Mona Lisa to the Louvre by its Italian thief figured in her recollections. Even the Bonnot Gang, that anarchist group who pioneered the criminal use of the motorcar in Paris, terrorizing neighborhood after neighborhood with their daring bank robberies, was beneath her lofty gaze. Still, she can be applauded for omitting Esperanto from her lexicon, made popular in France after the World Congress in 1905 at Boulogne-sur-Mer to promote the high-flown, ersatz language originally intended to break down barriers.

On an international level, it was odd that a young woman like Florence, who later claimed to have always adored Impressionist art, did not see the dangers lurking in Kaiser Wilhelm's headline-grabbing ethnic cleansing of the Berlin Königlichen National-Galerie of its French Impressionist collections. Kaiser Wilhelm was determined to undermine the dominance of France in all forms of the arts as a central doctrine of his war aims. His mantra was simply that Berlin must replace Paris as the seat of international cultural power. In Florence's defense, France, prior to the Great War of 1914–1918, felt its place as the world's cultural capital was secure.

Florence was well aware of Impressionism, Postimpressionism, Cubism, Futurism, Expressionism, Fauvism, Progressivism, avant-gardism, and more in fine art, literature, and music. She knew they divided thought and engendered debate as topics of conversation required of any salonnière. Still, her youth prevented her from understanding that these very changes in artistic tastes would impact her personal goals. Her singular determination to succeed was admirable, but it blinded her to the significance of the cauldron of emotions surrounding her and all of civilized Europe. It seems that Florence was never truly political until later in life; but then again, that may have been an illusion purposely created retrospectively through her living a life with mirrors.

∽

Just before the guns of August 1914 fired for the first time, heralding in the bloody Great War—known today as World War I—a young American man came to Paris. Henry Chittenden Heynemann, a former neighbor of the Lacaze family in Belvedere, California, was visiting Europe with his mother and older brother, James, and decided to look up Florence. Henry claimed publicly that the purpose of his European sojourn was to study architecture.[1] Florence proclaimed it was to woo her, and, frankly, not a minute too soon. Henry's father, Manfred Heynemann, was reputed to be a "blue jeans" millionaire; and since Manfred had died nine years earlier, surely, Florence and Berthe believed, Henry had come into a great deal of money.[2] That was their first greedy mistake.

Henry was the youngest child born to a Philadelphia society mother, Alice M. Hotchkiss, and immigrant father, Manfred H. Heynemann. Originally from Melbourne, Australia, Henry's paternal grandfather became a naturalized U.S. citizen in 1872. On Manfred's passport application, dated January 8, 1900, he declared a point of interest at the heart of the Lacaze women's dilemma: "I am domiciled in the United States, my permanent residence being at San Francisco in the State of California [since the age of six] where I follow the occupation of merchant; that I am about to go abroad temporarily, and that I intend to return to the United States inside of two years with the purpose of residing and performing the duties of citizenship therein."[3]

So, why did the twenty-three-year-old Heynemann choose the month before the outbreak of war to visit Florence? Was it to join his brother James, as some newspapers surmised? Or was it to study at the École des Beaux-Arts, as he told the newspapers later? Florence alleged, many years later, that they had never stopped writing to one another after she left San Francisco. Had Florence asked Heynemann to come, and if so, on what grounds? Was it purely out of old friendship, as she later pretended? Maybe it had something to do with her fear of being trapped in the coming conflagration. After all, she had already experienced two natural disasters, and should not have willingly put herself in the path of a war. Or maybe it was simply an innocent, open invitation extended without a thought or care that he would ever come.

Another possibility was that Charles Loeb had reported back unfavorably on Florence's and Isabelle's U.S. citizenships—and thereby any right to claim their inheritance from their father in the United States. Had it become essential for Florence to reside in California again, because Berthe was unwilling to go? Perhaps Berthe felt she could not achieve the same results as her stunning daughter, who could always act for her under a power of attorney. As it turned out, both mother and daughter felt that the most expedient solution would be for Florence to marry an American. Although Maximin's estate may have been negligible, Florinte's legacy was sizable. As Manfred Heynemann's passport application indicates, being an alien American, or expatriate, was—and still is—a tricky point for the government of the United States. This explanation might also reveal why Florence approached Henry, and not the elder son, James, the presumed heir to the Heynemann fortune. James was already a grown teen in 1906 when she left San Francisco, and would not have noticed a pretty child of ten.

Whatever the catalyst for young Heynemann's visit, there had been some change in the Lacaze family's circumstances. The lovely apartment overlooking the Luxembourg Gardens at 2 rue de Fleurus was no more. By 1914 they lived in a comely apartment at 143 boulevard Raspail in the heart of Montparnasse—the increasingly popular, yet more inexpensive, bohemian district of Paris. Cécile Tellier and her family had also moved to an apartment in the reasonably priced Montparnasse quarter at 10 rue Stanislas. Belts were tightened, too. Florence had yet to make any impact on Parisian society. Apparently, Loeb was frustrated, so far, in obtaining Berthe's inheritance or her rights to her husband's estate. Later in life, Florence told her friends that she was making "remarkable progress" as a singer by 1914. Notwithstanding her boast, the old professor was gone, and she was reduced to being accompanied by Cécile Tellier's mother, a piano teacher.

∽

At the end of June, Archduke Franz Ferdinand, heir to the Austrian throne, was murdered in Sarajevo. Everyone, except Florence and Henry, talked of war. Whether the young architecture student arrived in Paris on July 1, 1914, as a friend, childhood sweetheart, or potential victim of Berthe's necessity and Florence's wiles remains their secret. Staying at the Hôtel Matignon with his mother,* Henry wrote in his brown leather travel diary, titled "My Trip Abroad," that Florence was a "beauty" and

---

* By all newspaper accounts James was in Europe, but not in Paris, with his brother and mother. Florence's recollections bear out this point, too.

"a dream." Her sister, Isabelle, rated a mention, too, as very "Frenchy" without much English to her credit. Apparently, the three girls—Florence, Cécile, and Isabelle—showed him the cultural sights of the city unchaperoned by any parent. A trip to Magic City, the mock Coney Island amusement park erected near the Eiffel Tower, rounded off their evening, with Henry accompanying the three girls home just before midnight. While culture and amusement parks were grand, and the girls "swell," Henry hadn't traveled all the way from San Francisco to miss the City of Light's notorious nightspots. Already, Maxim's was the restaurant where one went to see the rich and famous. Then there were the dance halls—the most famous of which were, of course, the Moulin Rouge, featuring Yvette Guilbert, and the Folies Bergère, starring Gaby Deslys.[4] Henry frequented both, but not before depositing Florence home with her mother.

By day, Florence and Henry were chaperoned by Cécile and Isabelle. They visited the the Cluny Museum, the Pantheon, the St. Geneviève Library, the Louvre, and the Eiffel Tower. After supper, the foursome went out again to Magic City with its noisy rides and shrieks of joy. After midnight, Henry went off without the girls, time and again, to see the *real* sights of Paris—the Bal Tabarin and the Folies Bergère, where he hoped to make carnal conquests of its girls.[5] After all, Florence was not of their ilk.

While he seemed smitten with Florence, Henry continued his grand tour of Europe in the company of his mother. Within the month, they were joined by his brother James in Switzerland. Somehow, Florence extracted a promise that Henry would rejoin the Lacaze family in the southwest of France. He rather lukewarmly added the phrase "should time permit" in his letter to her. That tepid caveat speaks volumes. Seemingly, Henry's mother wanted to put some distance between her son and his steamy enchantress, Florence. She was so anxious, in fact, that the Heynemanns blindly traveled that July to Germany and Italy.

On July 29, the socialist leaders of Europe consulted with one another in Brussels in an atmosphere of "hopelessness and frustration."[6] The declaration of war that followed days later should not have been a surprise, since the newspapers burned with hourly updates. Still, for thousands of tourists—and particularly Americans—it was dumbfounding, leaving them slack-jawed. Horrified holidaymakers gathered in their hotel lobbies, gawping. Some wondered aloud what to do, and damned their hotel staff for not speaking better English. The male staff, meanwhile, quit their jobs to join the swelling ranks of marching men filing past their hotel windows toward glory. Female staff either made do or joined the nurses' training corps. Thousands of Americans scrambled away to seaports to hop on ocean liners to take them home. Thousands more were stuck for weeks. In an age before credit cards, the French government, in its infinite wisdom, froze all foreign currency transactions, making it impossible for banks to honor Americans' letters of credit or travelers' checks. Hotel bills couldn't be paid. Food couldn't be bought. Americans threw themselves on the mercy of their embassy, just as other nations' tourists clamored at their consulates' doors.[7]

Paris was bathed in chaos. On July 31, Germany published its ultimatum, or *Kriegsgefahr*, to Russia and initiated the preliminary mobilization of its troops. The antimilitarist French Socialist leader, Jean Jaurès, freshly returned from Brussels, attempted, but failed, to apply pressure on France's Parlement. Nonetheless, he wrote an article condemning the coming war, and left the offices of the newspaper *L'Humanité* at nine p.m. exhausted. As usual, he dined with colleagues at the Café Croissant nearby. While he was eating, and talking with his back to the open window on that steamy Paris evening, a young man appeared, pointed a pistol at Jaurès, crying out "Pacifist!" and "Traitor!" and fired twice. Jaurès slumped to one side and fell forward across the table. He died minutes later. The news choked the streets of Paris like the flames from the San Francisco earthquake. Cries of *"Vive Jaurès!"* reverberated everywhere. Anatole France sobbed, "My heart is breaking." All Frenchmen understood that without the calming voice of Jaurès, war was inevitable. As Austrian writer Stefan Zweig lamented, long afterward, "We all relied on Jaurès" to stop the madness. It was now up to Premier René Viviani to ensure calm. He issued an appeal for unity. The last thing France needed was the social unrest of which Jaurès had warned Viviani mere hours before his assassination.[8]

Most likely, soon after the assassination, Florence and her family headed south to the small spa town of Cauterets, near the Spanish border in the Haute Pyrénées, situated only twenty miles southwest of the celebrated town of miracles, Lourdes.* Florence later claimed that Cauterets had been the family retreat from Paris for summer holidays for years. Still, at the time, they would have been seen by those who remained in the capital as *froussards*—panic merchants—and frankly, unpatriotic. As Florence and her family left Paris, the *poilus*—common conscripts—flooded into the train station at Gare de l'Est, drunk with elation, or despair, to die for their country. By the time war was declared on August 3, 1914, Paris felt deserted, deprived of the bulk of its men of fighting age.[9]

The newspapers, however, reported only events depicting typical patriotic fervor. No one knew that this "War to End All Wars" would last beyond Christmas. While Berthe read the buoyant morning papers aloud to her daughters, hailing the "fresh and joyous" battles to come, they must have been concerned that the object of their desires, young Henry, was somewhere in Germany or Italy—deep within the borders of France's implacable enemies.

Whatever arguments or internal struggles Henry suffered, amazingly, he appeared on the Lacaze doorstep in mid-August without his mother. Mrs. Heynemann had departed for San Francisco. But why had she left for home without her son? Had they argued over the suitability of his attachment to Florence? Or had Henry, as his mother's youngest son, persuaded her that it was necessary for her to go home to prepare for his return with his bride? Had Alice Heynemann decided that by leaving her errant son alone in France, he might see his error, without the need to engage him in some unseemly squabble? Whether Henry told his mother before they separated that he intended to rejoin Florence remains unsaid, but Alice would have been an idiot (which she was not) if she hadn't guessed what would happen next.

This time, neither Berthe nor Florence would allow Henry to escape. He gleefully reported his encounters with the Germans, which were translated by a hungry press as his having been arrested for spying. Ap-

---

* Lourdes is where, in 1858, the Virgin Mary is believed to have appeared to Saint Bernadette (Marie-Bernard Soubirous). Known internationally for its Sanctuaries Notre-Dame de Lourdes, or the Domain, it is one of the most significant pilgrimage sites in Europe.

parently, "On one occasion, . . . when we were travelling homeward from Vienna,* the train was stopped by the military and the officers hearing us speak English asked us if we were of that nationality. 'Not by a long way,'" he replied, showing their American papers. The officer duly saluted and they were bothered no further.[10]

Despite his seeming devil-may-care attitude, the war had hit Henry hard. While the Europe of his dreams held the mysteries of the best of European architecture and rediscovery of his beauty, Florence, train travel brought with it the constant sight of wounded troops, suffering from horrific injuries. Refugee camps hastily installed along the railway tracks—filled only with women and children—were burned into his psyche. Thank heavens, he thought on more than one occasion, that America would not enter the war. He needed to forget all he'd seen, and Florence was just the tonic required. The lazy summer days in southwest France, where he was charmed by the countryside and his delectable girl, slowly performed their magic, but Henry still did not propose marriage. At the end of the first week, Florence knew she'd simply have to take matters into her own, rather more competent, hands.

On the morning of Alice Heynemann's birthday, August 21, Florence pounced. At seven in the morning, she entered Henry's bedroom and took the bold step of asking Henry to marry her. This was no mere ingénue's prim marriage proposal to a shy lad from across the gulf of the family sofa or living room. This was young Florence at her alluring best. Henry was still in bed. Her long wavy blonde tresses probably were draped over her shoulder as she was wont to do. She approached him with her feline walk, her swaying, uncorseted, shapely body seductively visible through her dressing gown.[11] As was her habit when vamping a man, she spoke softly, her hypnotic eyes locking his, her lips a mere inch from his own. Henry was flabbergasted, and frankly didn't stand a chance. Overwhelmed, he gladly accepted. It never occurred to him to question her motives.

Then the real performance began. An hour later when the happy couple broke the news, Berthe claimed that she felt Henry was too young,

---

* The Heynemanns were most likely originally of Austrian descent, since Henry's father, too, visited Austria whenever he could.

too immature, to marry her daughter. Still, she liked him very much. Alas, Berthe and her daughters were obliged to do the only sensible thing in the circumstances. They decamped the next day to Lourdes, *sans* Henry. Naturally, the moonstruck Henry followed. He was greeted cordially and pleaded his case, most likely proposing a marriage settlement to Berthe for spiriting away her lovely Florence to San Francisco. Berthe still did not give in. The Lacazes headed to Toulouse, where a mortified Henry in tow couldn't stop complaining of a toothache. Already, he was getting on Florence's nerves. When Florence protested that he was acting like a child, he promised he'd buy her a first engagement present if she took pity on him and brought him to the nearest dentist. His nerves were frayed by his toothache and Berthe's reluctance to acknowledge Florence's proposal of marriage to him. Fed up, Henry probably threatened to make a dignified retreat via Spain to catch an ocean liner back home if Berthe would not agree to their marriage.

Like any wildcat, Florence knew it was time to move in for the kill. She told Berthe Henry was ready to talk dollars and cents. If they didn't move now, they risked losing the squirming fish on the line. The marriage settlement agreed between Berthe and Henry has never been published, yet it should be assumed that Charles Loeb was advising Berthe behind the scenes via telegram. Henry would need to settle an income on her daughter—enough to help with Berthe's and Isabelle's expenses in Paris, too. Then he would need to compensate Berthe for the loss of potential income Florence could have earned as an opera singer. Then there was the matter of religion. The Protestant Henry must agree not to interfere with Florence's religion, and to understand that any children of the union would be raised as Catholics. Furthermore, Henry could not claim any of Florence's inheritance from her grandmother, father, or eventually, Berthe herself. It was a no-brainer for Henry: he'd seen the apartment on boulevard Raspail and knew they were living respectably but without any great fortune. At last, Berthe relented and gave her willing approval. A telegram was sent off at once to Loeb in Paris to draw up the necessary documents, while Henry bought Florence an engagement present of a fine gold wristwatch.[12]

Henry, at twenty-three, did not need parental consent, in either

America or France. But Florence was only nineteen. According to French law, the consent of her mother was essential, and Henry knew it. By shilly-shallying, Berthe had won significant concessions that were designed to resolve the family's financial crisis at a stroke, irrespective of the outcome of Florence's efforts regarding the inheritance in San Francisco. Berthe's telegram to Loeb stressed that time was of the essence. Henry was losing patience. To placate Henry, a trip to Carcassonne to see its famous medieval Cité fortress—now a UNESCO World Heritage Site—was planned to celebrate their betrothal.

Of course, Henry cabled his mother to let her know the news, and that he would soon be coming home with his bride—that is, once Alice settled her son's financial promises to Berthe. With all foreign transactions still frozen in France, it was suggested by Berthe that Spain might offer a viable solution to their problem. The suggestion seems to have come from Loeb; however, Berthe decided on her own embellishments.

Mother and daughter agreed that Florence should accompany the impressionable Henry to Madrid, where the letter of credit sent from San Francisco could be cashed. Perhaps Florence could marry Henry in Madrid, too, Berthe schemed. A further enticement, if Henry needed any, would be to show him the marvelous architecture of the great cities of Barcelona and the Spanish capital. Berthe agreed that Florence should go unchaperoned to Spain with Henry, on the pretext of marriage there. In that way, should Henry's mother fail to fulfill his financial undertaking, Berthe would be able to sue him (and her) for breach of promise and ruining Florence's reputation. So the young couple left for Spain on September 25, 1914.[13]

Once Loeb was made aware of Berthe's thinking, he must have advised that the proposed "marriage" in Madrid was impossible. While French law gave foreigners marrying in France the full force and benefit of its laws, publication of the bans of marriage was left to the national law of the foreigner. Since America didn't have rules regarding publication of bans, nor any public proclamation by summons of the people of the parish, the pair could readily be married in Paris—so long as Florence's family published the bans for her. French law allowed Florence to marry a foreigner (Henry) in a foreign country (Spain), so long as the marriage took place in the legal form of that country, and that publication of the bans and the written consent of the parents had been fulfilled in France.[14] Loeb was protecting his client from a grievous mistake, since Florence's nationality had been declared as French.

Soon enough, the would-be bride and groom discovered the difficulties of a marriage in Madrid for themselves. On announcing their intention at the American embassy, they were informed that American law would not apply to Florence until after the marriage—when she would automatically assume her husband's nationality. For the marriage to be valid, the bans needed to be posted on the walls of the Mairie de Paris (city hall) ten days prior to the marriage taking place.[15] Chances are, too, that Florence and Henry had consummated their union in anticipation of the marriage. For Henry, a properly brought-up young man, there could be no honorable way back.

While Madrid was not where they were married, contrary to many announcements in the press, it is where money arrived to complete Henry's side of the financial bargain struck with Berthe. On their return to Paris on October 13, the bans were posted and Berthe received her hard-earned payment in cash. Florence shopped for her trousseau, while Henry met up with old friends at the Imperial Club. Berthe gave her future son-in-law a diamond-studded tiepin in the shape of a swastika—in those days believed to be an ancient symbol of good luck. The new couple's passage was booked back to New York on the *Rochambeau*, due to leave Le Havre on October 31. Precisely ten working days after their arrival from Spain, on October 27, at ten in the morning, Henry and Florence were married at the Mairie de Paris. Florence's witnesses were her mother and Charles G. Loeb. Henry's two witnesses were Cécile Tellier's mother and Henry's friend from the Imperial Club, Henry Hargreaves. On cue, Henry pronounced his "oui" when prompted, and the pair were finally joined in wedlock. Once Florence obtained absolution for the sin of marrying a Protestant the next day at church, the pair were officially blessed by Abbé Chazot.[16]

Three days later, Mr. and Mrs. Henry C. Heynemann embarked on the *Rochambeau* for New York, surrounded by refugees, infants, and fleeing Americans. Meanwhile, J. P. Morgan and company had persuaded the French government to allow it to transfer enough letters of credit and American Express travelers' checks to fund the repatriation of any American who approached them. Only one American defaulted on the generous loan.[17]

What mattered to Florence was that she was once again American, and on her way to San Francisco to claim the family fortune at long last.

5

⌒⊙⊙⊙⌒

YOUNG MRS. HEYNEMANN

*If you are lucky enough to have lived in Paris as a young
man, then wherever you go for the rest of your life it stays
with you, for Paris is a moveable feast.*

—ERNEST HEMINGWAY

BACK THEN, FLORENCE LACAZE HEYNEMANN WAS EXPERT AT KEEP-
ing her thoughts to herself regarding her return to the United States,
and ultimately, to San Francisco. Having married an American, and
taken his nationality—or more precisely retaken it—Florence would
waste no time in settling the family's affairs in California. First, she and
Henry had to cross to the West Coast by steamer through the newly
opened Panama Canal.*

Originally, a generation earlier, the monumental project had been
undertaken by the Frenchman Ferdinand de Lesseps, builder of the Suez
Canal, but he had failed to complete the work due to outbreaks of yellow
fever and malaria in his workforce, and was thereafter dogged by financial difficulties. The United States took over de Lesseps's bankrupt company and began work on the project in 1906.[1] Florence never recorded
her impressions of this tremendous feat of engineering for posterity, as

---

* It was opened to its first traffic on August 15, 1914.

she neglected to do with so many other significant moments she witnessed in her long life.

The happy couple's return to San Francisco was heralded with a page-one news item in the *San Francisco Chronicle* headlined HEYNEMANN WELL-KNOWN and subtitled "Architect and his [*sic*] Bride Members of Bay Cities Society." At last, Florence had arrived as part of le gratin, albeit of San Francisco. Annoyingly to her, the newspaper article gave prominence to her husband:

> Henry Chittenden Heynemann is well known in the younger circles of society of the bay cities, and the announcement of his marriage to Miss Florence Lacaze, formerly of Belvedere and this city, was received with much interest by their many friends here.
>
> Heynemann received his degree in architecture from the University of Pennsylvania last spring, and it was following this that he went abroad to pursue his studies. He is the son of Mrs. Manfred H. Heynemann of Belvedere . . . and also had a number of exciting experiences in being mistaken for a spy by both the Germans and French.
>
> Miss Florence Lacaze, to whom Heynemann was married at Madrid [*sic*], on October 27th, is also a student of architecture, but more recently has been studying music abroad with a view to an operatic career.[2]

The flagrant inaccuracies contained in the article indicate that neither Florence nor Henry nor his family were consulted before printing. Although she had made page one of the biggest newspaper in the city, it was all wrong, and the article, rightly, rankled with her. It was her first important lesson in dealing with the press.

The *Oakland Tribune* featured a large picture of the couple with the caption beneath: MR. AND MRS. H.C.S. HEYNEMANN WHO ARE NOW ON THEIR WAY HOME TO BERKELEY AS THEY APPEARED ON THEIR ARRIVAL IN NEW YORK AFTER THRILLING WAR ZONE EXPERIENCES.[3] The article, contrary to the one in the *San Francisco Chronicle,* made it clear that Henry's elder brother, James, was not accompanying the newlyweds, in what would have been seen by readers as a breach of good form and manners. Nonetheless, the paper couldn't help but report the sensational ordeal that Henry allegedly endured: "Heynemann was captured in Europe by soldiers on three occasions, sentenced once to death, and finally met Miss Florence Lacaze with whom he had gone to school as a child in Belvedere. She had come to Paris after studying art in Madrid [*sic*]. She secured his release from custody and later they were married. They fled from Paris, arriving in New York to embark for the Pacific Coast via the canal."[4]

While a thrilling tale that made everyone want to congratulate Florence and Henry, it was more than an embellishment of the truth. Probably prompted by Florence, shortly after their arrival in the Bay Area, Henry made a statement to the *Oakland Tribune* that was reported in the December 11, 1914, edition. Still, they got other bits of the story wrong: that Henry "traversed in his trip 40,000 miles passing through nine of the war torn [*sic*] countries of Europe" being the most flagrant. Henry denied the rumors of his being captured as a spy, and explained why any English speaker needed to show his or her passport. The most accurate news the *Oakland Tribune* announced was that Mrs. Manfred H. Heynemann would be entertaining the newlyweds at the Century Club on December 19, in what was promising to be quite a lavish affair.[5]

New Year's Eve was spent partying in the Oakland area, with Henry showing off his exquisite bride. They were brought to the party of Mr. and Mrs. Hugh Hogan, as the guests of a French couple, Mr. and Mrs. Leon Maison. The Maisons were acquainted with Berthe and, most probably, with the cousins of Maximin Lacaze. Within ten days of arriving in the city, Florence had begun to discover what had happened to the family's inheritance.

In January, the couple moved to San Francisco proper at Florence's behest, because she claimed she needed the excitement and culture of the city. In truth, living in the city made her daily sojourns to resolve her family's affairs with lawyers easier. Within a month, it became evident to Henry that his bride had come "home" with more pressing matters in mind than sampling San Francisco's cultural attractions, much less being a wife.

Surprisingly, Florence wrapped up her family's affairs in relative short order. It can be presumed that Maximin had lived indebted to his cousins in his final years, and had not left an appreciable pot of gold. If he had, then Florence would have litigated to reclaim what must have been rightfully hers. Indeed, within a few years, she would demonstrate how she could litigate expertly from the shadows, and use the press to her advantage. Berthe's claim to her mother's inheritance was another matter. Florence could, acting under her mother's power of attorney, legally claim the inheritance for her mother, so long as she declared her intention to remain in San Francisco, and that Berthe would return to the city to live with her. She signed whatever paperwork was necessary and arranged for Berthe to countersign the required documents.

By mid-March 1915, the five-month marriage was already on the proverbial rocks, and Florence was gone. Henry was crestfallen, but remained determined to give a salutary lesson to other young men who intended to make international marriages—ninety percent of which ended in divorce. That April, Henry went public again, explaining eloquently to the world why, in his opinion, his short marriage was over:

> The personal equation was simply swamped by forces we failed to recognize before we were married.
>
> It was a case of love battling against environment, and in the end environment was too strong. But when she came here with me she left behind her all the refinement and culture to which she had become attached as part of her very life she was forced to abandon, and the tug upon her fine nature was too severe.
>
> My wife was a songbird, that I found in Paradise. I brought her away—from the atmosphere of art, music and the highest culture in the world, wherein she had been reared and to which she had become accustomed as part of her very existence. . . .
>
> She came here with me, to a land where people spoke a different language and where the very ideals to which she had been bred were changed.
>
> She found life as we live it—simple, crude in comparison to the culture of Paris, and art a mere smattering. She was not happy. She pined, as a delicate bird of paradise would when taken from its

environs. I knew she would not be happy here. She must return to her own home in Paris. So it was arranged. . . .

Paris is as impossible for me as San Francisco is for her. . . . I do not speak the French language. My business is here. I must make money here. There is the dilemma.[6]

Or, perhaps, there was the rub. Had Florence believed that she was marrying a fabulously wealthy, albeit younger son of a blue jeans millionaire? Perhaps she kidded herself that she had. After all, the Heynemanns made a generous settlement on her mother. If Florence truly believed it, she allowed her imagination to get the better of her. The glaring truth was that Henry was a man who had to make his way in the world by *working* for a living. He was merely a necessary tool Florence used to regain her American nationality and reclaim the family's inheritance.

Instead of admitting such cold and cruel calculation, Florence said that the error lay in her believing she could make her life in San Francisco. A life with Henry merely as his wife was not the life she believed she'd signed up for. She told her husband that she needed to return to Paris to continue her operatic studies—once the war permitted—at the Conservatoire de Paris. It was the only thing that would make her happy. Yet this, too, was a bald lie. Florence never attended the Conservatoire de Paris, either before or after her marriage to Henry. Indeed, her entire "opera career" was a mere sham.[7]

∽

While Henry remained pliable to Florence's will, what neither bride nor groom recognized was that things would need to get an awful lot nastier before any divorce could be granted. Understandably, Alice Heynemann and her other children pressed Henry to divorce Florence on the grounds of desertion. Yet, in 1915, this was still the ungentlemanly thing to do. From Florence's viewpoint, she needed grounds for divorce that met the strict regulations set forth in the French civil code.

In France, there were only three reasons for granting a divorce—or recognizing a foreign divorce. First and foremost was adultery by either the wife or husband. Second was mental or physical cruelty, which included publicly uttered grave insults. The third cause was the condemnation of one of the parties to an infamous crime or felony.[8] The third cause was a nonstarter. Still, unless and until she could prove adultery or mental or physical cruelty, Florence would never be free again to marry. Desertion was included in the civil code as part of the "grave insults" catchall intended to release unhappy couples, but Florence wisely was not prepared to take the blame for the breakdown of the marriage. That would spoil her chances of remarrying a wealthier catch.

Lawyers on both sides put their heads together to find the safest solution to meet the seemingly unending tribulations of dissolving an international marriage. At first Henry preferred the chivalrous way out: he would insult Florence publicly, calling her a "butterfly" in the press. While hardly an insult today, at the beginning of the twentieth century, it was unkind, even if perhaps true in Florence's case. To "butterfly" not only meant to flit or flutter, but was also politely used to describe someone without substance, a gambler, a sonneteer, or a young person without purpose.[9] Apparently, the insult was insufficiently grave to convince Florence or her lawyers that it would stand up in French law. Henry loved Florence utterly, and was prepared to set her free, even if that meant a scandal. So, a scandalous set of circumstances appeared in the press across America that he had committed adultery with a woman in the Midwest.

On August 11, 1916, Florence filed for divorce in San Francisco. Although the divorce papers were sealed, the *San Francisco Chronicle* reported that "the testimony of another woman may be brought out if the divorce is contested." It was not. Presumably, the couple agreed privately prior to the filing that the financial agreement with Berthe would remain unaffected. Since there were no children of the marriage, Florence's vow to the Catholic Church was irrelevant. The only consequence of a civil divorce to her would be that as a divorcée, she could not marry in the Catholic Church again without special dispensation from the Vatican.

Naturally, the good people of San Francisco were gnashing their teeth at the aspersions cast by Florence against their good city. To boot, the reporter's dander was up against the "Frenchy" wife of poor Henry. "The suit, it is said, will probably shock the friends and family of both young people, although it has been known for more than a year that temperamental differences existed between the two and that Mrs. Heynemann *frankly preferred her native and beloved Paris to the cruder environments* of a busy Western American city."[10]

Of course, to file for a California divorce, Florence needed to be a resident in San Francisco, and her lawyers arranged for her to stay anonymously at an undisclosed location when the press began to whir into gear. Reporters tried every trick to locate her for a quote, without success. Referred to in rough Western style as "dainty" and a "French woman," it was only the beginning of the onslaught against the soon-to-be ex–Mrs. Heynemann. Henry, on the other hand, left town. The *San Francisco Chronicle* reported that:

> Every attempt was made yesterday to surround the filing of the suit with the utmost secrecy. Mrs. Heynemann's attorney brusquely refused either to affirm or deny the suit. Mrs. Heynemann herself, although she is known to be in the city, kept her whereabouts concealed. None of Heynemann's relatives would discuss the case, other than to say that he is out of the state at present.
>
> Mrs. Heynemann was Miss Florence Lacaze of Paris. Her parents were old friends of the Heynemann family in this city, and when young Heynemann met her two years ago while studying architecture in Paris, he already had heard of her beauty and succumbed quickly to her charms.
>
> The wedding took place in Madrid [*sic*] after which he brought his dainty bride to San Francisco. But within less than a year, Mrs. Heynemann returned to Paris, and her husband admitted that he had erred in expecting her to be satisfied with conditions here. None of the Heynemann family would say yesterday when Mr. Henry Chittenden Heynemann would return to San Francisco.[11]

A month later, Henry and Florence were divorced without his contesting the charges on the fictional grounds of his having committed adultery. Florence remarked to her friends that she had wasted "a few months too many" on her San Franciscan boy-next-door and his overweening mother.[12] On a personal level, Florence showed the same signal sense of purpose in her twenty-two-month San Francisco escapade that she would demonstrate in later life. Nothing and no one would stand in her path to becoming the woman she believed she could be. Not even a war. Besides, war offered untold opportunities for an artful gambler like Florence. She was well on her way to becoming a dangerous woman.

6

HOME AGAIN, WAR, AND FOLIES

*. . . young women were wearing cylindrical turbans on
their heads and straight Egyptian tunics, dark and very
"unwarlike." . . . Their rings and bracelets were made from
fragments of shell casings from the 75s . . .*

—MARCEL PROUST

THE PARIS TO WHICH FLORENCE RETURNED IN OCTOBER 1916
was a distinctly different place. "Madame Lacaze," as Florence became
known as a divorced woman, gazed upon large billboards dotted throughout the city. These outlined where "the front" was located, with its infini-
tesimal advances and retreats from the trenches regularly updated. The
front had stalled only forty-five miles from the capital. From Montmartre,
frequent fireworks of mortar shells lit the night sky, entertaining the often blasé onlookers. Although the Germans had captured the industrial
heartland of the northeast, creating shortages of all manner of supplies,
including ammunition,* many Parisians seemed distinctly unconcerned

---

* American arms and munitions manufacturers were thrilled by the declaration of war since the
Allies—the Triple Alliance of Russia, Great Britain, and France—were unable to match Ger-
man production quotas, despite a huge increase in arms production and men-under-arms.
When the scandals of defective ammunition manufactured early in the war in France and
Great Britain became public knowledge, the American government and investment houses de-

with the horrific, and at times senseless, bloodshed reported daily. Two years of war had hardened souls.

Florence's beloved Paris was overrun with older men and young women, soldiers on leave and thinly disguised deserters. Many simply did not believe the war would last, or that the injuries to France's youth could be so devastating. Still, when their men did not come home for the first Christmas of 1914 or the one after that or the following one, everyone asked when and how it would finally end.

Florence, like so many others, was more concerned with how she could keep her mind off the air raids and nearby bombardments. The museums were closed. The Paris Opéra was dark, as were the theaters in the early years of the war. Only the music halls like the Folies Bergère and Moulin Rouge remained open.

Meanwhile, writers of a rainbow of nationalities volunteered for the various international ambulance corps. Natalie Barney's "Temple of Friendship" was where one went to hear the readings of works by poets killed in the war, accompanied by "sweet and sad music." Charity dinners were held by salonnières for the war effort, and it was at these that Florence had her chance to sing, and be discovered, at long last. Years later, in reminiscing about this time in her life, she said—in contradiction of all her other memories—that she hadn't settled on singing bel canto opera as her career.[1] There was, of course, no mention of her attending the Conservatoire de Paris, as it was a lie that could easily be revealed to all and sundry. Undoubtedly, her reception at these dinners fell far short of the adulation she felt was her due.

Patriotism was the order of the day. The reclusive, hypochondriac writer Marcel Proust skulked about the city in the early evenings to check on his investment in the gay brothel at the squalid Hôtel Marigny on rue de l'Arcade. He observed that the only form of patriotism on show was the transformation in fashion. Designers Jean Patou and Paul Poiret were working for the army, not only in creating chic uniforms, but also in the relentless search for an "invisible" blue. Their myriad outfits not only failed in their mission—after all, how much blood and guts and

---

lighted in extending France's credit to the breaking point so they could "buy American." Great Britain opted instead to correct its shoddy manufacture, fueled by war haste, at home.

mud does it take to render "unchic" and "unblue" even the most carefully tailored garment—but their dozens of shades of blue created confusion as to which one was the correct one for the uniforms of the French army. Still, their preoccupation with their fruitless commissions made way for younger, inventive designers like Coco Chanel. Unable to source exotic feathers or silks that proliferated before the war, Chanel, though still only a milliner, successfully adapted locally available fabrics to her simpler designs of straw hats and felt berets redolent of the French countryside of her youth. Wearing Chanel's hats caught on as a symbol of patriotism.

The military look became high fashion, and Florence was among the bevy of women clamoring for a Chanel hat and her own handmade pair of military high-heeled boots. Cosmetics, too, became a boon industry, and Florence, like so many young women, began wearing rice powder to remove the shine from her nose. Fashion, always a way of life for French women, had become a recreational pastime in war.

∽

Not all women, however, were occupied with selfish enterprises in the first two years of this nightmare war. As deaths and casualties mounted to the hundreds of thousands, the American upper crust of Paris stepped to the fore. Winnaretta Singer de Polignac returned to a stunned city in October 1914, just as Florence was sailing to America. Winnaretta saw the long queues of people lining the streets hoping to empty their increasingly worthless cash from their bank accounts. The Métro was no longer running, and many newspapers had to cease printing for lack of newsprint. With each month that passed, some young man Winnaretta knew and loved had died. Nephews Henri de Polignac and Jacques Descazes, the youngest of her sister Belle-Blanche's three children, were killed. It was time she put her fortune to work to stop the madness.

In March 1915, Winnaretta met with the first female Nobel Prize winner, Marie Curie. The scientist was attempting to buy automobiles that hadn't been requisitioned by the government to convert them into mobile X-ray units. Curie believed that by enabling field surgeons to more readily locate bullets, X-rays would facilitate battlefield surgery, and thousands of lives could be saved. It was a view not necessarily shared by the generals or government, due to lack of funds and short-sightedness toward innovation. Curie's mission would need, therefore, to be privately funded. Of course, Winnaretta donated one of her own automobiles and covered all the costs to purchase and install the radiological equipment. As Curie personally trained 150 female attendants to operate the vehicles and apparatus, Winnaretta shamed her other aristocratic friends into donating in equal measure to herself.[2]

She also joined the French branch of the pianist-turned-politician Ignace Paderewski's General Committee for Polish Relief, which distributed much-needed supplies to Poland. Working with Consuelo Vanderbilt, the estranged wife of the Duke of Marlborough, to fund the 350-bed hospital in Suresnes on the outskirts of Paris,* Winnaretta went on to become the driving force on the Franco-American Committee for the War Blind. She organized the purchase of a large old hotel in Sceaux, another suburb of Paris, as their lodgings. She tirelessly raised funds from friends, newspaper columnists, and press barons alike, while also securing the personal patronage of French President Raymond Poincaré.[3]

In the late spring of 1917, Florence, too, did what she could for the war effort. Like many society women, she volunteered as a nurse, and after her training, worked in a hospital in Limoges, in the southwest of France.[4] While Florence could hardly be called a "society lady" as a twenty-one-year-old divorcée of modest means, her infallible belief in herself allowed her to pretend that she was. Perhaps the only way she could convince others that she was a "society lady" was to go where no one knew her, far away from her Paris home. Naturally, it is also possible that, once she had volunteered for service, Florence was posted, like any soldier, where the nursing administration felt she was most needed. In the second war with Germany twenty-two years on, she boasted to her German writer friend Ernst Jünger that "I could stomach the amputation of a leg far better than a hand," without giving Jünger further insight.[5]

Whatever the reason for the Limoges posting, her patients there had been stabilized in field hospitals or in other centers near Paris before

---

* This would later become known as Hôpital Foch.

being shipped out, so the injuries treated were, generally, complications from surgery, the spread of infection, secondary amputations as a result of gangrene, shellshock—known today as post-traumatic stress disorder—or simply long-term convalescence.[6]

While Florence may have harbored daydreams of tending to the wounds of a major or colonel, who more than likely would be the son of a wealthy landowner, she was too shrewd to fall for the trap commonly set by doctors at the hospital who asked if she would like to tend to the wounded officers only. Yet it is here in Limoges that the first remarks about her loud laugh rang out. Her raucous sense of humor was tickled by the conscripts' salutes to those nurses who preferred ministering to officers. Often resentful of what seemed like shoddy treatment, the French poilus organized coordinated rear-gun cannonades, let loose to the chagrin of many an embarrassed nurse, who would scurry to the windows to let in the fresh air.[7] Florence was not one to blush, rush, or hide from insults.

Similarly, she regaled in the mockery made of some aspects of the war in the weeklies like the glossy magazine *La Vie Parisienne*, aimed at officers. *L'Illustration*, meanwhile, targeted amusing the general reading public. *La Baïonnette* pandered to the working classes, with fewer articles and more cartoons, pinups, and caricatures. A veritable humorous war of postcards broke out where "Tommies"—the British rank-and-file—joined a French poilu in spanking the Kaiser, or the poilus on leave bequeathed souvenirs of lice to the places they visited. In all the printed media, the Germans were reduced to the third-century barbaric Hun archetype, and their helmets, called *pickelhaubes*, intended to inspire fear on sight, became objects of ridicule. The naughty postcard of a lady's bent-over nude bottom with a likeness of the Kaiser painted on it and a pickelhaube perched atop was a bestseller.

Since the front was so close to the capital, it was unusually easy for writers who weren't serving in the ambulance corps or the army to visit and write about what was going on. Other writers were in the thick of it. Jean-Paul Sartre became a prisoner of war. Ernest Hemingway, e. e. cummings, John Dos Passos, Dashiell Hamett, and even Walt Disney all drove ambulances and ammunitions trucks at the front. Edith Wharton was one of many who made a tour of the trenches.* Gertrude Stein wrote, "The 1914–1918 war made everyone drunk . . . there was never so much drunkenness in France as there was then, soldiers all learned to drink, everybody drank." French soldiers were often ordered to drink tafia—100 proof alcohol straight from a frontline still—just before going "over the top" of their trenches. Good, properly brewed tafia was tested in a spoonful mixed with gunpowder. If it exploded, it was the genuine stuff. The African-American former boxer turned Foreign Legionnaire Eugene Bullard said, "It made us more like madmen than soldiers."[8]

∽

Although the United States remained neutral until the spring of 1917, there were thousands of American Francophiles who volunteered much earlier for the American Volunteer Corps and the Foreign Legion. The advantage for Americans stranded or working freelance in France was obvious: Not only could they help the war effort, but they could be fed at the French government's expense. The Presbyterian pastor at Princeton University, Sylvester Beach, a former chaplain to the American Cathedral in Paris, encouraged the university's 181 volunteers prior to America's entry into the war to join up. "In Princeton, we are all for war," he declared. His daughter, Sylvia, who was living in Paris at the time, had left the city to be an agricultural volunteer in the countryside so a farmer's son would be able to join the good fight at the front.[9]

With the arrival of the American forces, Florence took stock. Even though Russia pulled out of the war after the victory of the Bolsheviks in their October 1917 Revolution, it was a racing certainty that the entry of the United States would swing the balance of power in favor of the Allies. American men, fresh and able, as well as American war materiel, would make all the difference, Florence reasoned. Still, as these doughboys† appeared over the horizon like the legendary Fifth Cavalry, Florence

---

* Nellie Bly, a former star columnist for William Randolph Hearst's *New York Journal-American*, made ends meet while stranded in Vienna when she begged Arthur Brisbane, Hearst's right-hand man, to become the *Journal-American*'s reporter on the spot. Her harrowing tales about the war from the Austrian front won many accolades. Still, her mission had less to do with journalism than with saving herself from hunger and bankruptcy. (See Brisbane Papers, Syracuse University, New York.)

† The term "doughboy" came from the buttons on the American uniforms, which resembled balls of dough.

had to admit to herself that she was neither fully French nor fully American. To boot, the war had put her life and aspirations on hold. Her brief stint as a singer at charity galas in the homes of the Parisian salonnières in the 1916–1917 season was an eye-opener. She had kidded herself long enough that she was going to succeed as an opera singer. She was twenty-one, a divorcée, with few prospects. Still, she *could* sing popular songs, and she danced wonderfully. Besides, her shapely legs and ankles, along with her other undoubted attractions, made men remark that she was, quite simply, drop-dead gorgeous.

When, where, or how she had the idea to lower her sights to become a chorus girl remains Florence's secret. She never divulged her innermost thoughts to her friends except Cécile Tellier—and the devoted Cécile never spoke out. In fact, the only proof that Florence performed onstage at all resides in a series of newspaper articles dating from December 14, 1918, to September 14, 1919, in which Florence is named by the former dance hall performer Mrs. Edith Kelly Gould as the co-respondent in her divorce from American millionaire Frank Jay Gould. In one article, Florence is described as "a former Parisian beauty" who had "returned to the stage in Paris and at the time she is said to be acquainted with Gould while playing at the Folies-Bergère."[10] No wonder Florence's memory lapsed years on, when she claimed that she had met Gould in 1921, introduced to him at a salon by the French Brazilian pianist Magda Tagliaferro and newspaper caricaturist Sem.[11] If it were widely known among the gossips in the salonnière community that Florence had also become embroiled in a divorce suit with an American millionaire, all doors to le gratin of Paris would have slammed shut.

Still, there was more to it than that. Florence had always been an unmitigated snob. In 1918, the Folies Bergère was much more than the nude chorus girls its name conjures up today. While topless women appeared on its stage as early as 1907 in a pantomime entitled *La Chair* (*The Flesh*), where the cuckolded husband tore the clothes from his wife's body, the resulting lack of outrage was unexpected. The breasts revealed in *La Chair* belonged to the actress, and later writer, Colette, the second woman in France to achieve the rank of Grand Officier de la Légion d'honneur. The Folies star performer, Maurice Chevalier, who became her lover shortly after, wrote, "Colette was a superb example of the 1908 beauty. Plump, broad shouldered, a trifle stocky . . . with a high, full, shapely bosom, a bosom which is—oh, here goes—the most exciting, appetizing bosom in the world!"[12] Nonetheless, Colette was unhappy with her pioneering bare breasts at the Folies, but had little choice when directed to allow her violent disrobement. She was flat broke, kicked out of the marital home by her bounder of a husband, Willy, and living on the goodwill of her lesbian lover, the Marquise de Belbeuf. While Florence was not plump, broad shouldered, or a trifle stocky, her slender shape, bosom, and legs were often admired by Chevalier when they danced the rhumba together.

*

The Folies was not alone in pioneering scantily clad women. This was also the heyday of Florenz Ziegfeld and his Ziegfeld Follies in New York. From 1907 through to his final show in 1931, Ziegfeld launched the careers—and breasts—of some three thousand beauties. Some grabbed noble titles while rifling through their husbands' wealth, while the less fortunate were used and discarded into poverty, or eventual suicide. For Florence, the Folies was her means to grab the best future she could for herself with both hands and never let go.

When Ziegfeld was criticized for his wanton disregard for his performers' welfare, he replied that his nudes were never allowed to budge so much as a little finger. They were tastefully arranged in tableaus among the bucolic scenery, wearing strategically placed laces, rosebuds, or spangles. To Ziegfeld, he was re-creating artistic *tableaux vivants* reminiscent of fine paintings.[13] While Ziegfeld shocked Broadway, the chauffeurs of the "Four Hundred" still drove up to the theater to collect their patrons: Guggenheim, Rhinelander Stewart, Vanderbilt, Biddle, and Hutton. The Folies Bergère wove its own brand of magic in Paris, attracting its clientele from among le Tout-Paris and le gratin. Surely, there, Florence would be noticed?

After all, Anna Pavlova, the daughter of a laundress and unknown father like Berthe Lacaze, performed opposite Nijinsky there. Charlie Chaplin, aged only fourteen—forever "Charlot," the little vagabond to the French—enchanted audiences from the outset. Mistinguett sang and danced, sprinkling her Marseilles accent with the fairy dust of the new snobbery—an English accent. Along with her lover, the debonair singer Maurice Chevalier, the pair thrilled the audiences while fully clothed. Arletty, originally a fashion model for Paul Poiret and discovered, as many girls dreamed, while walking along the street, took to the stage with French matinee idol Jean Gabin in 1912. Clown acts, jugglers, magicians, circus riders, and female impersonators from the four corners of the globe were just some of the acts adorning the stage of the Folies Bergère.[14]

Still, with the war, even the Folies had to change its approach to entertainment. At the outset, young actors either volunteered to fight or to entertain at the front. Its current owner, Paul Derval, who had abolished the ladies of the *promenoir*, that scantily clad backdrop to the main revue, reintroduced his "small nudes." Gemma la Bellissima, a dancing girl in see-through green gauze, became the resident "Dancer in the Nude" and the crowds of soldiers on leave, newshounds, and deserters flocked in alongside the men who were too old to fight. "During the Great War," Maurice Chevalier wrote, "the breasts of the girls at the Folies became a sort of symbol of what a great number of troops briefly on leave from the agony of the front line thought they were fighting for." Indeed, when Italy entered the war, the Folies marked the occasion with a parade of "twenty magnificent girls" decked out in Italian uniform with one breast exposed.[15] Most of the chorus girls were English, having learned their craft at dance schools back home. They lived in a hostel nearby, jealously guarded by their English nannies to make sure nothing untoward happened to them.

When Florence appeared sometime in the summer of 1918, she was an exception in more ways than one. She was, of course, not English. She also lived at home with her mother and sister. Most significantly, she was no ingénue, and entered the life of the dance hall with her wits about her. She knew about the Guggenheims and Vanderbilts at the Ziegfeld Follies as much as she knew about le gratin of Paris and visiting royalty, who frequented the Folies. Perhaps she was one of the many gowned *mannequins habillés* (scantily dressed models) rather than a nude sporting her *cache-sexe,* or strategically positioned fig leaf. Perhaps not. Maybe she was a backup singer for Mistinguett or—more likely—Arletty, who became Florence's friend around this time. Sadly, again, Florence never said.

Instead, Florence recounted the fantasy to her friends that she first met Frank J. Gould when he heard her sing at a charity gala in 1921. He was so smitten with her beauty that he came up to her and proposed marriage on the spot. Her story was that she took two years to give in to his unswerving pursuit. The history, however, widely publicized at the time in France and in the United States, reflects a different truth.

7

⚬∽

THE MAN THEY CALL "FRANCK"

I think I've done well for myself.

—FRANK JAY GOULD

FRANK JAY GOULD WAS QUITE A CATCH ON THE ONE HAND, AND quite a handful on the other. He was the black sheep of the Gould family, leaving America in 1913 in a huff, declaring that he hated government interference in his private business affairs—and by the way, the new federal income taxes of 1913. It hadn't helped either that two years earlier, Frank was among a host of businessmen indicted for the alleged violation of the Sherman Anti-Trust Law.[1] Though already married to his second wife, Edith Kelly Gould, a British-born music hall singer and dancer, he had acquired a well-deserved reputation among le gratin as a drunken playboy. He had merely swapped the New York newspapers that reported daily on his antics as "the tear-away Frank" for the French press's wonderment at the free-spending American they called "Franck." Indeed, he was so generous with his money that the mayor of Maisons-Laffitte, where his horseracing stud was based, had him created a "Chevalier de la Mérite Argicole" in the first year of his arrival on French soil.[2] Still, the French press didn't understand just *who* the Gould family was in America.

At five feet nine inches, Frank was slim, trim, and the tallest of the sons of the notorious robber baron Jay Gould. He also had his father's facial features. Like two of his brothers, George and Howard, he had a penchant for actresses and all that glittered. Viewed from outside the family circle, as an expatriate American and inheritor of one-sixth of Jay Gould's immense fortune, Frank seemed a prime target for any gold digger.

All the same, that would be selling Frank, and the Goulds, short. Originally an English immigrant to Connecticut in 1647, Nathan Gold, as the Gould clan was called back then, was thought to be Jewish. Not true. Like many sixteenth- and seventeenth-century working families in the grab for surnames, the Golds took the name simply because they mined, worked with, or otherwise fashioned the valuable ore. Their very name made them rich, elevated socially, to their way of thinking. After two hundred years working the land and marrying into the best Puritan families, the Goulds were firmly eleventh- or twelfth-generation Americans. Sometime early in those generations, the spelling change to "Gould" was more than likely to do with the original English pronunciation than any desire to hide their nonexistent Jewish origins.

The Goulds of Delaware County in the state of New York were good Baptists. John Burr Gould farmed an ordinary 150-acre patch of land with a large white farmhouse near the village of Roxbury. His son Jason— known to all as Jay—had been a pain in the backside from the day he was old enough to talk. He always wanted more, thinking he was better than his own father and the good people of Roxbury. In 1850, Jay, aged fourteen, asked if he could go to the Hobart Academy to study engineering so he could become a surveyor. The boy would have to pay his own way, John Burr Gould said, and lose his share of the farm. There were the girls and young Abraham to continue in the family tradition, and if Jay thought he was better than the rest of them, then so be it.[3]

Jay Gould stuck it out at Hobart for six months before deciding he had already learned all the "business" mathematics he needed. So, in an age when degrees didn't matter much, he went on the road, offering his services as a surveyor. Rural New York was not much better than a Wild West frontier in the early 1850s. Jay became well acquainted with danger and hunger. He was swindled by his first employer, and decided that every man was out to fleece him. To fleece or not to fleece offered no dilemma to Jay.

Within six years, Gould became the partner of a savvy landowner, Zadoc Pratt, by convincing the old man to buy land richly forested with hemlock timber from the Delaware, Lackawanna, and Western Railroad. Since Pratt was in the tannery business, and hemlock was a prime source of tannin used to cure leather, he was minded to go for it, so long as Gould contributed financially. Gould not only bought the first lot of land, but a second woodland, too, that bordered the railway tracks. Naturally, the Delaware, Lackawanna, and Western was delighted to have a major new customer, not only for its redundant land but for the wood's carriage, and offered Gould and Pratt preferential freight rates. Before his twenty-first birthday, Gould was running the sawmills, blacksmith's shop, and tannery. Tanned hides were sold at the "swamp" on the edge of a meadow on the east side of Manhattan Island (as it was called in 1856), and Jay employed enough men to name his thriving little community Gouldsboro.

Lured by the buzz of Manhattan and the clever movement of money, soon enough, Gould set about swindling Pratt. He sidelined the profits from the sawmills and tannery, and set up his own private investment bank called Jay Gould and Co., of Stroudsburg, Pennsylvania. While, in theory, the tanning company owned the bank, Jay knew how to fiddle the books so that old Zadoc Pratt never knew the bank existed, until it was too late. While Jay made his first million with tannery money by speculating on the financial markets in New York City, Pratt was fleeced of a fortune. Soon enough Gouldsboro became a ghost town, but that hardly mattered to Jay.

He already had Charles Leupp, his next sucker, in his sights. It was Leupp who rescued Jay from the tricky situation with Pratt, putting up some $60,000* to prevent Pratt from foreclosing on the property he co-owned with Gould. Leupp drove a hard bargain for the bailout, as Jay expected from the seasoned Wall Streeter. Leupp reasoned that with the

---

* At an inflation rate of an average of 2.17 percent annually over 159 years, the $60,000 is worth $20,701,800 today.

tannery business in Gould's and his hands, they could make good money together in all forms of the leather trade.

All the same, the leopard didn't change his spots. Gould engaged in wild speculation on Wall Street without telling Leupp. When the New York City branch of the Ohio Life Insurance Company collapsed, investment houses crumbled, and Jay was unable to meet his margin calls. So he drew on Leupp's accounts to make some payments, and Leupp became an unwitting partner to his crimes. When the market failed on August 23, 1857, Gould, Leupp, and Leupp's brother-in-law lawyer, David Lee, owned all the hides on hand in the "swamp"—on paper, that is—and every hide to be delivered to the New York market for the next six months.[4]

Leupp's hard-earned reputation as a seasoned, honest investor was in tatters. When he finally pinned down Gould at his Stroudsburg investment bank in Pennsylvania, waving reams of bills and legal notices in Jay's face, Leupp expected Jay to be contrite. It was all in the unwritten rules of the game, Jay replied, and all that he had done was in their combined best interests. Yes, technically they were bankrupt, but all they had to do was hold their nerve. Then Jay shared a bit of advice with his partner that old Commodore Cornelius Vanderbilt gave out like confetti: to avoid being suckered, go out into the business world with the intention of doing it to someone else. The Commodore had a rare insight into the oxymoron of "business ethics."

Leupp was aghast. He had been betrayed and bankrupted by a scoundrel. He should have known better after what Gould had done to Zadoc Pratt, he fulminated. Gould remained steadfast: just hold your nerve, he repeated endlessly. That evening, a downtrodden Leupp headed back to New York City by train. When he got home to his Madison Avenue mansion, he walked into his library, locked the doors, took a revolver from his desk drawer, put the barrel in his mouth, and pulled the trigger. Charles Leupp became the first investor on Wall Street to blow his brains out, preferring death to dishonor.[5]

∽

Leupp's brother-in-law, David Lee, ensured that his death would be avenged. As he had done with Zadoc Pratt, Gould was parlaying differences in state law and the lack of federal legislation to play catch-up with such shady practices. Since the state of Pennsylvania did not recognize New York law in these financial dealings—and avenging Leupp's death was all that mattered—Lee hired fifteen gunslingers in Scranton, Pennsylvania, who successfully occupied Gouldsboro and its tannery. Gould hired fifty men in reply and the inevitable happened. Many were killed, others injured, some arrested, but the odds were too great for fifteen hired guns against fifty. Although Lee lost a costly battle, he won the war: Gould was undone by refusing to pay the six percent interest to Leupp and Lee originally agreed upon on the initial $60,000 loan to buy out Zadoc Pratt. Gouldsboro soon became a home for tumbleweed.

While Jay Gould's reputation was tarnished by fleecing his first two partners, he was already wheedling his way into the orbits of bigger men on Wall Street. Daniel Drew, George Law, and the biggest name of them all, Commodore Cornelius Vanderbilt, had been shaking up Wall Street with dawn raids on each other's, and lesser mortals', holdings. They suckered European banks of France, Germany, and England, which had put up huge blocks of capital for the expansion westward by rail in the previous decades. To build America's railroads, promoters came to Wall Street to sell stocks and bonds, just as cotton brokers came to New York to find the markets into the vast British Empire. It was an eat-or-be-eaten world, and Jay was hungering for a feast. In his first ten years on The Street, Gould and his new partner, Daniel Drew, enticed Commodore Vanderbilt onto the opposite side of a raiding war for the Erie Railroad. Vanderbilt lost.

Naturally, Vanderbilt was livid.[*] When a second raid on the Erie was mounted, Vanderbilt secured an injunction from his pet judge, George G. Barnard of New York State's Supreme Court, to stop Gould. The Erie would cost Vanderbilt $8 million, a great deal of money even for the likes of the Commodore. Gould and his coconspirators cashed in, tossing bundles of money into trunks and moving the Erie's headquarters to Jersey City—out of Vanderbilt's and Judge Barnard's jurisdiction. The Commo-

---

[*] Commodore Cornelius Vanderbilt already controlled the three railway lines serving New York City from the north: the New York Central, the New York and Harlem line, and the Hudson River Railroad, better known to commuting New Yorkers today as Metro North. Acquisition of the Erie Railroad was his next target.

dore couldn't help but pay Jay a powerful compliment: Gould was the smartest man in America. Even so, it marked the beginning of their life-long feud.

Mrs. Alice Vanderbilt, along with her friend Mrs. Caroline Astor, ensured that the Goulds were banned from New York's "Four Hundred."* Even in America, in an age when only men voted, it was the women who ruled society. Jay could have cared less. He had married the handsome heiress Helen Miller, and with backing from his father-in-law and what was left of the tannery money, he bought the Rutland and Washington Railroad, which ran from Troy, New York, to Rutland, Vermont. The Erie was his second major acquisition. Jay even bought his own newspaper, *The World*—sold later to Joseph Pulitzer—so he could tell his story at will. Other railroads would come later—so would his cornering the gold market. Soon enough, he was called the "Mephistopheles of Wall Street," or the "Vampire of Wall Street."[6]

Were the Goulds the kind of family that Florence had been looking for all along? Certainly by pinning her colors to Frank Gould's mast, it showed that she was a fearless gambler. What if Frank was anything like his father, or even worse, the "Franck" the gossip columnists smeared? The call of all those juicy millions resounded in her head, louder than reason. Besides, Florence had yet to meet a man she could not control, and surely the next generation was wildly different from Jay's.

Frank's brother, Edwin, resembled his mother in his religious devotion and unswerving dedication to charity for the needy. Helen, the eldest daughter, had been her father's housekeeper since her mother's death in November 1887, when she was twenty years old. When Jay died, Helen ran the family estate, Lyndhurst, in Tarrytown, New York, and converted the bowling alley near the dock into a center for teaching undereducated women to sew on the new Singer sewing machines. They were brought

---

* The "Four Hundred," the New York social elite, were determined by the size of Mrs. Caroline Schermerhorn Astor's ballroom, simply because that was the number of people it could comfortably accommodate. Naturally, there were more than four hundred millionaires in New York City at the time, so the jockeying for position began for who would be on the list of the four hundred for the next season.

to Lyndhurst's dock on the Hudson River by private boat, fed, and taught the skills Helen believed would serve them in good stead to better their own lives.[7] Edwin was like-minded, founding schools in Westchester County with his own foundation. Still, Helen was mocked by her other, more worldly siblings, George and Howard. The youngest children, Anna and Frank, grew to hate the puritanical atmosphere Helen created at home.[*]

Frank told Florence about his inheritance. If they were to become life partners, he wanted her to know just what she was getting into. Jay Gould died at the family's 579 Fifth Avenue residence on December 2, 1892, aged only fifty-six. At the time, he owned Western Union Telegraph Company, the Manhattan Railway Company, the Missouri Pacific and St. Louis, Iron Mountain and Southern railways, as well as extensive investment and property interests, making him one of the wealthiest—and reviled—men in America.

Despite Jay's terrible reputation, he was a wonderful provider to the wider Gould family, supporting his sisters and brother. He was abstemious, and a dedicated, faithful husband. He loved his children, too, after his fashion. Jay always knew he was building his empire for them, and set up a trust to protect his children from the prevailing tendency in society to be greedy for greed's sake, which seemed to follow a patriarch's death just as surely as night follows day. After bequests and payment of debts (including taxes) within the wider family, Jay's estate was estimated at $73,224,547.08. This figure did not, however, include Jay's shares in his companies Western Union, the Manhattan Railway Company, or large chunks of Wabash Railroad stock, Texas and Pacific Railroad, Consolidated Coal Company of St. Louis, Wagner Palace Car Company, and as much as $10 million in bonds of the St. Louis, Iron Mountain and Southern Railway Company. A far more realistic value to place on the trust was closer to $150 million.[†]

The lower calculation was made with an eye to inheritance tax, with New York estate tax set at roughly one percent on large estates. There were no federal income taxes or federal inheritance tax in 1892. Each of

---

[*] George was born in 1864, Edwin in 1866, Helen in 1870, Howard in 1871, Anna in 1875, and Frank in 1877.

[†] Roughly $4 billion today.

the six children shared their one-sixth equally. One of the other stipulations of the trust was that any children of his children needed to be blood children, meaning born in wedlock, to inherit. As both Anna and Frank were minors, George (with the guidance of Helen) would manage their affairs.

Helen was given 579 Fifth Avenue with all its contents. She also had the use of Lyndhurst until Frank came of age. A stipend of $6,000 a month from the estate was also set aside to maintain both properties. George received $5 million outright and $500,000 for each of the five years he had managed the Gould property portfolio. The Gould Family Trust was intended to remain invested in its entirety. With its heirs living off the interest or dividends, and if properly managed, Jay's children, grandchildren, and great-grandchildren should never know hunger or poverty.

George had already saved Anna from that fate by intervening with a marriage contract just before she wed Boni de Castellane. By becoming her guardian, he again saved her from bankruptcy when he bought Boni off. Even so, the best of intentions do go pear-shaped.[8]

With Helen's goodness shunned by Frank and Anna, her influence with George regarding their upbringing and family investments waned. Frank and Anna often called her "Sister Helen" behind her back, referring to her unswerving righteousness. While Howard, Anna, and Frank made their official homes with Helen, as Jay planned, Anna and Frank spent as much time as they possibly could at George's more fun-loving abode. Their foibles were indulged there, and both grew estranged from their well-meaning sister.

∽

All the same, did Florence already know about the Gould siblings' penchant for showgirls and actresses? Had she made a study of the Gould men and their fortune as she'd done with the salonnières of Paris prior to meeting Frank? Their tastes in women were certainly printed in society and gossip columns around the world. Jay Gould died while Florence was a child living in San Francisco. Is it unthinkable that she remembered the Gould name as the family who owned the railroad that carried her away from her home in 1906?

Within a year of Jay's death, Howard Gould joined the New York Yacht Club and began playing as hard as he worked. He also became smitten with a young actress named Bessie Kirtland, who used the stage name Odette Tyler. In March 1894, Bessie was given a $9,500 ruby ring by Howard, and she made sure that their forthcoming marriage became the steady diet of the Four Hundred gossips.[9] That is, until Helen intervened. She discovered that Bessie was *divorced*. Helen scolded Bessie for dishonesty, until the poor girl called off the wedding. Just over three years later, Howard married a more independently minded actress, Katherine Clemmons, and withdrew further from the family.

This episode, if Florence knew about it, would not have worried her. George had since married the actress Edith Kingdon, and had two children by his mistress, another showgirl, Guinevere Jeanne Sinclair. Frank told Florence all about the family reaction to them, while making his own feelings about George abundantly clear. George had spent the trust's money as if it were water. In fact, Frank readily admitted to the acrimony that existed between the brothers.

By 1905, George was spending millions on railroad building, hoping to fulfill his father's dream of a transcontinental railway.* But he was up against some mighty opponents like J. Pierpont Morgan and Edward Harriman, who were battling George to become the masters of America's rails. Nothing was too devious for them, including hiring snipers, making piratical forays onto the railroads, and fomenting strikes. The upshot was a heavy reckoning to be paid. Between 1908 and 1911, George would face the wrath of Frank and Anna, both of whom were already spending more time in France than in America. Both accused him of mismanagement and sued. Now, there was an interesting tidbit of information for Florence to lodge away for a rainy day.

Florence told Frank she wanted their relationship to hold nothing back. She wanted both Frank's heart and wallet. "To hold on to your man," Florence told friends years later on the Riviera, "you need to occupy him. You make love together for, what? An hour? Maybe only half an hour? Then you have twenty-three other hours to fill. How to occupy

---

* When the San Francisco earthquake hit, Helen gave $100,000 to help George's own railway workers, among others, to survive and get to safety.

that time, and your man, is only learned as one's lifework."[10] Florence, however, had no intention of being a geisha. Those twenty-three other hours could be filled in whatever way she saw fit to occupy Frank. The best solution, for the present, was her stating that she did not expect him to give up other women, any more than she should give up her dalliances. To have faith in such a relationship, Frank and Florence shared their most private pasts. There would be no secrets between them, they agreed, ever.

She avowed her "mistake" in marrying Henry Heynemann. Frank had made two mistakes of his own, so she was on safe ground. More doubtful is her recall of the scheming and plotting to hook Henry and take her back to California. She would have been mad to admit to such hardhearted behavior to a future stinking-rich husband. Her confidences made, Florence would have moved on as rapidly as possible to her attributes, including her athleticism, knowing that Frank was a sportsman millionaire and keen dancer. Dancing onstage was athletic, too, as if his lascivious eye hadn't noticed.

For Frank's part, yes, he was married when they met—twice altogether, twice unhappily. Yes, he had twin daughters by his first marriage, Helen and Dorothy. Yes, he had custody of the girls. Yes, his second marriage was in defiance of his sister, Helen, who some years earlier had married Finley J. Shepard, aged forty-four. Yes, he hated any government interference in his affairs—especially federal taxes. Yes, he was a staunch Republican. Still, he loved his racehorses, his dogs, and France. Then, significantly, yes, admittedly he drank far too much. Yet there was far more to Frank than that.

Frank had intended to go into the railway business after graduating from the school of engineering at New York University.* In 1901 he had fallen in love with and married Helen Kelly, the independently wealthy daughter of an old Wall Streeter and ally of Jay Gould. It all began so well. He worked in the family business for a while, but the social life of a millionaire in New York proved too alluring. He became a New York clubman based at the Union League Club, still situated today

---

* Frank thoroughly enjoyed his time at NYU, studying engineering under his cousin Alice's husband. He remained emotionally attached to the university until he died, and bequeathed a million dollars to a building that would bear his name. On his graduation, he gave $4,000 worth of equipment, even though he was not yet twenty-one.

on the corner of Thirty-Seventh Street and Park Avenue. He owned dog kennels and was the first to show St. Bernard dogs at New York's annual dog show at the Westminster Kennel Club.[11] Vying to beat his brother Howard for the title of "Gould Sportsman," Frank bought his first yacht from the Charles Seabury yard in Morris Heights, New Jersey.[12] By February 1909 he was elected the Commodore of the Seawanhaka Corinthian Yacht Club of New York as captain of his steamer *Helenita*.[13]

His divorce from Helen that same year was sensational and acrimonious, filling dozens of newsprint pages around the world. Eventually, it sent a woman to jail for perjury. The *New York Times* header declared: "MRS. TEAL'S TRIAL FOR PERJURY BEGINS—Miss MacCausland Tells of Offered Bribe to Swear Falsely Against Frank Gould." Margaret Teal, the supposed mastermind of the bungled affair, found herself facing the charges alone when her cohorts, Julia Fleming and private eye Harry Mousley, turned witnesses for the state. The case revealed a plot that could only benefit Helen Kelly Gould.

∽

In July 1908 after the Gould divorce case was announced, Margaret Teal, who was known to Mabel MacCausland through Mabel's work as a milliner, suggested that in exchange for promises of a sum of money and a trip to the country, Mabel "had, in March 1908, seen Frank Gould in the apartment of Bessie DeVoe, a chorus girl, in the Hotel Glenmore. . . . And while waiting for Miss DeVoe in the sitting room had seen Frank Gould leave the actress's bedroom."[14]

Mabel, an honest girl, had nothing against Frank personally, and thought Teal's story was morally wrong. So she told the authorities. Mrs. Teal went to jail, and a referee needed to be appointed for the Goulds to reach a divorce settlement. After some horse-trading, Helen Kelly Gould got her divorce, Mrs. Teal her comeuppance, Mabel acquitted herself with honor, but alas, poor Bessie DeVoe didn't bag her millionaire. She did get some modicum of revenge by publishing Frank's love letters to her, but only after Frank paid $10,000 for breach of promise to marry her.[15]

Instead, Frank married the English showgirl Edith Maud Kelly on October 27, 1909. An acclaimed singer and dancer, Edith was as beautiful as her sister, Hetty, who was young Charlie Chaplin's first love. Within

months of the wedding, Frank put his American investments and properties into the hands of managers and moved to France, making it permanent in 1913. His goal seemed to be to devote his life to his personal
pleasures and the life of a grand seigneur in France. He bought the domain and château of Le Robillard in Normandy, once the home of Dumas's real-life musketeer, Pierre de Montesquiou d'Artagnan. After some
$200,000 in renovations that included American-style indoor plumbing,
the domain was fit for a king—and Frank "settled down" to breed racehorses with his showgirl wife.[16]

That first year, his horse Leremendado won the mile-long race for two-
year-olds at Le Prix des Fourres at St. Cloud. The victory was all the sweeter
for beating William Vanderbilt's horse Garcero Duro. At Maisons-Lafitte,
Frank's Jerretière won the Prix Maintenon. July brought victory to his
horse Pauvrerose, as well as a purse of $800. In October, his horse Aimette
won the Prix de Ballon. Frank had thirty horses in training at his stable,
but only six horses ran. Between March and September, the racing calendar
season, he had won a piffling 69,995 francs to Vanderbilt's 800,000 francs—
but Vanderbilt had been racing for three years and had run more horses.[17]

Frank's pride and joy, though, was a bay colt, Combourg. While finishing only second to Baron de Rothschild's horse in his first race at
Longchamps, Combourg was "the chief feature of the day," *The New York
Times* reported. Combourg was the great stallion, son of Bay Ronald out
of Chiffonette. He won a purse of $67,000 in his first four years racing.
Combourg won the Prix de Nice, the Noailles, and the Greffuhle Stakes.
He placed second in the Grand Prix de Paris and won the Royal Oak and
the Prix du Cadran. And Combourg was only the beginning. Frank's
finest horse, Amphiction, a chestnut gelding, won sixteen races in quick
succession. Then, in the steeplechase at Deauville, Amphiction fell at
the Irish Bank hazard and broke his leg. It was a severe compound frac-
ture. Despite Frank's offering of $20,000 to any veterinarian who could
save his horse so he could live his life out to pasture, no vet came forward, and Amphiction had to be destroyed.[18]

❧

Frank's happy marriage with Edith was short-lived. Within two years,
he was drinking so heavily that on awaking at eight a.m., he would down

a quart of whiskey, then go back to sleep for the rest of the day. He'd get up in time for dinner, always holding a glass of some spirit in his hand, and serve himself from his collection of alcohol at the ready on the sideboard, until he passed out. On the nights when he left the house, he would invariably be brought home by his chauffeur or taxi drivers, legless. By 1913 he was a regular at Paris's finest *maisons de joie*—brothels—where he met a shady lady he called "Sonia." Whenever Edith was away from Le Robillard, Frank brought Sonia home. He had already granted the lady an allowance of $1,200 a month, an automobile, and, of course, jewelry. Given his daily stupors, it didn't take long for Frank to be caught with Sonia in flagrante, but rather than divorce him, Edith sent him to a sanatorium. Twice.

Frank spiraled downward, regardless. In 1917 he tried to kill Edith, breaking down the door to her bedroom and beating her. During that same incident, he tried to make her swallow a vial of something he claimed was poison, and when she refused, he threw the bottle at her. Then he called in the fourteen household servants to forbid them from ever serving Edith again. Frank had gone completely off the rails.

He rented an apartment for a demimondaine with the unlikely name of Leone Ritz. Each evening, Leone would serve up a menu of young girls, perhaps two or three at a time, so that Frank would never get bored. The apartment house residents complained to the owner, who informed Frank he must find his accommodations elsewhere due to his scandalous behavior. So Frank set up Leone Ritz in a suite of rooms at the Hôtel Meurice instead. Naturally, Edith could take no more. When she moved out of the family home in disgust in the spring of 1918, Frank incredibly set the wheels in motion for a divorce on the grounds of adultery. In the meantime, one of Frank's bevy of lawyers, Charles G. Loeb, had already introduced him to another client, Florence Lacaze.[19]

∾

In a story that ran for years, Edith contested the French divorce. Apparently, Frank had done the unchivalrous thing and hired a private detective to follow his wife. Shortly before midnight on Friday, October 25, 1918, Edith and her Mexican friend, Mario Casasus, the son of twice Mexican ambassador to the United States Señor Don Joaquin de Casasus, a graduate of Princeton and member of the American Ambulance Corps during the Great War, were arrested in a hotel for "improper relations." In accordance with French law, they were each fined fifty francs. But that was only the beginning.

The *Washington Times* carried a full-page spread in its Sunday, December 15, 1918, issue entitled "The One Almost Comic Episode in the Sombre [sic] Details of the Frank Gould Divorce Suit Which Has Startled Even Gay Paris." The article described a scene worthy of the best French farce. Apparently, in a dawn raid on Saturday, October 26—the morning after the midnight raid on Edith and Señor Casasus—three policemen stood guard outside the doors to rooms 208, 210, and 212 in a quiet hotel off the rue de la Paix. They had received a tip-off from Edith Gould.

The investigating officer, one Inspector Vallet, quietly opened the door with the pass key to room 208. A man in pajamas leaped from his bed. As expected, it was the American Frank Gould, as infuriated as any self-respecting millionaire could be. Gould sensed that this was Edith's swift retaliation. Still, the inspector could see, Gould was in bed alone. Then what of room 210? When that door was opened, Vallet saw that the salon had a dining table set for two. Then surely the young lady he was looking for must be in room 212, Vallet asked his fellow policemen rhetorically. When that door was opened, Florence Lacaze sat up, grabbed the sheets to her bodice in mock modesty, and demanded, "What is this outrage?" "Do you know the gentleman in room 208?" Vallet asked. "No," she replied with a pout, "I do not know him." Gould was asked the same question of the lady in room 212. "I have not had the honor of her acquaintance," he declared. Then how can he explain the dinner table set for two? "It is for me alone," Frank insisted. Florence asserted she knew nothing of rooms 210 or 208.[20]

Despite their protestations of innocence, surely Edith would have the evidence she required against her husband for a divorce and a juicy settlement? Yet Frank struck first, filing the divorce papers secretly. The unwitting Edith was "served" with the papers, tossed through the open window of her taxi. She claimed she never picked them up, assuming the packet was either mistakenly thrown into the cab or that it was part of some sort of prank. The next she heard about her Paris divorce was when she read the morning newspapers. Her lawyers were consulted and proof of the farce in the hotel off rue de la Paix handed over. How could this "divorce" be valid? She had never been properly served. The lawyers agreed. Although they tried to get the decree overturned—not least to receive an equitable divorce settlement—Frank triumphed. He was a drunk, he told Florence, but he was no fool. He was also very well connected, enlisting the still powerful, former French premier René Viviani to his cause. When her countersuit came to court, Frank's divorce was upheld as valid.

As the woman scorned, Edith determined to make Frank pay dearly for his ungentlemanly behavior. She raced to New York to file another countersuit to overturn the French divorce decree, naming Florence Lacaze as the reason for the breakup of her marriage. Naturally, the talons of the San Francisco press were out again to slash at Florence and her new millionaire. If Frank were to prevail, then "big things must be done if big fortunes are to endure and substance is not to fade into the shadow." Frank was painted as an utter ne'er-do-well, and his Parisian pad was drawn as a palace worthy of Nero with accessories that "Europe as a whole did never possess and probably never will understand." This wastrel's lifestyle, the *San Francisco Chronicle* declared boldly, included a "mirrored bath large enough for 100 to swim in at a time," and "the old Roman [Nero] would have given more than his empire that he burned and fiddling would have gone out of fashion in his own castle."[21] That was in November 1918.

❧

Florence remained, by and large, oblivious to the horrors of the Great War and how it had deeply changed the Parisian cultural landscape. She hadn't known a frozen apartment in the long winters, waiting interminably for rations of coal dust, straw, and peat called *boulets*. She was with Frank. They could buy anything at any price, and did; dispensing largesse where it could grab the most beneficial headlines for themselves by sending champagne and food to French soldiers. They were not among the National Treasures deemed worthy of boosting morale and the glory of French culture, and did not receive special treatment like the sculptor Auguste Rodin, who was dying of pulmonary congestion and was mercifully gifted a cartload of coal through the intervention of a cabinet minister. Nor did they help other cold and starving artists during the conflagration. They were too self-absorbed.

Foreign artists were less fortunate during the war and its aftermath. Picasso's first mistress, Fernande, was reduced to breaking up Louis XV chairs to make a fire for the visit of Foujita, the Japanese painter, to Picasso's studio. Sylvia, the daughter of clergyman Sylvester Beach, was psychologically scarred when she saw a direct hit on the church of Saint-Gervais that killed ninety-one worshippers outright. In his first bombing experience during the war, Ernest Hemingway stood near the Madeleine when the façade of the church was blasted to smithereens, and reported his near-death experience. More prosaically, potatoes, carrots, and beans were planted, uprooting the fashionable Luxembourg Gardens, among others, to feed the local population. Parisians' senses were heightened at the thought that they might die at any moment from bombardments or starvation even after the guns ceased firing.[22]

∽

In November 1918, the Great War was over at last. The United States flexed its muscles at the Treaty of Versailles, with its Fourteen Points laid down by President Woodrow Wilson. Reading about the unsavory antics of American millionaires like Frank within spitting distance of the blood-soaked Western Front made thousands of heads shake and tut-tuts be muttered at breakfast tables across America.

Rather than counterclaim against Edith's allegations and protect Florence's good name, Frank chose the wiser road, almost certainly on the advice of Charles G. Loeb. The French divorce was valid, the French courts said, and recognizable under international law. Edith was no longer an American citizen, since their divorce was recognized in the United States. There was simply no case to answer. The New York courts agreed. Several times over. Thousands of column inches, twelve court hearings, and four years later, Edith finally gave up. Or so it seemed. The question remained, however, would Florence ever be able to tame her Frank?

PART TWO

THE CRAZY YEARS

Beauty is only to be admired, only to be loved—to
be harvested carefully and then flung at a chosen
lover like a gift of roses.

> —*F. Scott Fitzgerald,* The Beautiful and the Damned

8

TAMING ALL THOSE MONSTERS

*A son may bear with equanimity the loss of a father, but
the loss of his inheritance may drive him to despair.*
—NICCOLÒ MACHIAVELLI

WHILE AMERICA AND THE ALLIES WERE HAMMERING OUT THE
peace in Paris, another war raged on. Frank had nearly fallen out with
his brother back in 1910 when George, as the executor of their father's
estate, refused to recognize Frank's second marriage to Edith Kelly.
George called Frank "a damned fool to marry that showgirl." When
George was proved right, Frank vowed never to forgive him.

George was a monumental hypocrite, Frank fulminated. It was gall-
ing that George and Guinevere Sinclair had two children without the
benefit of wedlock—since he was still married to Edith Kingdon Gould—
yet the children were educated, fed, and clothed from the family trust.
These births could not be kept a secret from the Four Hundred, nor
would the press be gagged. Helen Gould Shepard lamented George's affair
with Guinevere. Edwin was compassionate to the poor children. Howard thought it wildly funny; and Frank and Anna vowed revenge. George
also opposed Anna's second marriage to the Duke of Talleyrand, and
enlisted Helen's flat opposition to the union. Anna's resentment was more

to do with fretting that her income had dwindled to $750,000 annually than with family disapproval.[1]

Yet Anna's bitterness was nothing to Frank's fury. George had tried to stop Frank's marriage to Edith Kelly, and as sure as the sun rose daily, brother George would not approve of Frank's next choice, Florence Lacaze. While Frank ranted about George's mercurial nature, his extravagances, and self-indulgence, Florence—the arch-schemer—led Frank into hatching a plan. Time was on their side, she advised. Frank's French divorce was still contested by Edith. Until the outcome of her counter-suit was certain, they would be unable to wed. Besides, George was the soul of indiscretion, and everyone knew what he was thinking before he uttered a word.

Consequently, the "War of the Goulds" began. While Frank staved off Edith with one hand, Florence was masterfully wielding her new power in the campaign against George. Her love affair with Frank had been printed in most good newspapers as part of Edith's efforts to win a New York divorce. George, therefore, needed to be handled very much like any other important business transaction: coldly, with a great deal of forethought and the element of surprise.

The Gould family trust had dwindled steadily since the Knicker-bocker Panic of 1907, when on October 15, the F. Augustus Heinz Mercantile Trust Company experienced a run on the bank. One bank after another collapsed, while Heinz scrambled for cash to pay out its depositors, even borrowing $1.5 million from Edwin Gould. As the banks failed, the stock market fell, and billions were wiped off the value of most stocks. Railroad stocks were hammered, hitting the family trust hard. Fortunately, Frank, Edwin, and Howard had already taken their dividends and accruals and plowed them into less volatile investments, meaning that by 1907, the three brothers were earning their own fortunes outside the family trust. In Frank's case, he had the foresight to see that electricity and power generation would be the next big thing.

Whereas Jay would have known how, when, and where to invest instinctively, George proved too profligate and too unwise. Vast swathes of Gould railroad stocks were dumped at panic prices onto the market and scooped up by John D. Rockefeller, the Deutsche Bank (once swindled by Jay), and Kuhn, Loeb & Co. investments.* In the spring of 1911, these three minority shareholders grouped together to oust the Goulds from the Missouri Pacific, the Denver and Rio Grande, and the Western Pacific railways. George was forced to resign as president; and while all the Goulds remained shareholders, they no longer called the shots.[2]

∞

Now, eight years later, Florence was faced with the dilemma of how to help Frank without harming his fortune. The solution was simple: hit George hard with the truth. Bring in Anna as an ally. If they didn't throw all the dirt they had on George and the family trust before George started tossing brickbats in their direction, Frank would lose, just as he'd done back in 1910. Meanwhile, Florence fended off Frank's ardor. She intimated she would not marry him until his demons—ex-wife, family, and alcohol, though perhaps not in that order—were resolved.

Above all, Florence knew Frank needed to get to grips with his alcoholism. Treatments or solutions for dependency hadn't progressed a great deal since the Victorian era. Indeed, ever since the Roman Empire's philosopher Seneca classified alcoholism as a form of insanity, how to cope with it remained a hot topic. By 1918 the Victorian treatment of "waterboarding" had fallen into disfavor, where patients in sanatoria across Europe and the United States were placed in cold water in sealed baths and nearly drowned with a constant jet of cold water on their heads and faces. Still, there were myriad quack remedies available, from eating 231 lemons over precisely twenty-nine days to the use of cocaine to cure alcohol and opium dependencies.† Specialist profit-making sanatoria for alcoholism proliferated, with only the wealthy admitted for their cures. The Keeley Institute in the United States was one of the first, opening its doors in 1869 with its controversial "Gold Cure." Despite its cure's questionable medical benefit, the institute remained a pioneer in treating alcoholism as a disease.

Sadly, in 1918, the treatments available for alcoholism were still

---

* Kuhn, Loeb & Co. represented the interests of the estate of Edward Harriman for the benefit of his yet-to-be-famous politician and diplomat son, W. Averell.

† Absinthe, "the green fairy," a highly addictive drink, had been banned in France in 1915 due to its harmful effects and does not seem to have been part of Frank's ongoing dependency.

based on medical opinions formulated in the 1870s.[3] Men and women in Frank Gould's social strata were increasingly sent to "jitter joints," or fancy hotel-like sanatoria, to dry out and hopefully stay sober. Those unable to pay for "cures" were sent to city "drunk tanks" to dry out. Their only form of help came from the various Christian missions or temperance leagues that preached on the evils and sins of their dependency. Today's understanding that alcoholism or any dependency has medical, heredi-tary, social, and cultural causes was unknown in Frank's day.

Presumably, Frank went to the jitter joint of his own choosing to dry out, then was sent back into Florence's caring arms. Chances are, she knew her man well enough to devise a program of treatment that no in-stitution could possibly dream up. She understood his demons, his faults, and his aspirations. She didn't need to lecture or scold. That simply wasn't her way. More than likely she showed Frank just how good a time they were having when he was sober. She didn't mind his having fun with other women, gambling, or dancing to his heart's content. The subliminal message was: Life with her was beautiful and fun.

Crucially, she taught him, as no one else had done, how she lived in France as an American, and how the French thought. In her inimical and self-serving way, Florence handed Frank something no one else had cared to give: hope for the future. It was the perfect and most incredibly thoughtful gift for the yachting millionaire who had lost his way. Once he was sober, the key component to Frank's cure—a battle plan to free himself from his brother George's grip—was hammered out together with Florence. While seeming generous, it was not entirely altruistic of Florence. It made the vulnerable Frank fall more hopelessly in love with her. By 1919, he was determined to make Florence the third Mrs. Frank Jay Gould.

❧

Frank declared war on George in the New York courts in the spring of that year—while the family mistakenly thought that Frank remained preoccupied with Edith. The *Evening World*, once owned by Jay Gould and now part of Joseph Pulitzer's media empire, led with the page one headline: $25,000,000 LOSS CHARGED IN SUIT OF FRANK J. GOULD TO OUST GEORGE AS EXECUTOR. The equally potent sub-headings of "Sister

Joins Him in Petition Charging Mismanagement of Inherited Millions"
and "Fight over W.U. [Western Union] Sale" give the broad brushstrokes
of the litigation.[4] *The New York Times*, *The Wall Street Journal*, and *The
Washington Post* followed with similar banners. Some $34 million was
alleged to have been lost by George. How could one man lose so much
money? they all asked.

The New York Times printed George's reaction. George's opinion
was that this was merely a family row brought about by Frank's resent-
fulness concerning his wife, the showgirl Edith Kelly. Evidently, there
was more to Frank's claim than that. New York Supreme Court Justice M.
Warley Platzek signed an order requiring George to show "just cause" to
why he should not be removed as executor and trustee of the Gould
family fortune. The three complainants—Frank, Anna, and Anna's three
children by Boni de Castellane—were each represented by their own
lawyers.

George, in a trick worthy of his father, tried to evade service of the
claim by speeding off in his car, presumably to his New Jersey home,
with the court's messenger in hot pursuit. George was stopped by a New
York City traffic cop before he could reach the bridge. When he refused
to open the car door to accept service, the court's messenger threw the
notice into the car under the feet of George's chauffeur, who allegedly
tossed it back into the street. In view of George's obvious reluctance to
answer the charges, Judge Platzek ordered that he be constrained from
destroying or removing any personal or estate books from the jurisdiction of the State of New York.[5]

As indecent sons of a noted robber baron, neither George nor Frank
played fair. Each brought to bear his considerable influence on the courts
in whatever way he could. Frank inflamed George's children against him
ensuring that George's portion of the estate would become mired in
controversy. The children of George's marriage to Edith Kingdon were
warned that those born to George's mistress, Guinevere Sinclair, would
dilute their inheritance. Guinevere, too, weighed in: she fully expected
her Sinclair children to inherit. Then George's and Edith's daughter, Helen
Vivien, who had married the Irish hereditary peer John Graham Hope
de la Poer Beresford, 5th Baron Decies, was accused by Frank of taking
$180,000 from the trust in an illegal loan to her husband.

George's hands were tied. If he adopted the same tactic, then he'd have to drag his elder sister, Helen Gould Shepard, into the quagmire, as she had helped raise Frank's girls. Instead, George opted for a more direct approach. Frank, as a trustee, was culpable for the trust's losses, too, not least because Frank had turned his back on the family business shortly after marrying his first wife. Yet rather than countersuing Frank personally, George's eldest sons clubbed together to accuse Frank for his own role in the mismanagement of the family fortune.

Then George planted a story in the American press that Frank was engaged to be married to one of his showgirl paramours, Miss Elsie Janis, who also happened to be Florence's chum. The intended threat was to expose some unsavory ménage à trois. Frank, however, sent a telegram to his New York business manager, George H. Taylor, for immediate publication, saying that his engagement to Miss Janis "was absolute news to me." All reputable newspapers printed a page one retraction.[6] The more George tried to come between Florence and Frank, the more inseparable they became.

The unedifying case of the Gould family tearing each other apart publicly went to court and an expert referee was assigned to arbitrate. Yet it rumbled on for over seven years, with complaint and countercomplaint leveled at the other side. The latest mudslinging garnished the gossipy appetites of most Americans at weekly, if not daily, intervals.

Eventually, George admitted some substantial losses, while lashing out that his father's will was not upheld in the question of Frank's second marriage. Finally, the court agreed. Half of Frank's assets from the estate were seized while the court decided if he had ignored the terms of Jay's will; and if, too, he had some culpability in the loss of the family fortune. The Gould family trust documents stated clearly that any of Jay Gould's children "contemplating marriage must obtain the consent of the majority of the trustees." Foreseeing obvious pitfalls ahead, the wily Jay also included a provision that "any of his children disobeying his wishes shall forfeit the income from one-half of his or her trust fund."[7] While Frank filed lengthy appeals to overturn the decisions on the several lawsuits lodged, he was unable to claim half of his inherited wealth.

Yet life went on regardless, as it has a remorseless tendency to do. By 1920, Florence seems to have left the stage, more than likely as part of a bargain with Frank. He didn't mind sharing her privately with special male friends, but her performing onstage while she was his mistress was out of the question. In an age when women were only beginning to wear fashions that showed off their figures, Frank knew how men thought about showgirls.

It was fine for *him* to publicly ogle women on stage, but it was unrefined and unacceptable for the third Mrs. Frank Jay Gould to set out her wares so explicitly. All the same, Frank knew the theater business was a good investment, so long as his mistress wasn't for sale as part of the ticket price. As if to prove some point, in 1921 Frank said in a press release to the *New York Herald*, "Hawaiian orchestras and jazz bands have seen their best days in Paris." He planned to put his money on a revival musical comedy for Florence, much as he had done for Edith, when he bought a music hall theater in London as her recompense for leaving the stage.

Frank believed musical comedy worked successfully at the Folies, with Mistinguett and Chevalier as headliners. So he purchased the Mogador in Paris. Gould's minority share reputedly cost $200,000. He announced that his theater would show only light opera and musical comedy. By April, Frank's business partners outvoted him, agreeing that the Mogador would have more success if it followed the trend for "girly-girly revues." Disagreeing strongly, Gould bought out one of his associates to become a majority shareholder for an undisclosed sum. Light opera it would be.[8]

∽

While Florence may have had a hand in the purchase of the Mogador, and certainly encouraged Frank's newfound interest in light opera, what must have irked her to near breaking point were the ceaseless claims by, and actions of, Edith Kelly Gould. First, there was the battle of the hats. In 1921, Frank was ordered to pay for 8,000 French francs' worth of hats that had been bought before Edith fled the family home in terror in May 1918. The courts ordered that since the two were still husband and wife at the time, Frank must pay Edith's milliner.[9] Then, two months later, Edith's New York lawyer, Gustavus Roger, rattled Florence's cage again by saying that Edith would take her case to overturn

Frank's foreign divorce all the way to the Supreme Court of the United States. To Edith's mind, Frank was still legally married to her and if he did remarry, as was rumored, his third marriage would be bigamous.[10] Not only was the family against Frank's marrying his third wife, but Edith clung like a limpet to her man.

Incredibly, there was more to come. Edith knew precisely how to get under Florence's skin. She returned to London's stage as "Edith Kelly Gould" with a role in the wildly successful revue *Needles and Pins.* Taking two weeks off from her Spanish dance routine to press her claim with the New York Courts before Justice George V. Mullan, she admitted that she was nervous stepping behind the footlights after a thirteen-year absence. "I am glad I went back to the stage," a demure and vivacious Edith told the press. "It seemed as natural to me to sing and dance as if I had never been away for a day. . . . I have had many offers from American theatrical and moving pictures producers, but have been forced to turn them down because of my London contract."[11] Florence's pride must have taken a knock. Not only was Edith a success as a headliner in London and sought after in America, but, in contravention of French custom, Frank's second wife steadfastly clung to the Gould name.

Justice Mullan said the court would hear the Gould case. Mullan's colleague, Justice Guy, ruled that given "the question was of so novel a character" it was only appropriate that Edith's millionaire husband grant her $6,000 toward her legal fees for her appeal to their court, particularly since Edith Kelly Gould claimed she was still Frank's wife.[12]

Without missing a beat, Edith sued Frank in Paris for payment of her purchase of seventy pairs of silk stockings, but eventually, the French courts found in favor of Frank. February 1922 brought respite for Frank and Florence at long last: Edith's final attempt to overturn the divorce failed in the courts. Joseph Pulitzer's *New York World* headlined the verdict as SUIT OF THE GIRL WITH THE HIGHEST KICK FAILS. Apparently, Justice Mullan "dismissed the petition of Miss Edith Kelly, the well-known [sic] actress who appeared in 'Pins and Needles' at the Gaiety Theatre, London, for annulment of the divorce decree which her husband Mr. Frank J. Gould, the multi-millionaire obtained in Paris on the ground [sic] that she did not defend in those proceedings."[13]

Undoubtedly suspecting the outcome, Edith immediately filed for a portion of Frank's estate in Paris—an option that was not open to her so long as she pretended she was still his wife. Though finally free to marry, Florence and Frank held off. Why? Berthe Lacaze had long before admonished Florence by letter for being the mere mistress of her millionaire. "Your letter doesn't give me any hope," Berthe wrote to Florence on February 21, 1919, "nor do you give me any detail concerning any change in your current status, which is a false one. I would so love to see you married. What more could one desire than to declare one's love to everyone? I am suffering tremendously at your state of affairs which I would have hoped to be so different."[14] Three years on, nothing had changed, save that the affair was public knowledge. So why the delay?

Had the words of Magda Tagliaferro, "If Florence hadn't met Frank Jay Gould, she would have triumphed in my stead at the Opera," scorched Florence's heart as she strolled among the peacocks in the park at Frank's stud farm and estate at Maisons-Laffitte? Frank must have divined that some grand gesture was required, so he bought Florence her own *hôtel particulier* (mansion) in Paris on rue Albéric-Magnard, near the Ranelagh Gardens on the Right Bank. At last, Florence had arrived financially. Still, it was not quite enough.

Frank needed to assure Florence's acceptance into le Tout-Paris in her own right. It was a simple enough matter for him to arrange. Not only did Florence need to be happy, she deserved it for showing him how to sober up and stay sober, as well as giving him renewed hope for the future. Frank asked his tame press baron friend, Arthur Meyer, the director of royalist newspaper *Le Gaulois,* to step in and arrange it.

Meyer, the son of a rabbi, had converted to Catholicism in 1901. Despite this, he remained a target for the anti-Semitic league Action Française long afterward. Although Meyer had Jewish origins, he was a committed royalist and anti-Dreyfusard. His journal, *Le Gaulois*, had a relatively small circulation of under 30,000 copies, yet it was the newspaper of choice for le Tout-Paris and le gratin. The mutton-chopped octogenarian Meyer took an immediate fancy to the seductive Florence, and brought her along to the salon of Élisabeth Greffulhe—the longstanding friend of Winnaretta Singer, Princesse de Polignac.[15] As if proof were needed of Meyer's significance in Paris's high society, twenty years earlier he had been invited for an extended stay with the Princesse de Brancovan* alongside the princess's anti-Dreyfusard friends Winnaretta and Edmond de Polignac—at the height of the *Affaire*.[16]

The elegant Comtesse Greffulhe had long ago accepted another native San Franciscan expatriate, the avant-garde barefoot dancer Isadora Duncan, into her salon. Duncan's flouting of the social mores was well known. Duncan's daughter, Deidre, was the outcome of an affair with British theatrical designer Gordon Craig. Her son, Patrick, born in 1910, was fathered by Winnaretta's brother, Paris Singer. By 1921, Duncan had moved to Moscow and married the Russian poet Sergei Yesenin, eighteen years her junior. Florence's affair with Frank—himself eighteen years her senior—was tame in comparison. While Élisabeth Greffulhe was married to a wealthy count, she had no money of her own. She, more than anyone, understood the significance of using the Greffulhe salon as a stepping stone to negotiate entry into le Tout-Paris and welcomed Florence with open arms.[17]

It was Meyer who arranged Florence's true singing debut at the Greffuhle salon attended by the exiled Russian Prince Felix Youssoupoff and his handsome cousin Grand Duke Dmitri, the murderers of Rasputin. Also present were the actress Cécile Sorel; milliner turned couturier Coco Chanel; the "pewter king" of Argentina, the Marquis de Cuevas with his twelve Pekingese dogs; and the king of Spain, among others. Wearing a black velvet full-length dress and accompanied by Proust's lover, Reynaldo Hahn, on the piano, Florence sang a lullaby from Offenbach's *The Tales of Hoffmann*. This time, she was no soloist charity singer for the war effort. Nor was she a bel canto singer, obscuring the words with excessive fioritura, or floweriness. She was the soprano soloist, paramour, perhaps fiancée, of the American multimillionaire Frank Jay Gould.

✍

Yet, if she married Frank, Florence knew she could no longer perform onstage, or even in a salon. Edith's lawsuits had made that clear. Whether she ever asked herself if she could have *truly* been a successful headline singer and dancer is doubtful—Florence's monumental ego pre-

---

* Mother of the poetess Anna de Noailles.

vented that kind of self-analysis. Instead, if she became the wife of a millionaire, Florence saw her new role as part of le Tout-Paris and as a salonnière, dispensing largesse to those great mortals of little wealth who nonetheless possessed an artistic genius. Still, the rub remained. They weren't married yet.

Haunted by the specter of Edith Kelly and her lawsuit for half of Frank's French estate, while simultaneously the family litigation raged in the United States reclaiming half of his American wealth, Florence had plenty pause for thought. She must have wondered just where and when Edith's vindictive, litigious spree might end. As the years rolled on, the situation with George changed too. After the death of Edith Kingdon Gould in 1921, George married his Guinevere and moved with his second family to London.

No matter what the outcome of George's and Edith's counterclaims to his own, Frank proved to Florence that he was a man of his word. He had been sober for three years. He had bought Florence cars, jewels, and her own hôtel particulier on the Right Bank. He had arranged for her introduction into Parisian high society. Finally, he had made it quite clear that he was, separate from the Gould family trust, willing and able to keep Florence in the style to which she wanted to become accustomed. He owned several transit system traction companies including the Virginia Railway, and combined them into the Virginia Railway and Power Company that was capitalized at $42 million.[18] Most significant of all, hadn't they had oodles of fun? Frank asked. Florence had to admit that even without access to half of Frank's riches, he was an exceedingly wealthy multimillionaire.

Another year passed. Frank, now age forty-five, and Florence, already twenty-seven, were wed at last on February 10, 1923, at the Mairie in the bride's parish of the sixteenth arrondissement in Paris. Frank was Protestant, but this time, there would be no asking of forgiveness of the Catholic Church. Florence's witness was her accompanist, Geo Dequenne. Frank's was Charles G. Loeb. Neither Florence's mother, Berthe, nor her sister, Isabelle, were present. Berthe's pleadings for Frank to make Florence an "honest woman" and her remarks about his womanizing and ungovernable drinking were the most likely causes. As for Isabelle, she could not be trusted by Florence to keep her mouth shut about Henry

Heynemann. Florence would not allow anyone to hurt her chances of bagging her millionaire.

The *San Francisco Chronicle*, naturally, made the wedding their page-one banner headline: FRANK J. GOULD MARRIES S.F. GIRL WHO WAS NAMED BY EX-WIFE AS CORESPONDENT. Unlike complimentary articles that describe the bride's gown, or the groom looking handsome, no newspaper in the United States waxed lyrical about either Frank or Florence. Their eloquence was, surprisingly, present in the unwritten word.

If Frank and George had agreed to private nonbinding discussions on how to end the deadlock, they were cut short by George's untimely death of pneumonia on the French Riviera in May 1923. That autumn, Frank kept the litigation alive by refiling charges against George's heirs to the estate. If successful, Frank's lawsuit would sweep away the $4 million left to Guinevere in a trust fund George had set up to protect his widow.[19] By the time an eventual agreement between family members was reached "in the interests of harmony" on Christmas Eve 1926—and at an estimated cost of $10,000 each day in legal fees—the Gould family estate had shrunk to a mere $50 million.

⁂

Unsurprisingly, there was a vengeful wedding present from Edith to the happy couple, too. Edith—still calling herself Edith Kelly Gould—announced her intention to open on the Paris stage in a musical revue at the Alhambra Theatre in the autumn season. Frank and his bride were livid, and issued proceedings to forestall Edith. When that failed, Frank sued to make Edith drop the Gould name, which to his mind, she was bringing into disrepute.[20] She appeared on stage before the courts could hear the case, warning the press that Frank and his bride might wish to "crab" her performance. There was, and is, nothing like a whiff of scandal to make a box office smash. Still, justice prevailed in Florence's eyes. The scorned Edith lost both the Gould name and any right to Frank's fortune. Apparently, the French courts—rightly—took umbrage at Edith's long battle to prove the French divorce invalid, while later arguing that under French law she was entitled to half of all Frank owned in France.

An interesting statement made by Frank's lawyer in the dying embers of Edith's litigation indicated that "Frank never wished to abandon America, citing the fact that the millionaire evaded paying French taxes on the grounds that he paid U.S. income tax, and was therefore, exempt elsewhere. . . . Mr. Gould lives in France solely because he needs special treatment for an illness by French specialists and because he desires to train his race horses."[21]

Illness? What illness? Surely Frank's lawyer was *not* referring to his alcoholism, since it was not seen as an illness or disease until long after. Another recognized, and terrifying, illness springs to mind. Did Frank have syphilis, contracted during his days amused by the demimondaine Leone Ritz? Had he passed it on to Florence? If so, was her treatment for syphilis—the cocktail of the organic arsenic compound marketed under the trademark Neosalvarsan* as the preferred therapy to inorganic mercury—the reason she never had children? Or was it some other disease caused by his alcoholism? Whatever the "illness," Florence knew the best way to protect herself and survive well was to accept Frank's financial generosity for her many kindnesses. Self-preservation rather than love was her main preoccupation in the years immediately following the Great War, while she was still Frank's mistress. Of course, nothing more was said about his health at the time, though Frank's symptoms and actions would soon speak volumes.

And what about those taxes? There is no available record of Frank Jay Gould paying his U.S. federal income taxes to the Internal Revenue Service once he became an expatriate. There is, however, plenty of information available over many years that he neglected to file, much less pay, his American federal taxes on his substantial declared French income.

Just maybe Florence had met her match at last.

---

* Neosalvarsan (neoarsphenamine) was available from 1912, and was developed to replace the more effective, but more life-threatening, Salvarsan (arsphenamine). Both were highly unstable organoarsenic compounds. Sterility in women was one horrible potential outcome from the drug, but the most common side effects were extreme nausea and vomiting. It is equally possible that Frank, and even Florence, opted for mercury as a cure given the history of liver failure, severe rashes, and even death reported from Salvarsan. Its Jewish inventor, Paul Ehrlich, became a figure of hate for selling the drug at high prices. Still, the development of Salvarsan became the blueprint for the development of all pharmaceuticals in every clinical trial that followed everywhere in the world.

9

LEAVING THE PERFUMED AIR OF BOHEMIA

*The real voyage of discovery consists not in seeking new
landscapes, but in seeing with new eyes.*

—MARCEL PROUST

FLORENCE KNEW HER HUSBAND WAS IN FRAGILE HEALTH DUE TO
his alcohol abuse. If he suffered from syphilis, too, the "cure" would have
been as unpleasant as the disease. Given his history of violence toward
Edith and his memory lapses once he sobered up, along with other disagreeable symptoms, Frank probably also suffered from a chronic con-
dition dubbed "Wet Brain," or Korsakoff psychosis, after its Russian
discoverer.* Florence was old to be a bride at twenty-seven, but believed
she was too young and pretty to be Frank's compliant nurse. Above all,
she needed to ensure Frank's return to health—or they would end up
leading separate lives.

Besides, the roaring life of the twenties beckoned. Out of the madness, a new Paris was born. The salonnières were still "at home" to one
another, but the old rituals of le gratin seemed anachronistic to the new
beau monde (beautiful people) like the artist and writer Jean Cocteau,

---

* Prolonged alcohol abuse can result in Korsakoff psychosis in patients, particularly if they have
undergone several "drying out" periods as Frank Gould had done. It has as its root cause a
thiamine (vitamin B_1) deficiency that cannot be easily treated.

and Colette, who at last became a writer, too. At the outset, Florence had barely noticed the fresh wave of foreigners frequenting newer "bohemian" salons, save her old *bêtes noires*, the Russians. A host of homegrown and foreign artists like Marc Chagall, José Maria Sert,* Joan Miró, Francis Picabia, Juan Gris, Georges Braque, Marcel Duchamp, and Henri Matisse were integral to the new beau monde. Exiled Russian royalty and artists abounded. Paris was a wilder, rejuvenated beating heart of the art, fashion, and cultural worlds of the West.

Gertrude Stein held court at 27 rue de Fleurus with a host of young American writers, from John Dos Passos to Ernest Hemingway and F. Scott Fitzgerald. Irish writer James Joyce, championed by Sylvia Beach and soon to be published by her bookstore, Shakespeare and Company, proved eventually a bridge too far for Stein and her life partner, Alice B. Toklas. Despite the continued friendship with Sylvia and her lover Adrienne Monnier, Joyce was persona non grata at 27 rue de Fleurus. The "new normal" of the Parisian beau monde included aristocrats of the Right Bank—like Winnaretta Singer, Princesse de Polignac, Élisabeth Greffulhe, and Count Étienne and Countess Edith de Beaumont, famous for their spectacular themed costume parties in the twenties— mingling freely with the Left Bank artists, like Picasso and Braque. All, that is, except Proust. In the year of Proust's death, 1922, Picasso mocked Proust at one of de Beaumont's fabulous parties for speaking only to dukes.[1]

Paris became "a world somewhere between *Guermantes Way* and *Sodom*," Florence's new friend, the playboy Prince Jean-Louis de Faucigny-Lucinge, claimed in his book *Un gentilhomme cosmopolite*.[2] The secret world of the lesbos of the Left Bank was no longer discreet, or indeed, shocking. It was a tantalizing time to be young and a woman. The war had left women in charge on the home front, making them liber- ated and useful running businesses and the economy while the nation's working men were at war. More significantly, it marked them. Many like Adrienne Monnier, the owner of the bookshop La Maison des Amis des Livres, recognized that they might never have been alive had they been born boys. Others simply rejoiced that they had survived.

---

* Sert painted friezes for Winnaretta de Polignac's salon. His wife, Misia, was an artist in her own right.

Paris afforded vistas that were unimaginable anywhere else—as the poor black girl born Freda Josephine McDonald in St. Louis, Missouri, discovered when she became the exotic singing and dancing sensation known as Josephine Baker. When she opened at the Théâtre des Champs-Élysées, *The New Yorker* reported that Josephine discovered "Paris has never drawn a color line."[3]

The British cruise ship heiress, Nancy Cunard, fell into the arms of Henry Crowder, the African-American jazz pianist, crashing through another color barrier. Nancy moved to Paris in 1920 to escape her drunkenness, dizzying array of lovers, and life-changing mistakes. In Paris, she became a poet, writer, political activist, and publisher of the Hours Press. Janet Flanner, Cunard's good friend and *The New Yorker*'s columnist of "A Letter from Paris" for half a century, became the wittiest and most accurate portrayer of life in Paris for Americans back home. "For the most part we had recently shipped third class to France across the Atlantic, at that date still not yet flown over except by migratory sea birds."[4] Florence should have been in her element.

Paris had become an American home-away-from-home. Demobilized American doughboys stayed on, enamored with the French and especially just how far the American dollar could go. Searching for the Parisian legends, they could often be heard to drawl in English of any passing man, "Say, mister, now where is this here Maxim's?"[5] African-American musicians introduced the city to American jazz, and the international love affair was sealed. Harlem poet, Langston Hughes, waited tables, while Ada "Bricktop" Smith, the West Virginian daughter of an Irish immigrant father and black mother, sang at Le Grand Duc, until she opened her own nightclub Chez Bricktop in 1924. Other Americans, like the wealthy couple Gerald and Sara Murphy, famous for their wonderful parties and literary friends like Dorothy Parker, Ernest Hemingway, and F. Scott Fitzgerald, composer Cole Porter and his wife, Linda, were all attracted to France by its artistic flair and the cheapness of living well.

There was another, extremely compelling reason for the mass American migration of the 1920s: the Volstead Act and the ensuing nightmare of Prohibition. Americans didn't like the restrictions on their freedom one jot, and felt that cold breath of the Puritan fathers huffing and puffing down their necks. Even the apple-pie-and-Dolly-Madison-ice-cream *Saturday Evening Post* carried an article by Kathleen Howard in 1922 extolling life outside the United States. "Of course we were all expected to start drinking as soon as the ship pulls out of New York harbor, and keep one happy mood of booze until we face the stern customs official on our return trip," Howard wrote. The article also told of her thrilling trip to the Maisons-Laffitte racecourse and even the sex-mad music halls of the Moulin Rouge, Folies Bergère, and the Rat Mort, a famed Montmartre dive. "Then, of course, there's no experience," Howard effused, "like heading off at three in the morning to the restaurants near Les Halles, for the obligatory onion soup and beer."[6]

There was a darker side to the excesses of Americans—especially American women—traveling to Paris for "the atmosphere." The English-language newspapers warned daily of "counts" and "barons" sweeping fresh American divorcées off their feet and out of their fortunes, while the American ladies were on the hunt for a title to match their wealth. The days of chaperones and the "acceptable for the respectable" were over, and any woman of means might find herself dancing with a total stranger at the Château de Madrid in the Bois de Boulogne, only to discover that the stranger was really interested in the contents of her hotel room. Florence scoffed at the amateurs' ignorance, while applying a slash of red to her lips after luncheon.

American artists, writers, and even tourists drank in Parisian cafés and struck up conversations with perfect—or at times imperfect—strangers. Many lived among the *bouquinistes* (booksellers) lining the Left Bank. Later, they would discuss their finds with French intellectuals at Les Deux Magots, which had been serving alcohol to French literary giants like Verlaine, Rimbaud, and Mallarmé since 1884. Alternatively, there was always La Rotonde in Montparnasse, where the increasingly broke impresario Serge Diaghilev, his schizophrenic ballet dancer Vaslav Nijinsky, the yet-to-be-discovered American writer Henry Miller, and composer Igor Stravinsky chose to unwind.

Another big attraction for Americans looking to escape the provincialism and puritanism of home was, frankly, described by Mark Twain: "A Frenchman's home is where another man's wife is," he lamented late in his life when he had turned from Francophile to Francophobe. "It is a country which has been governed by concubines for 1,000 years." No wonder the notion that France was the land of loose morals at the end of the nineteenth century was nurtured in America. Writings by Émile Zola, one of the first to extol the virtues of prostitutes and bohemians of the Latin Quarter, made for much secretive bedtime reading.

Lesbianism and homosexuality were more than tolerated—they were celebrated. Lovers kissed in the streets. For heaven's sake, everyone kissed, everywhere. No one hesitated to make eye contact, and men palpitated at the sought-after invitation from a strange woman with a wee bit of leg revealed from her ever-so-slightly-lifted skirt, silently inviting him to "*Suivez-moi, jeune homme*" ("Follow me, young man"). One of the period's best guidebooks, *Paris with the Lid Lifted* by Bruce Reynolds, gave practical advice on how to react to such overtures: ". . . you zee little French Goddess tripping towards you, and she spies you at ze same moment and you look ecstatically at her and show your pearly teeth (if you still have them) and she gives you right back zat 'come-and-get-me-love-me-carry-me-away wiz you' invitation. You have to make good."[7]

Still, the greatest reason for foreigners to move to the French capital was that Paris was a cheap place to live. While most European economies suffered devastation during the war, the 1920s saw rampant inflation, particularly in Germany, and a heavily devalued franc. The United States had done well for itself, emerging as the world's economic powerhouse in the twenties. Boat passage to France from New York could be bought for eighty dollars. Hemingway wrote an article for the *Toronto Star Weekly* in February 1922 entitled "Living on $1,000 a Year in Paris." "The dollar," he boasted, "either Canadian or American, is the key to Paris."[8] The U.S. dollar was worth some twelve and a half francs, and the Canadian dollar, something over eleven francs.* The ever politically divided French Third Republic—torn between royalists, republicans, and now communists—was united in its distaste of the carpetbagging American businesses. As for American millionaires, well, they were simply ill-bred men who only respected wealth.[9] Still, the American migration

---

* In 1921, the exchange rate was 8.2 francs to the dollar. In 1924, the rate was twenty-six francs to the dollar, recovering to eighteen and a half francs per dollar by the end of the month and lasting until December 1924. By December 1925, the dollar was worth twenty-three and three-quarters francs and twenty-three and a half francs by June 1926. *Sources:* Statistiques journalière. Archives de la Banque de France and Federal Reserve Bulletin, 1929.

of rich and poor, literary and artistic, continued unabated. Paris became a new American Dream.

∽

That is, for most Americans other than Florence and Frank. Florence, who always sought to rise like cream to the pinnacle of society, was lost, searching for a new identity. She was just one American, who was also French, among fifty thousand Americans wanting to be French. Hers would be a different voyage of discovery. While she would return frequently to Paris, what to do with Frank had become her abiding concern. She concluded that to protect him and their futures meant they would need to abandon Paris soon. She portrayed her devotion to Frank as being his personal "Geisha," who had learned her métier with aplomb.[10] In fact, she was looking after Number One.

Florence later said that they went to Cannes for their honeymoon, but their first trip south together was in the summer of 1923, not in the winter season, as one might expect for a man in ill health immediately after his wedding. No one, except Americans Cole and Linda Porter and Gerald and Sara Murphy, had ever gone in the "off" summer season until that very year. Her claim was vintage Florence, trying to steal a march on others who had become the more famous and well-loved couples. In truth, it was the dreaded Edith's revue premiering at that precise time at the Alhambra that was behind it all. Given their combined anger at Edith's antics, and Florence's compelling need to remain center stage throughout her life, her true motives and what she later claimed seem to have become muddled. Besides, it was hardly an exaggeration to say "summer," which included August and September, even if one's arrival on the French Riviera was the last day of September.

Still, unlike the Porters, Murphys, and other Americans discovering the Riviera, Florence and Frank would make it their permanent home and attempt, rather successfully at the outset, to re-create the Riviera in their own image.

10

CARELESS PEOPLE

My life has got to be like this, it's got to keep going up.
—Jay Gatsby, *The Great Gatsby*

BOUNDLESS OPPORTUNITIES LAY BEFORE FLORENCE AND FRANK as they gazed at the dazzling blue Mediterranean. They drank in Cannes's raw beauty, its wild air, and fell in love. Frank felt that he had come home. Florence must have been reminded of the California coast of her childhood. Yet, for Cannes to become home, they needed to buy one. They immediately settled on a house called Semiramis, aptly named after the mythical Queen of Babylon, but apparently they slept there only three nights, despite owning it for some thirty years. Villa Semiramis, built in 1884 by the Cannois architect Vianay Laurent and originally called Château Saint-Roche, was not a suitable residence for the increasingly spoiled Florence. While surrounded by nearly four acres of parkland, with magnificent views of the sea, it was isolated from the town by a ten-minute car journey and had no private beach. Florence was unprepared to settle for any home without a private beach. Now that she had bagged her millionaire, she could afford to be demanding. Surely, the French Riviera must have something more to her liking, she urged. So they kept looking.

She was right to persevere in more ways than one. The presence of infinite possibilities on the horizon of opportunists like Frank and Florence needed careful planning, particularly if they were to set up a business on the Riviera (as Florence had been urging her husband to do), evidently thinking of those empty twenty-three hours. Besides, she longed to settle where they could make an indelible mark—even change history. Much had been done already on the French Riviera, but she was convinced that there was more to do, and with a shake of her pretty head and her radiant smile, she told Frank they were just the people to do it. The burning question was where. . . .

While they were initially impressed with Cannes, the resort was essentially a British invention. In 1834, Lord Henry Brougham, former lord chancellor of England, was the first foreigner to build himself a villa on a western hill high above the city in the old Suquet quarter. He regaled readers with his description of the region in his otherwise dry *Dialogues upon Republican and Monarchial Government,* claiming to be "enjoying the delightful climate . . . its clear sky and refreshing breezes, while the deep blue waters of the Mediterranean lay stretched before us; the orange groves and cassia plantations perfumed the air around us, and the forests behind, crowned with pines and evergreen oaks, and ending in the Alps, protected . . . by their eternal granite, from the cold winds of the north."[1]

While Brougham "invented Cannes," and its subsequent *hivernants,* or snowbirds, fleeing the damp northern winters, earlier seasonal migrant had been traveling to the French Riviera, or the Côte d'Azur as the French call it, for over a century. A hundred years before Brougham, Tobias Smollett published his *Travels Through France and Italy* in 1766. Shortly after, Laurence Sterne's *A Sentimental Journey Through France and Italy* appeared in print. Sterne happened to be Thomas Jefferson's favorite novelist, and so when the prospect arose, Jefferson traveled south to Nice and beyond in 1787. Though Jefferson, as American ambassador to France, stated his purpose was to recover from a poorly healing dislocated wrist, the possibility of learning the secrets of the Italian rice industry, to take back to the Carolinas in the hope of improving their rice crop, proved an exceptional enticement, too.

∽

The French Rivera had long been thought to heal whatever ailed you. Menton, the most Italian in feel of all French cities on the Riviera, was known as the region's sanatorium by the nineteenth century. Yet, it had been "discovered" long before by the Italian poet Dante Alighieri in the early fourteenth century, after he was exiled from Florence. His travels there were inspirational, a balm to his wounded soul, and he set his experiences down in his epic poems, most notably, in *The Divine Comedy*, completed in 1320.

When the English doctor and Menton resident James Henry Bennet published an article on July 7, 1860, in the British medical journal *The Lancet* and claimed that the climate of Menton was warmer than in "any part of the northern or central parts of Italy" or the French Riviera, and was thus ideal for anyone with respiratory illnesses, Menton's fate was sealed. Its cultural windfall of sculptors, writers, and musicians of all nationalities flocked there in droves: the Italian composer Niccolò Paganini, the Polish-American pianist Arthur Rubinstein, the English author and illustrator Aubrey Beardsley, Frenchmen Henri Matisse and Guy de Maupassant, Russian playwright Anton Chekhov, the German nihilist philosopher Friedrich Nietzsche, Scots writers Thomas Carlyle and Robert Louis Stevenson, Irish greats Laurence Sterne and W. B. Yeats, and New Zealander writer Katherine Mansfield.[2] All sought cures where none could be found.

The "Comté de Nice," as the region was known in Jefferson's day, was ruled from Turin by the kings of Sardinia of the royal House of Savoy, as a part of Piedmont. It became part of France in 1860. Before long, Americans began to settle there. Louisa May Alcott, author of *Little Women*, stayed in Nice and set part of her novel on the Promenade des Anglais. Edith Wharton's father died in Cannes in 1882, and while Edith and her mother returned to America, she felt happiest in her villa at Hyères on the westernmost reaches of the Riviera. James Gordon Bennett Jr., the eccentric American newspaperman who owned the *New York Herald* and later founded the Paris *Herald*, fled scandal in New York to relax in the quiet village of Beaulieu-sur-Mer, where he hosted, among others, the likes of Lady Randolph Churchill and her young son, Winston. While Isadora

Duncan spent much of her life in Paris, Nice became her final spiritual home. She died there in a spectacular car accident on the Promenade des Anglais when her scarf became entangled in the spokes of her speeding Bugatti, instantly strangling her.

The closed world of the aristocracy residing on the Riviera for centuries never mingled with either the beau monde or new immigrants, including Frank and Florence Gould.[3] Their loss was the Goulds' gain. Throughout their visits in the winter season of 1923–1924, it became one of those unique experiences for the Goulds to rub shoulders with real royalty. The success of the Bolshevik's October 1917 Revolution meant that the numerous Romanov clan who hadn't been hunted down, imprisoned, or killed fled Russia. Many became exiles in France. Czar Nicholas II's uncle, Grand Duke Michel Mikhailovich, headed a cast of "who was who" in exiled Russian aristocracy living on the Riviera. The drop-dead handsome Grand Duke Dmitri, once the lover of Czar Nicholas's morganatic sister-in-law Natasha and later Coco Chanel, sponged off his wealthier relatives—and played on Florence's unbounded sympathies, and more than likely, in her bed. The Romanovs' supporters were forced to escape, too, with whatever wealth they could—which, in some instances, was larger than the gross national product of many small European countries. One such oligarch was a railroad robber baron named Paul von Derwies and his wife, the Russian version of the Goulds. Understandably, Frank and Florence became close friends with them, and remained so long after the von Derwies' fortune evaporated. Gone were the days of envying the Russians.

Maharajahs, kings, queens, princesses, and their councilors visited regularly, as part of the French winter circuit of luxury, leisure, and health pursuits between Aix-les-Bains, Pau, Biarritz, Nice, Cannes, and Menton. Frank played tennis with the Maharajah of Pudukota, and dined with the flamboyant Indian captain of cricket, Maharajah Bhupinder Singh of Patiala, who allegedly returned to India with a dancer from Maxim's in Cannes tucked neatly inside one of his trunks.[4] American millionaires and those who were wealthy but of lesser fortunes, began to flock southward, too. The popularity of the Riviera had grown so much that Cunard Lines linked the French Riviera, via Cannes, to the United Kingdom and United States in 1921, with the first sailing of the steamship *Coronia*.[5]

The Parisian beau monde wintered in the season and were changing fashions apace. Florence's preferred designer and friend, Gabrielle "Coco" Chanel, was the new czarina of fashion, elbowing aside Paul Poiret, just as Poiret had done to Jeanne Paquin after the war. When Chanel disembarked from the yacht *The Flying Cloud* belonging to her lover Bendor—the nickname of Hugh Grosvenor, Duke of Westminster— "as brown as a cabin boy" in the winter season of 1923–1924 to join in the fun, the last of the Victorian taboos was shattered. Without any forethought, Chanel had created the most lasting of her fashions—the suntan. What had once been the trademark of fishermen, peasants, stonemasons, bricklayers, and the poor forced to work in the sun became chic, beautiful, and sensual in the summer of 1923.[6]

It might be said that Florence was quite like Chanel, since she had only two real loves: herself and money. Everything else was a passion of the moment, weakness, or adventure with or without calculation.[7] There were of course other differences, too, not the least of which was Chanel's rabid and enduring anti-Semitism, explained away by many as an unfortunate by-product of her convent education. Still, the main difference between the two women was that Florence could literally afford sexual escapades, inscribed into her unwritten marriage contract, where Chanel could not. Her fashion house was her love. Her lover Bendor, however, could—and did—open doors with money and his personal power.

The wife of the Spanish painter José Maria Sert (Marie Godebska Natanson Edwards Sert), or Misia, as everyone called Chanel's inseparable friend, tagged along too. Yet to think that Misia was some sort of groupie would be to underestimate her significance. Misia was an artist's model, muse, trendsetter, and painter in her own right. While she was a friend and patron of Diaghilev, Stravinsky, and painters other than her husband, she was pointedly the object of the affections of Sara Murphy's sister, Mary Hoyt Wiborg, or Hoytie.* It was Misia who introduced the Murphy set to the "Party King of Paris," Étienne de Beaumont, and others who were also friends with the Goulds.[8] Misia would flit in

---

* Misia and her husband "shared" his teenage model's pleasures in bed, until it became obvious that José preferred the model to his wife and divorced her.

and out of all their lives like a butterfly, but always remained faithful to her Coco.

∽

There was a foreboding that the new beau monde of exiles, expatriates, and the fashionable French were making the world a smaller place. In 1925, Donald Ogden Stewart, author of the side-splittingly funny *Mr. and Mrs. Haddock Abroad* about the misadventures of Americans in France, recognized the ominous signs of things to come. "The Hôtel du Cap was now more than half full of wealthy vacationers," Stewart lamented, "and the small exclusive beach on which the Murphy children and Dos [Passos] and I had run wild was now shared with a Mr. and Mrs. Pierpont Morgan Hamilton and assorted guests."[9]

As expected, the two camps did not acknowledge the other's existence. Florence and Frank preferred mingling during their stay at Hôtel du Cap with the Murphy, Dos, and Stewart clan, rather than the Pierpont Morgan Hamiltons, perhaps to Florence's chagrin. Frank's vivid memories of how his family had been shunned by the Four Hundred would never wash away with the years. Still, Florence was never a good joiner-in at other people's parties, always preferring the role of hostess as the star of her own show. Unless they could rival the Hôtel du Cap in some way, Florence, certainly, sensed her place on center stage was under threat.

Once they were back in Paris, any thoughts the Goulds considered for their Riviera future were interrupted by an unforeseen and unwelcome interlude. Frank began complaining of stomach cramps. Sometimes he would have memory lapses of recent events, or be unable to recall what he'd just said, then return to normal. Uncharacteristically, he became lethargic, not wanting to go out or even get out of bed. Occasionally, too, he'd have fits of anger, which he quite naturally blamed on his stomach pain. When Frank began vomiting, Florence called in specialists, but no apparent causes could be found, other than surmising that Frank was suffering from some long-term consequences of his alcohol abuse. Perhaps a change of diet might reduce the symptoms?

Finally, months later, Frank began to spit blood. He was rushed to the private clinic near their Paris home. By the time he arrived, blood was oozing from his mouth. The surgeons advised Florence that Frank needed an emergency operation. They thought he had a stomach abscess, and there was no time to hesitate. Florence swiftly agreed to the surgery.

Given Frank's perceived importance in international society, Florence felt it her duty to notify the press of his hospitalization. The *Chicago Tribune* reported on November 18, 1924, that "Mr. Gould had been in ill health for some time and had tried various diets and then an X-ray revealed a large abscess . . . the patient is as well as can be expected after coming out of the anesthetic." In the days before antibiotics, Frank's recovery was anything but certain.

Amusingly, at the end of the article, a little tidbit was added: "He is 47 years old. Florence La Caze, whom he married in 1923, is his third wife."[10] The separation of Florence's maiden name into this grander, even aristocratic form of "La Caze" may have been an error. Then again, it might have been at her own instigation, since it was repeated time and again in newsprint from that date forward. Just as she had told the American press when she married Henry Heynemann that her father was an important banker in France, it suggests that, for Florence, it was no accident, but rather an enhancement of her ancestry.

No details of Frank's operation or recovery were made public, but given the severity of the abscess, he most likely had a partial gastrectomy.[11] He was incredibly lucky to ward off septicemia, too, since the abscess was the result of a violent infection. It took several months before Frank was fit enough to think about the future, but throughout that winter of 1924–25 in Paris, he dreamed of a home bathed in the warmth of the sun-kissed Mediterannean. Florence had to curse her luck and wonder between gritted teeth if she would merely be a young nurse to her invalid millionaire husband.

Finally, with the spring of 1925, Frank's health improved. He wanted to travel south again to explore their options in the leisure property market. While neither had experience of operating casinos or hotels, as artful gamblers it was a business that attracted them, and they wanted to find out more.

From Florence's perspective, finding a home and things to do for Frank on the Riviera would kill two birds at once: he'd be happy to remain there while she could flit between both their Riviera and Parisian lifestyles. Though they had already owned Semiramis in Cannes for two years, both had agreed back in 1923 that it was not the right place for them. Besides, given the success of the Ambassadeurs Casino under the iron fist of the aging Eugène Cornuché, along with plans by the consummate casino operator Henri Ruhl to open a second casino, the Goulds reasoned that Cannes wasn't the place where they could immediately make their mark.[12] To become viable competitors to such formidable opponents, both craved something new and unspoiled.

Frank and Florence stayed at Hôtel du Cap at Antibes in the winter season of 1923–1924 and loved it. Crossing and uncrossing her legs at the bar, a bottle of champagne within easy reach, a cigarette poised at her lips, Florence silently plotted, while fully aware of most men's eyes drinking in her beauty. The quiet fishing village of Juan-les-Pins attracted her. An easy car ride along the coast road from Cannes to Nice, it was ideally situated for their purposes. Located on a small peninsula jutting into the Mediterranean that also sheltered the ancient fishing village of Antibes, one and a quarter miles distant from Hôtel du Cap, she immediately understood that this was their idyll.

Later, sharing her vision with Frank, their Bugatti stopped to allow them to absorb the unspoiled vistas across the pleasant arc of sea at Juan-les-Pins, redolent of the Bay of Angels (La Baie des Anges) that embraced Nice. Antibes lay behind them, some two miles eastward. Cannes stretched out about four miles in front of them. Frank already had a substantial acquaintance with the northern summer resorts at Deauville and Dinard, and knew instinctively that this little jewel he called "Juan" represented his next gold mine. They could build a resort to their own liking here, Frank and Florence agreed. Naturally, it would be a money spinner, too.

Florence might have seen that they could be big fish in a very small pond at Juan, which could suit her aspirations for Frank. Then, the more he shared his vision with her, the more convinced Florence became that Juan was the remedy they both desired. They knew from their stay at Hôtel du Cap that the multitalented Cole Porter had rented the Château de la Garoupe from Lord and Lady Aberconway not even a mile away in 1923. Porter also invited those elegant Americans, the

Murphys, to stay back then. Now the Murphys were building their new home, Villa America, within plain sight.* Florence also knew that Gerald Murphy was a talented avant-garde artist and had an enviable affiliation—from a beau monde perspective—with Diaghilev's Ballets Russes.

∞

Of course, everyone gossiped about the Murphys' American literary friends, the Scott Fitzgeralds. Picasso and his Russian former Diaghilev ballerina wife, Olga, were at Juan, and were also great friends of the Murphy set. Ernest Hemingway, still a fine journalist coming to grips with the leap to becoming a great novelist, but always a "man's man," joined in, too, with his first wife, Hadley. The Murphys' great friend and witty New York columnist, Dorothy Parker, was extolling the virtues of Antibes back home. All of them frequently stayed at the Hôtel du Cap or rented villas nearby.

Florence saw that by the summer of 1925, the coast of the French Riviera was an artistic and literary paradise, and saw herself as the future Queen of the Riviera. Scott Fitzgerald's most enduring book and masterpiece of life in the "Roaring Twenties," *The Great Gatsby*, had just been published by Scribner's to a lukewarm response. Few realize that it had to be rewritten in 1924 at the request of his editor, Maxwell Perkins, to "add believability" to his characters. So, in an enduring alcoholic haze, Fitzgerald knuckled down at Villa Saint-Louis in Juan-les-Pins and wrote about what he so keenly observed.† He saw how the rich and not-so-famous American "exiles" with pretensions to social status and in possession of great wealth lived on the Riviera. Then he transported them back to his previously imagined north shore of Long Island's fictional towns of West Egg and its aristocratic counterpart, East Egg. Fitzgerald wrote about how these society types were in love with money and had become "careless people"; how they "smashed up things and creatures . . . and let others clean up the mess they made."[13]

The Riviera's careless world of fast cars and fast people, gambling

---

* Cole Porter went to Yale with Gerald Murphy.

† Villa Saint-Louis became the Hôtel Belles-Rives in 1929 under the ownership of Russian émigré Boma and his wife, Simone Estène. Simone came from a long line of Antibes hoteliers.

with life, drunk on their own search for pleasure in the microcosm of Juan-les-Pins, became the canvas to paint into his novel. The essence of the Goulds' selfish world became that of the characters of Fitzgerald's greatest work. Naturally, the Juan exiles, like Florence and Frank, could not recognize themselves in the well-disguised mélange created from Fitzgerald's flat Long Island characters of his original story, as fully paid-up members of their crowd, throbbing with life through *The Great Gatsby*'s pages.

Back in America, it was the age of Prohibition, of gangsters and racketeers making fortunes and plowing their illicit money into various cash businesses. They grew richer, too, like Frank, by avoiding paying taxes. Gatsby himself was a bootlegger who had an ill-gotten, showy wealth, all to impress the love of his life, Daisy Buchanan. But Fitzgerald would not portray his Gatsby as an Al Capone, king of the Chicago racketeers and bootleggers. Gatsby had class, and belonged in the glitzy reflection of Juan-les-Pins that echoed soon enough, too, in the pages of *Tender Is the Night*. Fitzgerald began writing and rewriting that novel as well from the Villa Saint-Louis near the Juan-les-Pins casino.

Wherever Florence looked, there seemed to be pockets of artists, writers, and musicians. "The length of the entire coast," the crafty literary critic and novelist Cyril Connolly wrote, "from *Huxley Point* and *Castle Wharton* until *Cape Maugham* small colonies formed where giants thundered in literary exasperation."[14] D. H. Lawrence haunted Vence in the hills between Antibes and Nice, while Colette, by now the successful novelist of the bestselling *Cheri*, shocked the tiny fishing village of Saint-Tropez with her presence. What else could you expect from Colette? Her marriage to her second husband, Henri de Jouvenel, the editor of *Le Matin*, had ended the year before, due—so the gossip columnists said—to her affair with her sixteen-year-old stepson, Bertrand de Jouvenel.

Aside from Picasso, his great rival, Henri Matisse, had just taken an apartment in Nice to scour the new Victorine film studios for models. Painters Wassily Kandinsky, Paul Klee, Moïse Kisling, Max Beckmann, sculptor Constantin Brancusi, and Dadaist sculptor Marcel Duchamp (known for his urinal entitled *Fountain*) were well-known faces descending on patrons and friends, like locusts, in or out of season. American photographer Man Ray and his Montparnasse muse Kiki (born Alice Prin) scouted locations for his first film. Then, of course, where would those great gay colonies and home to the American Sixth Fleet, Cap Ferrat and Villefranche, be without the inimitable Jean Cocteau, its local artist and playwright? Whispers of the Riviera through the Mediterranean pines are hinted at in many of these artists' works from this period.

The Goulds learned all that they hadn't already known about this international beau monde from Antoine Sella, the owner of Hôtel du Cap. As incredible as it sounds today, Sella, a hotelier with an amazing sixth sense for trends, first kept open his *hôtel de grand luxe* on a trial basis for the summer season of 1923 with a skeleton staff—primarily for the Murphys. Like everyone who met them, Sella was utterly charmed by Gerald and Sara, and joined the ranks of those who wanted to give them anything they asked—just to be part of their lives. Their friend Archibald MacLeish remembered how "Person after person—English, French, American, everybody—met them and came away saying that these people really are masters of the art of living."[15] The hotel's summer "opening" was such a success that by the next year, Sella made Antibes–Juan-les-Pins a year-round resort. Simply to know the Murphys seemed to capture their friends in their successes and reflected golden glow.*

Florence may have envied them, but she could easily, in her opinion, better them. By then, she'd become a woman whom people daren't refuse, thanks to her sexually charged allure and Frank's millions. The novelist Pierre Benoit met Florence in those heady days, and fell madly in love with her. Benoit knew she was a man-eater with dozens of conquests already, but simply couldn't help himself, "as she could offer everything . . . of herself, and she was bored sitting on her pile of gold," Benoit sighed, "perhaps she thought she was Aphrodite, collecting lovers at her pleasure."[16] Still, she hadn't recognized—nor ever would—the difference between inviting illustrious friends as beloved equals to share in your golden sphere, as the Murphys did, and entertaining them at vast expense as your financial inferiors. Nevertheless, Florence set her mind to becoming a person whose art of living would become the envy

---

* Things soon went horribly wrong for the Murphys with the illnesses and deaths of their two sons. Their story was both beautiful and tragic.

of all—even the Murphys. To do that, Juan would become her first experiment. Although she was untrained, Florence remained a natural and extremely talented businesswoman. She saw clearly that by investing in Juan in 1925, just as it was attracting an international artistic clientele, the possibilities for fun and glamour were just beginning to unfold. With Frank's money and her flair, they could create a paradise on the grandest scale.

Like Jay Gatsby, Florence believed that her life could only "keep going up." So they bought a walled neo-Gothic villa called La Vigie with its own beach that had views to the east and west along the narrow promontory on the edge of Juan. Frank was in his element, scouting the competition, learning what people liked, what they didn't, and what the area needed for the future. They traveled the coast between Nice and Monte Carlo to see how other people with money passed their time. Casinos and luxury screamed out at them. It was the new way to get rich, just as railroads and power generation had been twenty years earlier. The French Mediterranean coast with its lavish, hedonistic lifestyle begged them to conquer the Riviera.

11

⟨⟨⟨∘⟩⟩⟩

AN AMUSING INTERMEZZO FOR MILLIONAIRES

> *We must select the illusion which appeals to our tempera-*
> *ment, and embrace it with passion, if we want to be happy.*
> —Cyril Connolly

FRANK WAS ESPECIALLY INTERESTED IN THE MONACO MODEL OF casino. While Florence gambled incessantly at its roulette and baccarat tables, her jeweled bracelets rattling like dice as she observed the punters and those who hung back from the action, Frank studied with envy how, nearly sixty years earlier, François Blanc created the modern-day Monte Carlo. For him, it was an amazing feat, and soon enough, Frank had Florence agreeing that bettering Monte Carlo would become their aim.

Blanc was the man Frank Gould longed to outshine. The famous clipping "Monaco is an earthly paradise, a fairytale land" from the influential newspaper *Le Figaro* dating from February 23, 1865, was beautifully framed and hung discreetly in the lobby of the principality's Hôtel de Paris. It hailed Blanc as Monte Carlo's founder: "M. Blanc has transformed this region, once pleasing rather than rich, into a veritable California; only he does not discover gold mines, he creates them."[1] So did Frank Gould.

François Blanc and his twin brother, Louis, learned their craft of misdirection at the feet of the former lawyer turned casino owner Jacques

Bénazet, who owned the two most profitable private gambling clubs at the Palais-Royal in Paris: Frascati's and the Cercle des Étrangers. These clubs, like all the 180 leasable units used for gambling, prostitution, intrigue, or other vices, were called *les enfers*—hells—by the French. Blanc swiftly became expert at financial forecasting, casino security, and publicity and understood from the get-go that the only way to win in a casino was to become the house.

So, when the landgrave Ludwig of Hessen-Homburg advertised that he was willing to sell the exclusive rights to gaming in his territory, François struck a deal to build a *Kurhaus* (spa) in exchange for the thirty-year lease for the landgrave's casino. Chronically underfunded, the brothers still managed to make it work and turned the backwater of Bad Homburg— which was no more than the landgrave's castle, a few hundred dependents' cottages, and a small inn—into the "must sample" resort fit for kings, their consorts, and millionaires.[2] It was their single-zero roulette tables, offering the best odds in Europe, that attracted the wealthy and aristocratic to their resort—rather than the spa—as most would later claim. The Russian royal Romanov family stalked the roulette tables, as did Queen Victoria's princely sons. Even Fyodor Dostoyevsky, a man who should have known better, amassed huge debts at Blanc's tables in the 1860s. The Blancs, naturally acting as the house, were the only ones to truly win time and again at the gambling tables. At Bad Homburg, François Blanc was crowned casino royalty.

Blanc realized soon enough that Bad Homburg's spring and summer season needed an overwintering business partner. The principality of Monaco—spanning a mere 499 acres, or half the size of Central Park in New York—beckoned. In September 1855, Société Anonyme des Bains de Mer et le Cercle des Étrangers à Monaco (The Sea Bathing and Foreigners' Circle of Monaco Company), known as SBM, was created, making Monaco the first place to offer gambling on the Mediterranean coast.[3] Still, Monaco was a tummy-rumbling three-hour coach journey from the railway terminus at Nice along a narrow mountain road, which was also frequently peppered with armed highwaymen. Coupled with French and Italian saber rattling that threatened war, Blanc chose to abstain from the bidding for the Monaco concession. Instead Pierre Auguste Daval bought the lease for 1,208,000 francs. Then, almost immediately,

Daval lost everything to the duc de Valmy when his casinos were forced to close in the political Franco-Sardinian Alliance against the Austrians. Blanc was a man who could read the future, Frank believed.

Fortunately for Blanc, as German politicking and talk of unification loomed, the political situation for Monaco became peaceful. The Comté de Nice was now part of France, stretching as far as Menton. By the time the casino called Les Spélugues on Monaco's plateau had opened its doors in February 1863, Valmy sat across the table from Blanc offering the lease on the casino for 1,860,000 francs. After ruthless bargaining, the deal was sealed for 1,129,000 francs—less than the price of the original lease eight years earlier.[4] That April, Blanc signed the contract for exclusive rights to operate games of chance in Monaco for the next fifty years.

Blanc immediately set to work with the Grimaldi prince's enthusiastic approval to build "a whole town," which he did, and of course named it after Prince Charles*—calling it Monte Carlo (Mount Charles). It was a perfect symbiotic relationship. Monaco shed its poverty while Monte Carlo became more than a mere casino. Blanc created an emotional bond between his gambling visitors and the town that enriched everyone beyond the sum of its gambling rooms. Blanc's advertising depicted a whole new way of life, a new patrician outlook for a fading aristocracy seeking relevance in a modern world.

Soon SBM, under Blanc's guiding hand, built Monte Carlo's Hôtel de Paris adjacent to the casino, modeled on Paris's Grand Hôtel on boulevard des Capucines. Café de Paris followed a few years later. Soon enough, Monte Carlo offered boules, water sports, a marina, four steamers to ferry guests between Nice, Genoa, and Monaco—and an omnibus to take gamblers to the front door of the casino along a fragrant avenue where mimosa wafted on the breeze.[5] Monte Carlo became, in fact, the first luxury destination resort, freeing its visitors to spend as lavishly as they lived, while they enjoyed Blanc's carefully crafted experience. It was this vision, the completeness of Monte Carlo in its François Blanc heyday, that lured Frank and Florence into the casino and hotel business.

---

* Charles III was the great-great-grandfather of Rainier III, Prince of Monaco, husband of actress Grace Kelly.

Florence Lacaze Gould, wife of millionaire sportsman Frank Jay Gould, for press shot "Popular on the Riviera," September 1930.
(Courtesy of the Library of Congress)

Aerial view of Lyndhurst and the Hudson River.
(Courtesy of Lyndhurst, A National Trust Historic Site)

First home of the Lacaze family in Paris, just opposite the Luxembourg Gardens.

Jay Gould (1836–1892). (Courtesy of Lyndhurst, A National Trust Historic Site)

Helen Gould Shepard (1868–1938). (Courtesy of Lyndhurst, A National Trust Historic Site)

Anna, Duchess of Talleyrand-Perigord (1875–1961), taken in 1939. Anna returned to Lyndhurst that year, acquiring the family estate from Helen's widower. (Courtesy of Lyndhurst, A National Trust Historic Site)

Anna with daughter Helene-Violetta, who as an adult was Gaston Palewski's lover and later wife. They became close with Florence after Frank's death. (Courtesy of Lyndhurst, A National Trust Historic Site)

Frank Jay Gould as a young man.
(Courtesy of the Library of Congress)

Frank Jay Gould posing for the New York World-Telegram, *1912.* (Courtesy of the Library of Congress)

Florence Gould, circa 1954, talking to Jean Cocteau (right). She is fifty-nine years old in the picture and is beginning to wear her dark glasses. (Courtesy of Archives Municipales Montrose, Cannes, France)

Portrait of Gabrielle "Coco" Chanel, 1936. Hand-colored photo by Brois Lipnitski (1897– 1871). (Private collection. Courtesy of Roger-Viollet, Paris/Bridgman Images)

Arletty starring in Le Jour Se Leve, 1939, *directed by Marcel Carne Arletty.* (Courtesy of Bridgeman Images, © DILTZ)

As captioned in the New York World-Telegram, *"Mrs. Frank Gould, society leader in New York and Paris, arriving in New York aboard the* Ile de France," *1934.*
(Courtesy of the Library of Congress)

Edith Kelly Gould demonstrating her "highest kick in the world."
(Courtesy of the Library of Congress)

Isabelle Lacaze (left), sister of Florence Gould, with Florence, holding their Pekingese dogs on the maiden voyage of the SS Normandie in 1935.
(Courtesy of Getty Images)

Florence Lacaze Gould aboard the SS Normandie *in 1935 with two of her Pekingese dogs. Both she and Frank were devoted to the breed.* (Courtesy of the Library of Congress)

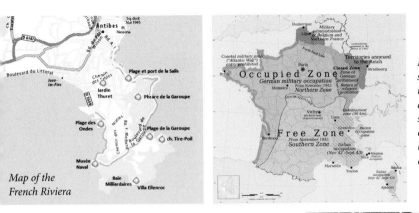

Map of the French Riviera

Map of France showing how it was divided at various stages of the occupation between 1940 and 1944.

Above: 129 Avenue Malakoff, where Florence held her wartime salon in her apartment on the third floor. (Courtesy of the author)

Above right: 133 Avenue Malakoff, home of Ludwig Vogel, Florence's wartime lover. (Courtesy of the author)

View from Florence's home in Cannes, Le Patio, renamed as Palais Gould today.

Left: View of Palais Gould today. (Courtesy of the author)

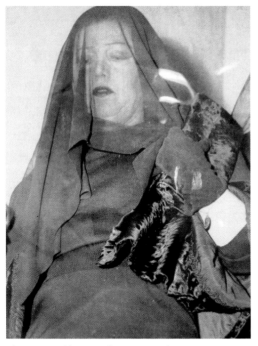

Florence Gould, 1956. This Associated Press photo was captioned "Mrs. Florence Gould, third wife of Frank Jay Gould, gets the bulk of Gould estate." (Courtesy of the Library of Congress)

Letter from Tom Hoving, director of the Metropolitan Museum of Art, to Florence Gould, dated April 6, 1968—a time capsule and a letter of thanks.
(Courtesy of the Metropolitan Museum of Art)

Promenade des Anglais in Nice with the Palais de la Méditerrannée in the background, circa 1929.
(Courtesy of Hyatt-Regency Palais de la Méditerrannée)

Front view of Lyndhurst.
(Courtesy of Lyndhurst, A National Trust Historic Site)

∽

Florence undoubtedly had more to do with Frank's decision to invest in casinos than the traditional role being the woman behind the man. If he were to make a full recovery in the move to the South of France, she recognized that he'd need an interest as all-consuming as racing his thoroughbreds had been at Maisons-Laffitte. During his illness and long convalescene, she had to face up to the bold fact that should Frank die, she would receive only the widow's portion of one-third of his French estate under French law. Her well-honed self-preservation naturally kicked in. Frank had two daughters, several established households in France, a substantial American inheritance, and a business of unknown proportions in the United States. If he died, without changing his will in her favor, she'd have a mere million or two, tops.

They had been married only eighteen months when Frank underwent his serious operation. She knew full well that her slice of the pie on his death was not—just yet—a slice worth the sacrifices she was making. Besides, Florence rightly thought, Frank's daughters, Helen and Dorothy, were young women now, and married. Chances were, there would be a battle for the third Mrs. Gould to get what she so richly deserved.

It would be underselling Florence to believe that she somehow was not at the heart of the decision to own casinos and hotels. Indeed, her widow's one-third portion of a thriving casino business could be worth more than all the rest of Frank's French estate. Fortunately for Florence, Frank's near brush with death and continuing illness made him more pliable and eager to please his lovely wife, who had, after all, nursed him back to health.

In Frank's eyes, casinos and hotels were great wealth generators. He had always invested in what was "new," and inevitably, it served him well. Frank knew the checkered history of gambling in the United States— from corrupt state lotteries in the mid-nineteenth century to the riverboat gamblers. It left horseracing as the only form of accepted gambling stateside, despite the practices of drugging horses or substituting horses bound to lose—and thereby chalking up huge odds—with winning "ringers." Frank also knew New Mexico and Arizona had to abandon gambling to gain statehood.[6] Still, the Goulds' vision for Juan would be different. It was gaming for people who should know better. It was gambling for those who could afford to lose their shirts.

Casinos and hotels as Blanc saw them—what the industry calls "destination properties" today—were an extension of the upper-class desire to travel in comfort. The Train Bleu, officially called the Calais-Méditerranée Express, which had been running again to Nice since December 1922, exclusively catered to first-class passengers. Frank and Florence did not gloss over the substantial fact that both casinos and hotels were huge cash businesses, where—if you knew how to manage it—only a portion of the income needed to go "on the books" to be reported for tax purposes. Florence was ever mindful of Frank's aversion to the taxman to other officials trying to dip their fingers into his hard-earned profit pie.

Florence's lovely green eyes widened at the possibilities. Her winning smile burst into life, too. With gambling tables, hotels, and restaurants, Florence's salon in the south of France aiming to capture the newer *Tout-Riviera* would be recalled long after she was gone, and on a canvas larger than any in Paris, where the competition was greater. She would turn their Mediterranean venture into entertainments that would even make her friends, the Étienne de Beaumonts and the Faucigny-Lucinges, green with envy. With Frank's money and her vision for entertainment and fun, all of Juan-les-Pins would become her party. Thereafter, who knew—perhaps Cannes or Nice? Indeed, Florence could become the uncrowned Queen of the Riviera, with all Parisian society clamoring to be admitted to her Mediterranean court. Still, dreams were one thing, and gambling houses and hotels another. So Florence and Frank set to work on their project with the diligence of students studying for a doctorate.

∽

The Goulds, a pair of natural-born gamblers, settled on a casino as their first venture. Frank invested in the Casino de Juan-les-Pins, with his French business partner and restaurateur Edouard Baudoin as its director and day-to-day manager. Aside from Baudoin's expertise in running the casino along the lines Blanc had devised, he understood the importance of greasing palms and close friendships—particularly when it came to the mayor of Antibes–Juan-les-Pins, Charles Guillaumont.[7]

Frank had learned the art of crossing state lines and bending the local political will to suit his business needs from the master, Jay Gould. At Juan, Baudoin would be the public face and take all the inevitable flack for the Goulds' actions.

Even Baudoin was amazed at how easily permissions to operate a casino and build a large luxury hotel came through the friendships he cultivated with Guillaumont and others in the corridors of political power. From the mayor's perspective, it was even more incredible how easily he was reelected with Gould money sloshing around in his campaign fund, not to mention Gould influence brought to bear on the press.

So, in 1925, together with Florence, the trio wasted no time and planned the construction of Hotel Provençal at Juan—a 256-bedroom luxury property fit for millionaires. In less than a year, all approvals were in place; and the hotel, set within its own parkland, rose to its full height on the Juan skyline adjacent to the casino. Considering that it took Henri Ruhl, the man who gave Deauville its "incomparable éclat," several years of negotiations plus two years to build his casino in Cannes some twenty years earlier, the Goulds had succeeded beyond all imagining.[8]

Of course, brickbats were hurled, mainly from the Ambassadeurs Casino's owners in Cannes, who saw the Goulds' project as dangerous and unwanted competition. While the accusations of corruption against Guillaumont were directly linked in the Nice and Cannes press to Baudoin, the Goulds, as the money behind the man, remained unscathed. In fairness to Guillaumont, he recognized—with the help of the Goulds and Baudoin—that gaming had transformed the fortunes of the bankrupt Grimaldi dynasty over fifty years earlier. Guillaumont argued forcefully that all he wanted was the same quality of life for the people of Antibes–Juan-les-Pins as that of those who had once been poor in Monaco.

Gambling in France had been closely regulated since the law of 1907. The Deuxième and Septième Bureau of the Sûreté (the detective investigation branches of the civil police) demanded approval over casino directors and their accounts. The government was mindful of the casinos' ability to create traceless cash transactions—and thereby avoid taxation–or use the casinos as meccas for criminality and illicit wealth generation. Its response was to legislate. Casinos needed to be owned by

French companies, sufficiently capitalized, and with French directors operating them.

While Frank remained American through and through, Florence could still be considered French by the government, given the right circumstances, and so she held shares in her own name and was on the board of directors. Frank had yet to meet a man who didn't find her persuasive, and knew she was a great asset. Besides, he naturally preferred to stay in the background, masterminding investments, sharing an architectural vision with Florence while both pampered their ever-present Pekingese dogs in public. Ultimately, both allowed others to run the tedious day-to-day routine of their businesses for them.[9] Florence reasoned that one should be mingling, animating, and encouraging everyone to enjoy themselves and spend, spend, spend. Frank's strengths lay in acquisitions and finance, not operations. What the French government hadn't come to grips with from Frank's perspective was the common practice of skimming money from construction contracts and hidden ownerships. In fact, Frank and Florence would become adapt at money laundering.

Significantly, the historic agreement of 1860 between Napoleon III and the Grimaldi princes stipulated that no roulette tables were allowed as part of the French casino offer on the entire French Riviera. This automatically gave Monte Carlo its continued preeminence. Nice already had two municipal casinos along the Promenade des Anglais— the Casino de la Jetée, built on stilts jutting into the sea, and the Municipal Casino at Place Masséna. The Casino Ruhl, named after its Swiss-born owner, Henri Ruhl, was the best private casino in the city. Cannes, too, had its casinos in its hotels, the Carlton and the Martinez, and, of course, the Ambassadeurs Casino. There were dozens of private gambling clubs—called *cercles*—each with its own set of arcane rules that members had to obey. More important to Frank, there were several casino owners—not to mention underworld backroom operations—that would stop at nothing to avoid new competition.[10] Frank and Florence believed that they could avoid that murky world— at least for now—since Juan-les-Pins afforded the unique opportunity of a virgin territory.

They spent a lot of time at the splendid Hôtel du Cap at Antibes and were befriended by its owner, Antoine Sella, who was furious when he heard of their betrayal in developing their new hotel on the doorstep of his magnificent oasis. Hadn't Fitzgerald written the lines about *his* beach and *his* hotel in *Tender Is the Night*: "On the pleasant shore of the French Riviera about half way between Marseille and the Italian border, stands a large, rose-colored hotel. Deferential palms cool its flushed façade, and before it stretches a short dazzling beach. Lately it has become a summer resort of some notable and fashionable people; a decade ago it was almost deserted after its English clientele went north in April"?[11] Hadn't Sella discovered the secret of keeping his property open on a year-round basis? Frank calmly replied that since Sella refused to sell Hôtel du Cap to him, at any price, he had been compelled to rethink his strategy. It was Sella himself, Frank reasoned, who wanted the competition on his doorstep. What Sella didn't know then was that the local restaurateur, Edouard Baudoin, who had bought the small casino at Juan the year before, was the Goulds' business partner in the hotel venture.

Under Baudoin's management, the Hôtel Provençal became an Art Deco rose-colored palace almost as famous as Hôtel du Cap in the twenties. With its white sugar-sand beaches, luxury suites, jetty suitable for yachts to dock, gourmet restaurants, bars, and casino, it quickly became a favorite for pleasure seekers wanting *la dolce vita*. Florence and Frank hobnobbed in Cannes at the Ambassadeurs Casino with the Parisian gratin like the Rochefoucaulds and the Melchior de Polignacs, and remained unsullied by the stain of "being in trade."*

Simultaneously, Florence befriended the wild and wonderful Scott and Zelda Fitzgerald at Juan. Rudolph Valentino, heartthrob of the silent screen, lounged in its bar. She joked with Harpo Marx while he thumbed tunes on the casino bar's piano. Suzanne Lenglen, the French Ladies' Tennis champion between 1920 and 1926, taught Florence to play tennis on the hotel's courts. The Murphys, Fitzgeralds, Picassos, and Hemingways danced in the Provençal's ballroom and even preferred its casino to the more formal one overlooking the rocky beaches of Monte Carlo.

---

* Marie Charles Jean Melchoir de Polignac inherited his mother's champagne business, Pommery, and was its hands-on managing director. While others may have thought he was "in trade," de Polignac carried a noble name and heritage. His cousin, Prince Pierre, was the father of Rainier III, Prince of Monaco.

It was the age of the "flapper," skirts above the knee, eyes rimmed and blackened by kohl, and bobbed hair. The Charleston, the Shimmy, and the Black Bottom dances gave way reluctantly to jazz. Florence embraced jazz quickly and initiated the first "Jazz at Juan Festival" in June to keep everyone entertained.*

Demanding to be the trendsetter in fashions, Florence harangued Chanel to design special beach pajamas for her. By day, Florence wore Chanel's beach pajamas. By night, these were sequined, or velvet, or satin, lined with extra-deep pockets to hold her spoils from the gambling tables. Florence's fashion-statement pajamas designed by Chanel caught on, and beach pajamas became the must-have item of clothing for the summer season of 1926. Even Paris's high-society magazine *L'Illustration* took an interest and dubbed Juan-les-Pins "Pyjamapolis." Still, the wealthy, notable, and even the hoi polloi winced as her shrill laughter rang out across the gaming rooms with each of her winning hands. The once quiet and honey-laced singing voice could carry a long way, even in a crowded room. Seemingly, it never once occurred to Florence to be discreet about her winnings at the tables. She was the queen, and they could—in the words of another dead queen—eat cake.

∽

In the twenties, like so many young women, Florence joined the flapper craze with gusto. A slash of red daubed her lips from then until the day she died. Her eyes, darkened with brown eyeshadow and kohl, made her look exotic, if somewhat forbidding. Furs embraced her face, her slouch hat pulled down over one eye, as she increasingly looked the part of the femme fatale she had become.[12] Not satisfied with playing in the casino until closing most evenings, she relished any sporting challenge she could find, daring others in her champagne-infused folly to join in. Freed of her waist-length tresses, Florence helped to popularize water-skiing, by setting up competitions.[13] Florence sparred with the French film star Arletty, who had married the shady "financier" Alexandre Stavisky, to race cars along the unofficial "Juan circuit" in her Hispano-Suiza or Frank's Bugatti. Living fast was the motto of the day. While

---

* The Juan Jazz Festival exists to this very day.

Florence portrayed life as one great roaring party—never going to bed before three in the morning—Frank preferred a less showy life than his wife. Known as the man in the old-fashioned wing collar and tie, he made fewer and fewer appearances among the glitterati who frequented his hotel and casino, preferring the company of his Pekingese dogs instead. Making the casino and hotel buzz, he believed, was Florence's job. She was the honey to attract the beau monde into his money-making propositions. She was also the glue that helped them hold it all together. And she was good at it.

∽

Then, in 1926, to the Goulds' surprise, the arms dealer turned casino owner Sir Basil Zaharoff suddenly sold his shares in the Monégasque hotel and casino company, SBM, after the death of his wife and long-time mistress, Doña Maria.* Dubbed "the Merchant of Death" in the press, Zaharoff's name instilled fear, even among the foolhardiest. "The destinies of nations are his sport," Max Aitken, Lord Beaverbrook, said, "the movements of armies and affairs of Governments his special delight. In the wake of the war, this mysterious figure moves over a tortured Europe."[14] Still, the Goulds coveted SBM.

Frank Gould knew Zaharoff. He also knew that the man was dangerous. Tall and thuggish with his Mephistophelian beard honed to fine points, Zaharoff had made his fortune as an arms dealer for the Allies in World War I. Born to Greek parents living in Odessa, as Zacharias Basileios Zaharoff, he returned with his family to Turkey in the 1840s. There Zaharoff sharpened his racketeering skills by exchanging money on the black market at hugely inflated rates, as well as making a living as a boxer and muscle-for-hire. His uncle Sevastopoulos made him a partner in his textile business, but neglected to pay him a living wage, commissions, or any share in the profits. So Zaharoff, by now calling himself "Basil," took what he felt was his due from the company and headed to London. Sevastopoulos pursued, and sued; but when Zaharoff produced the partnership agreement to the court, his uncle wept, and the case collapsed.

---

* Duchess of Marchena y Villafranca de los Caballeros was married to the institutionalized cousin of King Alfonso of Spain, making divorce impossible until his death.

Leaving London for Athens, Zaharoff was hired by the Swedish armaments firm Nordenfelt, and swiftly worked his way up from clerk to major shareholder. Zaharoff was the arms dealer to the Balkans in the run up to the Great War. After switching his allegiance to the British arms manufacturer Vickers, Zaharoff profited from every conflict worldwide, and was rumored to have prolonged the war by his astute whisperings to politicians of rival nations. The British knighted him for his help to the Allies, but Zaharoff always remained aloof, a mysterious mover behind publicly reported events.

By 1923, *The Wall Street Journal* named him the fourth richest man in the world—ahead of the Vanderbilts and Mellons. That same year, Zaharoff was an invited guest at the baptism of Prince Rainier Grimaldi, grandson of the reigning Prince Louis II of Monaco. *The Washington Post* wrote that the French diplomats present were concerned by Zaharoff's presence and gift of a large gray pearl since "no one doubts [Zaharoff] as being the true power behind Monte Carlo," and a British agent. The article concluded that "the superstitious are suggesting that the Zaharoff pearl may be an omen of ill-luck" for the Grimaldi dynasty.[15]

Indeed, Prince Louis's father, Prince Albert of Monaco, had been in financial difficulties since the end of the war in 1918. As a neutral power, the principality had been a hotbed of intrigue, and was even accused of operating a spy ring for the Germans from the casino. Newspaper articles, eyewitness reports of "Monaco as the secret backroom of Europe," and novelists all preyed on the German connections of François Blanc. "If you only knew the underground workings of the place, the mentality, the way in which everything is run," a Monte Carlo insider warned a friend in the 1922 novel *The Poisoned Paradise* by Robert Service, "why you're not living in the Twentieth Century at all. It's medieval."[16]

Still, Frank and Florence both knew to strip away the hyperbole and concentrate on the important fact that the Grimaldi monarch had depended on his share of the wealth from the casino, and later the SBM hotels, and knew that their takings had declined during the four-year bloodbath that consumed Europe from 1914 to 1918. François Blanc's son, Camille, headed up SBM now, and despite the Monaco's monarch asking him for help first, he refused to lend money to the cash-strapped prince. The Goulds had little trouble learning that sometime in 1918,

Zaharoff had loaned the prince the sum required, in exchange for his help in taking control of SBM.

As the Goulds were hoping to settle into the Riviera life in 1923, Zaharoff forced the resignation of Camille Blanc. Léon Radziwill, Camille's nephew, remained a substantial shareholder, and threw his allegiance behind the powerful arms dealer. A figurehead president and former associate of Zaharoff's working for the French forces in the war, Alfred Delpierre, ostensibly ran things until the high-handed René Léon took over the day-to-day management of SBM. Effectively, Zaharoff had made SBM's position in the world of gambling on the Riviera unassailable—and Frank knew to stay well away.[17]

Yet after his wife's death in 1923, Zaharoff suddenly sold his shares in the company to the Dreyfus Bank of Paris and a consortium of investors. Florence's playboy friend, Prince Jean-Louis de Faucigny-Lucinge became an SBM director, and she sensed it was time to seize their moment, too. By then, the Goulds owned three hotels in Juan-les-Pins and its casino. With Zaharoff out of the picture, they could expand eastward toward Nice, and, who knows, perhaps east again to Monte Carlo. A prime piece of real estate had presented itself on Promenade des Anglais in Nice, and when Zaharoff was known to have retired from his investments in SBM, they grabbed it. Frank's health had seemingly improved, and the time was ripe to give SBM a good run for its money.

12

TAKING STOCK

Life is a desire, not a meaning.

—CHARLIE CHAPLIN

DESPITE EVERYTHING, FLORENCE WAS UNFULFILLED—OR AS THE writer Pierre Benoit noted, "bored sitting on her pile of gold." Business was grand, and making millions fun, but it didn't quench her desire for fast living. She longed for speed, as all young people did in the Roaring Twenties. For her, the embodiment of that fast life was Zelda Fitzgerald.

Florence adored Zelda. She often told Frank how Zelda and Scott made her laugh. Perhaps Florence recognized something of their unhappiness and desperation in herself, because she saw nothing wrong in their drunken escapades and antics. Crashing cars, kidnapping hoteliers, covering opera singer Grace Moore's villa walls with obscene graffiti, or gliding a scoop of sorbet down the back of a countess's ball gown in a stunt akin to those of "the Little Tramp" Charlie Chaplin in the 1917 film *The Adventurer* were all taken by Florence in good heart.

Yet when Zelda unexpectedly got up from the dinner table at the Juan casino where she had been sitting with Scott and the Murphys, and lifted the skirt of her evening dress above her waist and began to slowly dance like a dervish for no apparent reason, Frank warned his wife that Zelda was not good for business. Casino guests ranged widely from the

Rothschilds and Rochefoucaulds to ministers of state and the perhaps more tolerant Hollywood stars. Still, Florence didn't judge her, and even envied Zelda's spontaneity. Like the Murphys, she saw Zelda's "tremendous natural dignity."

Florence understood, too, what it was like to be overshadowed by a more successful husband. Both women were frustrated artistes—Zelda as a writer and ballet dancer, Florence as a singer. What Florence had perhaps never understood was that for the real artists—writers, painters, musicians, actors, directors, and the like—she would always be a potential patron first; and a beautiful, vibrant woman who loved the arts a poor second. This simple fact blinded her to the shortcomings of Zelda and other artistic "friends," as they appeared to those outside the social world Florence had entered, and taken by storm, in marrying Frank.

Florence only realized that Zelda was deeply troubled when it came to the incident at La Colombe d'Or restaurant, when the Murphys and their friends were dining there. La Colombe d'Or was magnificently situated high in the hills above Antibes in the medieval village of Saint-Paul-de-Vence. Apparently, when Gerald Murphy drew attention to the overweight and aging but still magnetic Isadora Duncan, Scott sat at her feet in homage to the once great lady. Duncan was so flattered that she ran her fingers through Scott's blond wavy hair, calling him her "centurion." Zelda, unsurprisingly, was furious.

Without any warning, Zelda leaped over the parapet behind Gerald Murphy into the darkness. Everyone thought she was dead. Fortunately, she had landed on a stone staircase and was already on her feet—knees and dress bloodied—but otherwise unharmed by the time they dared, horrified, to lean over the wall to gaze at her corpse.[1] The story made the rounds of the Riviera rumor mill, and Frank feared the worst. Zelda was not someone he wanted in his hotel or casino. In their business, so he admonished Florence, there *was* such a thing as bad publicity. They catered to high-profile guests at the hotel. Even those from Hollywood never behaved as outrageously as Zelda. Certainly, none of them would have enjoyed watching her jump off the terrace at La Colombe d'Or.

Frank believed Zelda was unhinged. Despite his sound, if patriarchal and hypocritical, advice to his thirty-year-old flapper wife—who

was too busy enjoying the fruits of Frank's millions and her inher-
ent defiance of tradition—she remained loyal to Zelda, if somewhat
chastened. The final straw came, however, when Scott kidnapped the
hotel's orchestra until they agreed to play the music Zelda wanted. Frank
was unamused, and ordered Florence to cut off relations with the ugly
Americans—or else.[2]

✍

Of course, Florence knew she had gone too far too quickly. Frank began
to spend more and more time at the Casino de la Jetée on the Promenade des Anglais in Nice. There, he tickled his passion for dancing—
and he was a very good ballroom dancer—while also indulging in his
infatuation with the comic opera singer Regina Ardenti. Florence knew
Frank liked his girlfriends to have some stage presence, but disingenu-
ously, he couldn't bear for his wife to sing in public. Suddenly, she saw
the fate of Edith Kelly Gould looming like some huge wave before her
sea-green eyes. Divorce, and even worse, no financial settlement became an unfathomable possibility. True, she held her mansion in Paris
in her own name. True, too, she was a director of Frank's French companies with shares also in her name. Frank had paid for a house for her
mother, Berthe, in Cannes, too. Florence had invited her trusted friend
Cécile Tellier to live with her mother as a companion. Isabelle, ever envious of Florence, was provided for as well. Frank settled allowances on
them, too.

All the women Florence had ever cared for—or, in the case of her
sister, felt an obligation to provide for—could finally relax from the nag-
ging financial worries that plagued them. Possibly, Berthe tried to give
her daughter some sound advice. Florence had acclimated herself too
quickly to the lifestyle of the idle rich. She was bright enough to realize
that the fabulous wealth was not her own. As unpalatable as it might
have seemed to her, Berthe was right. There was no doubt that Zelda and
Scott Fitzgerald would have to be dropped. As had already become her
custom, when Florence turned her back on people, whether lovers or
friends, it was an absolute rupture, and this would be the fate of the
Fitzgeralds, Murphys, and others in their circle. Only Picasso remained
more than a nodding acquaintance.

Still, there is a curious passage in Gerald Murphy's notebooks that invites some speculation. "What would happen . . . if a family devoted to an honest, animal expression of sex suddenly came across someone who used sex dishonestly, sophisticatedly, as a tool or a weapon?"[3] Surely, Murphy must have been thinking of Ernest Hemingway or Pablo Picasso, both of whom lusted after his lovely Sara. Scott Fitzgerald held nothing of the predator in his sexual attraction to Sara, but made his thoughts known to both the Murphys.

It is tantalizing to ponder for a moment if Gerald Murphy had experienced this predatory nature in a woman for the first time in Florence. Had he observed her cozying up in the casino bar to Charlie Chaplin or Harpo Marx or Rudolph Valentino or Pablo Picasso or Scott Fitzgerald, or any of her other male guests, as she was wont to do? Was Murphy one of her unsuspecting prey? Had Murphy then seen her turn around, as if on a dime, and immediately latch on to the arm of her husband, flashing her radiant, adoring smile at Frank? Murphy would have needed to lose all his senses to avoid observing how Florence approached men with her feline walk, her seductive voice beckoning them to her with its sexy whisper, her face enveloping them, placed an inch—no more—from her prey. Then there were those green eyes, mesmerizing the object of her attack, while her soft breath begged him to kiss her lovely lips, as one of her salon authors, Paul Léautaud, would later write disapprovingly. Murphy, as few others, resisted because he adored his wife, his children, and his life. Florence was simply not his kind of gal.

Her behavior was utterly sanctioned by Frank, so long as she told him all about her evening's escapades over his breakfast in bed the next morning. Both Frank and Florence had taken several lovers. Florence recalled that "everyone slept with everyone else. It was fun; it was practical." Whenever Frank became bored with his current paramour, he would ask his wife to surprise them in flagrante. Florence dutifully played the role of the outraged wife, and the lover of the moment would flee, clutching her clothes to her chest. Should Frank *not* tire of his latest girlfriend on cue, Florence would shower the woman occupying his affections with dozens of jewels until Frank got the bill. He was a millionaire, twice divorced, and read his wife's actions loudly: it was time to dump his latest mistress, claiming, "I had to, the affair was costing me a fortune."[4]

The implied understanding was that a third divorce would cost him even more. While everybody slept with everyone else in Florence's parlance, at the end of the day, Frank had decided that three wives were quite enough. He felt an undying loyalty to, and admiration of, Florence for nursing him back to health. To boot, she had a fine sense of humor—and a keen business mind—to match her beauty. They thought alike on many levels, which was far more than he could say for either of his earlier wives. Besides, he hadn't met his match before, or a woman quite like her—ever. But the signs were there. Frank and Florence were growing apart.

∞

Their relationship was tested further when William Randolph Hearst's newspaper empire published the serialization of Boni de Castellane's memoirs entitled *How I Won and Lost Anna Gould's Millions*. Boni was pictured with a Russian wolfhound, a Borzoi, at his side, staring up the immense chimney breast at a framed likeness of Anna. "While I was endowed with ancestors of the highest social prestige, bankruptcy haunted me. The time had come for me to respond energetically. My thoughts turned to the very rich American heiress who I had to conquer," Boni boldly stated. "Napoleon won and lost an empire for France. The Count of Castellane won a rich American heiress for himself, and lost her," the article went on. "Boni is the pioneer of what would soon become the new sport of foreign nobility: the hunt for rich girls in the New World, where the title of countess or marquise is sure to seduce them."[5] Privately, Frank seethed for his favorite sister. Publicly, he had to swallow hard and say, "No comment."

Meanwhile, Florence was tasked with averting the negative publicity leveled against the Gould name. Rightly so. It was Florence's job to keep them both in the public eye and to organize all sorts of devil-may-care high-profile entertainments for their international set. Florence, who had been playing mixed doubles tennis with the Irish champion Tom Burke, his brother Albert, and sisters Patricia and Mimi, cooked up a scheme—with Gould money—to hold an international tournament at the Carleton Hotel in Cannes and include the Goulds' new property, the Gallia Tennis Courts, as part of the tourney. It was a wonderful publicity coup, Frank agreed.

So Albert Burke, the official promoter, leased the Carleton's courts, and pulled in the U.S. champion, Helen Wills of California, and French champion, Suzanne Lenglen, as the main event. Since Florence courted international tennis buffs who also had muscle in Hollywood, like Charlie Chaplin and Rudolph Valentino, she was able to land an exclusive "motion picture" deal that sold for $100,000 to show the ladies' finals match worldwide. That is, until Helen Wills had her say. Wills was outraged at the promoters' making "the match a business proposition." This was, of course, in the days when tennis viewed any outside sponsorship dimly, and the only monies earned were from spectators attending the tournament.

All other photographers and movie reel companies, including Pathé—which provided the bread-and-butter newsreels to theaters around the world—were excluded. Wills complained to the American Lawn Tennis Association. "The Californian does not attempt to hide her annoyance over the many circumstances showing commercialism in the Carleton tourney and the sarcastic comments made by some newspapers and tennis enthusiasts," the American Press newswire reported.[6] Then the American committee cabled Wills that "as you are receiving no financial consideration from the motion picture rights, there can be no criticism. By all means play."[7]

Florence may have breathed a sigh of relief. The last thing she wanted after Zelda's escapades *and* Boni's nasty revelations was to draw negative attention to the Gould name and their new tennis courts venture in Cannes. Any sighs were, however, short-lived. Wills said she'd play against Lenglen anywhere other than the Riviera. Refusing to compromise her principles or see other photographers and motion picture companies excluded from the tournament, Wills announced she would scratch unless the motion picture deal was withdrawn, and all photographers and filmmakers could work at the event. Frank was apoplectic. Burke feared the whole venture would be a catastrophe, not only financially, but also for his brother. What if Tom came under the watchful eye of the powerful voices in the sport? After several tense days of wrangling, Albert Burke and the

Goulds agreed that they had best cancel the exclusive motion picture contract. The match went ahead under the terms Wills demanded, but the tennis tournament was a public relations disaster.

✑

As is so often the case in the breakdown of a close relationship, both parties plowed their efforts into their business, keeping up, too, with the requisite society events and charitable donations. Florence had created wondrous music festivals and light opera performances at significant expense for the 1927 season. Yet Frank's millions still had far more scope for investments in bricks and mortar. The Juan Casino, Hôtel Provençal, and their new acquisitions of the smaller Hôtel Alba and Hotel des Deux Plages in Juan-les-Pins were only the start of their Riviera empire.[8] The eleven tennis courts in the California district of Cannes, near the Ambassadeurs Casino, were their first foray outside Juan. Perhaps their plan was to build a hotel there, too, although none ever reached the zoning stage.

✑

Meanwhile, Cannes partied on. The Dolly Sisters performed in several galas that year of 1927 at the Ambassadeurs, while the big bands played zippy melodies for dancing the Charleston and Black Bottom. Polish actress Pola Negri (made famous by her affair with Charlie Chaplin) was accompanied by her husband, Prince Alexis Mdivani, as she swanned into the casino at Juan.* So did Grand Duke Dmitri (Chanel's former lover) with his new wife, Cincinnati-born Audrey Emery, trailing rumors of her piffling six-million-dollar dowry in her wake.[9] These were the people Frank wanted to stay at his hotels, not the great artists Florence gathered to her—all of whom he called her "knights errant" or "zoo" or "circus." For now, Florence swallowed hard and agreed.

So they concentrated on their investments, rather than their personal relationship. European inflation was conquered, at last, due to loans from American banks. The Great War faded to a distant memory.

---

* Mdivani divorced Negri and married the original "Poor Little Rich Girl" Barbara Woolworth Hutton in 1933. He was Hutton's first husband, while actor Cary Grant was her third. She had eight marriages in all.

Surely, they were entering an era of ever greater prosperity in 1927? Consequently, when Frank spotted a choice real estate opportunity in Nice on Promenade des Anglais, he snapped it up, albeit for an extortionate price. Frank, like Florence, saw that Juan had become too small for them to expand their business further.

Both longed to break out into all the luxury markets in France; and Nice was the next logical step. Frank bought up the best part of a square city block, comprising the outdated Hôtel Royal and several private villas. Only one villa owner refused to sell, the aging owner Baron Roissard de Bellet, stating, "I will never allow myself to be bought by an American." Florence replied with one of her best one-liners, "Money doesn't care who owns it."[10]

Florence was thrilled that they were hobnobbing with the wealthy, the famous, and the notable, but to continue her rise—and Frank's cure—they would need to do more. Mary Pickford and Douglas Fairbanks dined at their table. Hollywood actress Gloria Swanson was hosted by Frank and Florence to announce her engagement to her third husband, Henry de La Falaise, Marquis de La Coudraye, while Swanson's part-time lover, Joseph Kennedy, looked on toasting them. Maurice Chevalier danced with Florence. Their next-door neighbor, Maréchal Philippe Pétain, dubbed the "Hero of Verdun," was often invited to join their festivities.[11]

Of course, they gave money to charities, and were active in the local balls—buying their plates and contributing to the charities' aims as required to keep their names favorably regarded in the press.[12] When they set up La Gauloise Sports Club in Juan, they were sure to give 5,000 francs to the poor of Antibes.[13] Monte Carlo had its François Blanc, Cannes its Lord Brougham, but Antibes–Juan-les-Pins had Frank Jay Gould.

There was, however, a very special charitable interest that was made public in 1927: Dr. Arthur Vernes and his Prophylactic Institute. Frank and Florence had become Vernes's main benefactors. It seems the good doctor found quick ways of detecting all sorts of major threats to life. In November 1927, the Goulds went public on his behalf, and the Associated Press (AP) wire services carried the story around the world. The headline in most newspapers read: "NEW METHOD ANNOUNCED—For

Determining Existence of Tuberculosis—Photographs Used." The article was short, sweet, and to the point:

> Paris, (November 7) A.P.—A photographic method of determining existence of tuberculosis in mankind, even when unsuspected, was announced today by Dr. Arthur Vernes, head of the Prophylactic Institute, whose work has been facilitated greatly by large gifts from Mr. and Mrs. Frank J. Gould.
>
> Vernes asserted that more than 15,000 tests have verified the accuracy of his method, which is based on a photometric test of the blood. Tuberculosis is frequently active when the lungs are entirely free of it, he said.
>
> The Prophylactic Institute has been specializing for many years in similar blood tests for other diseases.[14]

Tuberculosis was slowly killing thousands every year, including writers D. H. Lawrence* and Katherine Mansfield. What the article left out was that Dr. Vernes's specialty was a search for a friendlier cure for syphilis than Salvarsan or Neosalvarsan. For a crowd where "everyone slept with everyone else" to use Florence's words, Dr. Vernes offered the prospect of a less harmful cure where none existed, just yet. The Goulds' interest in Dr. Vernes suggests that Frank certainly, and Florence possibly, suffered from some of the side effects of the efficacious but deadly drug.

∾

The Goulds' French Riviera developments in Nice would run their natural course, obviously with the right push and shove to favored "friends in high places" so they could get their necessary building permits, licenses, and approvals. As expected, they did not view their payments to a local dignitary's preferred charities, or cash to officials, as bribes. What we call "corruption" was simply the way things worked in the twenties, the Goulds would reply in their defense. Frank always invested in ways that greased the wheels of commerce best. Casinos always attracted their

---

* He died in 1930.

share of cheats, high-stake gamblers, syndicates looking to break the bank, and other rackets. Equally, it was important for Frank to ensure that "good relations" existed between him, local police, and the mayors of the cities where he had establishments. A venal system was never far from their door.

Meanwhile, there were other destinations, perhaps easier pickings, nearer to their home at Robillard in Normandy that required their attention. When they had gone to take the waters at Bagnoles-de-l'Orne the previous year as part of Frank's round of natural "cures" for his ravaged body, they were appalled at the neglected state of the thermal baths and the beautiful lake choked with weeds. So they bought the spa and much of the surrounding countryside. Long associated with the Arthurian legend, this was the fabled Lancelot country. It was also once home to Alexandre Dumas (father), European aristocrats, Indian royalty, and prime ministers, but Bagnoles had become impoverished and merely hinted at its former glory. In 1927, the Goulds opened their art-deco-style Bagnoles Hôtel and Casino du Lac. Designed by architect Auguste Bluysen, today the buildings are protected and treasured historical structures. Frank and Florence had taken a medieval spa favored by the aristocracy in the Belle Epoque but ruined by the ravages of war, and from its ashes, rebuilt an entire thriving community. Yet their immense contribution to the community went unrecognized by posterity. For the locals, it simply represented the frenzied growth of the Goulds' French property empire, which in turn, mirrored the fascination with speed engulfing the younger generation.

13

⚬꧁꧂⚬

THE MONÉGASQUE FEUD FIT FOR A PRINCE

Some people can live more, better, faster, more enthusias-
tically in less time than others.

—Theodore Dreiser on MONTE CARLO, 1912

EDOUARD BAUDOIN, WHILE LOYAL AND A TALENTED CASINO OP-
erator, did not have the panache or flair of a grand hotelier like Henri
Ruhl. Another management structure was needed if Frank and Florence were to offer real competition to other hotel and casino owners. A
hotel manager, or perhaps even a partner, needed to be brought on board
to run the accommodation side of their business. As the old tourism
industry adage goes, the longer they stay, the more they spend.

Never slow off the mark, the Goulds had already pinpointed one of
Ruhl's great finds: Joseph Aletti. Not only had Aletti turned the spa town
of Vichy into a major international resort, but he also ran the Hôtel Ruhl
in Nice during its first winter season in 1918–1919 to entice the snowbirds to return south after the war. Henri Ruhl had chosen Aletti to run
his flagship Riviera hotel in the most difficult of circumstances, when
tourism was at an all-time low, and when Nice was still seen as a "leave
city" for the military and the injured. That meant Aletti had to be tops.

Better still, Aletti knew the political machinery in Nice. That was a
huge bonus to Frank, who had already crossed swords with local politi-

cians over the acquisition of the land for his Palais de la Méditerranée. Besides, word had it that Aletti had also conquered the political scene in Menton, when he opened the Hôtel Impérial for César Ritz and hired on the former general manager of Hôtel du Cap.[1] In a country where workers' rights were at the top of the political agenda, such a man was worth his proverbial weight in gold.

Yet Aletti, while flattered, did not immediately agree to the Goulds' terms. At the time, he was working in Nice at the Hôtel Majestic on boulevard Cimiez, overlooking the Baie des Anges. To have a beautiful hotel was one story, he told Frank and Florence, to have a luxury hotel that worked beautifully was quite another. Aletti had over twenty years' luxury hotel experience and was reluctant to share his expertise with a mere restaurateur and casino man like Baudoin, unless there was more to the proposition than merely managing the new Nice palace for the Goulds. Spurned, but unbeaten, Frank and Florence trumped Aletti and bought the Majestic.

Aletti worked for them now, like it or not, and they would prove to him that they had a vision equal to, if not better than, Aletti's own—and the bankroll to back it. Still, the hotelier shilly-shallied. Florence intervened. Hadn't Frank sold his shares in the Virginia utilities in 1925 for $11 million to underwrite his acquisitions in France?[2] Hadn't most French people thought they had more money than sense? Hadn't they been proved wrong? Florence cajoled. So, when Florence suggested that they decamp to the Majestic as hotel inspectors, Frank agreed.

Soon enough, they advised Aletti that luxury meant a private bathroom for every bedroom and that more sumptuous furnishings were necessary additions to his finely honed hotel service. Aletti was impressed. Work began immediately on refurbishing the property to standards that wouldn't become the norm until the late twentieth century. Cars, frequently Rolls-Royces or Bentleys, would have individual garages. Heavenly scented soaps were placed at the sink and bathtub for use by hotel guests. In-house telephones were installed. Plush towels and bathrobes adorned the marble fittings. The Majestic would be the first hotel in the world—even before the Waldorf Astoria in New York—to understand the significance of those little extras and the quality of service that made guests want to return again and again.[3]

The real sweetener for Aletti, however, was another pin in the map of France bought by Frank and Florence. The Goulds funded Aletti to front the purchase of several spa hotels and casinos in Vichy that Aletti had managed previously, making them the most significant hotel and casino owners in the popular resort. The Goulds also invested in a large villa in the spa town, as well as other real estate. With Aletti's experience and their money, Frank and Florence looked forward to the opening of their biggest project yet—the Palais de la Méditerranée.

∾

The Marseilles-born Joseph Aletti was a man Frank and Florence knew they could do business with. After graduating high school, Aletti went to London to train in the British capital's best hotels and become fluent in English. After all, the Meurice Hotel in Paris had been modeled on "English luxury," which was, at the end of the nineteenth century, still the pinnacle of distinction.[4] Hardworking, with a tremendous eye to detail, Aletti climbed through the ranks of hotel operations: managing the front office, food and beverage and banqueting, sales, marketing, redevelopment, and finally acting as general manager for a host of high-net-worth hotel owners from Baden-Baden and Montreux to Nice and Menton. Frank especially liked him. On a personal level, Aletti also thought like the Goulds: monogamy was for the unimaginative, not him.[5] Maybe Florence saw herself as another sweetener?

Aletti had another advantage. He understood Henri Ruhl, who despite his advanced age, Florence and Frank believed was their top competitor in Nice. While running the Hôtel Ruhl in Nice, Aletti had managed the spa hotel for Henri Ruhl in Vichy, which was renamed Hôtel Radio under its new ownership. Since those were the heady days when everything in a hotel was "badged" with the hotel stamp, from the sand in the standing ashtrays to pens, cutlery, napkins, bath towels, and tablecloths, a rechristening of the Hôtel Ruhl to another name with the same initials "HR" became a cost-saving necessity when Ruhl sold the property in 1920 to the Giorgetti family.[6]

Still, Frank and Florence had stronger competition in Nice than just Henri Ruhl. François Darracq, the industrialist owner of the Hôtel Negresco with is monumental domed lobby, worried—as most hoteliers always do—that his city was becoming overbuilt. The Casino de la Variétés objected to the Goulds' vision for their "Venetian palace" as well as their acquisition of the Municipal Casino, claiming unfair competition. The claim most likely had more to do with the city's outlawing the vogue for marathon dances among the young clientele at the Variétés than with any real threat from the ultra-luxury offerings at the newest casino and hotel.[7] But the Goulds' palace served a different clientele. It was Florence's task to bring in the biggest names in comedy and light opera to enhance the Palais de la Mediterannée casino's program for the public. Silently, the new owners of SBM's Casino and Hôtel de Paris in Monte Carlo watched and waited.

The Goulds' art deco palace of 187 bedrooms with baths and twelve suites was built in just under a year, by some 350 construction workers using steel-reinforced concrete for its basic structure. The sculpted façade of seahorses and classical goddesses was illuminated at night to give this huge hotel and casino—measuring some 9,000 square meters, or almost 97,000 square feet—its pride of place along the Promenade des Anglais. The lights illuminated the Palais's raw pulsating power, ten times larger than the Monte Carlo casino. Rumor had it that the Goulds backed the venture with some $5 million of their own cash.[8] Darracq of the Negresco, Henri Ruhl, and even René Léon of SBM in Monaco were not amused.

∽

Privately, Frank and Florence were patting themselves on the back for their impeccable timing. Their architects assured them that their Nice hotel and casino were due to open on time for New Year's Day 1928. They also had one eye to a takeover of SBM in Monte Carlo after their Nice venture, thanks to some fortuitous mishaps that had befallen SBM in the previous eighteen months.

Léon Radziwill, who was the grandson of François Blanc, was SBM's president, but he often deferred to René Léon for all decision making. While speeding through a small French town in his roadster, Léon lost control of his car and knocked down a girl. Panicked, he fled the scene. Somehow the girl, known only as Mademoiselle Magnin, lived, and identified the sports car. From there, it was only a skip and a jump to

Léon's door. Given his significance, and that the girl was a poor peasant, Léon was sentenced to a mere fifteen days in jail and fined five hundred francs. There is no record of his ever having served his sentence.

Of course, there was an outcry from the Monégasque press, screaming that if Léon had an ounce of dignity he should "pack his bag and leave the principality in shame." More allegations of corruption were hurled by the editor of Le Monégasque against SBM, claiming that French prime minister Louis Barthou had pulled some local strings. Fair enough: Barthou's brother was a top SBM director and a director of the Monte Carlo ballet. A little sideswipe at Léon as a Jew was also added to spice up the article, in explanation of his revolting behavior.[9]

That summer, there was a serious outbreak of typhoid in the poorest districts of Monte Carlo. Since SBM was also responsible for providing clean water in exchange for its exclusive gambling rights, the people and the press were outraged. SBM's indomitable publicist, the American Elsa Maxwell, knew that polluted drinking water was bad for business, and it needed correcting pronto. So she concocted a publicity stunt to overshadow the deaths SBM had caused. A lavish Christmas Eve party was held to herald the arrival of the new water purification and automated pumping system devised by Philippe Bunau-Varilla during his work on the Panama Canal.* Frank and Florence were invited guests at the party, wishing the Monégasques well through gritted teeth.

Still, the bad news kept on coming for SBM. On March 2, 1927, Radziwill was found slumped over in his chair. The coroner declared that he had suffered an embolism, but an autopsy revealed that Radziwill had died of an opiate overdose. The press had a rollicking good time, speculating that Radziwill had been poisoned by his mistress, a con artist called Marthe Dalbane, whom they nicknamed "The Death Flower." Demimondaines who haunted Radziwill's bedchamber were brought in for questioning, but eventually they were all released without charge.

Four days later, a twenty-year-old man from the Netherlands shot himself in the heart while gambling at the casino. Fortune smiled on him, and SBM. He survived his wounds. Soon after, Léon hit another car and fled the scene—yet again. Finally, in what seemed like a gangland-

---

* Essentially, the water was cleansed by injecting small amounts of bleach at regular intervals.

style murder, the body of a woman was discovered on a back road leading to the casino. She was missing four of her fingers.[10] Lady Luck,
Florence believed, rubbing her hands together metaphorically, was not
smiling on the object of their desires.

∽

Fortune, as most people know, is fickle—and often success boils down
to making one's own success. How Frank and Florence could think that
their rivals would take their meteoric expansion beyond the discreet
Antibes–Juan-les-Pins peninsula lying down shows their arrogance.
Suddenly, their luck, too, changed. Liquor licenses, gambling permits,
agreements that had been previously negotiated with the mayor's office
based on local taxes plus a share of the profits were once again up for
grabs.

Then, with only three weeks left until the Palais de la Méditerranée
was to open, the mayor's office pulled a fast one. The hotel was fully staffed
and in training for duty. The entertainment was booked. Seasonal
menus were printed and stocks ordered, and the companies operating
the casino and hotel were each capitalized for over four million francs.
The mayor pounced, unilaterally decreeing that unless the Palais de la
Méditerranée agreed to pay fifty percent more than its competition to
the City of Nice by way of its "contribution"—a tax in all but name—its
gambling license would be withheld. Further, the hotel would not be
allowed to officially open. To say that Frank and Florence were apoplectic with rage was an understatement. They had invested over $5 million
of Frank's money in the project. More irksome still was that their new
competition, due to open at the same time, the Hôtel and Casino Castellamare, represented by a lawyer with strong ties to Ruhl, Léon, and Darracq, was told it could pay 1.5 million francs less than the mayor's
office was demanding from the Goulds.[11]

When cornered by the local press, Nice's mayor, Alexandre Mari, revealed that, in his opinion, it was "amoral" for a hotel to offer gambling
under the same roof where "families slept," but that he had been persuaded by Joseph Aletti's and Edouard Baudoin's management case that
the hotel was a necessity to draw guests to their establishment. The management's argument was made even stronger by their one-thousand-seat

theater that was intended to book international entertainment. So, in a vain effort not to appear hypocritical, Mari made a public statement that it was in the city's interests that only *one* future hotel and casino be built, for the sake of "public morals." Unfortunately, unknown to the Goulds, the Hôtel and Casino Castellamare would be that hotel—unless, of course, they could persuade the mayor of the error of his ways with extra folding money.[12]

On the Goulds' orders, Baudoin posted a large poster throughout the city with huge red letters calling out "TO THE POPULATION OF NICE." It went on to say that "I decided to open the Casino de la Méditerranée on the 1st January 1928 with an opening which would have attracted the cream of the international set. Nonetheless, we are faced with a City which, instead of encouraging this hazardous and costly financial investment made at great sacrifice, proposes to charge me more than any other existing casino, and I therefore regret to inform the people of Nice that we will not be proceeding with the opening."

In smaller print, the poster asked the citizens of Nice to take heed of such actions and that Baudoin, who signed the poster, had expected as warm a welcome as he had received at Antibes–Juan-les-Pins a few years earlier.[13] Accusations and counteraccusations were hurled by each side publicly. The local unions, which of course had myriad employees expecting to work at the Goulds' hotel and casino, finally brought their own style of pressure to bear. Suddenly, from an intractable position on both sides, face was saved. Gould, using his front man Baudoin, agreed to pay the extra "taxes" for one year only. After that time, the other casinos would be brought into line with the Palais de la Méditerranée.

This first feud lasted for months, suggesting the usual venality in the greasing of palms and that an entente with the competition was reluctantly declared. It should be noted that there was some defense for the mayor's inscrutable reasoning. The overspend in the 1928 annual municipal budget showed an investment in the local hospital and the acquisition of the Imperial Park, amounting to an eye-watering 7.3 million francs—and it was only January, the first month of that fiscal year. As part of the truce, it is equally possible that the Goulds agreed to lighten the city's load by making charitable contributions toward the park and hospital, as a gesture of goodwill. Whatever the mode of peacemaking, the hotel and casino opened nearly four months late, at the end of April 1928.

Profits were budgeted at around 25 million francs, justifying, too, the ten percent of profits the city was demanding. That said, the real bottom line was more than likely closer to double that amount. As casinos are a cash business, no one could know for sure if Baudoin and the Gould owners were declaring their full income on their corporate tax returns. Government oversight was still lax in those days, particularly since there was no gambling tax yet in France.

∞

Despite the bitterness of the battle with the mayor and his council, the first year of operations in Nice was said to be wildly profitable. The hotel was full. Florence and Frank funded the local Nice opera. Yet all plans to mount operas in their hotel theater had to be rearranged, due to the delayed opening. Insultingly, Aletti was obliged to submit for "council approval" the list of performances, which included such famous works as *The Marriage of Figaro, Falstaff, The Barber of Seville,* and *Lucia di Lammermoor.*[14] They spent money on these extravaganzas that few would have contemplated. To boot, the Associated Press wire agency burned with the news that the Goulds were offering $50,000 in prize money for the Foster's Beauty Show to take place at their Nice casino, assuring the English-reading public that "an American beauty" would be represented, and that there would be international judges in attendance.[15]

The hotel and casino that Frank claimed "even Caesar could not have built" was finally opened. Nightly merrymaking was ordered by Florence. Americans "toasted the prohibition" with Florence while she gambled incessantly at the baccarat tables, thrusting her much-vaunted winnings into her deep-pocketed, sequined evening wear, giving rise to bawdy Mae West jokes about happy pistols in pockets. Spotters were employed not only to stop card counting and other forms of cheating, but also to slip enough money for the journey home into the pockets of those who lost their fortunes at the tables. Meanwhile, the private gambling rooms were thick with cigar and cigarette smoke, while the high-stakes rollers in tuxedos pitted their fortunes against the bank and, invariably, lost more than they won. Even the bad news received from New York in

December couldn't dampen their spirits. Frank's most trusted business manager of all his U.S. business affairs, George H. Taylor, had died at the age of sixty-eight of heart disease.[16] Maybe it was an omen.

The year 1929 dawned as one of promise. With Taylor's death, Frank sold most of his private stock market investments (as opposed to those still invested through the Gould family trust), until he could officially appoint a new permanent manager for his U.S. affairs. Then, on January 24, by decree no. 36.617, Florence joined her husband as a Chevalier of the Legion of Honor for her generosity to charitable causes.[17]

And there were other, more pressing wars to fight on the French Riviera. All the Goulds' major competitors, as far west as Hyères and east to San Remo in Italy, were balking at how the Palais de la Méditerranée was stealing their business. SBM grumbled about its poor season. Frank and Florence increased the pressure, and began to militate for roulette tables to be allowed in France. If countenanced, it would break the deal that had existed between Monaco and France since 1860.

A year after the hotel and casino's opening, the war of words and ill feeling that the Goulds harbored against their competition still simmered beneath the surface. Then, without an apparent cause, anti-SBM posters appeared on the streets of Monte Carlo, urging the Monégasque population to "STAND UP!" What should they stand up against? "A foreigner who has exploited us for years, the administrator of that gambling hell. Our freedom is not meant to be controlled by these wretched characters, these shady racketeers." Apparently, the posters were all over Nice, Cannes, and Juan-les-Pins, too. A detective known only as Duchamp of the French intelligence service reported to Léon at SBM that these posters were cheaply printed in an exceptionally large print-run in Nice by a group known to police as "The Four Devils," headed by one "Monsieur Noah." The only hitch was that Noah wouldn't have had the money for the printing. Léon told Duchamp to do nothing about the posters.[18] Two could play at the Gould's game.

≪∞≫

Black Friday and the Wall Street Crash of 1929 went virtually unnoticed on the French Riviera, at first. The American literati had to go home, of course, but wealthy Europeans had no idea that an American stock market crash would affect their own incomes. They hadn't thought for a moment that the newly insolvent U.S. banks, which had lent vast sums of money to France and Germany after the war, could demand early repayment. Nor did they fathom what an early repayment would mean. As far as Frank and Florence were concerned, George Taylor's death some ten months earlier had literally saved them millions. It also helped them to believe that they were unassailable.

As if to rub salt into the weeping wounds of the afflicted, Florence went on a spending spree bedecked in furs, frolicking in and out of Paris's rue de la Paix jewelers, where fortunes in canceled orders went begging at huge discounts. Similarly, Impressionist art hung on the walls for months on end at the big art dealers in rue de La Boëtie in Paris, giving Florence her first big haul of Bonnard paintings on the cheap. Real estate, that immovable commodity the Goulds snapped up wherever possible, became instantly affordable, like the property advertised as "For Sale, Cheap, Nice Old Chateau, 1 Hr. from Paris; Original Boiserie; 6 New Baths; Owner Forced Return New York Wednesday; Must Have IMMEDIATE CASH; Will Sacrifice."[19] If there was one thing Florence and Frank had in common, it was an opportunistic instinct.

Of course, they had no idea that René Léon was plotting his revenge. That December, the Goulds thought Léon was busy dealing with a simmered of all twenty-one members of Monaco's National Council, who resigned over SBM's failure to provide the public services as originally agreed upon with François Blanc. The American press reported on the "Tempest in a Teapot" rather unsympathetically, since the Monégasques were making untaxed demands on a private company. Léon struck in the middle of the furor. A British and French combination pitted their wits with the Greek syndicate headed by the "cleverest little man who ever dealt a hand of baccarat," Nico Zographos, to beat the Goulds' bank at the casino. Zographos had hitherto been the high-stakes gambler at SBM's Casino de Paris in Monte Carlo.

The raid on the Goulds' casino began on December 26. Florence and Frank were spending Christmas at their home at Maisons-Lafitte, when they were called urgently to Nice. By the time they reached the city some twenty-four hours later, the consortia had already taken the bank for some 9 million francs. Gould had seen off Zographos before at Juan, and knew that the only thing to do was to appear to be a sportsman, and increase the stakes of *Tout Va,* or "the sky's the limit." Over $2 million wafted across the gambling tables in the direction of the gamblers in the first forty-eight hours. Luckily for the Goulds, the casino's profits at all the other tables combined, were higher.[20] Again, the California newspapers couldn't miss the opportunity of reporting the hard-to-believe figures being wagered, and naturally also dredged up the old chestnut of "San Francisco born" Florence Lacaze and her short marriage to Henry Heynemann, who was, by then, on his third wife.*

With each passing day, and no definitive result, thousands gathered outside the room where the high-stakes game was being played. The United Press International newswire sizzled with its report that after seven days, the battle "where millions were scattered on the tables of Frank Gould's palatial casino" still had no outright victor, although the bank was ever so slightly in the red. Government inspectors, medical doctors, and French casino authorities took their positions lining the walls of the salon where the betting was taking place, in an effort to avoid what might end in several deaths from exhaustion—or perhaps suicide or murder if any signs of cheating were detected.[21] After two weeks of frenzied play, the casino was even, and the consortia that tried to bring Gould down quit in exhaustion.

Léon fulminated. The great journalist and historian William Shirer reported for the *Chicago Tribune*:

> There is a war to the finish along the Riviera, that Gold Coast spot of the Old World which about this time of year airs out its glittering hotel palaces, renaissance gambling rooms and restaurants, and opens them for such business as elderly American women with their young ideas, their husbands and European counterparts can be induced to steer that way. This struggle is mainly a war between Nice, Cannes and Monte Carlo, the three picturesque towns which look out over the Mediterranean and implore the gods to send them some gamblers to their half-empty casinos.[22]

---

* Heynemann was sued by his second wife, who lived in the Midwest, on the grounds of desertion in 1919.

Shirer makes no mention of Black Friday emptying the casinos of the Riviera, blaming the falling business instead on Americans finding equally brilliant watering holes stateside. Prohibition hadn't been repealed, but it was already seen as a failed experiment to keep America moral.* The article claimed the casino war's escalation began with unfair competition by Madison Avenue advertising men imported by Gould to the sunny Mediterranean shores.

Léon retaliated, yet again. It was time to lower the tone of those gambling in the Gould's palatial establishment. "Shady looking characters" were seen penetrating "Gould's shrine" rubbing shoulders with European aristocracy. Of course, Frank roundly blamed the appearance of these people of "questionable reputations" on his competition, since they not only comported themselves as anything but gentlemen, but also wore "dirty shirts and soiled waistcoats." Inevitably, "such an element mixing as it does with haughty crowds in the baccarat rooms and on the dance floor have ruined the atmosphere of the place." The local gendarmes evidently agreed. "Anyone trying to gain entrance who is not completely attired in formal dress, will be ejected by the husky gendarmes."[23]

The war between the casinos had begun.

---

* The Volstead Act was finally repealed on December 5, 1933, although after 1931, little resource was put into upholding the law. John D. Rockefeller, a lifelong teetotaller, had initially supported the Anti-Saloon League and Prohibition, but, along with many national leaders, realized the law didn't work and later demanded that it be repealed.

14

༄༅༅

HOLLYWOOD CALLING

Beauty is a very tangible asset in these days of fluctuating values.

—ELIZABETH ARDEN advertisement, 1932

THERE WERE OTHER RISKIER, HIDDEN CHALLENGES FACING FLOR-ence and Frank than the casino war. Florence believed the problems on the Riviera were no more than a mere bagatelle in their business affairs. In many ways, she was right. Frank hadn't touched his share of the inheritance from his father since the family lawsuit over a decade earlier, making him a multimillionaire through the family trust alone, despite the 1929 crash. Their casino woes could easily be resolved by the Gould millions, as Florence reminded Frank. Besides, hadn't she fixed countless things for them in the previous ten years? Although aged thirty-eight, she looked—and acted—ten years younger. Frank, on the other hand, was aging rapidly.

Florence needed the excitement of being admired, and of carnal love, something Frank was increasingly less able or willing to provide. Her trips to Paris became more frequent, and her sexual partners more varied. During the Parisian season of June 1930, she attended all the fancy-dress balls. After all, if she didn't, it would be almost uncivilized. Entertainment in the capital was always serious stuff, and something

Florence had longed to be a part of since reading about the exploits of the rich and noteworthy as a child. Still, the 1930 season was unusually frenetic, phantasmagoric, and mostly foreign. Those relatively unaffected by the Crash were anxious to prove they still had their cash. The stylish Daisy Fellowes, the niece whom Winnaretta Singer had raised from childhood after the death of Daisy's mother, Isabelle-Blanche Descazes, hired publicist Elsa Maxwell for one of the largest and most memorable masquerades of the season, where men cross-dressed as famous women. Florence attended the White Ball, where her friend Jean Cocteau won accolades with his wigs and white-plaster masks. All the formal balls by the Jewish bankers, the Rothschilds, were given in a single week, and were ironically dubbed *la Semaine Sainte*, or the saintly week. Much more to Florence's liking, however, was the As-You-Were-When-the-Autobus-Called Party, again designed by Elsa Maxwell, but this time on behalf of Señora Alvaro Guevara, the former Meraud Guinness.* Invitees were warned that "a charabanc would call for them at no specified hour" and that they "were to come in whatever attire was theirs when the chauffeur tooted his horn." Guests in varying degrees of "undress" included a lady who had only "exactly one side of her face made up, a gentleman clad in shaving soap and a towel, and several ladies in half-fastened skirts . . . the great life-class atelier of Montparnasse, is still discussing the charabanc party."[1] No matter where she went, or with whom, the child Florence, who'd been always on the outside looking in, was no more. Paris widely admired her, at long last, as a great "American" beauty.

By 1931, Florence had come into her own as a femme fatale and woman of the world. Cosmetics queens Helena Rubinstein and Elizabeth Arden were preaching what Florence had known since the age of fourteen: a woman's economic potential could be measured by the allure she created. As the Great Depression gripped the world, and the Goulds were faced with the competition striking at their great "Venetian palace" in Nice, Florence's allure became ever more significant in their business and personal affairs. After all, Hollywood was in its heyday of escapism,

---

* Meraud Michael Guinness (1904–1993) was an author, poet, and painter, born into the wealthy Guinness family. She lived most of her life in France, but studied art in London at the Slade School of Art, in New York, and in Paris under Francis Picabia. She married the Chilean painter Álvaro Guevara in 1929.

setting the scene—so she thought—for her kind of woman. The booming Hollywood film industry created a new archetype: a glamorous woman on the make.[2] It was as if the image were tailor-made for Florence.

She wore large jewels fit for a queen, most notably her pearl necklace valued at some 20 million francs. Admirers remarked on how they could hear the rumor of her pearls swaying against each other as she slinked, catlike, into the room. Frequently decked out in black satin or sequined dresses clinging to her shapely body and capping off the effect with thick luxurious furs of dark sable or mink, Florence completed her Hollywood image by donning fashionable, heavy mascara and eyeshadow, adding the finishing touch by painting her seductive smile with dazzling red lipstick. Combined with her wit and risqué humor, she became the almost-attainable version of Jean Harlow or Marlene Dietrich— the women most lusted after by men of the day.[3]

∽

Of course, back on the Riviera, the Goulds' enemy, René Léon of SBM, spread gossip that Frank had been ruined by the U.S. stock market crash. So Florence went on more buying sprees, and was reported in the gossip columns regularly. Faced with what many newspapers in France and the United States called the "ruin of the Gould fortune," Frank readily ensured their future publicly by buying Florence more diamonds and properties to show the world that they were far from bankrupt. She was his picture of opulence, sent into the public arena of Paris to defy the Riviera gossipmongers.

Florence, the consummate actress, played her part well. The Goulds continued to give to charities and put on charity events locally, too, splashing their names endlessly in newsprint. The loud noises that they were going bust withered to a mere whimper. Hadn't they invested $2 million to make the roads passable at Breuil in the Maritime Alps for their new hotel project there? Florence asked, the ever-present champagne glass in hand, rattling her outsized emerald and diamond bracelets. What other private investor would put money into such a vast infrastructure project when the government refused to participate?[4]

They were kind to their friends, too, Florence purred. Hadn't she arranged with Charlie Chaplin's brother Stanley, now retired in Nice, to keep Charlie in the news when his career was failing? It was quite a stunt they pulled, too. The president of France's train was running late for an important reception in Nice, so Chaplin—"little baggy pants"—was called in at Florence's behest on short notice to be President Gaston Doumergue's understudy. Unlike the tennis tournament in 1926, Chaplin's involvement proved a notable publicity coup.[5]

∞

For Chaplin, it was the beginning of his love affair with Florence. While still famous around the world, he was no longer the box office smash from the days of the Keystone Cops. Back in 1914, at the start of his Hollywood career with Keystone, he made thirty-five films. The following year, he made fourteen. Six films per year was his total output in the next two years, then a total of nine films over the next five—including *The Kid* in 1920.

His first film for United Artists, the film production and distribution company founded with Mary Pickford and her husband, Douglas Fairbanks, was unusually a comedy of manners entitled *A Woman of Paris*, based on the life of Peggy Hopkins Joyce, a collector of many husbands, wealth, and jewels. Chaplin wanted to show the rest of us how the rich lived. It made him the first director to bring a comedy of manners to the big screen—albeit in a silent film. While not successful in America, it was greeted as a great film in Europe. His single great hit afterward was *The Gold Rush*, although it ran into some costly production delays. After *The Gold Rush*, he produced only two other films until 1931. Desperate, Chaplin saw something in Florence, eight years after the release of *A Woman of Paris*, that made him wonder if Florence could not become his newest inspiration.[6] For him, that must include lovemaking.

That said, love and "progress" had cost Chaplin dearly. His divorces from his two teenage brides were cruel blows to his bank balance. His lack of faith in "talkies," or talking pictures, as movies with soundtracks were then called, was even more devastating. Talkies had taken the moviegoing world by storm three years earlier, but they were just a flash in the pan, he argued. Other comedians were less shy of their voice boxes, and Chaplin was rapidly eclipsed in front of the camera by witty newcomers like W. C. Fields, the Marx Brothers, Eddie Cantor, and the Hal Roach comic-duo Laurel and Hardy. To boot, these comedians had no skeletons lurking behind locked doors, like marrying underage girls or fights with their production companies. It was these comics who became the new American icons as the Great Depression deepened.[7]

Chaplin, however, like Florence, was an artful gambler. He had thrown three years' production costs into his newest film, *City Lights*. Worse still, his own United Artists told Chaplin he was charging too much to get the film into the movie houses. Chaplin gambled and hired his own private New York theater and raised the admission price from fifty cents to eighty-five cents to shouts of *"What!?"* from his business partners. After three weeks running in New York alone, Chaplin recovered all his production costs, and the film went into profit.[8] Still, it was a salutary experience. Chaplin was no longer number one in Hollywood. It had also been a long time since he had been in front of the camera, rather than producing and directing. So, searching for solid ground, he went to Europe and his ever-faithful fan base. In Germany, he discussed politics with Albert Einstein—as you do when you're Charlie Chaplin. After Berlin, he paid an extended visit to his brother Stanley in Nice. Evidently, he intended to renew, too, his relationship with the Goulds.

Florence's mise-en-scène with "Charlot" (as the French called him) paid off. A month later, the new premier Aristide Briand decorated Chaplin with the Legion of Honor medal for his services to comedy. Chaplin played boules and tennis with Florence and posed for photographs with the Goulds. He gambled at the Gould casinos, dancing the rhumba with Florence held closely in his arms—their hips swaying in sync while the Latin rhythms played into the wee hours of the morning—enchanted by her. Before leaving, Chaplin called on them to advise who he should meet to remain in the European limelight. In Monaco, it was the king of the Belgians, the Prince of Wales, and the ubiquitous publicist Elsa Maxwell. In Rome, Chaplin was ushered into a two-minute session with Benito Mussolini, the fascist Italian premier. Chaplin was unimpressed.

Despite everything, it was Florence who held his interest while he was in the south of France, and later in Paris. Other, younger women came and went during his Grand Tour, but Florence was always more than a simple one-night stand. Chaplin had decided to embark on the great wooing of Florence Gould. Besides, the oomph had gone out of the Goulds' twelve-year liaison. Florence may have felt that the excitement of Hollywood—not to mention the draw of a highly sexed, internationally famous movie star—was too great an opportunity to pass up.[9]

Newspaper articles began to appear across the United States that September. Charlie said that he had offered Florence a starring role in his next film, and he would write the script to suit her many talents. A week after this was leaked, a second report was sent out across the wire services by United Press International that Frank and Florence Gould were in amicable divorce talks. Lawyers for Mrs. Gould stated that "the chief obstacle in her accepting Chaplin's purported offers was understood to have been an agreement with Gould that she would not appear in any public performance after their marriage."[10]

Frank, so Florence declared, would give her a divorce, but she could lay no claim on the Gould millions despite her very active role in making his French hotel and casino enterprise a success. At the time of their marriage, they declared that their "fortunes" prior to marrying would remain separate. Florence could easily agree to that back in 1923, but years on, with all the work she had put into their "French Empire," the injustice would have stung her deeply. She could always claim that she had given birth to his French companies, but with no children to inherit, her position was weakened in law. She could try to fight Frank, of course, but she had seen how far that had gotten his second wife, Edith. So Florence thought about Hollywood and her "Charlot" and realized her heart belonged to Frank and his millions. She told the Little Tramp as much, too.

Chaplin understood. It had been worth a try, and there were no hard feelings on either side. He returned home to Hollywood, without his Florence, and the intensifying Great Depression. That's when he got the idea for his great social drama, *Modern Times*. Never one to be long without a woman at his side, Chaplin began to groom his next paramour, the former Ziegfeld girl Paulette Goddard as his new leading lady. In a logical next step, he made Goddard his third wife.

Florence never alluded to their affair, though she later made many references to "giving up her career" with regret. Years later, she told friends that after the fire had gone out of her sexual relationship with

Frank about this time, she'd nearly married a wealthy Romanian. Perhaps the fiction was to help her wounded pride, since Chaplin wasted no time in replacing her with Paulette Goddard. As ever the actress, and to give the illusive, rich Romanian some veracity, Florence told an admirer *after* Frank died that he had agreed to divorce her, with a small proviso. "Alright then. Let's not talk about it any further," Frank allegedly said. "And if, in a year from today, you still want to divorce me, then we will divorce."[11] Before the year was out, Florence had forgotten the "Romanian's" name.

15

THE PHOENIX RISES

Now I will believe/That there are unicorns . . .
the phoenix' throne, one phoenix
At this hour, reigning there.

—WILLIAM SHAKESPEARE, *The Tempest*

CHAPLIN COULD BE FORGIVEN FOR TRYING HIS LUCK. BY THE 1930s, Florence's beauty, charm, and fabulous wealth had become a deadly man magnet. She had already acquired a reputation as a lioness, devouring the men she wanted at will, but never allowing her head to desert her golden life with Frank. Strangely, he thought the way men fell for his wife slightly comical, naming them her "noblemen servants."

Among her admirers were the young and handsome French journalist Robert de Thomasson; Armand de la Rochefoucauld, the aristocratic president of the Jockey Club; and the Mumm champagne king, Melchior de Polignac. Still, Hollywood haunted her thoughts, and shortly after her liaison with Chaplin, Florence was seen everywhere with the Parisian matinee idol Henri Garat.[1] It was her old friend Mistinguett who discovered the dashing Garat at the Moulin Rouge. While he was a mediocre actor, he had the "Hollywood look" and a seductively deep voice that made women weak at the knees, and when Garat and Florence were out and about together, his young fans swooned before their screen idol.

Theirs was the first—and last—relationship in which Florence would find herself on the wrong side of a violent temperament. It was a stormy and brief affair, ending with Garat's threat of blackmail and the publication of Florence's love letters. The ungrateful actor forgot that Florence had made his entrée into Hollywood possible in the first place, but remembered all too well that she refused to follow him there. Garat also misunderstood the extremely tolerant nature of her relationship with Frank, and misjudged her entirely when he tried to claim money from her by threats. It is easy to imagine Florence telling Frank how "blackmail" was such a nasty word, but there it was—straight from Garat's beautiful lips. As her anger rose, she fulminated how she would not stomach anyone treating her so shabbily. She would have her revenge. She let it be known to her numerous and powerful Hollywood friends that they would be doing her a great favor if they no longer felt the obligation to give Garat work, since he was an untrustworthy lover. So, it came as no surprise to Florence when Garat's Hollywood days ended abruptly in 1933.[2] Still, once Garat was down and out, she doled out a few hundred francs, when the mood struck, to her former lover. Considering that she usually cold-shouldered needy discarded lovers, she must have felt conscious of some guilt.

∞

Of course, Florence still paid attention to the Goulds' business affairs in the early 1930s. The Palais de la Méditerranée and Hôtel Provençal on the Riviera remained profitable, and their casino and hotel at Bagnoles-de-l'Orne had recently reopened. Aletti made sure that their Vichy investments ticked along quite nicely, too, while Frank occupied himself with his Madison Avenue publicity hounds spicing up the latest round in the casino war, and promoting the newly opened hotel and casino at Breuil in the Alps above Nice.

The Depression had hit France late but hard. As American banks called in their debts, the beau monde searched for someone to bail them out. Florence was flying high, buying luxury real estate at massive discounts in Paris. Her great amusement was visiting pawnbrokers, auction houses, and discreet jewelry shops for bargains, gleefully palming her bejeweled steal-of-the-day into her nondescript tin that once held Lucky

Strike cigarettes, before sashaying away.[3] For a woman like Florence, who could sing the birds from the trees, her "rescue" of her more marginally wealthy friends appeared as generosity beyond the call of duty. They were blind to Florence's motives: armed with Frank's millions, this keen businesswoman knew that by holding Paris real estate for a while, the values would one day skyrocket. In buying their jewels and artworks, she was merely satisfying her personal pleasures.

While everyone else's eyes were trained on salvaging their fortunes, that rather loud, impassioned leader of the NSDAP (Nazi) party in Germany, Adolf Hitler, was ominously on the road to seizing power. Florence was too confident, too cocky, too savvy, to allow such political rumblings to disturb her fun. Besides, France—and all of Europe, for that matter—was facing the stark choice between fascism and communism. Like any good capitalist, the possibility of the communists winning out was unthinkable to Florence. So her parties continued unabated. Her Paris chums, ranging from Mistinguett and Maurice Chevalier from her old Folies Bergère days to the actresses Marie Bell and fellow road racer Arletty, were often thrown together like a fine French salad, mixing with Franklin D. Roosevelt's distant diplomat cousin and descendant of Lafayette, René de Chambrun, and his wife, Josée; Baron Maurice de Rothschild; Sir Oswald and Lady Cimmie Mosley; and other friends in the coterie of the future Edward VIII, known as David to his friends. Simply put, Florence was having a whale of a time.

In 1932, Florence met two women who would become central to her life. The Breton-born Magdeleine Homo, a former ice-skating star, met Florence at the ice rink in Paris and was invited to Florence's mansion on rue Albérique-Magnard for tea. After some negotiation and a second meeting, Homo agreed to become Florence's personal secretary. Within a few months, Frank poached Homo from his wife, allegedly without her consent.[4]

The second woman, Madeleine Manigler, attended Florence's 1932 Christmas bash at the George V Hotel, along with the great and the notable, not to mention the naughty, like her friend of long standing, Jean Cocteau. Madeleine Manigler was the guest of Florence's art dealer, Daniel Wildenstein. Florence, magnificent in her white, elegant, and simple Chanel gown, greeted Manigler as if she had been as old a friend as Wildenstein. Manigler, from Auvergne, was an art expert in her own right, who, like Wildenstein, had a passion for the artist Claude Monet. She was slim, well dressed, and quite pretty. In a flash, the two women became close—just how close has been a matter of some speculation for years. Manigler was quick-witted like Florence, and loved nothing better than sparring with words.

Their attraction to each other was instantaneous. Florence hated subservient and obsequious behavior in the people she wanted to keep at her side. Manigler would withstand the growing tyrannical streak Florence had begun to display, and could parry the millionairess's barbs with aplomb. After all, Manigler dealt with many wealthy and haughty collectors, as well as her boss, Daniel Wildenstein. Soon after, Manigler accompanied Florence on buying trips for Impressionist art, and helped solidify Daniel Wildenstein's hold over Florence's acquisitions. Still, there were more personal reasons for their "friendship."

Now in her mid-thirties, Florence had singularly failed to have made any close female friendships, aside from her childhood friend, Cécile Tellier. There could, naturally, be dozens of reasons for this empty space in her life, especially given Florence's man-eating reputation. Yet there is one explanation that should be explored briefly, given Madeleine's sexual preferences. By the beginning of 1934, Madeleine Manigler seemingly usurped Cécile's position and became Florence's closest friend in every way. This did not mean, however, that Florence was less attached to Cécile, who was, after all, Berthe Lacaze's paid companion. There was talk, but Florence waved it aside. She would do what she wished, with whom she wished, when she wished. More to the point, in society there was always "talk."

Considering the statement made by Florence that "in the Thirties, everybody slept with everybody else. It was fun. It was practical . . ." easily led those who heard her to believe that perhaps Florence was alluding to her own latent bisexuality. Given who she admired in le Tout-Paris as a younger woman, and how hard she had to fight for recognition in the world to which she hungered to belong, her possible bisexuality could have stemmed, too, as the natural extension of her burning ambitions. It is feasible that her new inseparable companion, Madeleine Manigler, provided Florence with a discreet outlet for any such urges she may have had. In the wild thirties in France, homosexuality and lesbianism were accepted. For Frank, however, bisexuality was anathema, and the very thought that his wife could sleep with women was the final straw. Later, Florence herself dated their estrangement as husband and wife to this period. Still, their business partnership and their public lives would continue as before. It was the most civilized and practical solution for both parties. After all, Frank was not in good enough health to go through another acrimonious divorce, particularly if Florence revealed the unpalatable reasons for his illness. Florence helped Frank pursue his own interests, as he would allow her to follow her own without recrimination. It was a very European arrangement.

Professionally, Florence oversaw the development of the Gould hotel and casino empire in France. Yet despite her efforts, she and Frank lacked a northern presence in their property portfolio in or near Deauville, which still attracted a sizable wealthy clientele. Then, after long negotiations, a fabulous newsworthy location became available. The Goulds announced their purchase of a resort town a mere stone's throw from the ever-chic Deauville. Their announcement of the acquisition of most of the town of Granville, along with every hotel in it, was reported by the Associated Press with Frank Gould quoted as wanting to develop one of the "most luxurious baccarat palaces in the world" and that the one at Granville would cost around $1 million.[5] Their intention was clear: They wanted to be the largest luxury hotel and casino owners in France.

❧

Back at SBM, Léon thundered on. Someone or something had to stop Gould and his Madison Avenue men from their negative publicity against Monaco, or the casino in Monte Carlo would go under. Gould's casinos were bigger, bolder, and more beautiful than the Monte Carlo casino. The Goulds' connections, particularly through Florence's efforts with le Tout-Paris and the beau monde equaled—if not bettered—Monte Carlo's. Her remarkable talent for making "friends" among the world's upper crust was quite simply unparalleled. Léon lacked her radiant smile and glamour. Prince Louis, Monaco's reigning monarch, was an aging, seemingly uninteresting figure.

That Monte Carlo might fail was an unconscionable thought. Prince

Louis was equally unimpressed with the principality's slide from grace in the public eye. The prince's income was wholly dependent on the success of SBM and the casinos. He was booed and jeered when he made public appearances. Something simply had to be done, he lamented. After some considerable reflection, Léon resolved to rid his prince of this turbulent American, his drop-dead-gorgeous wife, and their supersized casinos. Anonymous reports written to the police at the Sûreté's Deuxième and Septième Bureaus that the Goulds weren't declaring all their income were taken seriously. Initially, the complaints served only to highlight that every casino in the Nice area filed its annual licenses and renewals requests far too late, leading the police to suspect that none of them declared their proper income.[6]

That said, more serious charges were levied against the Goulds. They were "purposefully" withholding their income statements and "city contribution" payments for the casino. The Septième Bureau complained that it was impossible for them to audit the Gould establishments for malfeasance, breach of their license, or other illegal activities—and be expected to grant the new annual license in a timely manner. Unless the Palais de la Méditerranée cleaned up its act, the Septième Bureau would have to close it down. At the end of the day, Baudoin prevailed, and a penalty was agreed on instead for their late filing. Yet Baudoin failed to make the payments on time, merely halving them or rescheduling them unilaterally. Amazingly, the Gould's "Venetian Palace" remained open.[7] What more could Léon do?

∞

Predictably, in those times of greatest austerity, real disaster struck. The French government decided to raise a national tax on all baccarat gambling to help with its poor treasury receipts. Overnight, the big "bet a million" games took flight to Monte Carlo and San Remo in Italy. Even the Greeks, headed by Zographos, quit the French casinos overnight to avoid the additional two percent tax on their profits. Even worse, the Greeks announced that they would refuse to hold an "open bank" against the houses of the Riviera for the winter season of 1932–1933 and beyond, if the government did not climb down over the extortionate taxes. Without the thousands that came to watch the high-stakes gamblers, and play at chemin-de-fer, too (where the house made its greatest profits), all French casinos would suffer sudden death. The Goulds' Palais de la Méditerranée casino would be among the hardest hit by the high rollers moving elsewhere.[8]

Had Prince Louis whispered in the French government's ear? Probably not. The government of the Third Republic viewed itself as virtuous, if left-wing. Then, as now, it was the need for cash that drove any form of taxation on the rich or frivolous that would meet with broad public approval.

By November 1933, the Palais de la Méditerranée was running at a declared loss for the year of 3 million francs because of a combination of the casino war and absent American-dollar visitors. Frank's Swiss son-in-law, married to his daughter Dorothy, claimed the losses were more like 15 million francs. It seemed, too, that Baudoin was asking the Goulds to reduce his 3.2-million-franc lease at the Juan-les-Pins casino in what the local papers called its "*rocambolesque*," or fantastic, failure. The hotel the Goulds developed in the Alps above Nice at Breuil was an abysmal failure, too. Who wanted to ski in the morning, swim in the Mediterranean in the afternoon, and gamble all night amid this Great Depression, as the Goulds' advertising posters enthusiastically invited?

To boot, there were complaints to the Nice mayor's office that the employee profile at the Palais de la Méditerranée was not contractually correct. Seventy-five percent of all employees had to be French, as did the ownership of the casino. Since Frank and Florence were still the majority owners, they seemed to be thumbing their noses at the authorities. Irrespective of Frank's desire for Florence to play the part of the "dual national," the government classed her as "American by marriage."* Then, too, there were those 80,000 francs in "city contributions" overdue since February 1933 that Baudoin had rescheduled for payment with interest

---

* The automatic taking of the husband's nationality was changed at various dates in different countries following World War II, including in the U.S.A., France, and the United Kingdom. Today women or men marrying "internationally" need to apply for the spouse's nationality to become a dual national in accordance with current regulations. Still, in some cases, this can only be achieved at the risk of losing one's American citizenship. Frank's sister, Anna, had to re-apply for her American citizenship when, in March 1939, she returned to the family's Lyndhurst Estate in Tarrytown, New York.

at the end of November.[9] The only problem was that Frank Gould, as the primary owner, would have to pay the money from his personal pocket, or borrow it from some lending institution, since the hotel and casino were in the red. The debt would need to be paid no later than the date the hotel would reopen for the winter season—November 25.

As Frank and Florence pondered the various ramifications, quite unexpectedly on the blustery night before the opening, a fire broke out in their beautiful casino and hotel. What hadn't been destroyed by fire was ruined by the firemen's hoses. Were the Goulds behind it? Or was it SBM? The timing appeared to be extremely fortuitous for either party in the eyes of the press, and groundless speculation grew. Frank, though gutted, put on a brave face. Surely the city of Nice could wait for their back "city contribution" until the insurers paid out?

The damage, covered by forty insurance companies, was thought to be around $700,000. Officials immediately suspected arson, since the fire brigade reported that three fires broke out simultaneously in three separate locations: the hotel restaurant, casino, and kitchen. Eyewitnesses claimed that the suspected arsonist made his "quick" getaway on bicycle. The arsonist—who many claimed was a disgruntled croupier—was never caught.

Frank immediately put out a press statement. His palace that "even Caesar would never have built" would rise again from the ashes. The debt to the city would be paid forthwith. To alienate the mayor's office further would be reckless. Yet Frank's next task was to persuade the insurers that neither he nor Florence had anything to do with the blaze. A diplomatic decision was made by the police, with the help of the mayor's office, to drop any further investigation, since the two most suspected parties were either the Goulds or SBM.[10] Either way, the truth was bad for business. So the thorny question remained for the insurers: Would they or wouldn't they pay out?

ᴖ

The Goulds' problems were only beginning. France was gripped by the greatest scandal of its "virtuous" Third Republic—the Stavisky Affair. Florence's friendship with Mrs. Sacha Stavisky—the actress Arletty— had come into focus at the highest levels of government at precisely the same time as the Palais de la Méditerranée fire. Sacha Stavisky, also known as Serge Alexandre, had been running the most flagrant, fraudulent pyramid scheme to date, selling worthless bonds in the municipal credit institutions of Orléans and Bayonne, backed by nothing but thin air. He was also an inveterate gambler who had been banned from all casinos in the country, since these were the most obvious places for him to cheat and launder dirty money. Yet whenever he was on the Riviera, he made a point of gambling in the Goulds' casinos. Did Florence know what Stavisky was up to? If she did, perhaps she thought that the fire was a sign that Lady Luck was smiling down on them? After all, the casino's records were burned to cinders in the conflagration, too.

16

SCANDAL, AMERICA, AND SEPARATE LIVES

*I have slept with the Dear Lord, and the Dear Lord loves
me.*

—FLORENCE GOULD

FLORENCE TRULY BELIEVED THAT THE LORD GOD WAS PERSON-
ally watching over her, making her rich and responding to her every
prayer. The Heavenly Father was considered by Florence as her Grand
Protector—even her Great Banker—an Eternal Machine designed to print
dollars on her behalf. It was He, she believed, who had looked after her
and Frank with the casino and hotel fire. When it came to the Stavisky
scandal, He created her good fortune in keeping her investments out of
the public eye.

The financial situation in France was worsened by government
volatility. The 1932 elections created a coalition of the left, sometimes
called the second Cartel des Gauches. The Radical Socialists* in the coalition were led by Édouard Daladier for a second time in January 1934,
with the SFIO socialists (Worker's International Party) being the other
cogoverning partner. Maurice Thorez, leader of the French Communist

---

* Despite its name, it was a centrist party.

Party, would soon hold the power of "kingmaker" on the left. Rampant capitalists like Frank and Florence were increasingly in bad odor.

The main problem politicians faced was the economy. Neither the leftist coalition nor the right could agree on the appropriate program to save the nation from bankruptcy, much less find the money to modernize labor laws to twentieth-century standards or agree on a national budget. In other words, faced with the necessity to tighten belts, the French parliamentarians were at daggers drawn. Between December 1932 and February 1934, there were six French premiers leading six different governments. In the four years between June 1932 and June 1936, France would have twelve prime ministers. Instability reigned.[1] The last government to fall was that of Édouard Daladier on February 7, 1934, due to the organized right-wing riots in Paris caused by the Stavisky scandal. While Florence was celebrating Christmas Eve in Paris only six weeks earlier, the scandal finally broke.

The reactionary French author Robert Brasillach summed up the mood of the country well. "The last months of 1933 had shrouded France in a strange twilight of murder," he wrote in *Notre avant-guerre*. "One sign in the darkness, toward Christmas, the Lagny rail catastrophe, which left two hundred dead. . . . And we learned in a few lines, in the papers, that a humdrum swindle implicated the Crédit Municipale of Bayonne."[2]

∞

The humdrum swindler was Mendl, or Michael "Sacha" Stavisky, or Serge Alexandre as he became known after his first stint in prison in 1926. He was dubbed "Stavisky Don Juan" by *Paris-Soir* after his first acquittal for a 6-million-franc stock fraud in 1923. The trial took place shortly after the Ukrainian-born Stavisky became a French citizen. Journalists, many of whom were often aspiring crime novelists, like Georges Simenon, elevated the common swindler to romantic status. The right-wing *Le Journal* asked its readers if Stavisky was "Don Juan or Rasputin?" conjuring up the images of the French gentleman thief Arsène Lupin who consistently outwitted the bungling police.[3] Stavisky's film-idol wife, known to her adoring public as "Arletty," but called Arlette by her friends, was born in 1898 as Léonie Marie Julie Bathiat.

Known for her glamour, as a model for Coco Chanel, and, more recently, an actress with a sumptuous lifestyle on the Riviera and in Biarritz, Arletty was a former childhood classmate of Florence Lacaze Gould's from the Cours Dupanloup.[4] When Stavisky was arrested again at the end of 1926, Arletty was heavily pregnant with their son Claude. Simenon's romantic outcry in "The Love Story of Stavisky" about how Stavisky seduced his wife, who was left only with their baby son and her shattered illusions, sold newspapers in the tens of thousands. Although Arletty was never poor, like Florence, there was more than something of a gambler in her that made Stavisky attractive. Arletty loved high and dangerous living: the lifestyle that Stavisky afforded her.

An inveterate cardsharp, check forger, seller of worthless bonds and glass "jewels," Stavisky was barred from casinos, including the Goulds' casinos at Vichy, Juan-les-Pins, Bagnoles, Granville, and Nice for years. Yet due to Florence's friendship with Arletty, a blind eye was turned, as it was at other casinos owned by those who were beguiled by Stavisky's wife. Even more incredibly, for those who were not tempted to admit Stavisky, he miraculously produced a laissez-passer from the Sûreté Générale with the blessing of his former arresting officer, whose testimony had put him in La Santé Prison in the first place.[5] On one such occasion at the Ambassadeurs Casino in Cannes, Stavisky sat at the baccarat table on a Sunday in January 1932, playing with marked cards. The Greek professional gambler, Zographos, saw what Stavisky was doing, but by the time the policeman overseeing the action in the gambling parlor investigated, Stavisky had walked away with 270,000 francs.[6] With the help of the police and local officials in Paris and Orléans, Stavisky swindled millions more.

As the government was in utter disarray, Stavisky, always on the make, looked for ever-greater swindles. He found one in the Crédit Municipale of Bayonne. Similar municipal credit bureaus were dotted around the country, and were often the only means of "banking" available to traders outside of Paris. For some, it was an enhanced pawnbroker's service. For others, it served as a temporary payday lender. Some businesses used the services for short-term loans.

Envious, Bayonne's long-standing mayor, Joseph Garat,* saw no reason why the French Riviera should have three Crédits Municipales when
Bayonne had none. When "Serge Alexandre" appeared on the scene in
September 1931, Garat was thrilled that his small Basque town was receiving the attention it deserved at long last. The age-old warning "If
something seems too good to be true, then it probably is" should have
been embossed in gold on Garat's office door.

What Stavisky proposed to Bayonne was a simple nineteenth-century
banking solution: lend money at seven percent and issue bonds to investors at five percent. The two percent difference would be used to cover
the operating expenses and contribute to the general good of the town.[7]
It was what Stavisky did in Orléans, he explained to Garat. Stavisky
omitted to say, however, that the police were hot on his trail for his involvement in the municipal credit house of that city. What Arletty did
not know was that the Goulds used their local Crédit Municipale to help
fund their casino expansion and other short-term loans for operations.
What she might have known, however, is that Florence was an investor
in the municipal credit houses on the Riviera.

In essence, the scam consisted of Stavisky taking jewels, certificates
of deposit, gold, stocks, bonds, and any other valuables into his vaults
as "assets" to back the municipal credit's bonds over and above the
"loans" made. Often, the loans were made to "dummies," or cloaked to
Stavisky's cohorts, and the assets were sold before the owners could reclaim them. So long as Stavisky kept churning the sale of the bonds, and
he replaced the real jewels with paste or glass ones, he seemingly kept
ahead of the law.

Just before Christmas 1934, Stavisky went on the run, moving Arletty and their two children (their son was followed by a daughter) to the
Hôtel Château Frontenac in Paris. Stavisky was a "professional skipper"—a
term used in the hotel trade for guests who serially leave without
paying—owing the hotel over 35,000 francs. Then he took the last of his
wife's jewelry—three bracelets, her earrings, and a diamond—and told
her to find a furnished apartment to wait out the storm. His body was

---

* Mayor Joseph Garat and Florence's lover, the actor Henri Garat, were not related.

found a few weeks later, shot in an "apparent suicide," in a seedy hotel room in Chamonix near the Swiss border.[8]

Stavisky began life as a café singer, graduating to the romantic realms of bringing down a government. Bayonne's Mayor Garat was jailed, his thirty-year reputation in tatters. Paris's Prefect of Police, Jean Chiappe, was offered up as a sacrificial lamb to the people who demanded to know who in the government had been protecting Stavisky for years. Worse was still to come. The far right thundered its discontent in print and took to the streets calling on the entire government to resign and call new elections. Everyone on the left was corrupt, they screamed. The Radicals were muddied by the royalists; the anti-Semitic right-wing Action Française and Croix-de-Feu rioted in the streets of Paris, with forty thousand people attempting to storm the Chamber of the Deputies. Fifteen people were killed and more than a thousand injured.[9] In shades of Hitler's attempted Beer Hall Putsch some eleven years earlier, the alleged right-wing-inspired coup d'état failed before it could begin.

Still, it wasn't Bayonne or Orléans that brought down Stavisky, politicians, and the police who enjoyed the fruits of his embezzlement. It was Stavisky's greed in attempting to sell Hungarian agrarian bonds on the international stage. The scheme was halted by the Bank of International Settlement in Basel, Switzerland, when it raised all the right questions about "Monsieur Alexandre." In all, Stavisky took everyone for the approximate equivalent today of $268,778,000, ruining acres of politicians, not to mention miles of investors. The problem for Florence was that she had been one of his investors and her "friend" Arletty hadn't warned her or, indeed, given her inside information. Their longstanding friendship apparently cooled. Florence must have dreaded Frank's reaction if the Gould name was once more dragged into another scandal—albeit innocently.

⁊

While the loss of the money and the value of their shares in the Riviera municipal credits were a pittance in their vast fortune, Florence and Frank both knew that the repercussions of the scandal would deepen the Depression and further weaken the already tottering government. More instability could only harm business. Between their casinos (those "dens of vice," as politicians of any stripe called them), Stavisky, and Florence's showy decadence, Frank could be forgiven for believing that they might be the targets of some unknown reckoning.

Indeed, perhaps the time had come to look to reestablish their home in America, he thought. France, he believed, would lean farther to the left. Perhaps this was behind the Goulds' decision to rebuild the Palais de la Méditerranée and succumb to the relentless pressure from SBM? The timing of the decision seems to be more than a coincidence. The shock announcement about the rebuilding of the hotel and casino was coupled with SBM's press release that it would "buy the operations" for an undisclosed sum and an annual payment to the Goulds of $100,000. While the Goulds would still own the bricks and mortar, the decision made it easy to plan on going home, at least until the dust settled.

Days later, the government fell. Frank was right—there was a re-sounding victory of the left. To calm frayed public nerves, the new ad-ministration proclaimed that there would be a huge public trial with anyone affected by the scandal asked to bear witness against Stavisky and all those acres of politicians facing ruin. That, from the Goulds' perspective, was a nonstarter. They needed all the political goodwill possible from the city of Nice to get their casino operations trading again. They would need to swallow hard and avoid any further mention of the Stavisky name.

Did Frank forbid Florence from seeing Arletty, as he had done with Zelda? Was he aware of Florence's investment follies? More than likely, no, in both cases. Whether Florence privately helped the broken Arletty, as she would later do with other friends, remains one of her many untold stories.

Instead, arrangements were made to sail on the *Île de France* that October. While the *New York Sun* declared that Mr. and Mrs. Frank Jay Gould were aboard ship, Frank seems to have decided at the last min-ute—as was his custom—not to travel.[10] No reason was given, and no clarification was offered publicly if he had wired his approval to New York to allow Florence to act under his power of attorney with the new manager of his American business affairs, Mrs. Lola Walker. Certainly, Frank felt unable to "fit in" with Florence's traveling companions and former lovers Melchior de Polignac, Armand de la Rochefoucauld, and especially Madeleine Manigler.

Aboard ship, there were many others whom Florence knew, or aspired to know, too. The entire cast of Noël Coward's latest hit, *Conversation Piece*, were flattered by Florence's attentions. More than likely, the returning American millionairesses, Mrs. William Rutherford Mead, widow of the wealthy architect, and Mrs. George Davenport, whose family inherited the vast fur trade from the frontiersman George Davenport, were happy to make her acquaintance and asked Florence's opinion about *what the deuce was going on in France*?

Most prominent among those who joined Florence's entourage was Félix Wildenstein—of Wildenstein & Co.—the elegant and distinguished cousin of Florence's adviser in fine art, Georges Wildenstein. Georges was the ultimate employer of Madeleine Manigler. Nathan Wildenstein, the founder of Wildenstein & Co. and Georges's father, had already passed the reins of the French company over to his son while he headed up the New York gallery. This, too, could have been another reason for Madeleine's trip to New York. Rochefoucauld, as head of the French Jockey Club, was also a friend of Georges Wildenstein's, since the latter was a major player in thoroughbred breeding and horseracing. As for de Polignac, he, naturally, provided free champagne for all.

Despite press reports that Florence had come to New York to buy American silk stockings, her real reasons for the trip were masked. The previous year, Frank had changed his will to favor his wife, and Florence seemingly wanted to understand her husband's American empire. In anticipation of returning semipermanently to America, Frank had acquired a home in Ardsley-on-Hudson, in Westchester County, for $25,000, adjacent to the family estate at Lyndhurst. Given the proximity to the family home, it is probable that Frank's sister, Anna, had a hand in the negotiations. The magnificent mock-Tudor mansion of the style seen throughout Westchester County was called Mora Vocis after the time separation in Gregorian chants, where the vocal accent is on the last syllable. It had equally breathtaking views over the Hudson River as Lyndhurst's. Its previous owner, Justine B. Ward, had had the house built on North Mountain Drive some seven years earlier by renowned architects William Adams Delano and Chester Holmes Aldrich.[11]

But Florence didn't stay at Mora Vocis to get to know her new neighbors. The Plaza in Manhattan was more to her liking, and provided her with an easy base from which she could shop for all the antiques and furniture in New York City's best boutiques and auction houses that her new home deserved.[12] By night, she went to see Broadway shows like *The Great Waltz*, financed by Rockefeller money. Although opulent operettas were still popular in Paris and on the Riviera, in New York they were prohibitively expensive to produce, and often did not give the comic relief Americans craved. Florence was awed by the cast of 180, the hydraulic sets, and the fifty-three-piece orchestra. Another Broadway hit, *The Ziegfeld Follies*, struck a chord, too. Billie Burke, the widow of Flo Ziegfeld, worked with the theater-owning family the Shuberts to revive the popular 1920s format.[13]

By the time Florence's ticket was booked, she knew that the idea of returning "home" was no more than window dressing. In the one week that she remained in the United States, she also managed to visit Buffalo and Washington, D.C. Precisely why she chose Buffalo, unless it was to see the American side of Niagara Falls, she never said. It is particularly perplexing since she would have had invitations to see the Wildenstein stud at Saratoga Springs, some six hours away by car today.

She declared to the *New York Herald*, shortly before leaving, that she had come to "shop" and that while "New York was grand," the Goulds' primary residence would remain in France. She promised the reporter, however, that she and Frank would return together that winter.[14] Surely, Frank would be unable to brave the Atlantic winter seas, or survive New York winter.

The swift side trip she made to Washington, D.C., is easier to decipher. The public promise of returning to America was gauged to please, without a care for the truth. In fact, the Washington trip aimed to set in motion a resolution to Frank's federal tax problems. Apparently, no taxes had been paid in more than thirty years.[15] The purchase of their Ardsley home had a two-fold purpose: to prove to the French government that they were nonresident Americans, and, as such, they should enjoy a privileged tax status there; and similarly, to demonstrate to the IRS that they would become New York residents, hoping they might get away with paying taxes only on their U.S. income. As any expatriate American knows today, payment of U.S. federal taxes is not just on the sums earned in America, but rather on one's worldwide income. Frank and Florence were maintaining the inarguable from the viewpoint of U.S. legislation. The jury was out on whether the wheeze would succeed.

∽

On May 29, 1935, Florence was once again off to New York. Again, without Frank. This time, however, it was to be part of the gaiety and glamour of the maiden voyage of the French Line's newest, sleekest ocean liner, the SS *Normandie*. Designed by the former shipbuilder to the czars, the *Normandie* was not only the fastest turbo-electric steamship ever built, but also the first new liner designed to take the predominantly upper-crust passenger. With its main dining room swathed in Lalique glass, many commented on it as resembling Versailles's Hall of Mirrors. Still, it was longer at some 305 feet, wider, and higher than the Hall of Mirrors, too. The twelve full-height Lalique glass pillars made it a veritable city of light, able to seat seven hundred guests at some 157 tables.

A strange picture of Florence survives from the voyage. She is smiling radiantly, dressed in her white Chanel suit, black turtleneck, her pearls, and heels. To her left is an older gentleman dressed in a dark sports jacket and light trousers, smiling lasciviously at her. Next to him is a reasonably handsome man in a swimsuit with a towel draped over his shoulder. To her right, slightly behind that man, is a heavyset man in a gray tweed suit, who looks more like a bouncer or a bodyguard, gripping Florence's elbow tightly. In front of this man is a thin, elderly man— not Frank—but who rather has an air of an off-camera Boris Karloff. The "Boris" lookalike holds on to Madeleine Manigler's arm. As for Madeleine, she is dressed in a black swimsuit, her hair bundled up in a white turban, and a towel draped lazily to the front, hiding her legs.

Something stands out in this photograph: the lasciviously smiling man looking over Florence's left shoulder fancies his chances, and Florence doesn't acknowledge his existence. Two questions spring to mind, as well. Had Florence been aware that the Third Reich was already planting its spies aboard the best ocean liners, as reported a year earlier in the *New York Sun* during her stateside jaunt?[16] If so, would she have cared?

Evidently, the gulf between Frank and Florence had deepened. Even

Florence's charm could not undo the past. Was it her impressive gallery of collected lovers? Was it Stavisky, or Frank's loathing of his wives dragging the Gould name through the mire? Or was it her closeness with Madeleine Manigler? Frank's secretary, Magdeleine Homo, remained loyal to Florence and may have known his feelings, but she never revealed the family's secrets. Besides, who knows what goes on in the lives of couples—even the couples themselves?

∽

While the rest of France was bracing itself for the Stavisky Affair trial in December 1935, Madeleine Manigler bought Florence a Christmas present to remember: a two-month-old bear cub. If Josephine Baker could take her jaguar for a walk down the Champs-Élysées, Florence could do the same with her bear. The huge cage arrived at Florence's hôtel particulier on rue Albéric-Magnard on Christmas morning. Frank was furious. It was unconscionable to treat a wild animal like a toy. Not only that, but it was incredibly dangerous. Still, not to feed it would be murder, Manigler replied.

So Frank ordered his valet, Joseph, and his maid, Lucy, to feed it milk from a baby's bottle. Then he rounded on Madeleine and Florence, and told them to find a permanent home for the bear cub—*tout de suite*. Florence and Madeleine would be compelled to personally drive the animal to the local zoo in a hired van, where they claimed to visit him regularly. Florence's sister, Isabelle, certainly did, since she grumbled that the bear cub had eaten the sleeve of her mink coat.

Still, Florence's laughter about the purchase resounds loudly through her thank-you note to Madeline. "Thank you for the gift. It has cost me a fortune!" Simply put, Florence had decided that she adored bears, and bought four more bear cubs to roam the grounds of the Goulds' Maisons-Laffitte estate. Naturally, she had a huge enclosure sculpted within the grounds. The bears' arrival also meant that Florence had to employ her own keepers. Frank, certainly, was unamused.[17]

17

CRANO

DARK HORIZONS

As in law or war, the deepest purse finally wins.
—Mahatma Gandhi

SOMETIME BETWEEN 1934 AND 1935, FLORENCE MET TWO MEN who would alter her life for the next decade. One was an international wine merchant who married into a German sparkling wines family, and bought his aristocratic "von" from his wife's aging aunt. The other was a former drawing instructor. More than likely, it was the wine merchant she met first through the auspices of her friends, Melchior de Polignac and his American wife, Nina. The wine merchant's name was Joachim von Ribbentrop.

The former drawing instructor and high-school art teacher worked for Ribbentrop. He might have been another notch on Florence's belt, too. From 1934, he spearheaded the Franco-German youth movement, called the Comité France-Allemagne, or CFA, aimed at closer socioeconomic relations between their youth. He was tall, blond, thirtyish, and handsome. He was also married to a French woman, Suzanne, and spoke perfect French. His name was Otto Abetz.

Such Francophiles at the highest levels of Hitler's Third Reich were welcomed by French royalists like de Polignac, antiparliamentarians, and French fascists. Florence, like many entrepreneurs, was disaffected with the Third Republic. Left-wing politics was a costly irritant to business, and disrespect for all politicians was every bit as rampant as today. All the same, Frank was obliged to take any interest Germany had in the politico-economic affairs of France, since he'd been appointed the French Riviera representative of the Banque de France.

That said, neither Florence nor Frank were aware that the French secret services took a dim view of German interests in their country. Germany had represented a threat since the armistice of 1918 in clandestine defense circles. The French Service de Renseignements, or Intelligence Services, known as the SR, was comprised of several Deuxième Bureaus (Investigative Intelligence Services) for each branch of the military, with the army having the largest and best-funded department. In this finely tuned machine of state, information was passed from the SR to the different military Deuxième Bureaus for investigation, and if required, action would be taken. Embassy branches, too, supplied intelligence either directly to the SR or to the relevant Deuxième Bureau concerned with a particular burning issue.[1] As early as 1922, the chief of French military intelligence went so far as to report, "Humiliated by its defeat, Germany is obsessed with thoughts of revenge.... One single danger dominates all others at the moment, and that is the German danger."[2]

By the time Hitler seized power in January 1933, French Intelligence Services had become so alarmed, for so long, that its many governments seemed to think the agencies were crying wolf. Few were aware that after the publication of Mein Kampf in July 1925, Hitler dictated an even viler manuscript in 1928 that remained unpublished. In that work, Hitler declared that French power was a "question of life and death to Germany" and that it must be destroyed to "make it possible for our people finally to expand in another quarter."[3]

This was always at the heart of Lebensraum for the Nazis. Yet, from 1933, Hitler extended the hand of friendship, a steel fist disguised in a velvet glove. The men engaged personally by Hitler to enact that policy of rapprochement were Ribbentrop and Abetz. From 1934, any negotiations between the French and German ministers for foreign affairs involved Ribbentrop on the German side. His *Büro* acted as an unofficial, shadowy foreign ministry designed to suborn the official, and generally independent, foreign diplomatic services of Germany. Likewise, the roles of Ribbentrop and Abetz were personally determined by Hitler. The pseudo-aristocratic Ribbentrop's mission included sweetening diplomatic relations not only with France, but also with Great Britain. His office at 64 Wilhelmstrasse—opposite the foreign ministry—became the personal representative of Hitler outside Germany along with the Berlin headquarters at the "Brown House," where all NSDAP ideological decisions were made. To merit recruitment to Ribbentrop's office, applicants had to be dynamic collaborators and self-starters, whose initiatives had been proven in Europe and the USSR.[4]

No one fit the profile better than Otto Abetz. In 1934, Abetz proposed to Henri Pichot, the president of the Veterans' Services (UF)[*] that on the anniversary of the declaration of war twenty years earlier, German and French patriots should set bonfires on both sides of the Rhine border between the two countries, "the flames burning bright as a symbol of possible reconciliation."[5] While tempted, Pichot turned Abetz down, since he hadn't enough time to discuss the proposal with his other representatives. Rebuffed but undaunted, Abetz submitted a report on his proposal to the Reichsjugendführung (RJF),[†] which impressed Baldur von Schirach, head of the Hitler Youth. Von Schirach passed it on to Rudolf Hess, who showed it to Ribbentrop. Abetz was snapped up as Germany's mole in France by Ribbentrop, while he continued to work for the RJF and von Schirach.

✑

Abetz's first task was to win over the hearts and minds of the inhabitants of the Rhineland. With the plebiscite of the Saarland looming in January 1935, he created a propaganda campaign so that the people would not renounce Germany in favor of France. Many of the NSDAP's adversaries had settled there, since they had been persecuted by the Nazis. Catholics, too, were heavily represented among the electorate. Famously, Abetz pretended to not be a Nazi, and called out to the voters to

---

* L'Union fédérale des anciens combattants.
† Reich Youth Directorate.

support Hitler, who was after all "a man of peace; if one day, my conviction crumbles on this point, then I will run through the streets shouting *Red Alert!*"[6]

At the same time, Abetz returned regularly to Paris, where he dedicated most of his time to student exchanges. His articles appeared in *Le Figaro* newspaper, where he claimed that the youth of 1935 were suffering from poor relations between France and Germany and how "tomorrow France and Germany could be reconciled once and for all, and travel together forward as partners with confidence to tackle the true economic and social problems facing both countries. Everything else is a shriveled phantom."[7] In November of that year, Abetz became responsible for the CFA.

While peace and normalized relations with France could only be good for business, Florence's view of the CFA would have been based on who among her French friends had joined it. Her longtime admirer Pierre Benoit, introducer of the delicious Robert de Thomasson to Florence, was on its board, along with the father of her lawyer, René de Chambrun,* and, naturally, Melchior de Polignac. The right-wing writer and intellectual Pierre Drieu la Rochelle served alongside them, too.

De Polignac was, in fact, far more important than his nickname "Champagne King" implied. A lifelong friend of the founder of the modern Olympics movement, Pierre de Coubertin, de Polignac, served on the Olympic Committee that selected Berlin for the 1936 Summer Olympics and Garmisch-Partenkirchen for the Winter Olympics. In fact, it was de Polignac who convinced the Olympic Committee that Germany was the *only* place to hold the 1936 games.[8] Writing as the Marquis de Polignac, he waxed lyrical in his newspaper article for the right-wing *Le Journal*: "underpinned from the outset by the perfect understanding and dictatorial authority of Chancellor Hitler and by the faith of the Reich's sports minister . . . every detail was put into action methodically and with intelligence. . . . The German people have no desire to wage a modern war. . . . Its supreme desire is to protect itself from the ravages of the Soviet Union. . . . Would it be imprudent of me to

---

* Charles G. Loeb had returned to New York to practice law at Coudert Brothers during the late 1930s, but he remained on friendly terms with the Goulds until his death.

conclude that a great number of French citizens have a similar attitude as I do toward the Germans?"[9] Florence's reaction to the article and de Polignac's admiration for Hitler were never publicized. Perhaps that was because business in Nice was, once again, going rather badly.

∽

The Deuxième Bureau unexpectedly raised some queries about the old July 1934 request for the annual renewal of the gambling license for the winter season of 1934–35. The Goulds seemed confused. The request for the license came from Société du Palais de la Méditerranée when, in fact, this company no longer managed the casino or the hotel. Jacques Dalbouse, Chevalier of the Legion of Honor, and SBM's representative for the Société Fermière du Palais de la Méditerranée, managed to set the record straight with the city of Nice, and obtained a letter of release from the mayor's office, signed by Jean Médecin, the current mayor, theoretically setting their house in order.

Médecin's dispensation, however, was illegal, so the Deuxième Bureau investigative branch of the judicial police answerable to the minister of the interior wrote to Florence. It was strictly forbidden that "any casino where the licensee has become non-operational is not allowed to have its license renewed with or without notification."[10] The purpose of the legislation was to halt the flagrant disdain for casino laws. These laws were designed to stop potential criminal activity such as racketeering, tax evasion, and money laundering. Florence simply replied that SBM's company, the Société Fermière, was no longer running the casino. Yet the Deuxième Bureau determined that there had been a flagrant contempt for the law, and slapped down Médecin and the city of Nice, ordering the closure of the Goulds' casino.

At the heart of the controversy were three separate companies. The first was Société Immobilière du Palais Vénitien, which owned the building and all of its furniture, fixtures, and equipment. The files of the Deuxième Bureau state that this company was organized in accordance with French law, but behind it was a cloaked foreign company called General Motor, and cloaked behind that company was the eventual owner, Frank Jay Gould. His ownership was "camouflaged behind the screen of 'Holdings des Palais et Casinos' with his front-man, and Delegated Administrator being L.J. ASLANGUL, personal and private secretary to Mr. GOULD."[11] Some years later, the Sixième Bureau reported that Florence was in control of the company at the time.[12]

The second company concerned was Société du Palais de la Méditerranée, which was founded by the Société Immobilière, owned by Frank, and controlled by Florence. Its sole purpose was to operate the casino Palais de la Méditerranée. Its rights stemmed from a lease payable to the Société Immobilière du Palais Vénitien, or ultimately the Goulds. This second company had lain dormant for four years in 1935. Édouard Baudoin was its president and delegated administrator, presumably on behalf of both Frank and Florence.

The third company was the Société Fermière du Palais de la Méditerranée, which had operated the casino on a lease from the Goulds' Société Immobilière du Palais Vénitien since the time the hotel and casino were rebuilt after the fire. This third company was created and owned by SBM. Its official administrator was Mr. Dalbouse. This third company was the sole manager after the fire, and applied for the casino licenses through to the season of 1935–36. It was, therefore, the only company that could be granted a license to *continue* to operate the casino for the 1936–37 season.

That said, a news article in the *L'Éclaireur de Nice* announced on September 18, 1936—some two and a half months after the deadline for any license applications or renewals—that Édouard Baudoin would again head the casino operations. On October 1, 1936, SBM, through Dalbouse and the Société Fermière du Palais de la Méditerranée, countered Baudoin's claim in the press, averring that *it* would maintain the operations for 1936–37.

The Goulds created this confusion by using SBM's name for their own purposes to rebuild the casino and its business. Unsurprisingly, it was a difficult relationship, with the Goulds claiming that SBM was "walking on" customers to Monte Carlo, to the detriment of their Nice property. Perhaps SBM did, then again perhaps not. Florence decided in consultation with Frank, that after SBM successfully negotiated a three-year rolling renewal of the casino gaming license with the city of Nice, to boot them out without notice and replace SBM with their own company headed by Baudoin.

The Deuxième Bureau concluded that SBM's Société Fermière's contractual relations were severed by the Goulds, and that the Goulds acted in bad faith with the authorities. Since neither of the companies controlled by the Goulds applied for a license, and the Gould companies severed management ties with SBM through Société Fermière, *none of the companies* were deemed fit to operate the casino at the Palais de la Méditerranée. Furthermore, since the Goulds also held the management of the Municipal Casino in Nice, it was ruled that this, too, must come under review due to the Goulds' utter disregard for the law.[13] Frank was furious. Florence was the active partner in the administration of the business since he was in continued ill health. She was responsible for the illegality, and it was up to her to fix it.

A Gould appeal was lodged against the Deuxième Bureau's decision to foreclose on the casino, without addressing the allegations of possible racketeering or flagrant disrespect for the law. Instead, the Goulds blamed the city of Nice for its "misdirection" of the companies concerned, and ignorance of the ancient law of 1879 governing casinos. Florence argued that similar "illegalities" had occurred with other casinos in Nice, but that these casinos were not targeted. The appeal's success or failure rested solely on ignorance of the law and the defense that "everyone else was doing it, so why can't we?" Ignorance, as we all know, is no defense. Neither is pointing at someone else's success in flaunting the law.

The report blamed the Goulds, and not SBM, for the fire, since only the Goulds benefited from the blaze—something that was not entirely true, since SBM gained control of the Goulds' Nice casino and hotel. The Goulds were facing a humiliating defeat, and irreparable rupture with Nice's politicians. Seemingly, no amount of money strewn about locally could help.

Further police investigations proved that the Goulds, cloaked by Édouard Baudoin, were in cahoots with a Uruguayan former mathematics professor, Amleto Battisti, to fix the *Tout Va* bank at the casino, in a clear charge of racketeering. Battisti owned shares in Al Capone's favorite hotel in Havana, the Sevilla-Biltmore, becoming its sole owner in 1939, and intuitively understood the Goulds' requirements.

It hardly took a single sway of Florence's hips or a sensual, whispered conversation to persuade Battisti to step in. The loud jangle of casino chips bulging in her deep pajama pockets was the main attraction for him. Business in his home base of Havana, Cuba, had become rather difficult since the roar of American gunships and "diplomacy" rattled Cuban politics in 1933. By 1937, there were gunfights in the streets of Havana, making a business flirtation with the French Riviera, and Europe, a meaningful interlude.[14] Florence was undoubtedly aware that Battisti, while Uruguayan, was of Italian descent and was connected to the Mafia already. Battisti would later become known as the banker to the American gangster Meyer Lansky and through Battisti's bank, Banco de Créditos y Inversiones, would launder Lansky's casino profits in Cuba.[15] All that mattered to Florence was that Battisti could restore their fortunes.

The Deuxième Bureau's report falls just short of implicating the Goulds in an international money-laundering scheme, but their affiliation with Battisti tarnished their reputation by associating them with the "numbers king of Havana." Most damning was the belief that Battisti was brought in by Florence to recover the casino's operating losses of the first and second seasons; and when that failed, the fire was, in the opinion of the investigators, the only option the Goulds saw to extract themselves from the situation unscathed.[16] Battisti's personal reasons for moving in on their Riviera hotel are implied rather than made explicit.

Nonetheless, since it was Baudoin, as the Goulds' straw man, who arranged matters with Battisti, the criminal investigators needed to get hard evidence against the Goulds personally for their case to stick. What made matters more complicated for the Deuxième Bureau was the sudden disappearance of Amleto Battisti from the scene. While he was already closely linked to North American gangsters and the Cuban Mafia, too, including Santo Trafficante and Lucky Luciano and their "numbers rackets," Battisti's involvement in heroin trafficking remained unknown to French investigators.[17] In the aftermath of Battisti's disappearance, a Gould-inspired rumor flew around the world of high-stakes gamblers that he could no longer offer his 35-million-franc guarantee to the Palais de la Méditerranée. Given Battisti's connections to the international underworld, the rumor was untrue, and aimed instead at diverting attention away from an intended Mafia move onto the Riviera.[18]

Even so, it would be wrong to think that SBM was exonerated from any misconduct. The report concluded that SBM was replacing Battisti

at the bank for *Tout Va* with the Greek professional gambler and baccarat king Zographos. The final damning words in the Deuxième Bureau's
report against the Goulds were that "all of these irregularities were designed to hoodwink the Authorities: the Ministries of the Interior, Finance and Municipalities."[19]

As the owner of record, Frank was obliged to travel to Paris personally to dispute the ruling to the Septième Bureau, in whose power
foreclosure of casinos resided. Both Goulds argued their case passion-
ately, with Frank no doubt relying on Florence to charm their interrogators. Perhaps the Goulds contemplated, too, that a substantial gift of money
to police charities to smooth their ruffled feathers might help. Nothing,
however, seemingly worked. At the end of the day, Florence and Frank
were advised that the only means of keeping their casino open—albeit
with a sizable fine—was to declare peace once more with Société Fermière and its parent company SBM, which had applied for the licenses as
the operator of the casino legally and in anticipation of continuing as its
manager.

That, of course, did not address the burning issue of the foreclosure
of the Municipal Casino, or the stain that the Goulds' ownership and accusations that "cheating the system" represented.[20] It was a determined
Florence who went on a serious charm offensive to beguile Jean Médecin, Nice's mayor. She would not fail. She would contribute generously
to Médecin's campaign for reelection, and both would win, no matter the
cost.[21] If it required persuasion of a more personal nature, then so be it.
After all, Médecin was attractive and powerful. Soon enough, all talk of
racketeering was banished.

∞

Florence's Paris friends had their share of problems, too. Some twelve
years earlier, Coco Chanel had virtually given away the rights to her perfume business while watching the ponies gallop at Longchamp race-
track. She had asked to meet Pierre Wertheimer there, owner of Bourjois
perfumes, whom Chanel approached to produce and distribute her fragrance No. 5. When Wertheimer replied "why not," she never stopped to
think that he might try to swing a bad deal on her. Unlike Florence,
Chanel was bored to death by paperwork.[22]

By 1936, Chanel's lawyer, René de Chambrun, was in litigation for a fistful of years to regain the rights to Chanel No. 5, without success. Chanel's relationship with Bendor was over, too. Bendor needed an heir, and hardly required Winston Churchill's reminder that Chanel would never be accepted at court after the "Abdication Crisis." That said, Bendor remained on friendly terms with the couturier. Florence's old friend Étienne de Beaumont stepped in and helped Chanel design a new range of costume jewelry based on many of the real jewels that Bendor had bought for her. It became an overnight financial success.

Then, just as Chanel was riding high again in August 1935, her new man-of-the-moment, the handsome Basque illustrator and designer Paul Iribe, died of a heart attack before her very eyes while playing tennis at her Riviera home, La Pausa. Colette had called Iribe a "very interesting demon." Chanel was devastated, but was thankful that Iribe's defense of her quest to retake Chanel No. 5 was reinvigorated. He'd drawn Chanel as a martyred Marianne, grasped at by evil-looking men with obvious Jewish features, and published it in *Le Témoin*, awakening her supporters to the "enemies within" called "Samuel" or "Levy" and their "Judeo-Masonic Mafia."[23]

✑

While the Goulds struggled with the Sûreté and local politicians, the political and financial crisis created by the Stavisky Scandal—said to be on a par with the Dreyfus Affair and the Panama Canal scandal*—could still be felt. A godsend to anti-Semites, given Stavisky's Jewish origins, it also laid bare the decadent inner workings of the Third Republic's high society, in which Florence was a spinning cog, and corruption in its police force. At the trial of Stavisky "accomplices," Arletty, eyes fixed on the final pleas of her lawyers, smartly dressed in her dark Chanel hat and suit with an elegant broadtail collar, stood alongside Stavisky's other cohorts in crime, charged with the swindle. When the verdicts were delivered on January 16, 1936, once again the floodwaters of the Seine threatened the

---

* This occurred when a lottery, approved by the French Chamber of Deputies, to raise money to build the canal was proved fraudulent and mismanaged. The company funded by the lottery collapsed in under a year, eventually enabling the Americans to step in under Theodore Roosevelt.

city of Paris. Arletty waited in the courtroom, anxious to get home to her children. Nine people were convicted and eleven others acquitted. Arletty was among those set free. Apparently, her only crime was that she bore Stavisky's name.

Days later, Arletty slinked away with her children aboard the ocean liner *Île de France* bound for New York.[24] It is tantalizing to think that Florence may have been one of those who helped her escape the wrath of the French public, but Arletty was back in Paris by that October, broke as ever.

PART THREE

DARKNESS FALLS

&

Democracy is well and truly dead in Germany. . . .
The stability of the regime now depends on the
bayonets of the Reichswehr.

—Lt. Colonel Edouard-Charles Chapouilly to
General Maxime Weygand, June 1932

18

FIFTH COLUMNISTS AND FELLOW TRAVELERS

They should know that Hitler's triumph would be the death of the West.

—ANDRÉ SAURÈS, *Vues sur l'Europe* (1939)

FOREMOST AMONG FLORENCE'S LITERARY SET WAS THE ACADEMI-cian Pierre Benoit, who joined the ranks of the "Immortals" of the Académie Française in 1931. Benoit, whom Florence nicknamed "Bébé," was utterly captivated by her, much to the chagrin of Madame Benoit. "You have no idea how he wrote the most beautiful poems to me," Florence said, "and how he was sweet, soft, and round, like a baby. It was lovely. He was my baby."[1] The right-wing Benoit also possessed a great mind. To boot, he was a great admirer of the politics of Charles Maurras, author, poet, critic, and principal philosopher of Action Française, a political movement that was monarchist and anti-parliamentarist, and influenced Florence politically prior to the war.

More prosaically, it was Benoit who smoothed the way for the impoverished and seemingly friendless Arletty. In October 1936, Florence agreed to forgive her old friend for Stavisky's transgressions, on certain conditions. Arletty's only remark about the encounter was that she had to "first make nice to Florence's Pekingese dogs."[2] Florence's absolution

most likely took the form of financial assistance and a certain social reha-
bilitation among their set, for which Arletty remained silently grateful.

Benoit also raised Florence's hopes of a change of government to the
royalists or center right, which would be a friendlier regime for business.
Alas, both were sorely disappointed with the 1936 election results. That
April, there was a chilling victory for the socialists and communists.
Sylvia Beach reported to her father in New Jersey, "all went LEFT in
a landslide that has quite scared the old standpatters and canon-
merchants. Now they are trying to revenge themselves by sitting on the
franc so as to flatten it out."[3]

Sylvia also wrote about the "Friends" of her struggling bookshop,
which most patrons preferred to think of as a library and home away
from home. While Joyce was alive—just—the glamour days of Hemingway and Fitzgerald were past. André Gide had become the guiding spirit
for her French subscribers, as he was always a champion of the oppressed,
and he dramatically intervened to help her attract customers by estab-
lishing the "Friends" of Shakespeare and Company and contributing to
its readings during 1936 and 1937. Yet it was the unofficial friends who
privately rallied to support Sylvia's endeavors. Led by the major donor
and New Yorker Marian Willard, Helena Rubinstein gave $246, while
Anne Morgan, the daughter of her more famous father J.P., gave $460.
Paris needed an English-language bookshop, and "We women must
stand together! *Pour la culture!*" was the battle cry.[4] Florence did not
give copiously to this popular "American" cause and was apparently not
a customer. She preferred the high-society de Chambrun charities of the
American Hospital and the American Library.

Shakespeare and Company survived, thanks to Gide's efforts. He
arranged for Jean Schlumberger, founder of the literary magazine *Nouvelle Revue Française*, to speak that March. Then Schlumberger enlisted
his editor, the fifty-two-year-old Jean Paulhan, to read from *Les fleurs de
tarbes*, which wouldn't be published until 1941. Sylvia's companion,
Adrienne Monnier, likened Paulhan to a snake charmer, "the line of his
voice moved toward the idea like the sound of a flute, and the idea, un-
dulating, reared up like a cobra."[5] Paulhan's voice did indeed rise and
fall, and he moved about like a snake hoping to insinuate himself into
the listeners' thoughts, but the poem was incomprehensible to Sylvia. In

what may seem an unlikely turn of events, however, Paulhan would also become one of Florence's saviors within the decade.

∽

The real threat of war was on everyone's lips from the moment Hitler's troops strutted into the Rhineland in March 1936, in clear violation of the Treaty of Versailles. Nonetheless, Paris was still swaddled in its own importance. There were spring floods, once again. Would the Seine burst its banks, or not? Looking outward, ever so slightly, did they notice, the chattering beau monde asked one another, if the spring fashions held more than a mere hint of the military about them? Meanwhile, Condé Nast tore his hair out in New York because the fashion houses bent his French *Vogue*—nicknamed "Frog" by in-housers—to their will, with Chanel threatening to pull her entire collection unless no fashions from competing couturiers were shown on the opposite pages.[6]

The preoccupation with fashion disgusted leftist activists. How could fashion possibly matter while the bloody civil war in Spain raged on as the final proving ground for Hitler's war machine? How indeed, when French and foreign writers swelled the ranks of volunteers to save the duly elected left-wing Spanish Republic, among them, George Orwell. The writer Stephen Spender, later a British spy, visited Shakespeare and Company with Ernest Hemingway in tow traveling as a sort of antiwar correspondent for the North American Newspaper Alliance, on their way to fight in Spain. That May, on Hemingway's return, he gave a reading from his new novel *To Have or Have Not* to help his old friend Sylvia Beach. Spender and W. H. Auden would speak there, too, that summer.[7]

The national war of words between parliamentarians, communists, and socialists against royalists and fascists had been going on since the twenties. New far left and far right groups, fueled by the exile of Eastern Europeans and Italian and Spanish political refugees, served only to terrify le gratin of France. Though Florence had no friends on the left, she found many fellow travelers on the right. Hitler's fifth columnists, headed by Otto Abetz, seemed the most well-connected group to join. Besides, the conservative center ground in France was wafer-thin, and quite unfashionable. It would take a person of extreme conviction to remain indifferent to the rolling, boiling cauldron of political ideals of the thirties. Yet the only firm passions Florence held were those that bowed to her munificence, power, and beauty. With the coming war, these passions would stand her in good stead as a powerful survivor.

When the unlikely candidate Léon Blum, a Jew, miraculously became France's premier in the new leftist Front Populaire government in June 1936, Florence was, along with her royalist friends, aghast. The former legal adviser to Florence's favorite luxury car manufacturer, Hispano-Suiza, Blum held his first university degree in philosophy, his second in law. He was the author of books on Goethe and Stendhal; a devotee of Ravel's music; adored cats, flowers, objets d'art, and modern art. He was an enthusiastic cook, recited Victor Hugo's poems by heart, and his brother René was the director of the Monte Carlo Russian ballet.[8] Yet none of this endeared him to Florence and her friends.

Despite introducing social reforms, including obligatory paid holidays for the employed, Blum's ministry lasted a mere year. His government fell not because of its leftist leanings, or indeed his support for women's rights (he had three women serving in his cabinet even though they still couldn't vote*), but rather due to anti-Semitism among the right-wing political parties. The royalists even wielded the slogan "Better Hitler than Blum," bringing some conservative elements and socialists, too, into their swelling ranks.[9]

While Florence supported a move toward the right, she was not truly anti-Semitic, boasting the Jewish poet Max Jacob, briefly, as her lover, and adopting (and later protecting) her highbrow Jewish friends. Nonetheless, years later, even some of her close friends, like writer Dominique Aury (pen name for Anne Desclos), branded Florence "an American anti-Semite."[10] On closer examination, given Aury's knowledge of the Anglo-Saxon mindset—as she grew up in an Anglo-French home—her statement is a swipe at Americans as well as anti-Semites. In the late 1950s when she said this about Florence in a letter to her lover and editor, Jean Paulhan, the acceptable and understood face of the Jew to Americans was

---

* Women were not granted the vote until April 29, 1945. Women had been allowed their own bank accounts, however, since 1881, with the right extended to married women to open their own bank accounts without their husband's approval in 1886. *Source:* https://www.theguardian.com/money/us-money-blog/2014/aug/11/women-rights-money-timeline-history.

one who was wealthy, with a position in society, and with whom one shared a common "Christian" culture.

Florence's qualified acceptance of Jews can best be understood through Nancy Mitford's famous glossary definition of "U and non-U" terminology, the "U" standing, of course, for "upper class." If you were an "upper class" Jew (meaning a Jew with money), you passed for a "U" with Florence. So rich families who seemed more secularized and integrated, like the Rothschilds and the Wildensteins, were acceptable faces in Florence's lexicon. The poor, bedraggled Eastern European Jew, unable to speak the language, scrabbling for food or the means to make a living, devoid of friends or country, belonged to another past and future, and would never have crossed the threshold of any of Florence's homes.

That is not to say she shunned the poor. She was always good to her staff, who invariably arrived poor, if not Jewish. It was one of the many contradictions in Florence's personal world, where the poor were universally rejected unless they were *her* poor. As for the Jews, in her own strange brand of "evenhandedness," they were deserving of rejection, too, so long as they were not *her* Jews. Florence was, after all, a people collector. She chose to paste her own labels on those whom she met to suit their tastes.

Such caveats, however, isolated Florence into an ever-decreasing minority. As the Reich squeezed the lifeblood from its Jews, many sought refuge in France. Paris's Jewish population had doubled by 1936 to 150,000, as had the overall Jewish population of France to some 330,000 souls.* Where anti-Semitism fell away in the immediate aftermath of the Great War, because Jews served and died alongside other Frenchmen, the collective and favorable French memory became sorely taxed by the sudden influx of Jewish immigrants from Germany who spoke little or no French. The situation would only worsen as Germany made its conquests in the east.

◌∽

---

* France's 1936 population was approximately 41.9 million. *Source:* 1999/2003 "populstat" site: Jan Lahmeyer.

The fascist press was led by Charles Maurras's royalist and Catholic Action Française, in which it was impossible to separate culture and politics. The likes of Robert Brasillach, who edited Maurras's most popular journal from 1937, *Je suis partout*, claimed that anti-Semitism was "an important element in the process of the identification of the 'natives' . . . and was a manifestation of the 'revolt of the natives' against the foreign."[11] This statement, expressed as French literature, turned the violent and irrational into the reasonable. Fear spiraled and overpowered the population.

Few Frenchmen and women understood the implication of the Nuremberg Laws enacted by the Third Reich on September 15, 1935. Suddenly, anyone with a single Jewish grandparent was classed as Jewish. Anyone married to a Jew was urged, not so politely, to divorce on the grounds of the spouse being a Jew. Any children of that union were earmarked for the eventual "Final Solution," already actively researched by the hierarchy of the Nazi party before the war. Longstanding German supporters of Hitler, like Cornelius Gurlitt, whose son was Hitler's art dealer Hildebrand Gurlitt, fulminated, "My sons, I have to make statements, whether we are Aryans. This is very difficult because no one knows what an Aryan is. Was our ancestor, the monk Matinus Gorlitius, a German or a Jew? How can I deny my beloved mother? We have given our lives to Germany . . . there are four Iron Crosses in the family."[12]

This would become a familiar, ignored outcry throughout the occupied territories of the Reich by Jews, Freemasons, Gypsies, homosexuals, lesbians, bisexuals, and political opponents (including priests of the Catholic church) until the end of hostilities in May 1945. Florence most likely brushed aside the rise in anti-Semitism and horror stories from the east. They did not directly concern her. Besides, politics rubbed against the lifelong cultivated grain that Florence enjoyed: having a good time in high society.

That was a mind-set Florence shared with many others in the "U" world of galas, gaiety, and folly. Many believed that the German fascist wave would not affect them. How could it? Granted, while Florence socialized with the Duke and Duchess of Windsor, whose pro-Hitler stance made many a jaw go slack in despair in Britain and America, she was more interested in remaining at the heart of le Tout-Paris and le Tout-

Riviera, surrounded by her fashionable royalist and literary friends, than considering her world was about to end.

∽

By 1936, it had become increasingly impossible—even for Florence—to avoid the political turmoil. The Front Populaire of Léon Blum awakened the political spirit among her employees. At the beginning of July, all the personnel at the hotels, casinos, and restaurants in Cannes, Antibes, and Juan-les-Pins went on general strike to get their paid vacations and other improvements in employment that Blum had passed into law. The strike lasted for fifteen days. Much as during the general strike in the United Kingdom in 1926, it was all high-society hands to the deck. At the bar of the Palm Beach casino, Florence and her friends mixed cocktails themselves to the rattle of their jeweled wrists, the casino chits jingling in their pockets, and baptized their concoctions as "Bada-Blum" or "CGT King."*

Coinciding with the strikes, Florence decided it was time to glean her knowledge of what the politics of the future would hold, firsthand. So she acquired a taste for politicians, if not politics. The Belgian minister for transport, Marcel-Henri Jaspar, and the future general secretary for Quai d'Orsay, Hervé Alphand, were among her many conquests. Adding politicians to her litany of lovers provided her with the proverbial "killing two birds with one stone." She felt they could give chapter and verse on what was *really* happening, without her having to dedicate vast swathes of time and energy to reading about it—time that was better spent on fun and her investments. What better way to mix sex with pleasure? she mused.

Still, Florence did not give up her "pretty boys" or other friendships or her love of waterskiing, as seen in her devotion to her dim but gorgeous waterskiing instructor, Georges Ducros. Aged thirty-three, Ducros had been the European champion for the previous three years, and famously taught Florence the finer art of his "tricks" or "figures," which included dance-steps, a ten-yard jump, and other acrobatics while waterskiing.[13] Undoubtedly, the handsome Georges also taught her other tricks and contortions in the boudoir.

---

* The CGT is the Communist Union in France.

As war became increasingly inevitable in 1937, Florence divided her time between the hotels, restaurants, and casinos that comprised the Gould empire, acting as its main administrator. Frank had little energy and less inclination to travel, and especially had no desire to keep up with his wife. His mental capacity was diminishing, and was intermittently fogged by the effects of his increasing infirmity. Indeed, until the war broke out, there are very few sightings of Frank in Florence's company publicly.

Then a peculiar and deadly incident occurred in June 1937. The Italian anti-fascist exiled in Paris, Carlo Rosselli, went to the Goulds' hotel and casino in Bagnoles-de-l'Orne in Normandy to take a cure for his phlebitis. Rosselli not only headed a contingent of Italian volunteers to fight in Spain where he was wounded, but also developed a non-Marxist ideology he called "liberal socialism" and founded his own journal called *Giustizia e Libertà*, published in Paris.

After a week at the hotel, taking his mud cure in the morning, working in the afternoon, taking a drive, then going to the casino at night, on the afternoon of June 9, Rosselli and his historian brother, Nello, who had just joined Carlo to warn him of an attempt on his life, were gunned down. An unexploded bomb was found in the car. Had Florence whispered Rosselli's presence in Bagnoles-de-l'Orne—intentionally or not—into the wrong ears? By 1937, she was reputedly known for lacking discretion in some circles, especially after an evening of swilling champagne. Whether by design, poor investigation, fear, or her friends in high places, Florence was never questioned. The final verdict on the brothers' deaths was that they were assassinated by the Cagoule—an extreme-right sect known for their hooded capes. They were also tied to the French secret services and the secret society CSAR (Comité Sécret d'Action Révolutionnaire).[14] Given the affiliation, perhaps, too, if Florence spoke intentionally out of turn, it might have been part of the payoff demanded by the Deuxième Bureau to keep the Nice casino open. If the leak had been unintentional, then her gaffe was made almost certainly after midnight, when bottles of champagne made her less circumspect—not that she was ever known for her ability to keep a secret. It is quite possible that Florence never knew the truth of the situation herself, since she had become a habitual heavy drinker during her nocturnal escapades. As she traveled throughout France in her white convertible Hispano-Suiza, visiting some of their 1,200 glacier cafés, fifty hotels, numerous casinos, chocolate factory Rozan in Clermont-Ferrand, and various other real estate investments, she would not have thought about the incident twice.

Besides, she'd recently bought a new duplex apartment at 2 boulevard Suchet, a few fistfuls of doors away from the Duke and Duchess of Windsor. Ignoring Frank's wishes that it should be traditionally decorated, she decked it out instead in the latest art deco style with sleek, clean lines and modern furniture. Frank visited her there only as a matter of necessity, preferring a small apartment he kept elsewhere in Paris, where he could recall happier times when he could lure his mistresses for trysts. Now infirmity played on his nerves, exasperating him. In ever-failing health, Frank found it increasingly hard to muster the power it took to overrule his wife.

So her willfulness toward Frank deepened, with Florence's nightly social events among two or three hundred of her best friends (though not all at once) increasingly absorbing her. Parties would begin at the boulevard Suchet apartment, then roll on to Paris's nightclubs of the moment, Chez Florence or Chez Casanova or Chez Sheherazade, where the revelers would be joined by dozens of other "great friends" to dance and swizzle champagne until dawn, before adjourning to Les Halles for the mandatory onion soup.

At her Granville casino, Florence participated in the automobile "concours d'élégance." In Paris, her favorite haunts remained Maxim's for dinner or the Ritz for high tea. Even the Anschluss—the unifying of Austria and Germany—in March 1938, could not dampen Florence's social engagements, or her purchases from her friend Chanel or those of Jeanne Lanvin, a relation by marriage to Winnaretta Singer.

∽

Had Florence and her pals realized that Hitler's fifth columnists were infiltrating their ranks? Did they even care? Coco Chanel, while a brilliant couturier, was essentially a snob and headstrong, like Florence. Unlike Florence, she was a raging anti-Semite. Chanel did precisely as she wanted, when she wanted, with whom she wanted. As Europe plunged headlong toward war, Chanel's friends like Florence, the fashion editor Marie-Louise Bousquet, the expressionist painter Marie Laurencin, and society hostess Marie-Laure de Noailles were all adopted as part of the "führer's social brigade" sponsored by the "charming blond, blue and starry eyed" Otto Abetz. Foremost among this social brigade attached to the German embassy was an aristocrat, Baron Hans von Dincklage, nicknamed "Spatz" by his friends. The only problem was that von Dincklage had been in Paris since 1933, working as an agent for Hitler's intelligence operation, the Abwehr. Spatz was also among the many Aryan Germans to dump his Jewish wife, and subjugated French women to his clandestine work. In a 1935 Deuxième Bureau report, his maid, a member of a Nazi cell in Paris, apparently spied from von Dincklage's Riviera home at Sanary-sur-Mer. His villa was conveniently placed for espionage on all naval movements in and out of the military port of Toulon across the bay.[15] By 1938, he was Chanel's newest lover. Pillow talk traveled from Chanel's Place Vendôme apartment straight to Ribbentrop, and on to Hitler.

That said, Otto Abetz was the primary conduit to Ribbentrop, taking the literati of Paris into his web. It was easy for him to get to know writers and publishers, since his wife, Suzanne, was secretary to the influential right-wing journalist and owner of *Notre Temps* Jean Luchaire. In the guise of saving France from its socialists, Luchaire and Abetz became friends. Through the work of writer Annie Jamet, they founded the Cercle Rive Gauche, which organized conferences and discussion groups including the likes of Drieu de la Rochelle, Brasillach, Maurras, Jacques Benoist-Méchin, and Henry de Montherlant, as well as teams from the right-wing press. Many were published, wined, and dined in Germany throughout the autumn of 1938, and were thrilled with their newfound German market.

With a modicum of foresight, much less hindsight, the six-week-old Munich Agreement, declaring "peace in our time," was shattered by the events of Kristallnacht. Although the mass destruction of synagogues, Jewish places of work, and the rounding up of Jews throughout Germany were theoretically in retaliation for the shooting in Paris of the German diplomat Ernst vom Rath by a Polish Jewish teenager, Herschel Grynszpan, Florence and many of her friends believed the latest anti-Semitic violence had little to do with them.

Foresight, however, prevailed. When Abetz returned to France at the beginning of April 1939, he met his loyal followers of the CFA at the Hôtel Crillon on place de la Concorde. Among the invited guests were Gaston Henri-Haye, ambassador to the United States, and Melchior de Polignac. They were under observation by the French Deuxième Bureau, Henri-Haye said. Abetz was stunned by the uncomfortable questions posed by René de Chambrun and Pierre Benoit among others, and sensed that the CFA as "an instrument of propaganda and spiritual conquest" would implode. In May, it held its last heated meeting with the membership divided between closing down and continuing with its Franco-German rapprochement, now that the Nazi flag flew over Prague in an overt act of war. That June, Abetz was asked to leave the country, pronto.[16]

On July 1, 1939, without so much as waving Abetz good-bye, Florence and others in the "führer's social brigade" were among seven hundred close friends of the American hostess Elsie de Wolfe (married to the retired British diplomat Sir Charles Mendl) invited to de Wolfe's "circus party" in Versailles. In fact, only le Tout-Paris was invited, with the septuagenarian Elsie dressed to the nines as the circus ringleader with a diamond and aquamarine Cartier tiara, brandishing her whip, "as if to defy the fates" amid elephants draped in their Indian finery, led by handsome herders dressed scantily in only a loincloth.[17] Florence planned her entrance meticulously for weeks, ordering her costume from Lanvin.

But she hadn't reckoned on Frank arriving from the Riviera and demanding that just the two of them dine alone that same evening. Later her story was that there was no scene, no counter-demands, nor any fuss. She did just as Frank commanded, accompanying him to the Café de Paris, and afterward to Les Ambassadeurs before returning to their mansion at Maisons-Laffitte. That evening was the first of many "important" discussions about how to face the coming war and what their options might be. New York was back on the table for Frank, if not for Florence, and leaving Europe was a prospect both needed to reconsider. Again, according to Florence, he kissed her good night asking her to please be ready at eleven in the morning. For her disappointment, hidden so well the night before, he reputedly rewarded her with a visit to Cartier to buy her a magnificent diamond.[18]

19

FALL OF FRANCE

There are three non-military objectives to be controlled right away: Communism, the haute banque, the NRF.

—OTTO ABETZ, 1940

THERE HAD BEEN TWO FALSE ALARMS IN PREPARING FOR WAR IN France, the first in March 1938 when the British refused to back the French calls to intervene militarily to protect Czechoslovakia, and the second six months later, in September, with the Munich Crisis. Many viewed the August 26, 1939, alarm as another drill. It wasn't. On September 3, 1939, both France and the United Kingdom declared war on Hitler's Germany for invading Poland. The soldiers who gathered at Paris's Gare de l'Est railway station, decked out in their uniforms and steel helmets—but still carrying family blankets, clean socks, and handkerchiefs along with food from home—headed to their northern and eastern fortresses. Not for long. During the "Phony War," which lasted until May 10, 1940, soldiers watched and waited. Parisians, no longer able to kid themselves that war could be averted, nervously tried to get on with their daily lives.

The winter of 1939–1940 was one of the most ferocious on record in Europe, with temperatures in northern Spain reaching zero degrees Fahrenheit. While housewives complained of frozen spigots, soldiers at the front—watching and waiting—were freezing in the Siberian winter. Society ladies contributed what they could to relieve the suffering of France's soldiers, and foremost among these was Florence Gould. "We keep warm as best we can," Pierre Dux, a former member of the Comédie-Française, wrote in thanks to Florence, "with whatever falls into our hands, like vandals, including old furniture . . . parquet flooring, and by emptying the rum barrels that our Marianne of war sends to us, the generous Mrs. Frank Jay Gould."[1]

Yet before the real fighting began that spring, Florence suddenly rushed back to Nice on hearing that her mother had been hospitalized. They had remained close, if not always confidantes, or in each other's company. Florence had fulfilled her mother's dreams of their living well and becoming part of le Tout-Paris. If Berthe still disapproved of her daughter's wilder side, there is no record of any rift between them. On the contrary, Berthe lived among the Riviera's high society thanks to Florence's, and of course Frank's, largesse. Sadly, Berthe died on April 16, 1940, of heart failure before Florence arrived. Both Florence and Isabelle, dressed in designer black with black veils covering their faces, accompanied their mother's body back to Paris for burial at the Montparnasse Cemetery— allegedly in the same crypt where their father had been transported back for burial in 1911. For both, it was the end of an era, if not an end to the fictitious family history.

Isabelle, dark and slender, had never married. It is possible that her sexual preferences did not lie in that direction. Equally, she may well have preferred to live close to Frank, without commitment, and with his millions at her disposal. Many wagging tongues presumed that she had moved to the south of France to keep Frank company, rather than to look after her mother. Often, Isabelle could be heard at le Tout-Riviera parties, taunting her sister, wondering what artworks, books, or money Florence would leave her when she died. After Berthe's death, Isabelle was often seen at La Vigie in Cannes, or in Frank's company, walking along the beach.[2] Cécile Tellier would, of course, remain in Florence's employ, and was sent to make herself useful to Frank, ensconced at Juan. The increasingly infirm Frank was surrounded and catered to by Florence's staunchest allies. First and foremost was Magdeleine Homo, and now, Cécile Tellier.

∽

Meanwhile, France was facing its greatest threat. So, like many of the Parisian gratin, Florence responded to the national cry for volunteers to help make ready for the inevitable, preparing medical supplies, stock-piling food for the troops, working alongside her friend Hedwige princesse Sixte de Bourbon-Parme. As soon as the fighting began in May, she volunteered at Paris's Val-de-Grâce Hospital as a nurse. Arriving each day in her blue Bugatti, she was adorned with her ever-present pearls and bedecked with emerald and diamond brooches, jeweled rings, and gold bracelets to take up her duties. Florence claimed that one day when they ran out of bandages, she cut up her Lanvin blouse. Often, she would bring her chauffeur into the wards to help dispense champagne and foie gras to the wounded—of course flaunting the early food and fuel ration-ing. At times, she spontaneously gave jewels she had put on that day, or brought bottles of Joy perfume,* or some "old" evening gowns (worn a handful of times at most) to the staff nurses. Florence exuded an air of unreality and gaiety that must have made the staff nurses and patients wonder if she was some scary apparition or a fairy godmother. Even Frank moaned that "we used to talk about sports and parties in this house, but today we only talk of medicine and surgery." Still, Florence's parties continued undampened in spirit.[3]

In mid-May, the French ambassador to Madrid and "Hero of Ver-dun" Maréchal Philippe Pétain was recalled to a Paris in meltdown to become France's new prime minister. A military hero was just what was needed to lead France's army—the largest in Europe. The Goulds must have taken heart at Pétain's appointment. He was their next-door neigh-bor in Juan.

When the fighting began, defeat piled upon defeat and within days Florence and Frank cabled their legal team in New York. Their bags were packed; their passage booked; and they wanted to return home. When the reply came, they could be forgiven for reeling: The Internal Revenue Service awaited their arrival to discuss nonpayment of taxes. The cable

---

* Jean Patou's Joy perfume first appeared in 1929 and was the first fragrance marketed for its high price. It was a huge success, despite the biting Depression, and was voted "Scent of the Century" in 2000 by the Fragrance Foundation FiFi Awards—beating Chanel's No. 5.

may not have added "to take you in for questioning," but given the tax battles that followed, it was something that would have preyed on their minds. What could they do? Stay in France facing an extremely uncertain future, or return to the United States to face humiliation or worse. Perhaps things wouldn't be so bad after all with Pétain? At the end of the day, France had Europe's most powerful army. Perhaps, too, Florence could charm the old womanizer Pétain if need be?

While they mulled over their bleak horizons, by the end of the first week in June it was obvious that France would fall. Within days, the unthinkable happened. The French Army and the British Expeditionary Force were crushed in just six weeks after Denmark, the Netherlands, and Belgium fell to Hitler's Blitzkrieg. The only saving grace in the helter-skelter retreat to Dunkirk was the rescue of over 340,000 French, British, and Canadian soldiers by a ragtag flotilla of small ships that joined the Royal Navy. There were 469,000 casualties—including British forces—in the Battle of France. Approximately 350,000 French casualties including 112,000 dead, 225,000 wounded, and 12,000 missing in action in the short campaign, marking the bloody statistic for posterity. By June 14, it was all over. The Swastika flag of the Third Reich was raised along the Champs-Élysées and elsewhere in Paris. The city, however, had become a ghost town of empty streets and closed shutters to welcome Hitler's heroes.

As the German philosopher and writer Friedrich Schiller said, "No Emperor has the power to dictate to the heart." Millions of French citizens fled before the Wehrmacht's onslaught, often with less than an hour to spare in their race to freedom. Those who had time packed their scant belongings onto carts or baby buggies or simply took to the roads acting as their own packhorses. Unfinished meals were left on tables, as cherished family photographs were scooped up in the rush to escape. The northeast city of Lille, a bustling metropolis of 200,000 souls, lost over ninety percent of its residents in one afternoon. There would be no heroic Battle of the Marne in this war. By three a.m. on June 10, outriders had cleared the way for the government cavalcade to reach the small town of Gien on the River Loire, following the national art collection and other treasures into exile.[4] The Belgian gold treasury, sent to France for safekeeping, had been shipped to Dakar, capital of the French colony of

Senegal. France sent its own gold reserves to the United States.[5] On June 17, 1940, Pétain's voice crackled over the airwaves. The old man spoke as if reading from a crumpled note. At the request of the president, he announced he'd taken over the leadership of the government of France. "It is with a heavy heart," Pétain continued, "that I tell you today it is necessary to cease fighting." It was a unilateral decision, taken without consulting his generals or Churchill. Much of the government fled into exile again, this time to French North Africa.[6] Only Pétain and his henchman, former premier Pierre Laval, remained to form—they hoped—a new government in cooperation with the Nazi occupying regime.

Watching from the American embassy windows, the U.S. ambassador to France, William Bullitt, observed that the Nazis' "hope is that France may become Germany's favorite province—a new *Gau* which will develop into a new Gaul."[7] Bullitt, who had a radiant smile to match Florence's, and oozed old money from Philadelphia, rented the Parisian ambassadorial residence from her. Naturally, since Bullitt was footloose after his divorce from journalist Louise Bryant,* he had hardly asked his landlady to help show him the social ropes in France before becoming one of her conquests. Frequently seen with Florence at her favorite haunt, Maxim's, and at embassy balls, Bullitt was previously the U.S. ambassador to the Soviet Union before he was selected by President Roosevelt for the important follow-up assignment in France. He was Florence's kind of guy, too. Not only was he fun-loving, intelligent, and handsome—if balding—but he had FDR's ear. What made him even more attractive was that Florence, after receiving the bad news from the IRS, hoped Bullitt might be the man who could smooth the choppy waters hampering the Goulds' return to the United States.

Yet it was not to be. While Bullitt was the latest politician enlisted into her own private army for survival, he was a man aware of his loss of power in the maelstrom. When Bullitt told Florence about the wholesale looting of private collections across Europe by the art dealers working

---

* Louise Bryant was a journalist and author of *Six Red Months in Russia* as well as the widow of John Reed, author of *Ten Days That Shook the World* about the Russian Revolution. When Bullitt discovered his wife's lesbian affair with English sculptor Gwen Le Gallienne, he divorced her and was awarded custody of their daughter, Anne.

for Hitler, she asked him to please take two valuable tapestries into the embassy vault for safekeeping before the Germans took Paris. The compliant Bullitt was more than happy to be of service.[8] Later, however, Florence would tell a different story.

⁂

As was often the case, Florence's contradictory behavior frequently engendered confusion in peoples' minds. Yet in studying her actions rather than her words, some of her contradictions melt away. After the war, Florence claimed that she had taken part in the "exodus" of the tens of thousands from Paris with the nursing service of the Val-de-Grâce Hospital to Bordeaux, and "then went to the Caserne de Chanzy at Bergerac. . . . On 22 August 1940, I left Bergerac with my family to go to Juan-les-Pins where I remained until September 1940." Florence then said that she "returned to Paris at the time that the officers belonging to the reserve were recalled."[9] France had all but capitulated by the time of the exodus, so her claim that the French officers were being recalled was intended to mislead.

In fact, much of what she later claimed was hardly more than a thin tissue of lies and half-truths. In the particular instance quoted, if, as Florence alleged, she left the stricken capital with the nursing services in mid-June, when and how did she come to find her "family" when private lines of communication were at their worst? More important, why would she have told her friends after the war that she had been at Juan-les-Pins at the time of the fall of Paris?[10] Worse still, how could a Yugoslav officer known only as Vionovitch write her laissez-passer from the Occupied Zone to Juan-les-Pins, which "arrived in an envelope in the mail coming from Vichy," as she told her interrogators after the war?[11] There was no such mail service at the time. Her statements stand out as bald lies when considering that the new French government at Vichy came into being on July 10, 1940, by which time shadowy Vionovitch was allegedly in London with the Gaullist "government in exile."[12]

These are only the first of many dozens of serious contradictions that Florence would later swear to under oath to the Allies. What is clear is that as France was being carved into "Occupied" and "Free" zones, Florence and Frank decided, perhaps reluctantly, that they would take their chances with the Germans. After all, America was not at war with Germany. But the occupation decree of late June 1940 that "French nationals who had fled the country between May 10 and June 30" no longer had any rights enjoyed by French citizens, and that "their property could be seized and liquidated for the benefit of the French 'Secours National'" might have influenced their decision to remain.[13] While Vichy opposed the decree, believing it still represented France's independent voice, their protests served no purpose.

By mid-July, Frank would have been contacted as the local agent for the Banque de France by its new master, Karl Schaeffer. Schaeffer was now the most important person in the economic occupation of the country. Appointed to his post on July 8, 1940, Schaeffer either sent an emissary to see Frank or contacted him personally. Known as the "Eye of Berlin in Paris" he never wasted any time in exercising all his powers of investigation and action, as any experienced national banker in similar circumstances would do.[14]

∾

Florence's fellow travelers took different routes to find shelter, regroup, and try to make sense of the catastrophic turn of events. Countess Marie-Laure de Noailles[*] refused to leave her Parisian mansion for fear of losing her art collection of Veronese, Goya, and Rubens paintings to the looting Nazis.[15] Coco Chanel paid for Jean Cocteau and his actor partner Jean Marais to live in luxury at the Ritz, and soon joined them in her own suite as soon as the fighting began. Only those sympathetic to the Nazis could live there. The couturier also immediately closed her Paris fashion house. It was not the time to consider fashion, Chanel said.[16]

Meanwhile, Florence arranged for Baron Édouard de Rothschild and his wife; Arletty and her children; her friend Antoinette d'Harcourt; and Hervé Alphand, financial adviser to the French embassy in Washington, D.C., to flee to the Gould home at Maisons-Laffitte. Undoubtedly, Florence felt that hiding her friends, including the Jewish Rothschilds and Arletty (who had been married to the Jewish swindler

---

* De Noailles was nicknamed "la vicomtesse rouge" *not* because of any leftist leanings, but rather for a bloodthirsty affair when she sucked the lifeblood out of the young composer Igor Markevitch.

Stavisky), was not an act of bravery (which it was) but was rather something a friend should do. Florence's private code of ethics swung in favor of the vulnerable this time. Later in the war, she was reputed to have hidden downed Allied pilots, too, although neither Florence nor any pilots ever came forward with the proof.[17]

Others with something to fear fled as well. Colette took her daughter and went to the Château de Curemonte in Corrèze near Limoges. Matisse headed for the Riviera and Picasso to Royan, to weather the Nazi storm. Winnaretta Singer, the aged Princesse de Polignac, found herself in England at the time the Blitzkrieg against France began, and returned to the Wigwam near Torquay in Devon, where she wrote to her niece, Marie-Blanche, "my father came from Paris in 1870, fleeing the Germans and the Commune. . . . I feel less dispossessed [here] than elsewhere in England, where I spent my childhood. . . ."[18] Prince Jean-Louis de Faucigny-Lucinge, that wealthy jack-of-all-trades, was now a member of the French Economic War Mission in London, having joined Charles de Gaulle's "outlaws," as Pétain called them. Faucigny-Lucinge tried, unsuccessfully, to bring the Princesse de Polignac back to France.

The armistice agreement between France and Germany was signed on the evening of June 24, 1940, in the same railway carriage in the forest of Compiègne where Germany was humiliated by signing the Versailles Treaty, just a tad over twenty-one years earlier. A separate armistice agreement was signed by Pétain, effectively "willing" two-thirds of France to the Third Reich. A line west of Cheverny at the Loire was drawn southward to the Spanish border. The Atlantic and Channel coasts were to remain part of the Occupied Zone, with the Mediterranean coastline in France's "Free Zone" of Vichy. The new American ambassador to Vichy was Admiral William Leahy, an old friend of Frank's, who set up shop in the Gould palatial residence, Villa Inca, in the town.[19]

Simultaneously, the German high command sequestered hundreds of buildings in Paris and elsewhere to house their new machinery of state. The Luftwaffe took over the Ritz Hotel; the Gestapo, the Hôtel Le Meurice across from the Jardin des Tuileries. The Kunstschutz (ironically, this translates as the Art and Monuments Protection Office) was headquartered along with the Military Authority at the Hôtel Majestic on avenue Kléber. Counterespionage activities were based out of the splendid art nouveau Hôtel Lutetia, on Paris's Left Bank. The fearsome Jewish affairs bureau, or IEQJ,* sequestered the former headquarters of the Jewish art dealer Paul Rosenberg, at 21 rue de la Boétie. Rosenberg had already fled for his home near Bordeaux, and was en route to New York with his entire family. Finally, Otto Abetz, returned in style as the German ambassador to France, ordering only the best pieces of furniture and artworks to adorn the embassy, from the collections of Edouard de Rothschild, and the French art dealers and collectors Paul Rosenberg, François-Gérard Seligmann, David David-Weill, Alphonse Kann, and Josse and Gaston Bernheim-Jeune.

The Gould estate at Maisons-Laffitte and the divine duplex apartment at 2 boulevard Suchet were also sequestered by the German high command, along with the Goulds' other investment properties in the heart of Paris. The 2 boulevard Suchet duplex would eventually become the Paris home of the German navy, which also paid through the nose for the exclusive rights to Rozan Chocolats in a deal with Florence.[20] However, in 1946, Florence told her American interrogators that she had gone to Maisons-Laffitte in the company of a Swiss friend, Jean Guisan, where "two Adjutants of the municipality appeared and asked me for the requisition of the property. I told them that I was a neutral. I arranged this affair amicably and they gave me three weeks to remove all the objets d'art."[21]

There are several curious and later contradictory statements that stem from this period, too. Florence claimed that the ERR,† the art-looting operatives, under the command of Dr. Kurt von Behr's offices at avenue d'Iéna and led by General Franz Medicus, searched the house at Maisons-Laffitte for a cache of weapons early in 1941. The problem remains that ERR never searched for weapons, only valuable artworks. Nor was General Medicus an art expert. Of course, no weapons were concealed. Still, a fifteenth-century "valuable triptych and two precious single pieces were found." To save these from pillage, Florence maintained that if she agreed with General Franz Medicus then and there to offer the triptych to Göring, that he would, in turn, gift it to the Cluny

---

* Institut d'Études des Questions Juives.
† Einsatzstab Reichsleiter Rosenberg.

Museum in Paris "to which the Gould family had intended to will it." The two single and precious ivory pieces would remain in Göring's possession as recompense. "Mrs. Gould declared," so an official report by the German army states, "that she wanted to contribute the entire stock of wine for the soldiers on the Eastern Front; all the copper and brass, which filled an enormous cellar room . . . to [the] German war industry."[22]

However, this reported deal occurred much later in Paris, in March 1942 to be precise, once Florence was ensconced within the German hierarchy, and living a life of ease at Paris's Hôtel Bristol.[23] At that time, Kurt von Behr was no longer attached to the ERR, much less the Kunst-schutz, which, under the sympathetic Count von Metternich, truly tried to protect art in the first year of the occupation, until Metternich was transferred. From January 1942, von Behr, always decked out in his Red Cross uniform, headed the odious confiscation of Jewish and other "ownerless" property in France, codenamed M-Aktion.[24]

Another query arises from Florence's earlier reported date of the looting. If the confiscation of Florence's artworks occurred in early 1941, the former head of the "führer's social brigade" who was now Germany's ambassador, Otto Abetz, could have undoubtedly still intervened. Abetz and Florence had been well acquainted since 1934, and she would have felt that the only honorable thing for Abetz to do was to rescue her as the eponymous damsel in distress. But by March 1942, the ERR was operating under the misguided hand of Dr. Hermann Bunjes, and Abetz held no further power to either restitute or loot for his own account.

There was no love lost between Abetz and the ERR, who were con-stantly vying for power. Why hadn't the diligent and honest Count von Metternich, who was still involved at the Kunstschutz in early 1941, in-tervened? The report describes valuable medieval artifacts, yet there are other things that are quite striking about this incident, too. The report is essentially about the Rothschild family's valuables. It is silent about who told the ERR that Edouard de Rothschild had hidden at the Gould man-sion at 5 avenue Picard, Maisons-Lafitte, as the Germans were dismem-bering Paris. Also, if Florence's artworks were indeed purloined by the greedy Field Marshal Göring, why were they never reported as being officially looted to either the French or American authorities after the war? Was this all some sort of window dressing in the event the Roths-childs got wind of Florence's complicity regarding their looted valuables? Or had they ever belonged to Florence in the first place? Was she claim-ing ownership to cover up the more heinous crime in German eyes of harboring Jewish refugees? "'Curiouser and curiouser,' cried Alice" in her *Adventures in Wonderland*, as anyone might do in trying to com-prehend the diverse accounts of this one incident, since Florence would tell a completely different story to the OSS* after the war.

Still more curious was how Florence managed to swing a semiperma-nent laissez-passer between the Occupied and Free zones, and, incredibly, unadorned access to gasoline from the first days of the occupation. The fairy tale she would weave into the imaginary fabric of her history after the war was that Frank was able to handle only the assets in the Free Zone of Vichy, while she could handle only their northern investments. Noth-ing could be further from the truth. Florence was, from the time of the occupation of France, in charge of absolutely everything in the Goulds' French empire.

---

* The Office of Strategic Services (OSS) was the precursor of the CIA, and its first head of opera-tions was General William ("Wild Bill") J. Donovan.

20

LUDWIG

*The truth is incontrovertible. Malice may attack it, igno-
rance may deride it, but in the end, there it is.*

—Winston Churchill

SOMETIME SHORTLY AFTER JUNE 14, 1940, A FORMER GERMAN
Luftwaffe officer, Ludwig Carl Adolf Vogel, arrived at Bordeaux to take
over the French airplane manufacturing plant there. Tall, handsome by
all accounts, fair, and in his mid-thirties, Vogel was put in charge of, or,
to use the new term, Aryanized, the Bordeaux-based aeronautics company, Société Nationale des Constructions Aéronautiques du Sud-Ouest,
or SNCASO. Its owner, known only as Mr. Francezon, was deported
eastward on Vogel's orders, never to be seen again. Madame Francezon, however, continued to live a subdued existence in an apartment at
135 avenue Malakoff in the sixteenth arrondissement of Paris.[1] Soon
enough, Vogel became her next-door neighbor at number 133, thanks
to Florence's money. He would also become Florence's most significant
lover during the war.

While he was in the same place at the same time as Florence from
the summer of 1940 onward, and equally able to provide her with her
first laissez-passer from the Occupied Zone to Vichy, or the Free Zone,

Florence maintained that she met Vogel only after she returned to Paris to live in 1941. Her maid, Marcela Arnaud, asserted that Vogel was introduced to Florence by Jean Guisan, a distant relation of General Alphonse Joseph Georges, who was serving in the Resistance in North Africa. Guisan was also related to the commander-in-chief of the Swiss army, Henri Guisan. Florence said that Vogel was introduced to her by Werner Klingeberg, Melchior de Polignac's old friend from the International Olympic Committee and the German games.[2] Klingeberg also headed the DNA, the entity in charge of the press and all censorship in occupied France. Its main office was located at the infamous Hôtel Majestic along with the SS at the RHSA's* headquarters there.

So who was Ludwig Carl Adolf Vogel?

He was born in Stuttgart on May 26, 1909. His first trip to the United States was in May 1928, when he shared accommodation with a friend, Reinhold Schempp, also from Stuttgart. For his first three months in New York Vogel worked at Will & Bauer Candle Company before moving on to Rochester to work at North East Electric Company until June 1929. He tried, unsuccessfully, to be accepted at Cornell University to study engineering. As the Great Depression hit hard, he was forced to migrate from factory to factory, finding die-casting work in Pittsburgh and Harrisburg, Pennsylvania, before finally landing in Newark, New Jersey. When the last factory shut down, Vogel looked for another job in the tristate area for two months without any luck, and so he returned to Germany. He made his way home by working as a member of the crew aboard a steamer.

In 1930, Vogel enrolled in the airplane mechanics technical school FAG (Flugtechnische Arbeitsgemeinschaft Gruppe), earning his certificate of airplane mechanical engineering in 1933. At the same time, he learned about aviation at the nearby Deutsche Luftfahrt. In 1932, he was awarded his pilot's license, category B-2, for single-engine airplanes of any size. He also received his acrobatics license, and soaring and gliding

---

* The DNA was short for the Deutsche Nachrichtenableitung, or the German news bureau. Heinrich Himmler was the director of the Reichsicherheitshauptamt (RHSA). The former led the battle of words. The latter's duty was to "fight all enemies of the Reich" inside and outside its borders.

certificates at the same time. Then he was employed in a glider school near Stuttgart that advertised widely throughout Europe and the United States to attract foreign clients. In March 1933, the newly elected Nazi government in Germany militarized the glider school. That's when, Vogel claimed, he left.

Applying to emigrate to the United States again in May 1933, Vogel was told at the American embassy that he had to first sort out his "exit permit" that the new Nazi Germany demanded. When it was requested, so Vogel later told the authorities, he was threatened that if he left the country, his parents would come to harm. That is certainly one explanation for his disappearance from view for two months.

That said, he re-enrolled in the flying school to obtain his C-2 license to fly multiengine aircraft, while also working as an instructor for single-engine aircraft pilots. In what seems to be a rather apocryphal story, Vogel asserted that he created a mutiny among the instructors of the flying school, where all of them refused to join the air force when personally confronted by General Werner von Blomberg in 1934. Vogel further alleged that their rebellion went unpunished for all other officers except himself—since he was the ringleader—and that he was sent to Ohrdruf concentration camp for four weeks to become more pliable. Vogel swore that he remained an ardent anti-Nazi.

The hero story continues. On his release, he was snapped up by Emil Kropf at Standard Oil in Hamburg. There, Vogel was employed to organize flights, supervise test runs, test engines, help write Standard Oil's aviation handbook, and obtain contracts for gasoline supply to German aircraft manufacturing facilities, including the Göring Corporation and Focke-Wulf.

In 1935, Vogel landed Focke-Wulf as Standard Oil's biggest client. That year, he made several trips for his new client to Austria, Hungary, Turkey, Romania, Norway, Denmark, Sweden, Spain, and Russia. Five years later, Ribbentrop traveled to Moscow with Vogel and introduced him to Stalin. Again, curiouser and curiouser. . . .

In the 1936 international Olympiad flying rally, Vogel flew the Standard Oil airplane and won. Officially, he claimed never to have worked for the Göring Corporation, nor did he mention it as a client of Standard

Oil, even though the Göring Corporation sent him to France in 1936 to set up its sales organization there. In addition, the Göring Corporation became heavily affiliated with Focke-Wulf by 1937. Instead, Vogel admitted that he worked for the Focke-Wulf Corporation from 1939 to 1944 in Paris. In truth, he quit Standard Oil in 1937 to become a test pilot and the head of all export activity for Focke-Wulf, and was promoted to head up their entire operations in France in 1938.[3]

Finally, Vogel averred that he helped the French resist the German war effort, keeping SNCASO, which he directed beginning in June 1940, from collaborating with Germany through various ruses. In fact, his resistance began in 1943, when it appeared impossible for Germany to win the war. Vogel did refuse to sabotage the factories he controlled in July 1944, as Hitler's orders demanded, but then again, General Dieter von Choltitz also disobeyed Hitler when ordered to set Paris ablaze.

At no time, Vogel stated, had he been a member of the Nazi Party.[4] He hated the Nazis. Evidently, his memory had become clouded by the war, until it was later jarred by the OSS, which revealed that his Nazi Party membership card number 1335256 showed his membership in the NSDAP from 1932 to August 1933, at precisely the same time he tried to immigrate to the United States, and that he had served in the Luftwaffe during this period.[5] Later, the FBI questioned if he was a failed spy who had at last found success with the Nazis in the late 1930s. Oddly, too, Vogel did not recall that he was responsible for the deportation to a concentration camp of SNCASO's main director, Mr. Francezon.

Whatever the truth of Vogel's interrogation statements made after the liberation of France, he was married to a German-Bolivian woman, Elfriede K. Elsner, and had fathered a daughter, Renate Vogel, by the time he met Florence. For a portion of his work, he reported directly to a man known only as Dr. Colonel Bosse of the secret Organisation Otto, who, in turn, headed the confiscation of certain highly prized metals and jewels. Additionally, Vogel had significant authority within the dreaded Organisation Todt, the mass construction and slave labor outfit. Interestingly, when Florence's Italian butler, Diego Zanini, who had been in her employ since April 20, 1937, received his papers to report to the

Organisation Todt to "serve the Reich" in 1940, it was at her behest that Vogel had him spared.[6] So much for meeting Vogel in 1941. Florence never dreamed that in asking Diego to sing her praises after the war, she was exposing her own untruths to investigators.

Still, Florence's maid since June 1940, Marcela Arnaud, swore she became aware of the liaison between Vogel and her mistress only in the summer of 1941. When Florence returned to Paris to live at the Hôtel Bristol, "people she knew, but who were not of her circle before the war," like Jean Guisan, visited her regularly at her suite of rooms at the hotel. Guisan, as a Swiss citizen, would become crucial to Florence's ability to fund her activities during the occupation, as he was able—somehow—to pass in and out of Switzerland at will to cash Florence's checks drawn on her American account. Like many opportunists during the occupation, Guisan successfully provided a valuable service to like-minded survivors.[7] It was a great symbiotic relationship.

Above all else, Florence was determined to survive and to thrive despite the occupation, just as she had done her entire life. If that meant joining the legions of women who chose *la collaboration horizontale*—bedding Germans for a better life—then so be it. And bed them she did. If it meant paying bribes, she would. At the outset, she may have seduced Vogel, fourteen years her junior, with the sole purpose of getting her laissez-passers and surviving well, but soon enough, the pair became a couple, and they couldn't spend enough time together. They were both survivors, both opportunists.

Frank, of course, asked to meet Florence's new addition to her gallery of lovers, and heartily approved. According to Vogel, by 1941 Frank was no longer able to fulfill his functions as a husband. Still, did Frank know that Florence was keeping company with some of the more notorious characters in the SD and Gestapo, like the dashing Helmut Knochen, the Sicherheitspolizei commander in Paris during the occupation, or General Carl Oberg, the pig-faced high commander and police leader of France—who deported 40,000 French Jews to certain death? There were others, of course, just as Vogel had other mistresses, like Emma Schlesser, whom he used to take to "parties" given by the ubiquitous Dr. Colonel Bosse at the Villa Brandt in the Bois de Boulogne.[8] Before the war was over, Florence, too, would attend the parties there—including the colonel's farewell-to-France party, held on July 26, 1944, a month before the liberation of Paris.[9]

Yet in 1940, when Florence took up her residence in Paris at the Hôtel Bristol, almost all this history was still before her.

21

〇〜〜〇

THE "ANYTHING GOES" OCCUPATION

The World's gone mad today, and Good's bad today . . .
—COLE PORTER lyrics to "Anything Goes"

HÔTEL BRISTOL WAS LEASED TO THE AMERICAN EMBASSY AS A refuge for the thousands of American citizens still living in France in 1940—as it was the only hotel that had been kitted out with an air raid shelter in its basement that was impervious to poison gas.[1]

Until that June, America's Ambassador William Bullitt had lived high on the hog and virtually without any American loss in the city. That is, if the ambassador's consignment of 150,000 cigarettes that fell into enemy hands a month earlier during the Battle of France didn't count.[2] Bullitt was nominated by the fleeing French government to declare Paris an open city to the Nazis; was an eyewitness to the formation of the Vichy government; and warned President Franklin D. Roosevelt that July that Maréchal Pétain believed the Third Reich would allow his government to be headquartered at Versailles instead of Vichy. Versailles could then be declared a sort of Vatican City, able to grant sanctuary as required to French citizens.[3] Naturally, the ambassador knew better and warned his closest American friends to get out. Friends like Florence Gould.

The sultry millionairess and the footloose, debonair American ambassador had been close since his arrival in Paris in October 1936. Although the hotline of her old friendship with Bullitt cooled with his departure on special assignment to President Roosevelt in July 1940, he had given her good pointers on how to adopt a lower profile should she obstinately refuse to leave France.

Florence was far from being the only American citizen to remain. Gertrude Stein and Alice B. Toklas joined the exodus and hid out in the Free Zone for the duration. Josephine Baker devoted her ample efforts to resisting and spying for the Allies from the get-go. Florence was otherwise inclined, unwilling to let politics or war get in the way of her life story. Yet, like many, she feared—or claimed to fear—the rough handling by the occupiers.

That said, friends of the occupation were, unexpectedly, treated with iron fists, while perceived enemies were not only tolerated, but courted as emblems of Nazi reasonability. Two extreme examples were writer Robert Brasillach and Pablo Picasso. The virulently anti-Semitic and fascist Brasillach joined the French army at the time of its mobilization, and was captured. He remained a POW in a camp reserved for French officers for ten months—just enough time to finish his play *Bérénice*. Brasillach was released in April 1941. Picasso, too famous to disappear into a camp as a degenerate artist with communist sympathies, eventually returned home to Paris, and had the most prolific period of his painting career.[4] Although clearly a master of "degenerate art," Picasso exhibited and continued his career as before the occupation. He, like Matisse, who remained on the Riviera, was offered asylum in the United States. Both refused.

Where Matisse endeavored to find "his own way to limit the moral shock of this catastrophe" through "the narcosis of work," artist Pierre Bonnard—Florence's favorite painter—tried to emulate Picasso. "I immediately went back to work so as to recover my equilibrium," Bonnard wrote from Nice in September 1940, "but here there are such low spirits, such widespread fear that Nice may be occupied at any moment that, through contagion, my work is difficult, unproductive."[5] In this confused atmosphere, the Salon d'Automne at the Orangerie took place as usual with works by French masters leading the rich tapestry of artists. Soon other art exhibitions followed, like the Salon des Indépendants and the

Salon du Dessin et de la Peinture à l'Eau, with living artists needing to declare that they were (a) French and (b) not Jewish, Freemason, or communist to exhibit their works. These salons required, of course, collaboration with the occupiers each step of the way. As the satirist Jean Galtier-Boissière put it, "Collaboration is: give me your watch and I'll tell you the time."[6]

In the literary world, writer André Gide believed in the Soviet ideal, until he went to the Soviet Union and wrote *Retour de l'U.R.S.S.* Gide was crestfallen at the total absence of freedom of thought there, stating, "I doubt whether in any other country in the world, even Hitler's Germany, thought be less free, more bowed down, more fearful (terrorized), more vassalized."[7] He wrote that in 1937. Gide took a different road than Picasso, and most French writers, by bolting to French North Africa.

Literary life in France was a cauldron of politically motivated viewpoints on the left and right long before the occupation. After, Jean-Paul Sartre claimed that there were only two stark options set before the French people: collaboration or resistance. He was guilty of oversimplifying the dilemma facing those who made their living through the arts. He also conveniently neglected to recall that he—who thought of himself and his coterie at Café Flore as resisters—staged his plays *Les Mouches* and *Huits clos* to audiences during the occupation.[8]

This was the troublesome nub of the problem. Were musicians, singers, dancers, and actors meant to cease work entirely and starve to prove they were good French men and women? Were writers to stop writing to prove they were not collaborators? Were publishers to cease all publications, putting their employees out of paid work and making them targets for the draft into the deadly Organisation Todt as slave laborers? Were restaurant owners to close; grocers to bar clients from buying food; trains and buses to stop; all to prove they were not collaborating with the occupier? Life, and any public interaction, imposed collaboration of some nature on the people of the Occupied Zone and Vichy alike. Jean Cocteau wrote in his diary three years into the occupation, "At no price should one let one's self be distracted from serious matters by the dramatic frivolity of war."[9] Florence agreed wholeheartedly with her friend Cocteau. Others took offense at the perceived decadence of these enfants terribles.

Brasillach returned to his fascist best with his pro-German, pro-Vichy journal, *Je suis partout* (*I am everywhere*), in which he verbally assassinated the former prime ministers Blum, Daladier, and Reynaud for France's humiliation, naturally spicing his deadly commentary with anti-Semitic diatribes. He hit a bull's-eye when he wrote that one of the greatest fears among French writers, artists, singers, dancers, and musicians was that they were passionate about French cultural institutions staying alive: operas must be played; French books must be written; French cinema must be acted and produced; French art auctions and art exhibitions must continue. For them, this was not collaboration. It was keeping France for the French. That the fabric of society was being "vassalized," in Gide's parlance, didn't matter. Florence convinced herself that she was doing her bit for French culture during the occupation, too.

∽

Otto Abetz perceived that there were three great powers in France: banking, the Communist Party, and the *Nouvelle Revue Française*. The first two were easily dispensed with by the occupation. Banks were taken over by the Reichsbank, and any Jewish bankers either went into hiding, emigrated, or were eliminated. Communists were on the same watch lists, and received an equivalent treatment, if caught, as political opponents of the Nazi ideal.

The *Nouvelle Revue Française*, however, was groomed and polished for the Nazi cause. Jean Paulhan, a secret resister, had been the editor of the *NRF*, as everyone called the publication, since 1925. This made him one of the most powerful men in France, since his magazine was adored by the French intelligentsia. Yet to continue with the *NRF*, its publisher, Éditions Gallimard, was forced to accept a deal with Abetz, whereby the German ambassador's good friend and pro-Nazi Pierre Drieu de la Rochelle would replace Paulhan. In exchange, Gallimard could continue to publish authors not particularly sympathetic to the Nazi cause, so long as they were not overtly anti-Nazi or Jews. Unsurprisingly, German classics and other propaganda publications made up for French proscribed books, keeping the figures for books published during the occupation artificially high.[10] Gaston Gallimard became one of the occupation's most cooperative, self-censoring puppets, under the pretext that at least French thought was assured of pursuing its mission. Paulhan, meanwhile, began the underground press Les Éditions de Minuit, with the print works often manned by Paulhan himself, at some considerable risk to life and limb.

Having bent the three most powerful forces in France to his will, Abetz turned his attentions to his first love—looting France's treasures—leaving censorship in the capable hands of the German Institute's chief, Karl Epting, and his Francophile head of literary censorship, Gerhard Heller. That's not to say that Epting, too, did not indulge in a bit of grand larceny, as was the Nazi predilection. While he tried to literally "break into" the lucrative art-looting trade, Count von Metternich of the Kunstschutz soon put a stop to Epting's disgraceful sideline. Where Epting succeeded, however, was in his thefts aimed at changing history: purloining thousands of documents for eventual destruction or rewriting from the Foreign Ministry, including the original signed Versailles Treaty, along with the table on which it was signed. Both were sent to Berlin as presents for Hitler, while the other documents awaited the Nazi Party's pleasure. In case there had been any doubt as to his motives, Epting told an assembled audience of French intellectuals soon after that they "must give up the idea of being world leaders."[11] With Abetz's full-blooded support, the German Institute became the heart of the new French cultural world.

Meanwhile, the German literary censor of the Propaganda-Staffel at 52 avenue Champs-Élysées, Gerhard Heller, became a great friend of Florence's, remembering her fondly in his retrospective biography of the occupation years, entitled *Un Allemand à Paris*, published in 1981. Undimmed by the passage of time, his memory of the occupation is nostalgic: dining pleasantly at the Ritz; having a good chinwag with his French author friends, like Jean Paulhan and Marcel Jouhandeau; or enjoying the sybaritic lifestyle as the invited guest of French *Harper's Bazaar* petite chain-smoking editor, Marie-Louise Bousquet, or Florence Gould. What Heller does reveal despite himself, however, is that the Wehrmacht had instantly halted all publishing from the time of the occupation until his arrival on the scene some four months later, with all manuscripts awaiting his censorship sword. Only those authors holding Nazi viewpoints were spared. Some 2,242 tons of books and manuscripts were pulped just on his say-so, in one of the greatest book-burning exercises of the war.[12] Despite his selective memory, Heller wielded tremendous power.

There were a few writers who somehow managed to maintain a sense of humor, and had the good sense to write it down for posterity. Drieu de la Rochelle was knocked off his crowing perch about his prediction of a German victory four months into the occupation by the journalist Jean Galtier-Boissière. Back in 1915, Galtier-Boissière had founded the satirical weekly paper *Le Crapouillot* while fighting in the trenches—the French version of the equally aptly named British *Wiper Times*. While Drieu was in full flow praising the new German ambassador, Galtier-Boissière spoke his mind—as he always did—and told Drieu to expect a long war and an English victory. Drieu met this incredible prediction with a Gallic shrug. Galtier-Boissière was relentless: "My dear Drieu, I'll bet that you will be shot." "What about you?" Drieu asked in reply. "Me too! But in my case . . . by mistake."[13]

Florence lived by Cocteau's maxim, believing that war and the occupation inconveniences could be overcome. She would remain true to her fun-loving, sexually charged, hedonistic self, sensing the game to be played as merely more exciting. With a king's fortune at her ready disposal, it rarely occurred to her that she was playing a deadly game. Even then, those lucid moments emerged from the whirligig of the upper crust's self-indulgence only when close friends were in danger, or finally, with the glaring recognition that Germany would lose the war. Arrogance had its virtues.

When she took up residence in the autumn of 1940 at the Hôtel Bristol, Florence continued to receive friends. At the outset, the only recognizable difference was that some of them were in a Nazi uniform. So, while the occupiers whitewashed France's everyday life of Jewish, communist, anti-Nazi, and Freemasonry influences, Florence went to

Maxim's with friends, nodding to Göring and Abetz seated nearby, or enjoyed the dining spectacle among the most select of le Tout-Paris at the sequined floorshows at Chez Carrère. Unashamed and fearless, she donned her best gowns and jewels when attending performances at the opera and ballet, and often went to see her old friends Mistinguett and Maurice Chevalier perform at the Comédie-Française.

Florence could not stop indulging herself. She attended auctions of "ownerless" and "degenerate" art, in Nazi parlance, bidding alongside Hitler's art dealers at Hôtel Druout, or down the road a hundred yards at Galerie Charpentier; sometimes winning, sometimes not, but always paying dearly. The definition of "ownerless" meant looted from Jews and other enemies of the state. On the other hand, "degenerate" meant modern, unfinished (like the paintings of the Impressionists), or not to Hitler's tastes. While the artworks became "ownerless," the Paris art market thrived.

Florence enjoyed going to lavish parties at the German embassy given by Abetz. Hobnobbing with Marie-Laure de Noailles and her salonnières in the film industry or attending the musical salon of Winnaretta Singer de Polignac's niece, Marie-Blanche, heir to the fashion house of Lanvin, or joining her friend Marie-Louise de Bousquet in her literary and musical salons made the occupation quite pleasant.

Most notoriously, Florence and Bousquet headed up a network of *souris gris*—"gray mice"—who were society women willing to prostitute themselves to high-ranking Nazi officials in exchange for all sorts of favors besides cool cash. To call them "mesdames" or "procuresses" would be to denigrate their role. Florence saw a business opportunity alongside Bousquet, and became her silent financial partner as well as an active participant in the "gray mice" scheme.[14]

Indeed, of all the women Florence befriended during the occupation, Marie-Louise Bousquet proved the most significant. The gray mice network had given Bousquet—and by extension Florence—unprecedented access to all the German high command, including the German navy, the German embassy in Vichy, the German secret service (counterespionage services) at the Hôtel Lutetia, and the German high command offices at Hôtel Crillon, offices of the *Kommandatur* of Greater Paris. Bousquet used Florence's apartment at 2 boulevard Suchet for her secret rendezvous with the pug-faced "Colonel Patrick"—better known as

Colonel Arnold Friedrich Garthe, chief of the Abwehrleitstelle (counter-espionage) of Paris. The friendship of the two women, abetted by their German lovers, enabled Florence to conclude a lucrative deal with the German navy for the exclusive rights to the chocolates manufactured at the Goulds' Rozan factory at Clermont-Ferrand. It was also instrumental in setting in train the machinery for Florence to become a first-class black marketeer.[15]

As any good businessperson would do, Florence developed her own connections from the earliest days of the occupation. Often in the background, facilitating and smoothing over the cracks in the pavement of this new, uncharted society, was a parade of Nazi lovers, each entrusted with a specific task by Florence. As she would later brag over a glass or ten of champagne, "men are not worth a great deal, they can be bought for very little."[16]

Werner Klingeberg, aged only thirty when Florence met him, fell for her charms from the outset. As a friend of Melchior de Polignac from their Olympic Committee days, Klingeberg was greeted warmly by Florence on her return to Paris in the autumn of 1940. Klingeberg was director of the 1st Kommando SS in Paris and was the first to provide her officially with many favors, beyond her freedom of movement proffered by his laissez-passers. Klingeberg became Florence's loyal barometer of who to trust, or not, within the Nazi hierarchy. He would introduce colleagues to her, one by one, with the intent of making the occupation as pleasant as possible for his part-time lover.[17] From Florence's perspective, Klingeberg and all other Nazi uniforms, save Ludwig Vogel, were men she used to protect her personal interests, her piles of gold, her collections, and her husband, who was integral to her continued good fortune.

Initially, Klingeberg used his lieutenant, George Kremling, to deliver the travel passes to Florence. Then, for some reason, a man known only as Captain Krausen of the rue de Galilee bureau entered the scene, replacing Kremling. Suddenly, Krausen demanded a 20,000-franc bribe for delivery of the passes. Additional permits allowing Florence to "bring funds from the South Zone" as well as a laissez-passer for her secretary, Mademoiselle Arnaud, were also included in Krausen's demand.[18] Later, Florence pretended that it was the mysterious Yugoslav Vionovitch who was directing these operations, not Klingeberg or Kremling. Within the year, however, it seems Kremling left Paris, having permanently blotted his record, and found himself posted to the punishing eastern front.

Another facilitator for Florence's passes was Walter Steffens, chief of information services at the Hôtel Claridge in Paris. Steffens worked directly for Colonel Garthe, Bousquet's lover.[19] Florence asserted that she was introduced to Steffens through the ever-industrious Jean Guisan. Later, Florence credited Guisan—again erroneously—with her introduction to Major Willy Praeger-Gretsch a counterintelligence officer based at the Hôtel Lutetia. Who could blame her for such misinformation? After all, she could hardly admit to outsiders that she was performing an essential service to the officers at the Lutetia through the gray mice network, could she?

Then Praeger-Gretsch "asked" Florence to hire a girl known only as Miss Galliard as her secretary for 2,500 francs a month, a short time later.* Florence complied, knowing that the girl was not only Praeger-Gretsch's mistress, but also a spy within her household.[20] Yet Florence continued to do as she wished, refusing to learn the art of discretion or the desire to dissemble. She knew she had become untouchable.

◦∕∘

Steffens was probably not Florence's lover, but rather someone tasked by the Nazis to discover the fate of the fifteenth-century tapestries that Florence had secured through Bullitt at the American embassy in Paris before the occupation. In a rather confusing story told after the war, Florence maintained that Maynard Barnes, a U.S. representative at Vichy, placed the tapestries in the already mothballed American embassy in Paris. This was a physical impossibility. Interestingly however, Steffens failed to report on the tapestries' whereabouts, and seemed unduly concerned about the Gould relationship with Admiral Leahy, the U.S. ambassador to Vichy, who was living in the Gould mansion in the town. Florence told Steffens repeatedly that Leahy was just an old friend of her

---

* An extortionate sum given that, in 1973, I was earning a "good salary" in France of only 1,800 francs a month as an executive secretary.

husband's.[21] Frank, meanwhile, remained at Juan-les-Pins, with Magde-leine Homo, Cécile Tellier, and Florence's sister, Isabelle.

Steffens was no freewheeler, out to get the Gould art for himself. He was asking on behalf of his greedy masters for the purposes of "safe-guarding" the tapestries and the rest of the valuable Gould collections. Frank had a fine medieval collection in his own right, acquired since the beginning of the century. While Florence's newer purchases were mainly Impressionist works, Göring and others had already traded works by Renoir, Monet, and Gauguin for their preferred Renaissance artists, or, if need be, in foreign exchange to buy armaments.

In Florence's dizzying, revolving door of German men between 1940 and 1942, only one remained constant: Ludwig Vogel. He traveled with Florence several times to the south of France to see Frank, and steadied the tiller through the rough waters of the early occupation, allowing Florence to continue to live exactly how she wanted. They were both like-minded individuals who held a strong attraction to one another.

Still, was it an honest relationship? Deeply buried in the archives of the DGER in Paris, Source D, as he is called in the OSS documents, states that Vogel was a Gestapo agent. Was Florence taken in by a handsome opportunist, or was she aware, as the DGER claimed later, that she con-veniently aided the Germans until 1943 in partnership with Vogel, then began helping the Allies when the outcome of the war was more certain?[22] Honesty and occupation are never easy travel companions.

Nonetheless, from October 1941, Florence and Vogel would become virtually inseparable. Florence, certainly, was deeply attached to him. He often stayed at Hôtel Bristol when Florence feared detention or arrest. Steffens warned her that year of several threats to the Gould businesses and to her personally. At Vogel's behest, she decamped to the Riviera for a month that spring.[23] Often she would tell her friends that she was vis-iting her husband at Juan-les-Pins when, in fact, she was staying with Vogel in his apartment at 133 avenue Malakoff.[24]

Vogel had his other attractions, too. As an "approved" black marke-teer of the Luftwaffe, he could lay his hands on virtually anything. Un-believably, when Göring put a stop to the laissez-faire activities of Germans who were impeding the war effort with their greed, Vogel sur-vived. How? He was part of Organization Otto, which would be tasked by Hermann Göring to head up *all* black markets throughout France after June 13, 1942. His direct superior and good friend, Dr. Colonel Bosse, was responsible for the section called MUNIMIM (MUNItions-MInisteriuM), located at 33 avenue Champs-Élysées. Its purchases were designated as metals, tools, machine tools, cables, milk products, butter, eggs, canned goods, and fresh vegetables.[25] Florence had chosen her lover well.

∽

Toward the end of 1941, many Parisians had grown accustomed to the "new normal" of food and fuel shortages. They dreaded another cold winter without coal or wood. France was paying 400 million francs a day to Germany for "maintaining" the occupation, for which the Germans exported crucial manufactured goods and foodstuffs without payment.

It had been eighteen months since anyone outside Florence's circle of friends had seen chocolate. A blend of roasted barley and chicory passed as coffee in cafés and at home. The ration of bread was a mere three-quarters of a pound a day; children had less than two pints a day of milk and adults had no milk; and butter was limited to six ounces per week, which made baking pastries a thing of the past. Stocks were low, and always outstripped by demand. Jean Guéhenno wrote in his book about the occupation, *On vit mal* (*Life Is Hard*), "A kilo of butter costs a thousand francs. A kilo of peas forty-five francs. A kilo of potatoes forty francs. Still, one must find them." By 1942, there was no coffee, chocolate, confectionary, or cooking fats available—even on the black market.

Les Halles, with the largest wholesale meat market in Paris, could no longer afford to display chicken, turkey, or even rabbit at any price. Two days before Christmas in 1940, Les Halles had been without any meat whatsoever for three days.[26] Yet Florence's table never lacked a thing. Nor did the restaurants like Le Tour d'Argent or Maxim's, frequented by le Tout-Paris and their Nazi masters.

Worse came that winter. With coal production more than halved, Paris froze. Florence and her lover Ludwig Vogel, however, prospered.

22

⟨∞⟩

IN THE GARDEN OF EARTHLY DELIGHTS

Happiness depends more upon the internal frame of a person's own mind than the externals of the world.

—George Washington

AS FRANCE BRACED FOR ITS SECOND WINTER UNDER THE OCCU-
pation, Florence began to see the light. Blind eyes, including Florence's,
were averted from Jews made stateless by the occupier's laws of October
1940. Jews alone, she believed, would have their possessions Aryanized,
with German or French Catholic managers put in their places.

Within two months of the fall of France, art gallery owners fell like
nine pins before the roaring Nazi machinery of state. The Bernheim-
Jeune gallery was sold for a few pennies on the dollar to a known collaborationist. Daniel Kahnweiler made his gallery over to his Catholic
sister-in-law, Louise Leiris. Paul Rosenberg's gallery became the headquarters for the Institut d'Études des Questions Juive (IEQJ), the French
arm that instituted and enforced its heinous restrictions on Jews. Private
collectors like Alphonse Kann, Adolphe Schloss, the Rothschild cousins,
and hundreds of others fled, in extreme haste, trying to protect their art
as best they could. Only Florence's great friend and art dealer, Daniel
Wildenstein, managed to negotiate when and how his establishment
would be Aryanized, entrusting the business to his loyal employee Roger

Dequoy. The deal reached was agreed to with Hitler's art dealer of long standing, Karl Haberstock, in a "4 to 5 day" period at Aix-en-Provence.[1] Madeleine Manigler remained safe, working for Dequoy, while Wildenstein sat out the occupation in New York.

Florence was seen after September 1940, bidding for "degenerate" Impressionist art at the auctions, taking advantage of the sudden influx of otherwise unavailable modern masterpieces. Manigler and Dequoy continued to advise Florence in Daniel Wildenstein's enforced absence, and she did well out of the auctions. Still, Vogel warned her that sooner or later, the United States was expected to join the British against the Reich, and she may have to prepare herself for an Aryanization of her property. As long as America remained neutral, however, she need not fear. When the attack on Pearl Harbor took the United States by surprise on December 7, 1941, Vogel's suspicions became a reality. War on Japan was declared the following day. The inevitable declaration of war on the Third Reich came on December 11.

Florence spent Christmas 1941 with Frank in Juan-les-Pins, discussing once again if they should leave. Frank repeated that he was too ill to travel, despite Vogel's offer to fly him to safety in a private plane.[2] Frank insisted on remaining; however, he told Florence she could do as she wished. At last, even the Goulds were compelled to face up to reality: holding on to their French empire required Florence's contacts within the German occupying forces. Without her complicity, all would be lost. For a man who had been seriously ill for over twenty years, facing such a future had to be a daunting prospect, even with reassurances from his multitalented wife and her lover, Vogel. That is, if Frank could reason clearly after years of memory problems brought on by Korsakoff Syndrome. Still, the three of them knew that it could only be a matter of months, if that, before the occupiers would come after the Gould fortune. If Florence hoped for René de Chambrun's advice, she would have been disappointed. Chambrun's father-in-law and Vichy's prime minister, Pierre Laval, had been arrested on December 13, 1941, on the orders of Pétain.

~

Early in 1942, Florence returned to Paris, still living at Hôtel Bristol or with Vogel at 133 avenue Malakoff, when time and circumstances permitted. Then Vogel arranged "vacant possession" of a huge eight-room apartment in the neighboring building, at number 129 avenue Malakoff, for Florence. Who had lived there before is unknown, but since Vogel's apartment belonged to a Jewish family, it is reasonably safe to assume that Florence's was owned by a Jewish family, too. Both buildings had been requisitioned by the Nazis, but only Jewish families and a select group of "politically incorrect" owners had been forced out.[3]

The chosen address was not only convenient to Vogel's apartment, but was also a familiar one for Florence. It faced the "pink palace" originally built by Anna Gould for her marriage to Boni de Castellane.* The rent on Florence's new apartment was reported variously as 30,000 and 60,000 francs annually.[4] No matter the cost, she determined she would not be hounded out of her place in society, or her world, or let external considerations intrude on it.

While the apartment was made ready with its art deco furnishings, Persian rugs, and dark blue silk sofas, modern lighting, Middle Eastern glass objets d'art that Frank had bought, and Oriental-style black lacquered tables for the dining room, Florence received her writer friends at Hôtel Bristol for sumptuous lunches, dinners, and even high teas.[5] Hungry writers queued up to be on the invitation list, save the Café Flore habitués like Simone de Beauvoir and Jean-Paul Sartre and the virulent anti-Semitic writer Dr. Louis-Ferdinand Auguste Destouches, better known under his penname, Céline. Drieu de la Rochelle kept his distance, too. Yet Gerhard Heller, censor extraordinaire, attended these lunches with the publisher Jean Fayard.[6]

At forty-six, Florence retained all her sex appeal and allure. "She was pretty, tall, with dark blonde hair," Heller described Florence in his biography, "a woman of thirty years of age, and terribly attractive; a woman who knew everyone; and had a tremendous love of literature . . . her dinner table knew no bounds."[7] While his was a flattering portrait of the middle-aged Florence, she readily admitted she knew little about books. Instead she prided herself that she knew a great deal about authors, who were, after all, for the most part men. The legend created by Marie-Louise

---

* The "pink palace" was demolished in 1969. Anna moved back to New York permanently in 1939.

Bousquet and Florence during one of Bousquet's salons was that Bousquet suggested that Florence start her own literary salon. What no one else knew was that Florence had already begun to fit out her first proper salon for writers that February at 129 avenue Malakoff. But the project was put on hold, slightly delayed due to a fractured leg.

In trying to attract the "big names" in French literature for her first salon, Florence had asked Pierre Benoit to attend. How could a man who wrote the line "I could not resist the desire to speak to you, to write your name. . . . It is terrible, you know, to have a power like yours," say no to her?[8] What Benoit did not voice was that all great writers—even the "Immortals"—were required to be the obeying subjects of the world of high society and their individual patrons. After all, without patrons, who could afford the extortionate cost of becoming an "Immortal"?

One "Immortal" who did manage to say no was Céline. No amount of pleading, cajoling, tears, sexual prowess, or taunts of easing his penury could persuade Céline to enter Florence's circle. Even Céline's long-term relationship with Dr. Verne's Institut Prophylactique at 32 rue d'Assas, which treated prostitutes for venereal diseases and was financed by Gould money, couldn't make him budge. In desperation, Florence arrived at Céline's home one evening with actress Marie Bell in a horse-drawn buggy, armed with dinner and oodles of champagne. Céline was outraged. "I who never entertain anyone was forced to receive them," he ranted. "She said she wanted to buy my manuscripts, but I wasn't interested. I refuse to owe anything to an American millionaire." Florence was already drunk by the time Céline made himself clear. Céline admitted that she wasn't disagreeable or foolish, but was instead an unmitigated snob. Eventually, he showed her the door, and she stumbled down the stairs, breaking her leg.[9] He refused to visit her during her convalescence.

On March 28, 1942, while still living at the Hôtel Bristol, Florence received Gerhard Heller and Marcel Jouhandeau at her avenue Malakoff apartment. Heller thought she'd be pleased to meet his new friend, Ernst Jünger, the dashing World War I flying ace who had been decorated with the legendary Blue Max for his bravery. Jünger was also a fine writer, world-famous for his *Storm of Steel* and more recently *On the Marble Cliffs*, published in 1939. Heller had gauged Florence's love of handsome men well, particularly handsome writers. "All writers are *cocottes*,"* she often said, laughing.

Jünger, attached to the military headquarters based at the Hôtel Majestic, had been working on intelligence-related matters for Operation Sea Lion for the invasion of the United Kingdom. Once Sea Lion was canceled in February 1942, Jünger was at a bit of a loose end. Provisionally he was reassigned to censorship of private letters, but the assignment held little job satisfaction, nor did it make good use of his talents. So Jünger, an arch-observer, became a *flâneur*, or promenader, through Paris, leaving us with his reflections on the occupation. While he was amorously involved with a lady doctor in Paris prior to meeting Florence, he was entranced by Madame Gould. Jünger's first remarks about her in his Paris diary are about her intellect. "She made some excellent reflections," he wrote, "among others that the experience of death is one of the rare things that anyone wishes to snatch away from us."

He was equally impressed with her attitude toward politics, and that the key to living with political animals was to "not be afraid." Jünger asked her to clarify her thoughts on the matter. "One evening when I was in the tropics, I saw a butterfly by the light of a lamp in the garden," she explained, "alight onto the back of a gecko. It was a symbol of the greatest assurance." Later, Florence talked of Mirbeau's depiction of a terrifying landscape, and how it attracted her. "Its charm lay in its power," Florence said, "perhaps a power that will live on once all the fun and games of the idle rich have been exhausted."[10] It was the beginning of an intimate relationship between Florence and Jünger, Heller claimed.[11]

Heller tells the story of his own first encounter with Florence. It was at Marie-Louise Bousquet's concert featuring Pierre Fournier in the spring of 1941. While standing between Heller and Jouhandeau, Florence announced that she wanted to create a literary salon, intimating that it had been the suggestion of Marie-Louise. More than likely, neither Heller nor Jouhandeau knew of the ladies' gray mice enterprise, and had no idea that the salon would also expand their network in that field of endeavor.

---

* *Cocottes* in this sense means "little darlings."

At the time, Heller was preoccupied with the organization of an "artistic exchange" of French writers and artists to Germany. Jouhandeau, already smitten with the rather good-looking Heller, only wanted to find himself in intimate circumstances with the German, and immediately agreed to go. The German censor, meanwhile, claimed to be immune to Florence's ample charms. It was widely accepted, even in 1941, that "in the past, as in the present [and in the future], Heller did all he could to make people forget who he was."[12]

Florence wanted to make her salon surpass any other. Like the triptych *The Garden of Earthly Delights,* painted by Hieronymus Bosch around the end of the fifteenth century, Florence's salon embraced complex, layered notions of creation, heaven, and hell set amid an erotic madness in the minds of her faithful acolytes. Those who took part understood that her Thursdays were more than sumptuous black-market feasts where perhaps literature, business, food, and art were discussed. Florence's Franco-German literary Thursdays at 129 avenue Malakoff were juxtapositions of love and hate; *collabo* and *résistant*; rampant sexuality and closet homosexuality; French art and literature versus its German counterparts; German master and French supplicant; American money and French poverty; and even nihilism pitted against an ever-elusive hope. Yet despite the incongruity of the participants, these opposing individuals and their belief systems remained attracted to one another, entwined in a macabre cultural dance.

The first "Thursday" organized by Florence at avenue Malakoff took place in April 1942. The writers present were editor Marie-Louise Bousquet, Pierre Benoit, novelist Marcel Arland, Jean Paulhan, and the high-school teacher and acerbic writer Marcel Jouhandeau, whose sole claim to fame was his anti-Semitic lampoon *Le Péril Juif,* published in 1938. Since Thursdays were the only days her newfound friend Jouhandeau had free, and Florence had taken a distinct shine to the unprepossessing teacher, who was scrawny and grew a beard to hide his harelip, Thursdays it would be. Others invited were Marie Bell, Arletty, and of course the ubiquitous censor Gerhard Heller. Jouhandeau remained a good friend of Paulhan's, even though Jouhandeau's harpy wife, Élise, denounced Paulhan to the occupation authorities that same month, fortunately without dire consequences.* As far as all the attendees were concerned, the first salon chez Florence was a resounding success, replete with fine wines and food they hadn't seen in ages.

Each Thursday brought a varied guest list, with Jouhandeau acting as cohost. Though he lived only a block away, Jouhandeau lied to his harridan wife (who had been an intimate of Jean Cocteau and the Jewish poet Max Jacob prior to marrying the bisexual Jouhandeau) that he was going to the popular bistro "Chez Florence" to meet his students. During the occupation, Florence's literary circle would eventually expand to include writers Colette (by then married to the Jewish journalist Maurice Goudeket) and writer Paul Léautaud; artists like Jean Dubuffet, Marie Laurencin, and Georges Braque; as well as entertainers Sacha Guitry, Arletty, and Marie Bell.

∽

The mighty external forces rolled on. In the summer of 1942, French POWs remained in camps until a peace treaty with France could be signed. It was a peace treaty that would never come. Pétain blamed France's defeat on "our laxity. The spirit of enjoyment destroyed what the spirit of sacrifice had built."[13] Forty percent of all French production had gone to the Germans by the autumn of 1940, offset in part by the "cost of maintaining the occupation." The percentage could only increase once Pierre Laval struck his deal, called the *relève*, that came into effect in June 1942. Three Frenchmen were sent to Germany to work *in exchange for* the release of one French prisoner of war. Seeing that there were 1.58 million able-bodied men held prisoner, it was a deal that defied basic mathematical logic. For every Frenchman employed by the Germans, a German was freed up to become a soldier. Over 30,000 German guards were released under the shortsighted scheme and transferred to active combat duty.[14] René de Chambrun helped structure the appalling trade.

As summer took hold, and the tiresome demands of the occupiers increased, Florence had Vogel arrange an exemption for her from weekly reporting to the police. Dated July 3, 1942, and addressed to her at Hôtel

---

* Paulhan forgave her, since he believed everyone should all take people as they find them, and not try to change them.

Bristol, though she then lived at avenue Malakoff, the order is signed by the German commander of the police and internal security, SS Obersturmfuehrer Nährich. Without too much inconvenience, Florence became exempt from any reporting to police until further order.[15]

Florence, however, wove an alternative tale after the war. She swore that she was "interrogated" by Colonel Garthe for the first time in July 1942 because she had "taken up singing and was engaged by the Opéra-Comique. I never even made my debut because Mr. Gould did not want me to."[16] Yet Heller wrote that Garthe, under his alias "Colonel Patrick," had barged in on Florence in her boudoir in March 1942, interrupting his and Jünger's visit, ministering to Florence and her broken leg.[17] Had she confused the dates, something which she claimed she never did? Or was it rather a classic case of misdirection, since she rambled on nonsensically in the same statement, declaring, "I have nothing in common with Mr. Gould's preceding wife, who under the name of Gould went to dance in a music-hall. Mr. Gould in a lawsuit had her forbidden from using his name."[18]

In truth, Garthe was taking an active interest in the Goulds and their fortune. While Florence was personally protected from arrest, relations with the United States were hostile, and there was a great clamor in the Nazi hierarchy to Aryanize, or put under administration, all the Gould assets. For Florence that meant that it was time to consider directing her own personal Aryanization program to stay one jump ahead of the Nazis, much as her good friend Wildenstein had done. It was time to call on Vogel again for help.

23

⌒⟋⟋⟍⟍⟍⟋

THE OCCUPATION, 1942–1943

Light . . . does not always illuminate an agreeable spot.
—Ernst Jünger

VOGEL FERRETED OUT THE MOST APPROPRIATE AND PLIABLE OF
Aryan administrators for the Gould assets in consultation with the
German restaurateur and hotelier known only as Mr. Horscher, who
had taken over as the Aryan manager of Octave Vaudable's famous restaurant, Maxim's. In the 1930s, Horscher had bought a franchise from
Vaudable for his own Maxim's restaurant in Berlin. Horscher was well
connected in the international hotel and restaurant trade, and was intimately aware of those whom the German high command would tolerate.
The "suggestion" of Hans Dietrich Warzinski was accepted by Florence,
once a Wildenstein-style negotiation took place over a period of several
days.[1] Florence was fortunate indeed to have such good friends as Vogel,
Madeleine Manigler, and Roger Dequoy operating on her behalf. The
scurrilous rumor told by artist Marie Laurencin to author Paul Léautaud
on their way home from one of Florence's Thursdays that the Vichy properties had not been Aryanized until June 1944 was entirely untrue.[2]

Other Americans, and friends of Americans in France, fared less well
at precisely the same moment. René de Chambrun's mother, Clara, kept
the American Library in Paris open under watchful German supervision

and strict orders not to lend books to Jews. His father, Aldebert, worked tirelessly with Dr. Sumner Jackson to keep the American Hospital in Paris free from any investigation into its underground network for downed British airmen. Both remained, however, under the gravest suspicion. Meanwhile, René was blamed by the American government for instigating the reinstatement of Pierre Laval as prime minister in Pétain's government. Although Laval was at his desk again, henceforth he would share only a mutual distrust with Pétain.

Meanwhile, there were some 173 American men imprisoned at Compiègne in January 1942. René de Chambrun was instrumental in appointing André Masson as a new liaison for returning French prisoners of war. The hope was, if they stayed silent about their maltreatment as slave laborers, more prisoners would be released. Chambrun's thought process was also behind the beginning of the ill-conceived *relève*. At one time a close friend of *Time* magazine's owner Henry Luce, Chambrun received America's disfavor when Luce published his name on the blacklist of the "Frenchmen condemned by the underground for collaborating with the Germans."[3] Florence, however, did not rate a mention.

That July, Florence was told by Vogel to hide out on the Riviera, and not to return to Paris until he let her know it was safe. She, in turn, warned her old part-time lover, journalist Robert de Thomasson, that there would be an attack on his friendly *maquisards* resisting in the Free Zone, before she packed her bags and the salon went on holiday.[4] Vogel had been privy to information regarding how to deal with *résistants* and suspected that it would not be long before there would be an escalation of hostilities between occupier and occupied. He was right. As the United States rounded up alleged fifth columnists at home, the Nazi occupiers in France seized their opportunity.

During the summer, the Nazis hardened their position regarding the *résistants* and hatched a plan to imprison the highest-profile Americans possible. This would afford them the best bargaining tool for a trade of German spies, captured in the broad net cast in America. Beginning on September 24, 1942, the Nazi occupiers rounded up 1,400 Americans. Among them was Dr. Sumner Jackson of the American Hospital in Paris. Other Americans included Charles Bedaux and his son, Philip. Bedaux had been working with the Nazis to build a trans-Sahara pipeline.

Infamously, in June 1937, Bedaux and his wife put their chateau at the disposal of the former Edward VIII and Mrs. Wallis Simpson—now the Duke and Duchess of Windsor—for their June wedding.[5] Charles Bedaux would end his war in another prison, this one in Miami, Florida, accused by the Americans of trading with the enemy and treason.

That September 24, Madame Fern Bedaux joined Sylvia Beach,[*] painter Katherine Dudley, and actress and radio commentator Drue Tartière, known in America as Drue Leyton, alongside 350 other women taken by "salad basket"—as the French called the police vans—to the monkey house at the Jardin d'Acclimatation in the Bois de Boulogne, near Dr. Colonel Bosse's Villa Brandt. "Mrs. Bedaux said in a very loud voice," Drue Tartière recalled, "that she did not expect to be with us long, and that she was waiting for Otto Abetz . . . to come and get her and her sister released." Other American women who were not well connected to powerful politicians or big business in the United States were also arrested. Sylvia Beach observed that, "There were Americans coming from every kind of milieu. . . . A number of artists . . . a number of French war-brides of American soldiers from World War I, some teachers, some whores, some dancers, a milliner or two, a poet or two, a lady who lived at the Ritz."[6]

Madame Bedaux was right. Before the women were settled in their internment camp at Vittel in Lorraine near the German border, well-dressed French collaborationists accompanied by German officers came to release her. They even helped her pack her bags. As for Sylvia and the others, they were marched from Vittel's train station to Frontstalag 194, where the British women, interned since 1940, greeted them with wild cheers and songs.[7]

Of course, Florence knew what had happened that September. But it did not concern her as much as Coco Chanel's mad affair with her German lover, Spatz. Equally, Florence kept up to date with the latest in Arletty's steamy romance with her German lover, Hans Jürgen Soehring.

---

* Beach would remain at Vittel for six months, hiding her precious books in an upstairs apartment after she refused to sell her last copy of *Finnegans Wake* to a Nazi soldier. While Hemingway personally "liberated" her bookshop in 1944, it never reopened for business during her lifetime. Beach lived until 1962. Today the bookshop flourishes and is owned by Sylvia Beach Whitman.

Both friends lived at the Ritz, as all the best arch-collaborators did. That October, Florence, too, longed to be reunited with Vogel and reestablish her salon.

∽

On November 8, the Allies invaded North Africa while the Battle of Stalingrad was still raging. In retaliation, the Nazi occupiers of France invaded the Free Zone of Vichy. The choice of the date of November 11, 1942, was no accident, for Hitler loved symbolic gestures. Armistice Day for World War I was to be remembered forever by the French as the invasion of the Free Zone by German and Italian forces.

Frank, at Juan-les-Pins, was trapped by the Italians who had taken over Corsica and the Riviera as far as Toulon, and parts of France north to the Swiss border. In Paris, nothing had changed, except the thirst for knowledge of what precisely was going on.[8] Florence relied heavily on information from Vogel and Oberg for her news, when she was unable to glean stolen tidbits from loose-lipped Nazi officers frequenting her gray mice network. She took her usual break to be with Frank at Christmas, but she never mentioned what, if anything, was different on her voyage south.

On February 22, 1943, the office of the prefect of police wrote that it was unable to ascertain "any information whatsoever about the racial quality" of the Goulds. The note found its way into General Carl Albrecht Oberg's in-tray. Oberg, already well acquainted with Florence and her circle, had masterminded the anti-Jewish policies throughout France. So he sent his top man, Walter Odewald, SS Sturmbahnfuehrer of the *Kripo*, or criminal police, to question Florence.[9] In order not to alarm her too much, Odewald, who took a lively interest in black-market activities in addition to sending Jews and enemies of the Reich to their deaths, asked to be introduced to Florence by Vogel.

Evidently, Odewald fell victim to Florence's many charms, since his first request for information went unanswered. On April 19, then again on May 31, a second and third request for the same information about their "Jewish race" were made in identical, patient language. By June, the official report was filed. "As far as the racial quality [of Frank Jay Gould] is concerned, an investigation which permitted us to establish his Aryan race was undertaken in the United States by our [Vichy] Ambassador,

Mr. [Gaston] Henri-Haye. The conclusions reached by the ambassador are on file with the Interior Ministry at Vichy. As for his wife, who was originally French, her first and middle names and her maiden name allow us to suppose that there is no Jewish blood in the family." The same report also mentions that Frank, too, was exempt from reporting to the police.[10]

The most interesting part of the story, however, was that Frank's birth certificate had a blank space where his name should have been. More than likely, his parents hadn't agreed on a name at the time of his birth, and forgot to fill it in officially. Frank's birth certificate resided at the passport office in New York City along with an affidavit from his sister, Helen Gould Shepard, attesting that the blank birth certificate for the December 1877 birth of a baby boy was indeed that of her brother Frank Jay Gould. It is difficult to imagine that Frank was ever under any real threat by the Nazis in these circumstances. The Germans did not investigate very hard, since if they had, they would have found abundant tittle-tattle by Wall Streeters that Jay Gould *was* Jewish, and best friends with Jesse Seligman, head of the Jewish banking family.[11]

Still, that was not the end of the affair. In July 1943 a certain Mr. T. Rombaldi, the new Italian chief of the regional directorate of the IEQJ, wrote a note suggesting that despite the documents provided via the Swiss legation and Vichy ambassador Henri-Haye, there remained a strong belief that the Gould family had converted from Judaism. Rombaldi requested that the IEQJ director judge personally if the genealogical family tree in his possession was the same as the one indicated by the Swiss legation and the French ambassador. The file reached General Carl Oberg's in-tray again to investigate.[12]

The problem was that Oberg, who worked from the Maisons-Laffitte estate owned by the Goulds, had an increasingly more tolerant opinion toward Jews. That January, his boss, Heinrich Himmler, demanded that Oberg remove 100,000 "criminals" from Marseille as prisoners and blow up the "crime district." Oberg knew Germany was losing the war, and was disinclined to carry out yet another war crime. Odewald was consulted again, and a meeting was set up with the troublesome Italian Rombaldi in Lyon.

Meanwhile, Colonel Helmut Knochen, senior commander of the Si-

cherheitsdienst and Sicherheitspolizei, and the most powerful of Florence's part-time lovers, was aware of the French irritation with the
Italian occupation. Laval complained to him directly about Italian interference, after telephoning the Italian embassy in Paris. Laval was ada-
mant that the Italians could not "stand between the French government
and citizens of third countries on French soil" and asked Knochen to
intervene.[13] Had René de Chambrun put the Vichy premier up to the
calls?

Knochen was wrestling already with how to cultivate an anti-Jewish
sentiment among the French, and concluded it was impossible to succeed
without some sort of pecuniary interest. "The offer of economic advantages much more easily excites sympathy for the anti-Jewish struggle,"
Knochen claimed. He wondered in his memos, too, if it should be the
Italians who ought to offer money to the French. While enlisting the Italians could only mean trouble for Florence, it is unlikely that he ever
shared these thoughts with her.[14]

Instead, Florence was alerted to the danger through Vogel. She
quickly arranged to "hitch a ride" with Colonel Garthe, Vogel, and Odewald as far as Lyon.[15] Frank had been examined under the microscope
by Schaeffer of the Reichsbank ever since the occupation began, Florence
told them. Surely the German high command held sway over the occupying Italians? Of course, they did, Garthe replied. Florence was urged
to be patient.

On September 8, 1943, as part of a bigger slap in the face, the Italians
retreated from their French occupation, leaving the Nazis in charge. With
the Allied invasion of Italy, they had real wars to fight at home. Frank
remained happily exempt from reporting weekly as an "enemy alien" to
the police and was not troubled ever again by the Germans.

∽

German power was rocked back outside of France, too. With the fall of
Stalingrad to the Soviets that February, the North Africa campaign won
by the Allies in May, and the invasion of Italy that September, French
fascists took up the cudgels on behalf of their German masters. Their
nefarious paramilitary organization was called the Milice. Originally
formed as the "only French Legion representing civic, social and moral

action between the wars," Xavier Vallat, the head of the IEJQ, claimed that by 1942 the Milice had become the eyes and ears of the Vichy government. Charged with the serious duty of keeping its ear to the ground for any rumor of public opinion, the Milice also became the mouthpiece of Maréchal Pétain's government.

Pétain stated that it was their "duty to transform the physiognomy of the country." Long before the German takeover of the Free Zone, the Milice was the enthusiastic French arm of the Gestapo, wielding its own raids, or *rafles,* to rid France of its Jews and perceived political enemies.[16] There is no record anywhere in the archives of this distinctly French network that the Milice took any special interest in Frank or Florence. The Goulds remained under the protection of the German Sicherheitsdienst, the SS's security arm.

Nevertheless, the ever-resourceful Vogel tried to persuade Frank that he could secretly fly him to safety at any time he wished. Was this behind Vogel's flights to Germany—twice with Florence—to inspect German military airfields? Was Florence's use of a false identity and passport during these trips also aimed at helping her husband? Hardly. The reason for Florence's sojourns into the heart of the Reich was purely to be alone with her lover Vogel. Interestingly, too, Florence never passed any of the crucial Luftwaffe information learned on her trips to her *résistant* friends de Thomasson or Marie Bell. It might have saved hundreds, if not thousands, of lives. Despite her claim that from December 1943 she was working clandestinely as part of the OSS in France, her failure to pass on information regarding the German airfields and the movement of aircraft to the OSS demonstrates that she never worked officially for them.[17]

❧

Throughout it all, the gaiety of Florence's salons continued unabated. Jünger visited her apartment on May 8 upon her return from a Riviera sojourn, in the usual company of their friends. She was ebullient, quoting Frank as having enjoyed *On Marble Cliffs,* and claimed he said, "Now, here's someone who can make dreams a reality." Jünger judged that was a pretty intelligent remark coming from an American millionaire. Two evenings later, he returned to avenue Malakoff to be alone with Florence.[18]

June 23, July 6, July 20, and August 4 were also spent at Florence's avenue Malakoff apartment enjoying the fruits of her black-market table
and sparkling conversation.

Interestingly, Jünger and Florence also had the thriving Parisian art
market in common too. On May 13, he had dinner with Heller at the
Chapon Fin at Porte Maillot, a stone's throw from Florence's apartment.
Their invited guest was Dr. Erhard Goepel—the avaricious art dealer
who worked with Hildebrand Gurlitt (one of Hitler's four official dealers) and Kajetan Mühlmann, the greatest looter of Poland and the Netherlands. They discussed the Paris art market in some detail, including
the Oppenheim collection, and how Oppenheim made his greatest coup
after buying Van Gogh's *White Roses*. Goepel agreed that possessing
great works of art conveyed "a real and considerable magical power."[19]
Undoubtedly, Jünger shared this conversation with Florence, along with
many other similar conversations, for Goepel was invited to Florence's
home on at least one occasion.

Aside from gossip, good food, and conversation, her Thursdays were
also an opportunity to show her acolytes her priceless objets d'art—ancient
unguent boxes and lachrymatories from Egyptian tombs—her Impressionist art recently acquired at auction or chez Wildenstein, as well as
illuminated manuscripts and medieval engravings. She often retold the
story of how she had even "ripped out three pages of engravings" to
give to an admiring visitor. Jünger was suitably impressed.[20] The following year, for his birthday, Jünger would be presented with an Impressionist painting at Florence's by Goepel. It is unclear if Florence or
Goepel had been the purchaser.[21]

∽

In November 1943, Jean Paulhan knocked at the door of his crusty septuagenarian writer friend Paul Léautaud to invite him to his first lunch
chez Florence on November 22. "Well!" Léautaud exclaimed in his
journal. "I don't regret going to this luncheon at this Madame Gould's.
Pretty, pressing against you when she speaks to you, around thirty-five
years old, chestnut brown hair, tall, thin, supple, poured into a tight-
fitting long dress in the old style, more elegant than today's fashions . . .
When coffee was served, she sat next to me and stared with her singular

cat-like eyes. I told her that I liked cats most of any animal and with her face ever so close to mine she said, 'I have the eyes of a cat, look at them.' Singular eyes, I repeated to her, but there is more of the she-cat in them, a sort of languor and warmth."[22] Although a latecomer to the festivities, Léautaud would become the eyes and ears for posterity into Florence's gatherings.

At the outset, Florence was less charitable about Paulhan's inclusion of Léautaud, who became the acerbic chronicler of her salon. "How could Jean Paulhan decide to invite Paul Léautaud to *my* lunch?" she exploded one day at Marcel Jouhandeau. Her cohost's reply was that Paulhan "is a magician. He'll show you many other wonders."[23]

Soon, however, Léautaud tired of Florence's eccentricities, of her loud laughter, and of being received, along with other men, in her boudoir. "Truly, let me say immediately, I have no taste at all for these meetings. These shrieks, this need to talk, this feeling of being invited as some sort of rare object," Léautaud moaned to his journal. "I am used to being alone, eating alone, my nose in my plate, reading a newspaper if I have one, or eating with someone I need only speak to if I must." He thought Florence was endowed with "an unending stream of words . . . impossible to halt her flow or place one word." Marie-Louise Bousquet hardly fared better, with Léautaud describing her as "this Madame Bousquet whom I met at *that* American's home" who was "overly exuberant," meaning odious in Léautaud's book. As for Florence's fancy medical friend Dr. Arthur Vernes, he was presumed initially as wise, but Léautaud soon changed his mind, dubbing him "an idiot and pretentious." Cocteau was "affected and false" as ever, and the actual salon seemed more akin to "a bordello or an orgy" than a literary gathering.

Occasionally, Florence dispensed largesse in the form of coal for the coldest winters of the century on record. When Léautaud felt obliged to repay her generosity, he went to great lengths to provide her with some warmth in the form of coal, too. Weeks passed. At last, when he procured a few kilos and offered them to Florence, she replied that it wouldn't be necessary as she had an eighteen-ton truck arriving the next day filled with coal, just for her.[24]

It is not surprising that the only thing that kept Léautaud coming week after week and month after month was the food. He eked out his meager existence by writing articles for the collaborationist press, and, like so many in Paris, was always cold and starving. So, when Florence gave him a pound of leftover roast beef from lunch to take home, he knew he had hit the motherlode.[25] At least he would have one good meal a week, he wrote, and he so looked forward to her "goodie bag" that he could share with his beloved cats, not to mention her "impossible" gifts of real coffee and chocolates.

Léautaud was not alone. Even the secretive Jean Paulhan was honest about his reasons for visiting Florence. He wrote that these "guilty secrets" were dishonest, but that it was hard to renounce life's little pleasures.[26] Marie Laurencin took advantage of Thursdays to stock up for the week, too, as well as to sketch Florence to later paint her.

Léautaud not only left a chronicle of Florence's salons, but also a fifty-year chronicle of literary life in France. A rare treasure. Florence's true gift during her lifetime was her fifty-year-long salon, first at the Hôtel Bristol, then at avenue Malakoff, and finally at the Hôtel Meurice. Modeled in her eyes after those of Winnaretta Singer de Polignac, who died in London in 1943, it became the seat of her power both during and after the war. While she would be questioned about her salon by the OSS in the aftermath of the liberation, it was her involvement in one of the biggest banking scandals of the war that would be her undoing.

24

FLORENCE THE BANKER

*Women are like teabags, you don't know how strong they
are until you put them in hot water.*

—Eleanor Roosevelt

DESPITE THE OCCUPATION, FLORENCE HAD AN ENVIABLE FREE-
dom of movement throughout France that was unparalleled for most
German officers, much less French collaborators. To a certain extent, that
could be explained by the vast Gould entertainment empire, since, even
with Warzinski as her Aryan supervisor, she had the magic touch in
keeping things running much as before—save for hiring Jewish staff and
entertainers. Having friends in high places, like Vogel and Knochen, was
incredibly useful. Yet there was more.

Florence expanded her personal financial interests opportunistically
wherever possible, not only in black-market activities like the gray mice
network, but also in partnering with a new cast of characters in other,
unrelated fields, including textiles. Florence, like anyone, could see that
most women in France had begun to look shabby after years of occupation, and more than likely reasoned that anything she could do to restore
a modicum of chic and style would be worth the price. Still, it would
take peace, Florence was heard to say while powdering her nose, before
the displeasing clip-clop of those wooden clogs on the pavements would

cease. It was the Germans who had ordered that leather was better used for all things military rather than to adorn ladies' feet. The clicking shut of her compact signaled an end to the observation, just as it indicated the end of her literary lunches.

With Vogel's help, Florence took risks and associated openly with people—other than the Nazi hierarchy—who would be deemed as undesirables should the Allies win the war. Her shrewd business judgment, always led by self-interest and money—and oh, how she *loved* money—had become impoverished by her very successes in overcoming the German occupation.

Among her undesirables were gangsters and bankers—in an age when it was still possible to tell the difference. Some were quite important bankers Florence had met through her many years working with the Gould investments. Still, the Gould name opened every door in America, making them targets for the Third Reich. An investment banker, and German resident alien in America, August T. Gausebeck, president of Robert C. Mayer & Co., an investment brokerage company located at 50 Broadway in New York City, was the banker who would succeed in embroiling the Goulds in his treasonous activities as early as 1941.

Since 1933, Gausebeck's Mayer & Co.'s mantra was to help the Third Reich obtain foreign exchange to lift Germany out of its financial doldrums caused by the hyperinflation of the early 1920s. Gausebeck had fulfilled his banking functions for his homeland since the bloody days of the Great War, and by 1936, Germany's wealthiest investors backed Mayer & Co.'s various projects to obtain foreign exchange in accordance with Hermann Göring's Four-Year Plan. The first imperative of that plan was to fund the new German Luftwaffe.

Gausebeck knew from personal experience that Germany's greatest industrialists lusted after a stronger Germany. Gustav Krupp and Fritz Thyssen—German parallels of the American robber barons of the late nineteenth and early twentieth centuries in remaking the country—were foremost among Nazi Germany's supporters. Socially, politically, and economically, they were the equals of any Rockefeller, Morgan, Vanderbilt, or Gould. Unlike their American counterparts, they actively participated in the asset stripping of Hitler's enemies.

German industrialists applauded Finance Minister Hjalmar Schacht's newest scandalous money-making idea: importing foreign goods, then blocking payments to the exporter. Schacht would renegotiate the initial deal with barter agreements of German-manufactured goods as payment to the unsuspecting importers. It was financially criminal.[1] A combination of these blocked payments were handled through Swiss banking trusts, Gausebeck's Robert C. Mayer & Co., a German-inspired investment company called the New York Overseas Corporation, the British investment bank J. Henry Schroder, and eventually the Chase National Bank. All were complicit in the theft of millions from Jews fleeing Germany.

Their pièce de résistance was something called the Rückwanderer Mark Scheme that lasted from 1936 to 1941. Literally meaning "returning home," the Rückwanderer Mark was designed to allow Germans living abroad who wanted to return to Germany—on a temporary or permanent basis—to buy Rückwanderer Marks at an advantageous exchange rate. Gausebeck was in on the deal from the get-go when the Reichsbank allowed any returnees to Germany to exchange half of their dollars at the favorable RM 4.10 rate, even though the real exchange rate was only RM 2.48. How could the German government afford such largesse? Simple: the surplus was paid from blocked accounts and assets once owned by refugees fleeing Germany, mostly Jews.

The refugees lost an additional twenty-five percent minimum through a mechanism called a "flight tax," which was often as elastic as a rubber band. The elasticity stemmed from the official practice of (a) restricting refugees to one small suitcase to take with them and (b) valuing any non-monetary assets for two or three cents (pfennigs) on the Reichsmark. "The German government," the FBI noted, "thereby netted a profit in dollars of nearly 90 percent."[2] Companies trading Rückwanders needed to pay wholesalers, among which were a host of travel companies, including American Express, the Hamburg-Amerika Line, and the Swiss import-export firm Interkommerz, run by Henri Guisan, son of the commander-in-chief of the Swiss army. Jean Guisan, a close family relation and Florence Gould's young friend who cashed her checks in Switzerland, was also related to the French General Alphonse Georges, who was fighting in North Africa.[3]

Florence was aware of Gausebeck's scam when she entered into a business relationship with him, but paid no attention to the detail. Instead, all she saw was the opportunity to make oodles of money. The devil, as always, was absolutely in the details. By 1940, Jean Guisan was on the board of the Goulds' Société Anonyme Immobilière Gauloise, Société Lunchs et Glaciers, and Société Immobilière des Sports, employing around 20 million francs of the Goulds' capital.[4] Henri Guisan's Interkommerz would eventually make a fortune on providing wood for "hutments" in Germany, better known as the wooden barracks at the concentration camps at Sachsenhausen and Dachau. By 1943, Interkommerz was investigated by the British, and put onto the proclaimed list of "neutral" firms doing business with the Axis countries. It was then barred from Allied markets. In August 1944, Hermann Göring Works sold its shares in Interkommerz through Switzerland.[5] Florence was keeping very bad company indeed.

∽

The Neutrality Act in the United States prohibited loans and gifts to belligerent nations. J. Edgar Hoover, FBI director, was told in October 1939 that "Representatives approach investors and indicate to them that Germany will undoubtedly win the war . . . and that marks will undoubtedly increase many times in value."[6] Hoover was onto the scam like any mollusk clinging to a juicy rock. What attracted his attention was Gausebeck, that German resident alien who was secretly funding the anti-Semitic campaign of Father Charles Coughlin on the radio; Coughlin had sponsored the Wagner-Rogers Bill of 1939 that aimed to bring 20,000 Jewish children to the United States with Nazi money.[7]

In July 1941, Treasury Secretary Henry Morgenthau, investigating the entire Rückwanderer scheme separately, froze German assets and outlawed the scheme's continuance. Still, it was left in place for its counterintelligence value. Every purchaser of Rückwanderers was individually investigated by the FBI. The first arrest made was that of August T. Gausebeck, who had become, quite bizarrely, the consul general of Bolivia in New York, and was described as a dangerous criminal.[8]

The only problem was that by June 1942, Chase and other American banks possibly enmeshed in schemes to help Nazi Germany were deemed "untouchable" by the new attorney general, Francis Biddle,* on the grounds of conspiracy, espionage, or acting as agents of an enemy power. Still, the case rankled with the young Justice Department lawyer in charge, Frederick Rarig, who kept plugging away to indict Chase National.

Gausebeck, meanwhile, was arrested on December 9, 1941, and held in custody until May 9, 1942, when the Swiss government intervened on his behalf, and he was deported back to Germany.[9] Gausebeck remained in Berlin with his wife throughout 1943, courted by many, but waiting for an opportunity worthy of his significant talents.

∽

Florence carried on regardless, not caring that the tide of the war had turned, despite it being obvious to many Germans that Hitler's Reich would lose. Until her involvement with Gausebeck and Guisan, she had merely entertained the enemy in her home; bought "ownerless" art; provided setup, running costs, and women for a high-class prostitution ring; consorted with and traded in the black market with the Germans—hardly serious offenses given what others were doing. Gausebeck, Guisan, and three other men would change all that by luring her into a banking proposition in Monaco.

While most people knew that the neutrality of the principality was a mere silken veil, even a fiction, Florence rightly believed that any investigation of her war profiteering would be the last—rather than the first—action the Allies would contemplate. Still, if there were to be a battle for Paris, meaning that the Allies were going to win the war, prudence dictated that she obtain residency for herself, Frank, and even her troublesome sister, Isabelle, in Monaco. Besides, there was always the tantalizing lure of SBM.

∽

The hotel and casino company remained unfinished business for Florence—her only corporate "failure"—but it was never forgotten. Besides, hadn't she cozied up to two men in the textile business earlier in

---

* Appointed September 5, 1941, after Attorney General Robert H. Jackson became a Supreme Court Justice.

the occupation, since they had already put themselves in pole position to win control of SBM? But there were other attractions to Monaco. Its low tax regime, no wartime restrictions, no blackouts, no interruptions to public gatherings, balls, or casino gambling all made Monte Carlo an oasis, a thriving hub of pleasure. It was her kind of place.

Still, to invest and reside in the rarefied world of Monaco, Florence would need partners with connections in high places, partners who could cloak her activities: enter the two textile entrepreneurs in whose shady pies Florence already dabbled a finger. Each was quite different from the other. The suave, American-influenced stock speculator Pierre Du Pasquier—an avenue Malakoff neighbor—was the president of the textile and ancillary services house Experta, based in Lille. He also owned Du Pasquier & Co., Inc., in New Orleans, an American exporter of cotton to Experta. Du Pasquier was also a friend of Prince Louis II of Monaco *and* the French government representative in the principality.[10] The other textile merchant began life as a street trader in Moscow and worked his way up to a purveyor of cloth to the czar's army. Since the war began in 1939, he had provided cloth to the Kriegsmarine. His name was Michel Szkolnikoff. He was an exiled rag-and-bone merchant turned millionaire thanks to his associations with the biggest Marseille gangster Paul Carbone and the German security police chief, and Florence's good friend, Helmut Knochen.

Du Pasquier was at the top of the food chain of investors and industrialists, controlling a twenty-five percent stake in the object of Florence's desires, SBM. He was also on its board of directors. Szkolnikoff, through his business associate at Société des Textils du Nord, Marcel Boussac, also a friend of Florence's, held shares in SBM, too. Szkolnikoff was not without other German friends in high places, including the ubiquitous General Carl Oberg.[11] Yet both Szolnikoff's and Du Pasquier's business affairs were controlled by the German trust company Deutsche Waren Treuhand-Aktiengesellschaft,* which gave instructions to both men on behalf of the Third Reich.[12]

The final piece in this complex jigsaw in which Florence became embroiled in Monaco required a crook influencing the seat of power. Prince

---

* Translated literally as German Wares Share Trust Company.

Louis II was frail and old, and fretted over the loss of his properties in France. He was also entirely under the thumb of his minister of state, Émile Roblot. A small nervous man and chain smoker, Roblot had startled eyes that darted constantly behind his thick, milk-bottle glasses. At the age of fifty-two, Roblot became the plenipotentiary minister of Vichy to Monaco. He was, nonetheless, a man on the make, and was quick in spotting any opportunity to cash in on millions. As early as 1941, Du Pasquier tried to put together a new international bank based in Monaco that would be a fifty-fifty Franco-German enterprise. Together with Roblot, he even sought to provide Switzerland's navy with Monaco's quay as the port for the "cruelly deprived" Swiss as part of the deal.[13] The object of such a bank from a German perspective was the decade-long search for consistent foreign exchange. When the war began to ebb away from the Reich, its endless search for the reserve currencies of dollars or British pounds redoubled.

In May 1943, during the Italian occupation of Monaco, Du Pasquier was instructed to start buying luxury hotels and casinos on behalf of Mussolini. Top of the list was SBM. When Knochen and his superiors got wind of the Italian plan, the German reminded Du Pasquier that Szkolnikoff was already handling this same plan directly on behalf of the Reich. Again, hotels and casinos were viewed as prime sources of foreign exchange. Szkolnikoff was buying hotels on behalf of the Germans with unprecedented speed and an unexplained cash windfall. So, then, why were the Goulds' hotels and casinos left unscathed? It boiled down to the fact that the Goulds represented far more than mere foreign exchange: They were long-term targets as the highly acceptable face to Nazi trade within the United States.

With the retreat of the Italians in early September that year, Du Pasquier might have thought that his own dilemma of having to choose between Hitler and Mussolini was resolved. Not so. Thirteen days later, a filial institution of the Reichsbank, Aerobank, received the green light from Roblot to set up a wholly owned subsidiary of Aerobank in Monaco. Gausebeck agreed with Walter Schellenberg's AMT VI wi*

---

* The RHSA was divided into different bureaus, or AMTs. AMT VI was foreign espionage, and the "wi" stood for *wirtshaft,* or economy.

(foreign economic espionage division) that the ideal front man for the proposed bank was a naturalized French citizen from Switzerland, Johann Charles, who was touting for business at AMT VI in Berlin that autumn.

Schaeffer of the Reichsbank in Paris had only one candidate to stand as Banque Charles's chief: August T. Gausebeck. Sadly for Du Pasquier, his flirtation with the Italians toppled him as the Germans' chief financial poodle in Monaco. As a nonresident German with most of his own money in Switzerland, Gausebeck could be considered a Swiss banker, Schaeffer asserted. The ambitious young Walter Schellenberg, head of counterintelligence (SD-Ausland), with direct access to Heinrich Himmler, agreed.[14] All they needed now was a strong American name.

In a letter written by Schaeffer dated September 5, 1944, he states that he traveled to Nice to see Frank personally, accompanied by Baron Charles. Schaeffer believed that Frank was "enthusiastic" and even proposed to put some of his own money into the new bank.[15] Undoubtedly, the year 1944 was a typographical error. The Germans had already lost France *and* Monaco by September 5. More credible is the year 1943, when, at last, Banque Charles was becoming a reality. Of course, Frank would have been enthusiastic in 1943—when he, like many listening to "fake news" behind enemy lines, was far from sure of an Allied victory. Yet, Florence was not to know that Schaeffer had made separate overtures to Frank.

∞

Aerobank began life as an extension of the Reichswerke Hermann Göring, a major steel and manufacturing group in Germany aimed at the creation of the Luftwaffe and weapons. In 1942, Aerobank became the Luftwaffe's Bank der Deutschen Luftfahrt. It was obvious to anyone examining Banque Charles that Aerobank represented a significant flight of public and private Nazi capital of the highest order.[16] Gausebeck knew from his year-long visit in Berlin that top private Nazi capital needed to find a secure home in the event of defeat, and that Göring, Himmler, and Ribbentrop had already begun to safeguard their personal capital on foreign shores. Nonetheless, Gausebeck also knew that the bank's existence needed to be guarded from Hitler. Such an institution would be quashed by the Führer as defeatist.

Given that Gausebeck was stripped of his alien residency and deported from the United States, he could not appear as the main director of the bank. But Gausebeck had the idea of involving an American "cloak" in the new bank. Someone who would be above reproach for the Americans. Someone who naturally had business in the United States and France, and who was sympathetic to Germans, if not the Reich.

Florence's name—rather than Frank's—was thrown against the wall, probably by Vogel since he had strong connections to Aerobank. It stuck. Not only did she fit the description given by Schellenberg to Gausebeck—that is, if the Americans hadn't known about her other activities during the occupation. To boot, she owned all those lovely hotels and casinos that were such a rich source of foreign exchange. Besides, she was already involved in separate business endeavors with Guisan, Szkolnikoff, and Du Pasquier.

Consequently, a well-primed Baron Charles was introduced to Roblot by Gausebeck on November 26, 1943. The bank would be capitalized at 100 million francs and the license granted would be for the benefit of Aerobank. It would be "a limited partnership, Monégasque, funded by German capital and independent of any German bank."[17] In a show of goodwill, Gausebeck opened an account at Crédit Lyonnais in Monaco, depositing 5 million francs. Roblot, naturally, gave the nod. Schaeffer of the Reichsbank remained involved, too, at long distance from Paris.

∽

Florence's version of her involvement with Banque Charles was that she met Charles through Vogel, at Vogel's 133 avenue Malakoff apartment, in the spring of 1944. Feigning distaste, she said with a curled lip, "He called himself 'Baron.'" At the same time, she was introduced to Gausebeck and his American wife. "It was understood with my Commissarer Warsinski [sic] that I could remove 8 million francs [from the Gould French operations] and that I could become a silent partner in a bank at Monte Carlo having a capital of 80 million francs," Florence said. When asked what transactions had taken place, she did something quite revealing. She repeated the question.

"Transactions of the bank?" she asked. Everyone who faces a difficult question in a deposition knows that they should always repeat the question to give themselves time. "It did not do any business but it was to have done international operations." The question was about transactions, not whether it had any operations. Transactions would include any monies Florence, or others, put into the fledgling bank. Again, when asked about Charles's role, she repeated the question. "What role was Charles to have?" she asked. After a further pause, she said, "He had funds in Germany and he claimed his German nationality so that he could recover his funds in Germany."[18] The replies were short, which is safest, but not entirely truthful.

Among the pack of lies she told after the liberation of France was another revealing tidbit. Florence said that her only Swiss connections stemmed from her stepdaughter, Helen Gould, who had married Henri Guisan. Helen's first husband was Baron Jean de Montenach, whom she divorced before becoming Mrs. Helen G. Marat of Lausanne, Switzerland.[19] Helen never married Henri Guisan, son of Switzerland's army chief. Jean Guisan, that some Guisan close relation and member of the board of several of the Gould companies, was never mentioned.

In May 1944, with D-Day widely anticipated in Paris, Florence invested 5 million francs, not 8 million as claimed, in Banque Charles. Gausebeck invested 25 million, as did Charles and a third limited-liability partner, the Thibergian Group, helmed by one Guillaume Lecesne and headquartered in Marseille. Ultimately, however, the Thibergian Group's owner was none other than Michel Szkolnikoff.[20] Lecesne was a fanatical pro-Nazi banker, a member of the loathsome Milice, and like Florence, his involvement was intended as a cloak for the Nazis. Equally, Lecesne was privy to the Italian-inspired Marseille investigation into Frank's ethnicity the previous year.[21]

D-Day on June 6 was the determining factor for Aerobank to give Gausebeck the green light to activate the bank. The mayor of Monte Carlo and notary, Louis Aureglia, registered the company with Roblot's approval, stating specifically that "in no way is this an importation of capital" to Monaco, in a bald lie.[22] Over a billion francs in Nazi money would be invested in Monaco in the closing days of the occupation of France.

Six weeks before the liberation of Paris, Florence invested a further 2 million francs in a separate account for herself and 200,000 francs in the name of her sister, Isabelle Lacaze, who was already ill with stomach cancer. Despite a total 7.2-million-franc deposit, Florence had no right as a signatory. She had all the obligations of a limited partner without any of the advantages.[23] Or had she?

∾

How, if at all, was Vogel involved? Florence said that he had introduced her into the network serving Aerobank. He had worked for the Göring Corporation and later for Focke-Wulf in Paris before becoming the Aryan supervisor of SNCASO. On July 13, 1944—six weeks after D-Day—20 million francs were deposited into an account called ELBAG at Aerobank in Paris. Account number 1050P belonging to the Luftfahrt-bedarf, or Luftwaffe Air Transport, received a credit for an additional 10 million francs. A second account number, 1050H, for the Luftfahrtbe-darf was credited with a further 20 million francs. Banque Charles was then ramped up with "aero" funds.

Karl Schaeffer said that "for Germany, the purpose of Banque Charles was to take up a financial position in a neutral zone from where it would be easier to begin afresh after the war, particularly with America." It was precisely what Henry Morgenthau had wanted to avoid, and as the Allies breached the beaches of Normandy, a plan called "Project Safe-haven" was launched to prevent the Nazis from setting up or benefiting in any way from a flight of its capital from the occupied territories.

Banque Charles bought the Rococo-style Villa Millaflores on boulevard des Moulins in Monte Carlo. The sellers were Du Pasquier along with Jean Guisan and Interkommerz. The title to the property passed through SBM's books on April 11, 1944, and was sold three months later, on July 27. In passing through SBM's books, Szkolnikoff became part owner/seller of the property and benefited personally from the sale.

Reichsbank director Karl Schaeffer found the first half of the 36 mil-

lion francs required for the purchase, fronted from the Austrian indus-
trialist Bernhard Berghaus, a notorious financier of the Nazi Party.
Aerobank provided the rest of the money at the end of July.[24] Meanwhile,
Florence was seen by Allied informants coming and going from Villa
Millaflores, and was mistaken as Charles's lover, not his business part-
ner. What they didn't know then was that Florence was negotiating the
Gould residency permits through Charles.

Simultaneously, Szkolnikoff approached Du Pasquier with a plan to
merge his luxury hotel group—the old Henri Ruhl hotels, comprising
some twenty-eight properties—with SBM. It was a first step toward
Göring's personal goal of controlling the luxury hotel and casino market in France. A second acquisition of the Goulds' fifty-odd properties
would complete his goal. The textile merchant and millionaire Szkolnikoff was both the SS's and the Luftwaffe boss's cloak, just as Florence
became Gausebeck's.

Still, the Banque Charles conspiracy had terrible timing. Szkolnikoff's 614 million francs provided by the Germans, as well as the assets and cash of Banque Charles, needed to disappear quickly. Before the
funds could be funneled into other investments, preferably in the United
States, the Allies liberated France. Spain held both Banque Charles's and
Szkolnikoff's only salvation.

∽

The net seemed to be closing in on Florence in New York, too, when Attorney General Biddle finally agreed that the Justice Department's
lawyer, Frederick Rarig, could move toward prosecution of Chase National in January 1944. If the prosecution went ahead, it would pave the
way to follow the trail of breadcrumbs left behind by Gausebeck that
would eventually lead to Florence. Unfortunately for the Justice Department, Chase hired one of the smartest and "best lawyers in the country,"
John T. Cahill. The Justice Department was "privately and firmly
apprised" that Cahill intended to introduce into evidence that Chase
officials had "cooperated directly with the Bureau, as well as Army and
Naval Intelligence." The promise that FBI secrecy, its sources and methods, as well as those of U.S. Army Intelligence, would be blown in open
court was suddenly at stake. The Justice Department told Hoover he had

no alternative other than to back down.[25] The victory for Chase in 1944 would become one for Florence in 1945. John T. Cahill also became Florence's lawyer.

Still, the ups and downs of the final days of the occupation left Florence clutching for steady ground. That February, Frank took his safety into his own hands, and went into hiding with the help of Anne Marie Vilbert de Sairigné, a resistant based in Nice. He did not bother to tell his wife where or with whom he was hiding; or indeed, that he had written de Sairigné a check for $400,000 for her troubles.

25

⟨⟨⟨∞⟩⟩⟩

LIBERATION AND TREASON

Paris must not fall into the hands of the enemy, or, if it
does, he must find there nothing but a field of ruins.
—O.K.W./W.F.St./Op. (H) Nr. 772989/44, 23.8.44, 11
hours, order to destroy Paris

FOR MANY, THE LIBERATION OF PARIS ON AUGUST 25, 1944, CAME TOO
late. Since the end of 1943, resistance to the occupation and general dis-
sidence had become a real worry to the Germans. On Ribbentrop's
orders a new edict came into effect on January 7, 1944: the preventative
arrest. Tens of thousands of Frenchmen and women were detained for
three different types of agitation. Those who distanced themselves from
Pétain's regime or refused to cooperate with the occupiers filled the first
category. Next were high civil servants within the government machinery, and last were the intelligentsia and those who spoke out against Pétain or the Germans, along with their elected officials *prior* to the
occupation. The borders to other occupied territories were closed to prevent anyone absconding.[1]

For those who survived that bitingly cold winter, the normal fat allowance for cooking had been reduced from ten ounces a month to two
ounces. It had been four years since an adult had been allowed a milk
ration. Children were born who had never seen a banana. Bread was

rationed to six ounces daily, but that was a moveable feast. Often rations were cut as a form of reprisal for acts of resistance.[2] After enduring a sub-zero winter without any heat, a snowy spring, and a summer without food, the French were in a state of desperation. Florence's table remained, nevertheless, full of delectable treats; her home warmed by ample coal fires; and her friends maintained through her generosity.

Léautaud recorded how he hated himself for sinking so low as to be seduced by *real* coffee, many cups, and a chocolate dessert that could have sufficed for his entire meal.[3] Marcel Jouhandeau, one of the writers who went to Germany on the propaganda mission organized by Heller early in the occupation, was disillusioned, too. "Marcel Arland knows better than I, what one can say and when one must be quiet," Jouhandeau wrote to Paulhan in November 1943. "His presence is perhaps all that is left by way of 'reason' with our friend [Florence]." A few days later, Jou-handeau dreamed he was levitating above Florence's art gallery in the avenue Malakoff apartment. His dead mother entered, unsurprised to see him floating on the ceiling.[4] To be chez Florence was to lose one's equilibrium.

Still, her all *résistance* friends like Robert de Thomasson and Marie Bell were aware, like Marcel Arland, not to trust Florence with the details of their activities. All Florence knew was on which side their baguette was buttered. While she painted a different picture of herself to the various factions frequenting her avenue Malakoff abode, both occupier and re-sistant had learned long before that they could count on Florence's gen-erosity but not her discretion. Too much champagne, drunken late-night phone calls, and the irrepressible desire to be the enfant terrible, flaunt-ing her power and wealth, saw to that.

Even Frank knew when not to tell Florence the truth in these dangerous times. Seemingly unaware that Frank had gone into hiding, Florence instigated a plan to "kidnap" him with the help of her *résistant* friends Marie Bell and Robert de Thomasson at the beginning of August, then bring him to safety with the help of the FFI* leader Captain René de Treville.[5] Where safety was precisely, however, was never mentioned or explored. Events moved too quickly for them to act.

---

* Forces Françaises de l'Intérieur.

∽

The D-Day embarkation had been widely anticipated by the Germans since the beginning of May. In fact, it occupied all minds—both French and German. By mid-May, the German high command felt that there had been insufficient manpower in Paris to keep its increasingly belligerent population under control, so regiments of crack Mongolian fighters* in Nazi uniforms—redolent of the "yellow hordes" of Genghis Kahn and just as terrifying—flooded the Métro and the streets of Paris, to the stupefied gazes of Parisians.[6]

On the night of the D-Day embarkation, June 6, 1944, Ernst Jünger remarked that although it had been expected, the scale of the invasion took everyone by surprise. Two days later, he lunched at Florence's. During their feast, the telephone rang and she excused herself from the table. Returning moments later, she announced to her friends, "The Stock Exchange has reopened. [Where the French played, and lost, at war], we do not play at peace." Jünger wrote in his journal afterward that "money seems to possess the best antennae, and bankers judge the situation with more care and prudence than the generals."[7]

On June 22, Heller joined Jünger at Florence's, announcing that his train from Berlin was attacked by enemy air fire. Jünger replied that the German embassy was packing up and preparing to leave the city. It was total chaos. Night bombs fell in the courtyard of the Hôtel Majestic, setting alight a huge store of gasoline. Jünger discovered later that from then until the liberation, Allied bombs fell daily on the outskirts of Paris. Despite the unsuccessful attempt on Hitler's life on July 21, Jünger remained in the French capital, visiting Florence regularly. His July 26 visit took place in the evening, but not at 129 avenue Malakoff. Instead, he called on Florence at Vogel's apartment to get "inside knowledge" about the assassination attempt from him. Jünger bid his final adieus to Florence on August 10, since the "Americans were already at Rennes." Florence's good friend, the princesse Sixte de Bourbon-Parme, was also there to say good-bye to the charming German. The sighs and tears could

---

* Mongolian nationalists, fearful of being swallowed up by either the Soviet Union or China, looked favorably on Hitler's NSDAP, adopting it as a movement to preserve their "national identity," just as Hitler had done in Germany.

be heard along with the rustle of satin as the women kissed, hugged, and wished Jünger safe travels, along with their sincere promises to see one another again in peacetime. By August 23, the Allies were on the outskirts of Paris.[8] Peace in Paris was still days away. An eternity after four years of occupation.

∽

Meanwhile, the *épuration sauvage* (savage purging) of collaborators had begun. The first to suffer were the *collabos horizontales,* or the women who slept with the enemy. Coco Chanel, though briefly jailed in August, secured her safe haven in Switzerland—many think with the help of Bendor and Winston Churchill. Arletty was less fortunate. Daisy Fellowes, that niece whom Winnaretta Singer had taken to live with her as a child and allegedly was the best-dressed woman in France, faced a different ignominy. Her daughter, Emmeline de Casteja, spent five months locked up with prostitutes in Fresnes Prison.[9]

Florence went into hiding with Ludwig Vogel. As Charles de Gaulle marched his Free French army down the Champs-Élysées to cries of joy, women who had fraternized or slept with Germans had their heads shaved in the tens of thousands across the country, as an outward sign of their shame. Others were paraded naked through the streets, while still more women who consorted with Germans were kicked, beaten, or brutalized publicly. Some died at the hands of their avengers. Indiscriminate revenge attacks and denunciations became the food of the starving masses. Hundreds of thousands were accused of being members of the Gestapo or Milice.

Florence's "zoo" of writers—notably Jouhandeau and Léautaud—feared for their futures. Jouhandeau was receiving hate mail and death threats by telephone.[10] Drieu de la Rochelle attempted suicide once, and failed. Céline retreated with the occupiers in search of safety. Brasillach was arrested and awaited trial. Paulhan tried to reassure Jouhandeau, while wistfully wondering whether Heller and Jünger were safe. Though a resistant editor of *Les Éditions de Minuit*, Paulhan believed both Germans were friends of French literature.

Unsurprisingly, de Gaulle was named by the Allies as the president of the new French provisional government. He tried to put a halt to the savagery redolent of the French Revolution by introducing the offense of *indignité nationale* into law. Collaborationists convicted of the crime could expect the death penalty. Those who took the law into their own hands faced severe punishment, too. Anyone found guilty lost their right to vote and was banned from public service or the right to work in the media or trade unions. Further sanctions, depending on the severity of the crime, included confiscation of property and jail. Drancy, which had once held Jews and *résistants* en route to eastern concentration camps, now housed collaborators. Arletty, who gave such pleasure and so much escapism through her films during the occupation, was thrown into the dungeon of La Conciergerie, where Marie Antoinette had been imprisoned before her execution in 1793, until she was transferred to Drancy.[11]

Florence knew that her own role as Vogel's lover—not to mention her relationship with one of Germany's biggest war criminals in France, Helmut Knochen—put her at the forefront of the hated *collabos horizontales*. She hadn't been starving or without succor, as so many of the poorer women of Paris had been, and had no excuse for her blatant fraternization with the occupiers other than egotism, self-gratification, and opportunistic investments. Worse still was her knowledge of Vogel's activities and his role in the black market, where his responsibilities for MUNIMIM netted the Reich 3.588 billion francs in essential war materiel such as wolfram and radium, as well as converted funds from looted diamonds, platinum, machine tools, and quinine.[12] Vogel, too, was at the heart of the nefarious organization that helped prolong the war and starve France. Now that "liberation" had come, Florence, as if merely changing her chemise, preferred to see herself, henceforth, as a fellow victim of the occupier. Her instincts for survival were at their most acute.

∽

As an intelligent woman, Florence recognized that the French—not to mention the Americans—would certainly believe the worst. As an unmitigated snob and egotist, she gave a Gallic shrug, knowing that Gould money would talk in the end. If the Allies ever discovered Vogel's real role, then so be it. The Banque Charles debacle was bad; but it was nothing she couldn't handle. Still, did Florence know that both the Abwehr and the Gestapo viewed her as one of their own?[13]

With the arrogance of the super-rich, or perhaps the hardened criminal, Florence thought that she could hoodwink the Allies with the fantasy that she had invested in Banque Charles purely to save Frank. Besides, the attempted kidnapping of her husband in Nice was proof she was concerned. That Frank was unable to walk any distance or lie down to sleep made absolutely no difference in her mind to the veracity of her claims.[14]

So, in late August, Florence and Vogel first sought sanctuary at the Prophylactic Institute of Dr. Arthur Vernes, just as she had done in the early days of the occupation. From there, they went to other homes belonging to her or Frank. Once she could be sure that the Kriegsmarine had vacated her duplex apartment at 2 boulevard Suchet, the couple hid there. It was at boulevard Suchet that they agreed on their separate futures and the necessary course of action to protect each other in the aftermath of the liberation.

Toward the beginning of September, Florence moved Vogel to the home of the Italian pianist Joseph Benvenuti at 6 rue du Colonel Moll. Benvenuti had gone to Spain on several occasions for Florence, handling clandestine activities that, for the most part, remain her secret.[15] Simultaneously, further instructions were issued by Florence to Benvenuti regarding a proposed rendezvous with Szkolnikoff in the Basque city of Santander in Spain.

Vogel, too, was still gambling on making a fortune. While he declared that he was never an ardent Nazi, and probably never was, he took advantage of the chaos that reigned in Paris just before the liberation. Like a common thief, Vogel emptied the Focke-Wulf's bank account of 5 million francs before disappearing with Florence. His theft made it impossible for him to return to Germany. He told Florence that he was desperate to immigrate to America before his own war crimes were discovered by the French. Had Florence been in on the "heist" from Focke-Wulf beforehand? Were the 5 million francs meant to compensate Florence for her losses from investing in Banque Charles? Or had she agreed to help him hold on to his booty? Their precise plan or her involvement never came to light.

On September 6, 1944, Vogel finally surrendered to the French and was taken to Fort Noisy-le-Sec prison. During his incarceration there, Florence funneled over 75,000 francs to safety for him.[16] Still, Vogel quickly came to the attention of his Americans co-jailers since he was successfully getting messages out of prison to Florence. He was immediately transferred to Drancy. It was the Americans, not the French, who became suspicious of Vogel's American lover. Evidently, Vogel claimed that Florence would vouch for him. If that was what they had agreed, it was a mistake. The Americans asked the French military security to investigate Madame Gould as a matter of the utmost urgency on October 7, 1944. A week later, a second but still urgent note was penned demanding discreet inquiries by the French military police.[17]

Florence's Aryan supervisor, Hans Dietrich Warzinski, escaped to Spain, as did Horscher of Maxim's. As had long been suspected, U.S. agents discovered close links between Warzinski and Horscher in the hotel business in Germany prior to the war. When the Allies liberated Monaco at the beginning of September, they found that many of the subjects of their economic warfare investigations, like Michel Szkolnikoff and August T. Gausebeck, also had bolted to Spain. Gausebeck was last seen in April 1945 at the Hotel Ritz in Madrid, before suddenly decamping to an unknown address in Barcelona, presumably to handle the affairs of Banque Charles there. In the same wire from Madrid, it was agreed that Szkolnikoff would be blacklisted.[18] Baron Charles, however, was held in custody in Monaco while the military investigators poured over the paperwork relating to the bank named after him.

At the same time, Szkolnikoff met with a representative, more than likely Benvenuti, in Santander, Spain, to conclude a deal with "a private American group owning hotels in France." The object was to sell the Americans his investment portfolio of buildings, hotels, and his fictitious stake in SBM. Given that all his acquisitions had been made with German "flight capital," it was a dangerous deal to contemplate on all sides. Hidden in plain sight on the cover of one of the Szkolnikoff files at the National Archives in Paris are the scribblings of its main investigator, who wrote "Gould chases the hotels." On May 29, 1945, *The New York Times* reported that the Goulds were behind the Anglo-American group offering $10 million for a controlling stake in SBM.[19] The U.S.

army intelligence officer Lester Blumner, stationed in Nice, took an immediate interest in the affair, and linked the Goulds to Szkolnikoff.[20] But could Blumner prove it?

What Florence, Vogel, and even Szkolnikoff more than likely ignored was that the London Treaty of January 5, 1943, declared that the Axis Powers serving the Third Reich and all neutral territories were put on official notice. The Allies "intend to do their utmost to defeat the methods of dispossession practised by the Governments with which they are at war against the countries and peoples who have been so wantonly assaulted and despoiled."[21] In other words, since the Third Reich made the murder of millions of civilians and the looting of their property a cornerstone of its occupation and its primary objective of the war, the Allies were intending to make economic warfare waged by the Axis Powers a serious war crime. Any flight of personal or private Nazi capital to evade capture after the treaty date became a war crime. Anyone aiding and abetting risked treason charges. Given these facts, Florence should have realized that a file numbered RG 65—"RG" for record group and "65" being the number assigned to treason files—was opened in her name from the moment Vogel began talking his way out of his tight corner inside Drancy. Florence was, indeed, in hot water.

∞

On October 19, 1944, Florence was called to her first interview with the DGER, the Direction Générale des Études et Recherches, Deuxième Bureau, which investigated high crimes against the French state. She did not acquit herself well, being described by several DGER officers during her interviews as "haughty, arrogant, and part of the worldly set." The officers insinuated in their reports that Florence took advantage of her position in high society and her vast fortune to flout the black-market regulations and continue to live well. Vogel was also named from the outset as her lover. While they noted that she was concerned for her ill, rather than invalid, husband, the tone of the initial report is very dry.[22] At that point, DGER questioned only her economic activities at Banque Charles. No one asked why she brought paintings from her home at Juan-les-Pins to Paris in 1942 or later. No one asked about her purchase of looted art or art made available through forced sales at Hôtel Druout, Galerie Charpentier, or from Wildenstein's man in Paris, Roger Dequoy.

Meanwhile, Florence was a woman on a mission, setting in motion the Vogel plan, calling upon all the American contacts she could muster to have him freed from Drancy. She bigged him up with the new American ambassador, the veteran diplomat and somewhat laconic Jefferson Caffery, claiming that Vogel had significant military information that he wanted to share with the Allies. She even used the tapestries stored at the American embassy before the occupation as impressive proof of her wealth and status. Frank became embroiled, too, contacting old friends in high places, intimating that Vogel could be of tremendous use to the Allies, particularly in the location of airfields. While Frank was estranged from his wife, obviously he felt that was no good reason to abandon Vogel.

Some ten years later it emerged that "during his incarceration secret papers belonging to him [Vogel, were] concealed and protected by Mrs. Gould." The letter quoted was addressed to the Inspector General of Special Investigations of the Air Force and written by FBI Director J. Edgar Hoover. Hoover elaborated further, writing that Vogel was "released from incarceration through Mrs. Gould's efforts; secured employment and protection of the U.S. Army through Mrs. Gould's efforts" and that Vogel was "employed by X-2 [foreign unit] (from December 1944); rendered information to the American and British air services concerning production, location of plants, and German personalities."[23]

Although the conditions in which the French and American jailers held their prisoners were not as horrid as those under the Germans, each day that Vogel spent in captivity risked revealing his main activities in the economic warfare machinery of the Reich, not to mention his victims sent east to certain death. Florence knew the stakes she was playing for, but not taking the gamble was more dangerous for both of them. Her work paid off. Vogel was released on October 29, 1944—after seven weeks a prisoner—and taken into the protection of the U.S. Army. Still, Vogel remained in danger so long as he stayed in the European theater of war, where French and German eyewitnesses could point the finger at him.

Florence appeared before her French interrogators again on November 2, only four days after her last deposition to free Vogel. Again, they grilled her about her relationship with him and other, more prominent, Nazis. Again, she was described as haughty and quite above the whole sordid procedure. What she didn't know was that a captured German prisoner of war, under interrogation in England, had declared that she was an agent of the Abwehr.[24] The French saw through her silky lies but, for the moment, concluded that since she claimed American citizenship, and the Americans were in France, she could be their problem.

Florence believed that it was all over. She had saved Vogel, herself, and Frank. Vogel was posted to the multilingual X-2 unit, actively fighting against his former colleagues and betraying their secrets. No one understood that Vogel also left her with 500,000 francs in cash, presumably from the 5 million stolen from Focke-Wulf. Nor had they learned yet that she was licensed by the Abwehr to carry a concealed weapon during the occupation, making her a person of some significance and trust to the Nazis. What Florence did reveal, however, were some of the secret documents that Vogel had also liberated from his employers' offices in Paris, proving that halting any investigation of Vogel, and protecting him, could prove beneficial to the Allied war effort.[25]

Frank, by now, was aware of the kidnap scheme and Florence's true role in Banque Charles. He decided that their alleged enforced separation brought on by the occupation should become a separation in deed. Too much had happened that divided them. Florence, too, was troubled by Frank's payment of $400,000 to Anne Marie Vilbert de Sairigné for her help at the precise moment that Florence had paid Marie Bell and the Maquis to kidnap Frank for his own safety.

Simultaneously, the Americans discovered the Banque Charles affair. In February 1945, Florence was hauled back in for questioning. Jouhandeau remarked to Paulhan that something seemed to be preying on Florence's mind—perhaps it was the sudden departure of her butler Diego? Or perhaps it had something to do with Benvenuti? Two weeks later, Jouhandeau declared, "I can't intervene on behalf of Diego . . . don't you think that Madame [Gould] is in danger if her valet who has seen all and the rest is captured. . . . Florence faces a Cornelian dilemma, Hobson's Choice, between the Devil and the Deep Blue Sea, if you will."[26]

Jouhandeau was right to pick up on Florence's mood swings and worries. The previous December, the French had tipped off the Americans that Florence was a principal in a company "organized for the purpose of removing German and collaborationist capital from the jurisdiction of the French authorities." On August 23, while the Allies were breaching the outskirts of Paris, the capital of Banque Charles was increased from 80 million francs to 150 million. By February 1945, Treasury Secretary Morgenthau and FBI Director Hoover were already on her case. "Our hostess is distracted," Jouhandeau wrote to Paulhan, "detached, almost aggressive."

Florence fought back in the most public way she knew how. She contacted her old friend Joseph Kennedy and asked for help. The former American ambassador to Britain gave his son Ted, remembered today as Senator Edward Kennedy, the nod. At the time, Edward Kennedy was a war correspondent for the Associated Press. He wrote how Mrs. Gould's plight had been created by a desire to save her husband from being sent to a concentration camp. "It was a sort of blackmail payment, the business manager for the former Florence Lacaze asserted." Mrs. Gould told the younger Kennedy she "undoubtedly was 'the wife of a very prominent American' mentioned by Secretary Morgenthau as being under investigation by the French authorities."

Privately, Florence was enraged with Morgenthau, since she knew from her interview with the French that it had been within his power to protect her and Frank from a new investigation. At that point, she most likely hadn't realized that her RG 65 file for treason was becoming ever thicker. "I haven't the slightest fear of this investigation," she brazenly told Kennedy. "Not half this story has been told. Mr. Morgenthau should have known the full details before he spoke." What she hadn't counted on was the equanimity with which the younger Kennedy would approach her dilemma. When Morgenthau was asked to comment, he confirmed that "the United States had told the French government it would assist in a French investigation of a 'very famous' American couple suspected of collaboration with the Nazis."[27]

Kennedy then detailed Frank's personal and family backgrounds: Frank's father, his ex-wives, his horses, hotels, and casinos. In a more revealing exposé than Kennedy perhaps wanted to make, he belabored

Frank's eye for the ladies, and, unwittingly, Florence's ability to put on a great show as an actress. Kennedy continued:

> She received me in her home in the most fashionable part of Paris, a large and beautiful apartment but chilly for the lack of fuel like the poorer homes in the city. She wore a heavy blue robe that hung down to her ankles, and a thick fur piece on her shoulders. Mrs. Gould said that she had spent the first part of the war as a nurse in a Paris military hospital, assisting surgeons during operations. Just before the occupation of southern France she attempted to go to Bordeaux with her daughter* in hopes of getting to America, she added, but was blocked by the Germans and became a nurse at a military hospital in Bergerac.[28]

Florence insisted to Kennedy that the sequestration of the Gould assets by the French was a mere "administrative one." After all, "if I were a collaborationist would I be here now? Of course not. I wouldn't be free."[29]

⁓

Frank must have been outraged by his careless wife. Hadn't he avoided interviews in the past, or, when confronted unexpectedly, simply replied, "No comment"? The article raked over the embers of his past life, making public some of their most private matters as a couple, too. It painted him, a proud man, as impotent in the most public forum. The very last thing Frank wanted was to upset the men in American corridors of power, men like Henry Morgenthau. Now the Banque Charles investigation would bring out into the open the reckless way Florence had acted and her real economic collaboration with the enemy. Business remained a matter to be conducted in private for Frank, particularly as he hated paying those federal taxes. He knew how the most innocuous business transactions could be open to misinterpretation, much less ones where an opportunistic prospect was pounced upon. Whether Florence had intended to "save" him or not, the entire affair made him appear as an invalid publicly. It was deeply distressing. He would never forgive her.

---

* This might have been her stepdaughter Helen, though it is doubtful the event occurred.

What was not in the published article by Kennedy was his private interview with Donald L. Daughters, lead investigator in the postwar allegations against Florence. Kennedy explained that Florence told him that the "*commanditaire*" arrangement at Banque Charles was one "whereby an investor might participate in the bank without liability in the case of its insolvency."[30] It begs the question why Florence should have been concerned it might become insolvent when it had the backing of the Reichsbank. What Kennedy did not know was that the commanditaire arrangement also meant that she could not make decisions on behalf of the bank.

The Daughters report includes a more tempered assessment of Florence's activities from Source D, or the files of the DGER. They state that "the Subject displayed an understanding and cooperative attitude toward persons working in the French Resistance. On occasions [*sic*] she is said to have offered shelter to individuals sought by the German authorities and to have offered sums of money for use in Resistance activities. Subject is reported to have accumulated important information and to have communicated it to Resistance leaders, particularly information concerning the manufacture of arms in French plants, movements of German troops, war materiel, and plans of the German attacks on the French Maquis." She reportedly gave the sum of 1,200,000 francs to Resistance causes. Yet at the bottom of this shining paragraph—with no other mention elsewhere in the report—is the name Mr. Mandel, among many others, as having been a source of the information.[31] This was one of the aliases of Michel Szkolnikoff.

∽

The month of March was spent obtaining testimonials of Florence's good character from the likes of Marie Bell, General Georges, Robert de Thomasson, Jean Paulhan, the princesse Sixte de Bourbon-Parma, and even Florence's butler Diego Zanini, who swore how both Florence and Vogel had saved him from being sent as a slave laborer for Organisation Todt—the very organization Vogel worked for. Magdeleine Homo wrote a letter attesting to Florence's generosity in giving to all the right causes, including 800,000 francs to the 8th Battalion of Zouaves fighters; 400,000 francs to Marie Bell for the *Résistance*; gifts of ambulances and the generous donation of her time as a nurse. Homo also outlined in the letter how Florence had been threatened with arrest by the Gestapo on August 20, 1944, and "destroyed all the compromising papers."[32]

What Homo writes was undoubtedly true, and the purpose of writing about "compromising papers" was to infer that Florence had been actively working with the *Résistance*. What Florence hadn't realized was that the FBI already understood that the October 19, 1944, testimony under oath to the OSS bore little resemblance to her several later declarations to the Americans, most notably the statement that she was afraid of what the Germans would do to her husband.

Based on the recommendations of all the departments investigating Florence's activities with the Germans during the occupation, J. Edgar Hoover sent forward Florence's treason file to the attorney general for advice and/or action. How or when Florence employed the services of John T. Cahill as her lawyer—the same lawyer who had outsmarted Hoover in the Chase National Bank case—is not in the files, only that he was her lawyer in this matter. Weeks passed without further written documentation. Those weeks became months before Hoover received Assistant Attorney General Theron L. Caudle's reply, dated November 2, 1945: "Reference is made to your memorandum dated September 17, 1945, and its enclosures. The Criminal Division is of the opinion that no further efforts are justified in order to develop a possible treason case against the subject. You are requested, however, to furnish this Division with any further information which you may receive concerning this case."[33] The case was marked "pending."

Though the war had been over for nearly six months in Europe, experience had already taught all those who were investigating war crimes, looting, or collaboration that they did not know all the facts—yet. Besides, there were far bigger fish to fry than Madame Gould. After more than a year under investigation, Florence knew there would be no further action. Not only had she evaded treason charges, but to her mind she had also succeeded in convincing the American military to take on Ludwig Vogel, albeit in the fighting X-2 multilingual unit. While she turned fifty in July 1945, her powers of persuasion seemingly had not dimmed with the years. The only real casualty of her living dangerously was her relationship with Frank.

Florence could be thankful that no one twigged how she fit into the gigantic puzzle which Michel Szkolnikoff and his Nazi holdings represented. No one had connected Benvenuti and Szkolnikoff. While a few newspapers like *The New York Times* had picked up the story that "Frank J. Gould" was seeking to buy the former Ruhl empire along with SBM and thereby corner the luxury gambling and hotel market in France and Monaco at the end of the war, no journalist or investigator understood what that meant. Yet if Florence kidded herself that somehow the DGER or FBI would forget what she had done, or even that her RG 65 file for treason in America could be put behind her, she was seriously mistaken.

PART FOUR

STILL A GOULD

I mock everything, except myself.

—Florence Gould to Marcel Jouhandeau

26

ㄱ╰╮┐

NO SAFE HAVENS

It's true, it's true, I love money.

—FLORENCE GOULD

WHILE FRANCE TRIED TO COME TO GRIPS WITH ITS DIVISIVE COLLABO-
rationist and resistant recent pasts, Florence's salon continued as though
nothing had happened. German officers were replaced seamlessly by
Americans. In the months that followed, Florence, Léautaud, and Jouhandeau periodically mused whether Heller and Jünger had survived
the war in Germany. Marie-Louise Bousquet and Marie Laurencin
remained fixtures, always sparring with their hostess. Artist Georges
Braque joined in the festivities. Florence's old flame, resister Robert de
Thomasson, came back into the limelight. Jean Paulhan, who had been
in hiding in the final days of the occupation, was again in attendance,
and inspired Florence to pay for printing a book by Jouhandeau.

Chronique d'une passion, financed by Florence,* appeared in 1944,
but was beset by problems. Jouhandeau, who feared arrest like Brasillach,
had gone into hiding. By the end of October, he resurfaced, thinking
he'd somehow escaped censure. That December he was cited in *Les*

---

* There were only a hundred copies printed at her expense. In 1949 her Éditions de Quatre Jeudis
  printed a second edition, and in 1964 Gallimard printed a third.

lettres françaises—an index of dishonor—pinned to the chests of fascist writers that included Drieu de la Rochelle, Brasillach, and many others. Academician François Mauriac urged writers like Albert Camus in his *Combat* to denounce calls for denazification in France. The country had suffered quite enough and needed to heal itself.

Still, retribution took its various forms. January 1945 brought Robert Brasillach to trial for inciting to murder through his articles in *Je suis partout*; denunciation of individuals; and all sorts of collaborationism. Sensationally, Brasillach's homosexuality was linked to his *collaboration horizontale* with German officers. Despite hundreds of signatures by the literati of France, including Camus, de Gaulle refused to pardon him. Brasillach became the first writer to be executed for the crime of supporting the occupation. That March, Drieu de la Rochelle finally succeeded in committing suicide. Although he had usurped Paulhan's position at the NRF, Paulhan was devastated.[1] In May, Jouhandeau's "collaboration dossier" was reviewed by the judicial police. A month later, Jouhandeau went into hiding once more.

∽

None realized that the investigation into Banque Charles, Florence Gould, and Ludwig Vogel continued in secret in both France and the United States. The Allies, during 1944, worked together to annihilate the Axis Powers through shared intelligence. Investigators knew that the Goulds had over 300 million francs in assets sequestered by the Germans in 1940. Yet their businesses were only Aryanized as "enemy assets" after the American declaration of war. Unless and until the Allied sleuths could question Hans Dietrich Warzinski, however, they did not have absolute proof whether this was a "soft" maneuver to protect the Goulds or no. Then came the revelation that, in January 1944, Warzinski advised Florence that her assets had been transferred to Aerobank.[2] The Americans believed that this may have been the real impetus behind the investment in Banque Charles. Given the Gould name and connections at the highest levels of society, believing was one thing, proving quite another.

The French, however, became increasingly concerned with the scandals engulfing Monaco and the role their own plenipotentiary minister,

Du Pasquier, played. Du Pasquier's cohorts, including Jean Guisan and Szkolnikoff, were trying to take over the French luxury hotel and casino industry. Had Szkolnikoff also used Guisan to squirrel away his 2 billion francs in Switzerland? investigators asked. Banque Charles was a second scandal somehow linked to the first, but just how, puzzled them. Evidently, Banque Charles was the vehicle through which German flight capital would be laundered before being converted into dollars, and Szkolnikoff's empire was part of that scheme.

To make matters even trickier, Szkolnikoff allegedly absconded with some crucial and embarrassing papers to assure his own safety. The French were determined to find these documents. With the endgame of the war in play, and more war crimes coming to light, the DGER decided it needed help, but not from the overstretched Americans. In all innocence, they employed the services of Experta—which controlled Szkolnikoff's companies on behalf of the Reich through Deutsche Waren Treuhand-Aktiengesellschaft. It also formed part of eighteen trust companies dedicated to auditing the Reich's accounts.[3] At the time the investigation was undertaken by Experta, France was still at war with Germany.

No road runs smoothly in war, but the decision to use the German-controlled Experta with strong links to Florence's go-to man for Switzerland, Jean Guisan; the French plenipotentiary minister to Monaco, Du Pasquier; and Szkolnikoff showed a clear lack of understanding of the interplay between them. Experta, originally set up for the protection of French and white Russian loans against the Bolshevik Revolution of 1917, had moved with the times and was—during World War II—one of the main vehicles used for the Aryanization of French property. Experta also handled Aryanization of American assets in France. Helena Rubinstein's French cosmetics subsidiary's audit was carried out by Experta in 1942, despite Rubinstein having transferred ownership of the business to her French lawyers.[4] That said, Experta apparently did not handle the audit of the Goulds' properties for the Nazis.

Prince Louis's closest confidant, Émile Roblot, also linked to Experta, had been stripped of his official standing by then, but was, nonetheless, tasked with helping Experta and the DGER to discover the truth. From that moment, Szkolnikoff, still on the run in neutral Spain, was doomed to take the fall for his German masters. His body was found by the road-side, beaten and drugged, on June 10, 1945, around twenty-two miles from Madrid, in an alleged bungled French secret service attempt to repatriate him to France.[5] The incriminating papers he had stolen were never discovered.

American military investigators inadvertently led Szkolnikoff's as-sassins to him, advising the DGER of his whereabouts. Only the British and Americans felt that Szkolnikoff was a key to unlocking the mystery of Banque Charles; Florence Gould's shareholding; and ties to Argentina for Nazi flight capital. Precisely how they were intertwined was crucial to the success of unraveling this particular thread for Operation Safe-haven. Szkolnikoff's surprise appointment as Argentina's vice-consul in Spain enabled the U.S. Secretary of State, Joseph Grew, to lodge an offi-cial complaint with the government of Argentina and U.S. ambassador Jefferson Caffery in Paris regarding the seriousness of this link in Brit-ish and American eyes. Lodged in the Operation Safehaven files, there was a serious and credible link between Banque Charles, Argentina, and Szkolnikoff.[6]

Safehaven investigators also worked on this network from other angles. They listed Florence's contacts within the Nazi hierarchy, which when considered plainly, made for damning reading:

That her participation in the Banque Charles was an outgrowth of many close and congested relations she had with the Germans (in-cluding the Gestapo) and notorious French collaborators during the occupation. That her explanation of her participation in the bank (as set out before) does not correspond with the explanation she gave to the OSS, Paris, on October 18, 1944. "During the occu-pation, Florence Gould had social relations with the following principal German and French collaborators: Werner Klingeberg, Director of the Deutsches Nachtrichten Buro [sic], Paris (German Newspapers); Willy Praeger-Gretsch of the Abwehr; Walter Stef-fens of the Abwehr; 'Colonel Patrick' Garthe of the Abwehr; De Lestandi of the Le Pilori, one of the most fascist of French newspa-pers; Marcel Peter, director of Le Petit Parisien; Odewald of the Gestapo; General Medicus; Knochen of the German Secret Service; Countess de Chambrun, daughter of Laval; Carbuccia of the collaborationist newspaper [Le] *Gringoire*."[7]

Hoover had been told to close the Florence Gould RG 65 file, but the OSS and British and American officers working in Operation Safehaven were actively pursuing the Gould-Charles-Szkolnikoff lead. Florence had the Soviets to thank for saving her skin. The heating up of the Cold War, rather than Florence's cunning, meant investigators were called off the case. But none of this information appeared in Florence's OSS or FBI files. It resided in the Ludwig Vogel file dated June 6, 1946.

27

PAPER CLIPS AND FRIENDS CAST LONG
SHADOWS

*When one has friends, it is to defend them, not to attack
them.*

—FLORENCE GOULD

VOGEL HAD BEEN SUCCESSFULLY EMPLOYED AT WRIGHT-PATTERSON
Air Force Base in Cincinnati, Ohio, since September 15, 1945, some nine
months before FBI agents reported back to Hoover on June 6, 1946, in
writing. Florence had succeeded in getting Vogel sent to America as part
of the secret program called Operation Paperclip, to bring German scientists to America.

Vogel joined the company of the elite scientists such as rocket scientist Wernher von Braun, who was instrumental in the NASA space
program; Dr. Hurbertus Strughold, who developed manned space flight;
General Reinhard Gehlen, former head of Nazi intelligence in the Soviet
zone, who continued his work for the U.S. at the outset of the Cold War;
and Dr. Gerhard Schrader, a scientist at I.G. Farben, which manufactured the Zyklon-B gas used in the concentration camps, and who was
also one of the two inventors of the deadly gas sarin. These were just a
handful of the hundreds of top German scientists brought to America
for Operation Paperclip.[1] Even the former German General Franz Medicus, who worked from Florence's sequestered Maisons-Laffitte estate,

was part of the program as a valued medical man.* Yet Vogel was no scientist.

Hoover was unamused that Vogel, who was termed a "glider instructor and pilot" in his FBI files, should be among the illustrious and notorious list of Paperclip scientists. Indeed, Hoover discovered shortly after Vogel's arrival at Wright-Patterson in Ohio that he had been of very limited assistance to the Allies as part of the X-2 unit. Vogel interpreted interrogations of German prisoners, but didn't reveal significant information regarding air force bases, number of planes, or armaments, as promised by Florence. To boot, after three years in the United States, Vogel applied for American residency. This was behind Hoover's launching on October 5, 1948, a "SPECIAL INQUIRY—DEPARTMENT OF JUSTICE—GERMAN SCIENTISTS UNDER THE PROTECTIVE CUSTODY AND CONTROL OF THE JOINT INTELLIGENCE OBJECTIVES AGENCY" with a "particular emphasis on the internal security aspects of the immigration of Vogel to the United States for permanent residence. . . . All offices should be alert in obtaining information concerning the activities of Vogel prior to his coming to the United States and fully develop any allegations of a derogatory nature against Vogel."[2] Along with Hoover's letter was an enclosure of Vogel's relationship with Florence, and her derogatory information.

The bulk of the information of a "derogatory nature" unsurprisingly regarded Vogel's joining the Nazi Party in 1932, and Florence Gould. Vogel signed an affidavit attempting to explain away his membership to the Nazi cause, which, given that no one could testify to the contrary, had to be taken at face value—for the time being. A letter from the War Crimes Office in Berlin dated June 21, 1947, stated that they had no record of Vogel. His old boss at Standard Oil in Hamburg wrote that Vogel had been an exemplary employee.

Only Wolfram Hirth, Vogel's glider pilot trainer who had known

---

* Medicus's father so loved living in the United States that he gave his son Franz the middle names "Horace Greeley." Medicus, too, had affectionate memories of the United States, like Vogel. He was viewed by Abetz with suspicion. Medicus liked to portray himself after the war as a gentleman scholar who was forced to do as ordered. See Charles Glass, *Americans in Paris* (London: HarperPress, 2009), 134–135.

Vogel since 1933, gave a full picture of Vogel's personality in his affidavit of February 1948, reproduced here in part:

> Vogel pursues his aims with great energy and tenacity. In order to reach his goal he unscrupulously applies any means, as far as they are not expressly violating existing laws. His effort to exert himself successfully, to play an important part and create [for] himself a distinguished and profitable position are the motives for all his thoughts and activities. Here he possesses a sound egotism. He clearly and steadily pursues his aims and tries to eliminate all his competitors and enviers with relentless energy. Yet none of his efforts was prejudicial to his looking [an] adroit and sociable person, who is sure to make a good impression everywhere, in particular with women. Most of his comrades and collaborators did not like him, as his cool-blooded endeavors were often interpreted as unfair to his associates. Yet I do not think that this was the case. He possesses a sound ambition and business ability of a strong man who disregards the weaker, and who follows his way knowing about his own abilities and the right of the strong. After all, I think him an honest, respectable and valuable man. . . . Vogel has no political interests at all. . . . His attitude is liberal. There is no room for narrow national policies in his cosmopolitan mentality. As he disregards everything beyond his own success, he never took any interest in National Socialism, for the latter could be of no use to him.[3]

Vogel was a man after old Jay Gould's heart. No wonder Florence had fallen for him. No wonder Frank liked him. While Hirth's affidavit was no glowing endorsement of Vogel, it did let the FBI know that he always worked within the law. Still, Hoover sent the Vogel file to the attorney general's office. A reply came back: "The Assistant Attorney General has now requested the bureau to conduct [an] additional investigation in Paris by contacting appropriate intelligence sources for any additional information reflecting on Vogel's activities which may tend to verify the report that Vogel was a former agent of the Gestapo. Your particular attention is drawn to page twelve of special agent, Donald L.

Daughters. . . . ."[4] The intelligence source reply affirmed that no further information could be obtained in Paris.

Hoover spread his net wider. Having "met Vogel on many occasions," Commander William H. Munson, Vogel's commander when attached to the U.S. Navy, swore that he was not "impressed with him as a person of great character, but as a person ready to improve his own position." Commander Richard F. Thoeny, Air Documents Section, "stated that Vogel had been very secretive about his [wartime] activities" but did not consider him a security risk. Colonel H. M. McCoy believed that Vogel remained valuable to the United States for his contacts in Germany.[5]

Those who knew Vogel during the war, like General Georges and the princesse Sixte de Bourbon, had only high praise for Vogel and how he had saved them and their loved ones from deportation to Germany or worse. First Lieutenant Stewart French, who served with Vogel through the end of the war in the OSS in Munich, thought Vogel executed his duties with care and had strongly held views that were the opposite of fascism.[6]

Vogel used General William Donovan, former head of the OSS, as a reference. General Donovan did not recall Vogel, but said that his associate B. Meredith Langstaff of his law firm knew Vogel well and gave him a clean bill of health. Hoover was compelled to allow Vogel's request for permanent residency in the United States to go ahead. He'd lost a battle, but there was a war yet to be waged.

ം

Meanwhile, in France, the case against Florence and Banque Charles was building. On September 20, 1948, the French government put forward Florence's DGER file to the Ministry of Justice to bring her and her accomplices in the Banque Charles case to trial. In interviews with Karl Schaeffer of the Reichsbank; the French Ambassador to Monaco Georges-Picot; the former Secretary of State Émile Roblot; Du Pasquier, as a close adviser and friend of Prince Louis II; and several others, it emerged that the Monégasque bank project had been in the offing since 1941. Florence Gould, the judge reported, was earning four percent interest on her 5 million francs invested.

All her co-investors vehemently denied that there was any blackmail involved in her investment in the bank, or any innuendo or threats against her or her husband. That she deposited a further 2 million francs in her own account, in addition to another 200,000 francs in her sister Isabelle's name, when she was not obliged to do so, was a clear indication of her complicity in the flight of Nazi capital. The judge concluded: "Although it is unproven that she had committed a crime of intelligence with the enemy, it is certain that we have nothing to congratulate her for by her attitude." Sadly, the investigation was called off because of lack of manpower, and a belief that the evidence was insufficient to bring in a verdict of guilty against the parties. With evident regret, the decision was made that no charges should be brought against Florence or her associates in the Banque Charles affair.[7]

And so the show went on. Throughout the next two years, Florence's salon flourished, be it at avenue Malakoff with its new additions like Gallimard editor Jean de Noël, who would eventually replace Marcel Jouhandeau as her master of ceremonies; at Juan-les-Pins in summer, courting Elsa Maxwell or Henri Matisse; or at Maisons-Laffitte tripping down memory lane with Jean Cocteau in the town of his birth. Paul Léautaud continued his astute but biting comments as before, on the "idiocies" pronounced at Florence's Thursdays, yet condemned himself for being weak and unable to keep away from her table. Florence, who publicly proclaimed that "When one has friends, it is to defend them, not to attack them," similarly said within months, "Ah, Léautaud, he was truly horrid. . . . He put rice powder on his nose and rouge on his cheeks. When he was truly angry with me, he would call me a 'comedienne'—but since his mother, whom he loved wholeheartedly was a comedienne, I angered him more by pretending it was a compliment."[8] What really mattered to Florence was the *idea* of friends, and that they would remain at her beck and call.

There were, to paraphrase Shakespeare, many entries and exits. Some of these were directly related to her collaboration and Florence's increasingly acerbic words with her female courtiers. Marie Laurencin seemed to take great pleasure trading vile barbs with her hostess, though there was never any clear reason why. Marie-Louise Bousquet, while affiliated with *Harper's Bazaar* since the 1930s, was at last made the Paris fashion editor in 1946, working closely with Carmel Snow in New York. In what must have felt like a slap to Florence, Marie-Louise resumed her own Thursdays, attracting those buzzing around the fashion world. Meanwhile, the gray mice returned to their former lives. . . .

Arletty was less blessed than Madame Gould. She faced what can only be termed a hearing, rather than a trial, for collaboration with the enemy. The charges were, however, more than *collaboration horizontale* with her handsome German lover, Colonel Hans Soering. Arletty was the intimate friend of both René de Chambrun and his wife, Josée (also up on charges),* and had met Soering one evening when she went to a concert with Josée. Soering set her up in style at the Hôtel Ritz, but alas for Arletty, he was also a close associate of Hermann Göring's. Eventually the de Chambruns would be found "not guilty" of collaboration at a proper trial, but Arletty had no such luck.

Few people in France excited more argument both for and against the punishments meted out for collaboration. Arletty was well loved, and had given the French escapism during their darkest hours. While de Gaulle's provisional government wanted to make an example of Arletty in a strictly political sense, they also wanted her hidden from view. The *épureur*—a judge in the purges—recognized that putting her in a Paris prison might incite her fans to riot. Not giving her a custodial sentence would send the wrong message. Her punishment for collaboration was to be placed under house arrest at some locality at least thirty-one miles from Paris.

By sheer luck, Jacques and Lelette Bellanger, who admired Arletty, offered their Château de la Houssaye to the court as Arletty's place of imprisonment. When the judge discovered that Bellanger had been in the Resistance, he agreed to send Arletty there. What he could not know was that Arletty and Lel, as she called Lelette, would develop a very close relationship during her eighteen months' house arrest, although just

---

* Chambrun's father-in-law Pierre Laval, like Pétain, was put on trial and found guilty of treason. Laval was executed but Pétain was spared due to his age, ending his life in prison.

how close is a matter of conjecture. Unlike Florence, Arletty had well-documented lesbian affairs.[9]

∽

It is easy to ponder what happened to Frank during this tumultuous time, and what his reaction to these investigations might have been, but there is no publicly available record. Apparently, just after the war, the family home at Juan-les-Pins, La Vigie, was rented out to Picasso temporarily. The master of modern art decided to thank his hosts for the house by painting murals on the villa's walls. Frank disliked modern art, particularly Picasso's work, and so had the murals painted over in disgust when he saw them. This also begs the question where Frank lived between 1944 and 1946.

Having obtained, thanks to Florence, Monégasque residency, was he in Monte Carlo? Or perhaps he was camping out with Anne Marie Vilbert de Sairigné in Nice? What is certain is that after 1946 he officially removed himself from his wife and her boisterous coterie by installing his household at his small villa in Juan called Le Soleil d'Or. Frank never commented publicly on Banque Charles after the war, nor on Vogel. All that is known for certain is that Magdeleine Homo remained his secretary, and more than likely, his untrained nurse and dog walker—for Frank still adored his Pekingese dogs. His happiest moments were spent in his studio, dismantling and reassembling rare mechanical toys that his old friends sent him from around the world.[10] As with many older or infirm people, Frank needed the peace and solitude his wife was unable, or unwilling, to offer.

What we do know, thanks to a bizarre twist in the tale, is that on February 25, 1947, de Sairigné cashed the check for $400,000 that Frank had written for her hiding him from the occupiers and their minions in 1943–44.[11] The check was dated February 20, 1944, payable at the United States Trust Company of New York located at 45 Wall Street. Why she waited over three years to cash it is anyone's guess, unless she had gone into hiding for her own activities as part of the resisting Maquis during the war. Nonetheless, in the interim, Frank had apparently stopped payment.[12] De Sairigné's lawyer, Martin J. Kelly, lost his client's case in New York's federal district court. It seems that back then there was no such thing as a stale check, and it was not on those grounds that Frank's brilliant lawyer, the ubiquitous John T. Cahill, fought the case. Having brought the case in federal court, Kelly had to continue his appeal up through the federal, rather than state, court system.

Kelly argued that Gould had been out of danger certainly since the occupation of France had ended in September 1944, if not before, and yet waited until February 1947 to stop the check. No affidavit by Frank was submitted, nor affidavits for others on his behalf. Cahill wisely argued that the federal courts had no jurisdiction to find in favor of the plaintiff de Sairigné because she was a French citizen, suing an American citizen (albeit resident in France) in the U.S. federal court system. On this strong technical point of law, the New York State Appellate Division found in favor of Frank Gould.[13] A writ of certiorari, or a writ by which a higher court can review a decision in a lower one, was served, and the case went to the Supreme Court of the United States.

De Sairigné's case, case number 541, went before the Supreme Court in the October term 1949, and was filed in February 1950. Cahill and his team argued that *forum non conveniens* in the New York federal circuit court had been properly applied, just as in the appellate division. Technically, this involves a discretionary power allowing courts to dismiss a case where another court is much better suited to hear it.[14] This dismissal does not prevent plaintiffs from refiling their cases in the more appropriate forum or higher court.

Cahill also argued that neither Frank Jay Gould nor his attorneys nor any other authorized agent had ever been served with a copy of the summons or complaint, and that as both Frank and de Sairigné resided in France that there was "no sound reason for bringing this action in this country rather than in France," particularly as jurisdiction over Frank "under the laws of France" was not in question.[15] It was an accurate and compelling argument, irrespective of the contract implied by the check on which Frank had stopped payment. The U.S. Supreme Court found in favor of the defendant, claiming no jurisdiction in the matter.

So why did de Sairigné go to all the expense and bother of suing in the United States in the first place, particularly as Florence was under investigation for most of that time for her collaborationist activities in the war? Perhaps de Sairigné felt that by making a "stink" in America,

Frank would back down? If so, she didn't know Frank. Or was it to avoid a confrontation with Florence? If it were the latter, it could be that Florence, not Frank, had in fact stopped payment on the check. If so, then it is suggestive that Florence threatened de Sairigné with exposure in court—and thereby in public—of Frank's diminished mental state if she were compelled to defend stopping the $400,000 payment on his behalf in a French court. These possible explanations, as well as others, remain just a few speculations to dozens of unanswered questions.

∽

By the early 1950s, the Goulds' manager, known only as Mr. Gallauziaux, rebuilt their hotel empire, and financed two further properties. Gallauziaux was Frank's man, and had singlehandedly saved the Goulds' millions from Aryanization as early as 1941. Instead of repaying Frank's loans to his companies in cash, Gallauziaux had the foresight to wipe out the holding company loans by converting them into three notes: 10 million francs falling due in 1943; and 50 million due at the end of 1944 and again at the end of 1945. Warzinski twigged only the first note falling due during 1944, but with Gallauziaux's prevarication, and the German retreat, Warzinski was unable to collect for the Reich. As Gallauziaux told investigators during the Banque Charles investigations, there was no reason whatsoever for Madame Gould to put money on deposit with Aerobank or Banque Charles.[16]

Fortunately, Florence never knew what Gallauziaux stated in his deposition. Otherwise the competent Gallauziaux would have been fired. Besides, Frank had been dying, ever so slowly, for years. Florence concentrated on living a worldly life. The time had passed long ago for changes to her modus vivendi. She would wait out the end, confident of her financial position.

So while Gallauziaux toiled on their behalf, Florence was ever more involved in charities, "generous to a fault, as always." Some of these were pet projects of the American consul to Nice, Quincey Roberts.[17] Memories everywhere had become increasingly short. Everyone who didn't come to trial or faced an *épureur* was suddenly a *résistant*, in a mood of forgetfulness that swept across all Europe. Florence's claims of having joined the OSS in December 1943 were among the least offensive of the tall tales told. It was time to forget, to move on, and live life again.

～

At long last, French women could vote for the first time in the October 1946 elections. Surprisingly to some, de Gaulle was heading for a crippling defeat to the Communists, who won twenty-six percent of the vote. The Socialists and Moderates together claimed another thirty-nine percent, with de Gaulle's MRP retaining twenty-five percent.

Two weeks later, de Gaulle sent his head of cabinet, Gaston Palewski, to the National Assembly with his letter remitting his powers to them. Yet the National Assembly voted nearly unanimously for de Gaulle to head the new coalition government alongside the Communist majority. Where de Gaulle was violently anti-British and anti-American, Palewski was a converted Anglophile, had spent time at Oxford University, spoke beautiful English, and headed de Gaulle's private office while in exile in London. Interestingly, Palewski, who also had been Nancy Mitford's lover since they first met at the Allies Club in London in 1942. He was also the inspiration for the character Fabrice, duc de Sauveterre, in Mitford's novel *The Pursuit of Love*.

Despite Palewski's cooler hand on the tiller, de Gaulle's government lasted barely a month. De Gaulle's legendary stone wall of pride could not brook any compromise, even at Palewski's urging.[18] Although the Communists were in power, Palewski remained committed to de Gaulle and became instrumental in the formation of the Gaullist Party, the RPF (Rassemblement du Peuple Français). More significantly for Florence, Palewski became a member of the National Assembly in 1951 for Paris, and from 1953 through 1955 he was the vice president.

Yet there were those in France, even in the 1950s, who felt that Florence's conduct and collaboration during the war merited punishment. Despite the investigation into Banque Charles reaching a dead end in the courts, the DGER was determined to rid France of her presence. No amount of money nor charitable donations had swayed them in the intervening years. On October 1, 1954, the DGER put forward a document for counter-signature demanding Madame Frank Jay Gould be deported.

Frank could remain, since he had done nothing during the entire war to indicate that he was collaborating with the enemy. Florence's cherished life risked an abrupt end.

Only the Communists or a man of Palewski's powers of persuasion could possibly halt such an action. Given that Palewski was having an affair with the Gould's niece, Hélène-Violette Talleyrand-Périgord— Anna Gould's daughter—and that she had given birth to Palewski's son while still married to her first husband, it is not a leap of faith to think that he came to Florence's rescue.[19] After all, Palewski was a reckless and outrageous womanizer, and could hardly say no to any attractive woman.

Besides, Palewski had a fluid approach to collaborators. In September 1944, he came to the rescue of the extreme right-wing publisher Alfred Fabre-Luce in a delicate situation. The publisher's wife just happened to be the sister of Prince Jean-Louis de Faucigny-Lucinge of SBM fame, and she telephoned her brother for help. Apparently, Fabre-Luce managed to escape a dawn raid on his home, but his butler and a houseguest were arrested. By the time Faucigny-Lucinge arrived at the apartment, the Duchesse de Brissac, wearing only a fur coat over her underwear, was being questioned by the police. She, like Arletty, was taken to the Conciergerie. Frantic, Faucigny-Lucinge telephoned the Duke de Brissac, but he refused to help, since his wife had evidently been caught in flagrante. Soon after, Faucigny-Lucinge thought of Palewski, who managed to rescue the daring duchess from Drancy after a mere four weeks' incarceration.[20]

Even the best archives are incomplete, often for matters of state. So whether Palewski intervened directly or indirectly in Florence's case is conjecture. Nevertheless, someone of his political standing and power would have needed to become actively involved to save Florence from deportation.

⁓

Six months after the document requesting Florence's deportation was drafted and awaited the counter-signature that never came, Ludwig Vogel applied for security clearance to become a consultant to the U.S. Air Force. Hoover was again brought in to investigate. He forwarded the file to the assistant chief of the Counter-Intelligence Division and the inspector general. Florence's name featured as a primary reason to deny Vogel his security clearance—ten years after the initial investigation against her.

The year 1954 was among the darkest of the McCarthy era, when Americans were chasing "reds under the beds," as the saying went. While no one ever accused, or suggested, either Vogel or Florence of being a communist, America had been thrown into a maelstrom of fear by Senator Joe McCarthy's speech on Abraham Lincoln's birthday, February 12, 1954. He baldly accused the administrations of Franklin D. Roosevelt and Harry S. Truman of "twenty years of treason."

President Eisenhower's vice president, and later president, Richard M. Nixon went further. Adlai E. Stevenson, governor of Illinois, was running for president against the beloved incumbent and former leader of the Allies, "Ike," when Nixon claimed that "Mr. Stevenson has been guilty, probably without being aware that he was doing so, of spreading pro-Communist propaganda as he has attacked with violent fury the economic system of the United States and has praised the Soviet economy."

J. Edgar Hoover and other senior FBI officials had their own political agendas that included smearing the Roosevelt and Truman administrations for being soft on "commies." At the same time, Hoover was doggedly pursuing Florence's long-dead case and looking to envelop Vogel in the Nixon-alleged "6,000 security risks" cleared under the Truman administration. Hoover put thousands of innocent Americans seeking more liberal expressions in politics under surveillance.[21] If Florence or Vogel knew what was going on, either could be forgiven for wondering when and how this would all end.

28

A FORTUNE TO GIVE AWAY

C'est la femme aux bijoux, celle qui rend fou.
(It's the bejeweled woman, who will drive you crazy.)
> —1930s song thought to have been inspired by
> FLORENCE GOULD

FLORENCE'S ENDOWMENT OF THE ARTS AND GENEROUS GIFTS TO CHARI-ties continued unabated, often including vast and expensive parties, and invitations of the notable, great, and good. The first Cannes Film Festival, delayed seven years by the war, finally took place in September 1946, featuring Billy Wilder's *The Lost Weekend* and David Lean's *Brief Encounter*. Naturally, Florence was among those treading the red carpet, as she would try to do for every Cannes Film Festival during her lifetime. With each progressive year, Florence's svelte figure became more rounded and her sunglasses darker. Her fabulous triple string of pearls, once cherished for their magnificence, now served to hide her wrinkled neck. Since she hated the idea of plastic surgery, Florence tried to defeat age instead with more mundane accessories.

Despite age, she would remain at the heart of all that mattered to her. Her lunches continued to be her crowning glory, with her rejoicing in a table plan that brought together artists from different worlds with an apparent luck-of-the-draw nonchalance, though she had meticulously planned that Maurice Chevalier and Salvador Dali should sit together opposite her—so she could enjoy the sparkle of their mischievous eyes.[1] When the conversation somehow drifted away from having her at the center, she always brought it back where it belonged. For example, at her Malakoff lunch on May 20, 1948, while discussing the Cold War and the current diplomatic talks in London, Florence announced in front of Jouhandeau and Léautaud that if the Soviets pushed the Americans too far, "It will be war . . . you understand, I am again working 'undercover' (as I did during the German occupation). . . . All that I say is absolutely under the seal of secrecy. Do not repeat it to anyone."[2] Perhaps she was tipsy or her old friend William Bullitt, America's former ambassador to France, had whispered something to her since his return to Paris after the war. Not that Bullitt was in the know any longer. Her assembled guests had the wit to realize that her working undercover for the United States was simply preposterous.

∽

As the years drifted past, another way her loss of personal good looks manifested itself was in seeking beauty in external pleasures. Thanks to Daniel Wildenstein's return to France after the war, Florence added substantially to her Impressionist art collection. Wildenstein was five years old when Florence first came into his father's home, and since that time, had admired her beauty, good taste, and generosity. From 1923, when she married Frank, she was a regular visitor to the Wildenstein gallery, then run by Daniel's grandfather, Nathan, who dubbed Florence "the most beautiful woman on earth."[3] Impressionist art and fine jewels had always been foremost in her many passions, but as the mid-1950s dawned, they would also be her comfort.

Her jewel collection had become world-famous. In January 1951, her incredible thirty-three-carat emerald was stolen from her strongbox she kept at their hotel at Juan, and a cheap glass imitation was left in its place. She pointed the police to her hotel manager, who had given her the wrong key, swapping it with one for the box of a Paris industrialist. French police traced the emerald to Spain, then back to jewel cutters in Paris, where the stone was refashioned into two smaller pieces that were easier to disguise for resale to an unsuspecting buyer. The four thieves were caught and charged, and Florence was left with the two lesser emeralds as her recompense.[4] The outstanding question never asked at the time was if anything else of value was stolen from that box or others to which she had access.

∽

In 1952, Frank, harking back to the happiest days of his life, gifted another $1.5 million to New York University. Halfway through the year, Frank took to his bed, ostensibly never to leave it again. Three years later, NYU's Chancellor Henry T. Heald came to Juan-les-Pins to confer an honorary doctorate on Frank in person. He was so thrilled that another gift of a million dollars and the home at Ardsley-on-Hudson were conferred on the university.[5] Frank's generosity was undoubtedly from the heart, but it also heralded a personal recognition that his life was drawing to a close. The question that might have lingered in Florence's mind was whether Frank had changed his will.

Then, in June 1952, another robbery occurred at their other Juan-les-Pins hotel, Hôtel Alba. The weekly pay of the hotel employees, some $3,000, and $286,000 in bearer bonds were stolen from Magdeleine Homo's office. Around the same time, Frank's daughters, Dorothy and Helen, became suspicious that their father was not free to contact whomever he wished to keep him company or to decide his affairs. By 1953, they felt that Magdeleine Homo was preventing them from having contact with their father unjustly, and that he had become a virtual prisoner. Still, it is entirely possible that Frank simply issued an order for peace and quiet, just as it is possible that Florence may have decided that Frank needn't be bothered by his difficult children. Dorothy even appeared at Frank's home unannounced shortly before his death, and was turned away by Homo.[6]

That same year, Florence's drinking became a matter of some consternation, too, particularly to Jouhandeau, who received late-night, drunken, nasty phone calls from her. It would take over a year—and unquantified largesse—before she would be forgiven for her vile behavior.[7] Others remarked that as her beauty faded with the passage of time, her tyrannical streak grew exponentially and was measured by how much she'd had to drink.

The inevitable happened at six a.m. on the morning of April 1, 1956.

Sometime in March, Frank had slipped into a coma theoretically caused by uremia. While uremia was listed as the cause of death, it was more the final symptom of the health issues that had plagued Frank for nearly fifty years. Given his medical history, the uremia was more than likely caused by gastrointestinal bleeding and decreased kidney function.[8]

Frank's daughters were informed at once, and struck out against Florence. Two days later, Dorothy's lawyers had all the Juan-les-Pins properties sealed and all her father's bank accounts frozen. An estimated third of his fortune was said to be domiciled in France in the form of property investments and stocks. The rest remained invested in America.

Given the family history, it was a wise maneuver. A family war was declared, even as it came to the disposition of Frank's corpse. His daughters thought he should remain in Antibes; Florence wanted to see him buried in his doctoral robes and placed in the Gould family mausoleum at Woodlawn Cemetery in New York. A compromise was made, with the funeral eulogy delivered in Antibes by its mayor Marc Pugnaire, with the pastor Lazare Pellier presiding, before Frank's coffin was sent to New York.[9] Florence, Magdeleine Homo, and Cécile Tellier would accompany the body to its final resting place in the Gould crypt.

Frank's assets worldwide were estimated at some $120 million. The only last testament found was dated April 14, 1936, and deposited at the United Trust Company in New York. It was read by Frank's lawyer, John T. Cahill, at Juan-les-Pins, and gave Frank's daughters $100,000 each, plus an equal one-third of the French investment properties. Florence, minus additional gifts of $300,000 to various individuals, would receive her widow's one-third portion of the French investments in accordance with French law, and the remaining totality of Frank's American interests. Various small gifts to household staff and others included Dr. Vernes ($15,000) and Isabelle Lacaze ($25,000). Sadly, Isabelle who was suffering from stomach cancer, lived only another few months. Magdeleine Homo was singled out as receiving nothing.[10] This spurred Dorothy to believe that Homo was somehow disliked by Frank, when in reality Homo had just begun working for him in 1936.

Had later wills, as Dorothy and Helen suggested, been destroyed or even stolen in the previous two robberies that took place in their father's final years? Florence denied any such wrongdoing. Dorothy was determined to challenge the will in France and New York. Helen blanched at the thought. A mere ten days after her father's death, she made a statement under oath to her Paris lawyer, Russell Porter, who forwarded it on to the U.S. embassy in Paris. On May 17, a translation was sent to J. Edgar Hoover at the FBI, who disseminated it widely to other government departments. It contained *new* information in the "Gould Treason" case, namely:

> In early 1944, Fl. GOULD listed as 'sympathetic' to the Gestapo, was "recruited" in Paris by JOHANNES EUGENE CHARLES ... who had been given a mission by the Reichsbank Section of the Ministry of Economics. ... Fl. GOULD lent herself to this operation knowingly. Its purpose was to "attempt to maintain abroad a financial institution to maintain the interests of Germany." In theory, the bank was to receive funds later from German industrialists, one of whom was BERNHARD BERGHAUSS [*sic*] of Berlin (18 Million).
>
> During her visits to Monaco, Fl. GOULD, through CHARLES, was put in contact with the German colony of the Principality, and principally with KAGENECHT [*sic*], former Gestapo Chief, and HELLENTHAL, German Consul General.
>
> ... HANS GROM, Swiss Citizen, Gestapo Chief at Annecy ... declared that "he had been contacted in July 1943 by one Franz GOERING,* SS Untersturmfuhrer ... who had proposed installing him on the Riviera or at Chamonix with a view to the execution of a plan of the German services for the installation in France of German hotelkeepers *destined to work for them after the war*."†
>
> ... in October 1943, he was put in contact with one BIRKNER, SS Hauptsturmfuhrer of the S.D. in Paris, who sent him to WARZINSKI. ... The latter told him that he had at his disposal hotels belonging to Mrs. Fl. GOULD, a Nazi sympathizer, and offered to set him up in one of these establishments on the coast.

---

* Seemingly not a close relation of Hermann Goering.
† Italic emphasis is the author's.

Mrs. Fl. GOULD was reportedly also in contact in Paris with one VON MERODE, who claimed to be the illegitimate son of LEOPOLD of Belgium and who was Economic Counselor of the Reich, having relations with HERMANN GOERING.[11]

A number of interesting points appear in this new information. Dorothy's version of events gives an alternative and suggestive scenario as to the seriousness of Florence's collaboration, and specifically how she was favorably viewed by the Germans. Grom's testimony, given to American military officials after his arrest, further demonstrates that the idea of resurrecting a Fourth Reich from the ashes of the Third Reich was not mere scaremongering by the British and Americans, but an actual plan. Even more illuminating is that Franz Goering, who was the assistant to Chief of Counter-Espionage Walter Schellenberg by 1944, was intimately involved in using hoteliers as the affable face of sleeper cells for the Fourth Reich. The Goulds' hotels and casinos were firmly in Franz Goering's sites. Perhaps this gave rise to the postwar adage in the hotel sector: *There are no German hoteliers, only Swiss ones.*[12] Even more revealing is that Schellenberg was intimately involved in the bizarre tale of Coco Chanel's attempt to declare a truce with the Third Reich by approaching Bendor and Churchill on Schellenberg's behalf. Finally, Hoover made no comment whatsoever on the file, other than to pass it on to the Internal Revenue Service (IRS) and the Immigration and Naturalization Service (INS).

New York attorney William L. Matheson of 10 Gracie Square, Manhattan, was also hired to represent Dorothy. Again, Cahill triumphed. It was agreed that Florence would relinquish the entire French fortune in favor of the American one less its $300,000 in various gifts, on the proviso that Dorothy, who resided in Mexico City, agree to drop her claims. Given that Dorothy had no real proof of any wrongdoing, she was urged to accept by Matheson. The matter was resolved out of court.

Yet the saga continued. Frank had the outstanding issue of nonpayment of federal taxes going back decades. With Florence taking on the U.S. fortune, representing around two-thirds of Frank's wealth. As she was still Frank's legal wife, there was no inheritance tax to pay. Sadly, Frank also had an issue with his French taxes. Since his daughters were liable for inheritance tax, the settlement became quite a costly matter.

On March 6, 1958, L. Harold Moss, an IRS representative in Paris, notified the U.S. legate that he was investigating Florence Gould to determine if her French assets might become liable for U.S. taxes.[13] The list of Gould assets provided by Donald L. Daughters in 1945 was handed over to the IRS. This letter is proof that resolving the matter of Frank's taxes dragged on for at least two years after his death, and more than likely, some while thereafter. Nonetheless, Florence settled the matter to the satisfaction of both the United States and French tax authorities, since it was no longer referred to in her copious RG 65 file thereafter.

Hoover, however, rekindled his interest in her. William L. Matheson, Dorothy's New York lawyer, was deposed by the IRS on August 28, 1958. He made some damaging accusations against Florence, Magdeleine Homo, and Cécile Tellier. He "indicated that the 1936 will was preserved through the combined efforts of FLORENCE GOULD and her secretary, MAGDELEINE HOMO, and by keeping FRANK GOULD in virtual confinement in his latter years. MATHESON who described HOMO as a lesbian and Communist alleged that HOMO had become FLORENCE GOULD'S protege [sic] because of the fact that they were both sexual deviates." Matheson reiterated all the earlier charges of collaboration against Florence, and claimed that Homo had given money to the Communist Party. Matheson also stated that Homo and Tellier would be visiting the United States again soon aboard the U.S.S. *Constitution*. So Hoover ordered that all ports in and out of New York be watched.[14]

Matheson may have been embittered by his earlier defeat at the hands of Cahill and was passing off his feelings as fact in his deposition. He knew full well that such allegations would be of interest to the FBI, and was playing to his eventual reading audience—J. Edgar Hoover and the IRS. By 1958, all war criminals and collaborators who would be punished had been adjudged for their crimes—save those who remained in hiding like Adolf Eichmann. Hoover's determination to find something— perhaps anything—that would stick to Florence at the height of the Cold War was both unfair and a fantasy.

In the year of Frank's death, 1956, Ludwig Vogel applied for U.S. citizenship. Hoover remorselessly reopened the file replete with its statements and innuendo, evidently in the hope that something might turn up now that the war dust had settled. Nuremberg and the horrors of the Holocaust were already fading as everyone strove for a return to some kind of normalcy. The pan-German dream harbored by Germany since the days of the Kaiser was erased with the rise of the European Economic Community's six core nations: Germany, France, the Netherlands, Belgium, Luxembourg, and Italy. Economic closeness was the way that France and Germany expressed their own cries of *"Never again!"* These echoed, too, in the newly founded state of Israel. Still, political mistakes continued to be made. Suez, Korea, Cuba, and Vietnam, to name names.

Since no affidavit had been forthcoming from Vogel's former employer in France in the 1948 investigation, Focke-Wulf, Hoover ordered that contact be made with the company. Special Agent James T. McCue came up with the goods.

Christian Neyer, the personnel manager at Focke-Wulf in Bremen, was interviewed in November 1955. Neyer confirmed Vogel's employment for the company from 1937 until the liberation of Paris in August 1945. Vogel, according to Neyer, terminated his employment with the firm "on the day of the surrender of Paris, France and is not eligible for rehire for the following reasons[,] Arrangements had been made to evacuate Focke-Wulf employees to Germany upon the surrender of Paris, however SUBJECT failed to do so and disappeared. SUBJECT had access to the Focke-Wulf bank account at the Aero Bank, Paris, France, in the amount of 250,000 Reichsmarks (the equivalent of 500,000 Francs) and since SUBJECT'S disappearance the bank account has never been located." Vogel's former secretary, Irmela de Haas, whose married name was Cunningham after the war, confirmed Neyer's statement. She also confirmed that Vogel was the only person working at the company who could have absconded with the funds.[15]

This time, everyone was contacted. It was Hoover's last chance to stop Vogel. Even Vogel's former wife was contacted in Santa Cruz,

Bolivia, but all she could tell them was that Vogel had come to see her and their daughter in the beginning of 1949 in the hope of getting back together. The former Mrs. Elfriede Vogel, by then remarried as Mrs. Gasser, clearly stated to investigators that Florence Gould was the cause of the breakup of their marriage and their subsequent divorce in 1947. Vogel was meant to support both his ex-wife and daughter, but nothing had been paid before she remarried, primarily because she sought no payment. Gasser said that Vogel was a good man and she hoped he would succeed.[16]

With the benefit of eleven years of hindsight, the attorney general's office felt that Vogel's actions could well be interpreted as a means of slowing down the further production of airplanes, and showed his commitment to the Allied cause. Furthermore, nothing in his time in America pointed to his being anything other than a model citizen and businessman. It ordered that Ludwig Carl Vogel should be granted his American citizenship. The FBI file on Vogel was ordered closed, finally. Florence's treason file would be closed only in 1959.

∽

Hoover's determined work would take second or even third place to the investigations into Florence's two main German contacts, or persons of interest, in the parlance of today. Colonel Helmut Knochen and General Carl Albrecht Oberg (nicknamed "the Butcher of Paris") were both sentenced to death. Knochen was sentenced in a British trial for the murder of British parachutists landing in France in August 1944, a year after the fact. Oberg, too, was found guilty of mass murder by the British. Yet it was only in 1954 that both men were tried in a French court together, and again, sentenced to death.

Notwithstanding the two death sentences, both men were released together at the insistence of the German postwar chancellor Konrad Adenauer. Apparently, on January 18, 1955, Adenauer protested in the strongest terms to Pierre Mendes-France, a Jew and member of the French Resistance who was president of the Council of the National Assembly,* that both men were merely "Waffen-SS soldiers" performing their duty

---

* Mendes-France later also became prime minister of France.

as any other soldier must do. Knochen, Oberg, and others had already been convicted and served their time in the intervening period. The pair, despite being responsible for the deaths of tens of thousands, were the beneficiaries of the new realpolitik of the Cold War and were set free in October 1958, it is suggested, as part of a global reparations deal for 250 million Deutschmarks to the French "victims of German National Socialism."[17]

∞

The new decade—the 1950s—was half over and the shadows of World War II receded, making room for new conflicts between nations, and new personal friends for Florence. Florence's crimes and misdemeanors would go unpunished, as would hundreds of thousands of similar crimes across Europe. Operation Safehaven would die an unnatural death, just as the work of the Monuments Men in restoring looted assets would do. Both had the vastness of their tasks—including the impossible denazification program in Germany—to thank in part, but it was the Cold War and shameful McCarthyism that truly killed off their well-intended efforts. Florence, like so many others, would never come to trial or be deported from France. Whether she ever saw Vogel again before he married a pattern designer for *Vogue*, we shall never know. Vogel was by then part of her rich and varied past. She did, however, meet up with Ernst Jünger while traveling in Switzerland in the late 1940s, and agreed to finance a translation of his Parisian diaries.

She hired the writer Henri Thomas to translate these in 1950—that is, until he asked for more money than Florence believed he was worth. "Florence believes that he [Thomas] wants to diddle her," Dominique Aury wrote to Paulhan. "I suppose," she continued, "that he has it in for her because she refuses to give him what he demands [as payment]. . . . There was a terrible moment when I was seated next to him on the patio, and he looked up at her with hatred in his eyes . . . she rounded on him and said 'he pisses us off. Yes, you. You piss us all off.'" What Florence really held against Thomas was that she had already paid him 200,000 francs, and he hadn't produced anything. To boot, he refused to bathe. He literally stank.[18] Thomas was, of course, fired. Frédéric de Towarnicki and Henri Plard became the translators.

∽

In the 1960s, Maurice Chevalier decided to write his memoirs. He, too, became a regular at Florence's Meurice lunches, championed by her to meet and greet all the great and good in publishing worth knowing. It was a new endeavor for the singer, and he was grateful to his hostess, a "Great Lady of the Arts." Chevalier added to Florence, "Why do you wish to hide it?" He later admitted that "I courted her in a shameless but sincere way at the time. In my new life, in a new world where I was treading water to survive, her friendship and advice were of paramount importance. I said to her, half-seriously, "In truth, Madame, you are the godmother of an amateur writer of eighty-one years of age."[19]

It was time to party on.

29

⟨∞⟩

QUEEN OF THE RIVIERA

*The more one ages, the more one surrounds oneself with
things that are pleasurable.*

—FLORENCE GOULD

WHEN FRANK DIED, FLORENCE WAS JUST SHY OF HER SIXTY-FIRST BIRTH-
day. One of her first acts was to announce to her menagerie of friends
that she was giving up sex. While hardly a genuinely uttered remark, it
put down a marker that whatever any man might claim, she had no intention of remarrying. Nor would she allow any man to dig his clammy
claws into her hard-won fame and fortune. Roger Peyrefitte, author of the
scandalous book *The Jews,* detractor of literary prizes, and one of Florence's writer friends, wrote in his autobiography, *Propos Secrets,* that she
wished to marry him. He would be one of many, including Pierre Benoit, who misinterpreted her continued flirtatiousness for serious overtures. "A gigolo," she famously said, "would cost me more than a
painting."[1] Florence ceased to care who were her friends, her court jesters,
or her parasites. All comers were accepted equally at her parties, so long
as they knew how to play her game.

Florence's main preoccupation was to begin the rest of her life in the
way she intended it to continue. While the gaiety rolled on seemingly
forever on the Riviera, avenue Malakoff was consigned to the past.

Instead, Florence's Thursdays took place at her new Parisian abode, the Hôtel Le Meurice, where Frank had entertained his personal madame, Leone Ritz, some forty years earlier. At Le Meurice, Jouhandeau ceded his preeminence to Florence's new master of ceremonies Jean De Noël, a sensitive editor at Gallimard. The hotel luxuriated in her gatherings of the famous and notable, hosting the political, cultural, and social leaders of the day. André Gide, now a Nobel Laureate, backed her in the dogged and successful quest to make Jean Paulhan one of the "Immortals" of the Académie Française in 1963.

For all her generosity to French culture, including millions given for the museums at Versailles, Nice, and Angers, as well as contributions to the arts, Florence was awarded at long last the great honor of becoming an officer of the Legion of Honor. Ten years later, she became an elected correspondent member of the Académie des Beaux-Arts. Today, she is listed as one of the major benefactors of the Musée d'Orsay in Paris.

After the brouhaha with Frank's daughters was settled, Florence embarked on a project to mark Frank's passing in some way that would show the world that, despite their differences, she held a deep respect for him and all he gave her. Thus, the Frank Jay Gould Foundation and Museum was born. Or was it? The file for this venture in the French National Archives is still extant, but beguilingly empty. The local archive files in Cannes, too, are silent on the fledgling foundation.[2] After 1956, a serious project for the conversion of the Gould tennis courts into a primary school was undertaken by the town of Cannes; but, it, too, was beached on the rocks of political wrangling in 1960.[3] Instead, a fitting memorial to Frank was found in the form of a building named after him at New York University.

⁊

While Florence still received friends at La Vigie, shortly after Frank died she acquired the former home of Lady Orr Lewis, a Canadian railroad heiress, called Le Patio. Built in 1933 by the American architect Barry Dierks, on avenue Gazagnaire in Cannes, it had commanding views out onto the Mediterranean and the Lérins Islands—as well as that all-important private beach. Redubbed Palais Gould by its new owner, it combined all the elements of a high-security house in a city with the creature comforts of a lovely home with an immense patio at its heart. As the invited guest of Prince Rainier and his bride, Her Serene Highness, Princess Grace,* and other royal families (such as the Aga Kahn, King Farouk), Florence wanted Le Patio to be perfectly fabulous.

Old friends, too, were invited. In the spring of 1976, Ernst Jünger appeared on the terrace of Le Patio, dressed in white, tanned, with his piercing blue-eyed gaze that defied the Mediterranean with its brilliance. Aged seventy-six, with a full head of white hair, he stood erect like the soldier of old, still oozing every ounce of charm he exuded more than thirty years earlier. Florence was feasting her eyes on him when he recoiled slightly at her Pekingese dogs encircling him. Jünger never liked dogs, preferring cats. Yet he stooped to point out the cutest of her litter and said with a brilliant smile, "We will make an exception of this one because he is so beautiful." Then, without batting an eye, he added, "How do they satisfy their sexual urges?" Quick as a flash, Florence lifted her chin at him and replied, "They have none." Like the click of her compact signaling the end of her lunches, the conversation was brought to a close.[4]

✍

It was at Le Patio that Florence's large collection of Impressionist art was displayed at its best. Philippe Huisman, the antiquary and right-hand man of Daniel Wildenstein, advised her on future purchases when Wildenstein himself was unavailable. Often, Wildenstein would fly down to Cannes in his private plane, filled with Impressionist masterpieces that he felt would tickle Florence's fancy. These would be left "on approval" until the next visit—or the one after that—so that she could contemplate her new friends in their home environment, seeing how the light played on the canvases at different times of day. Florence, always with an eye to fashion, determined that Renoir's *La Bohémienne*, while initially seductive, had "too much of a bad hairdo" to please her. When Florence asked for a Van Gogh, Wildenstein produced one. She turned it down because of its black background. On the death of Daniel's father, Georges, Florence was delighted to buy the *Three Dancers* by Degas that had hung in Georges's office.

---

* They had married in April 1956.

Her tastes also ran to older artworks. She bought an El Greco and art from the English School of the eighteenth century. Courbet and Corot as precursors of the Impressionist movement were important additions to her collection, too. Bonnard's seascapes and beach scenes stole her heart. In fact, she would acquire eleven Bonnards through Wildenstein. Some of these artworks had been the property of Jewish art dealers, like Gaston Bernheim's *Vue de l'atélier* by Bonnard.[5] It is significant to note that the painting was bought through Daniel Wildenstein.

Some of the Wildenstein art, however, may hide dubious provenances. An Alfred Sisley, *La Machine de Marly et le Barrage*, sold to Florence by Wildenstein in 1969, was exhibited at Galerie Charpentier in 1945. Galerie Charpentier had been one of the hotbeds of Nazi looted art during the occupation. Another, a Manet still life entitled *Pêches,* was allegedly sold by Marcel Bernstein of Berlin in 1932 to Madame Kurt Hermann of Prettsfeld in Bavaria, and then miraculously reappears in 1976 in London. The 1945 date at Galerie Charpentier could easily mask a painting that was looted during the occupation. The alleged Bernstein sale of 1932 could have actually taken place in 1933. Other paintings with a Daniel Wildenstein provenance have since been shown to have a manipulated past.

The 1960s, however, remained a time of carefree buying, without the same research into art provenance regarding Nazi looted art as there is today. Back then, provenance was intended to assure the buyer that the painting was not a fake, first and foremost. Given that Daniel Wildenstein's name on a provenance has become a reason to exercise caution today in restitution departments of auction houses around the world, it also casts a dark shadow on the entire Florence Gould collection of art. Toward the end of her life Florence thanked Daniel's wife, Sylvia, for their years of friendship and service by giving her a thirty-five-carat emerald ring—one of only five of such a size. It was sold at auction in 2009 for € 500,000 along with its matching earrings and brooch.[6]

The hostess of Le Patio also excelled in collecting first edition books, perhaps with a little less fervor than she had collected their writers in her younger days. Art books by her favorite artists, such as Bonnard, Braque, Derain, Jean Dubuffet, and her particular friend, Salvador Dali, took pride of place. Matisse wrote a dedication in her copy of the 1948 *Les*

Lettres portugaises de Marianna Alcoforado, which he illustrated: "Dear Florence Gould, how your dress is beautiful. The white and blue and all its lines and florets that come to a point around you . . ." accompanied by a pretty little picture that he had sketched for her.[7]

Her crystal and porcelain collection was also worthy of a prince. Not only did she own a service for twelve that had been given by Count Orloff to Catherine the Great of Russia, but she also possessed an eighteenth-century dinner service from the French East India Company of 279 pieces engraved in gold with the letters "N" and "J" in commemoration of the marriage of Napoleon Bonaparte to his Josephine.[8] Florence had surrounded herself, indeed, with objects of great beauty—and value.

∽

Still, hobnobbing with royalty, politicians, and social hostesses would have taken its toll if it were not for her most intimate friends Cécile Tellier, Magdeleine Homo, and Madeleine Manigler. Family and close friends had become ever more important with age. Perhaps it was for this reason that Hélène-Violette, Princess de Sagan, and her lover and later husband, Gaston Palewski, became frequent guests. Whenever Palewski traveled to New York for business (as de Gaulle had become the eighteenth president of France in 1959, and founder of the French Fifth Republic), the threesome often visited Anna Gould at the ancestral home of Lyndhurst, until Anna's death in 1961. In a move that must have made Florence think about her own mortality, Anna gave Lyndhurst to the nation, and set up a charitable foundation to preserve it in perpetuity.[9]

More recent friends, like the cosmetics multimillionairess Estée Lauder, provided Florence with a fresh entrée into New York society. Until the launch of her perfume Youth Dew in 1953, Lauder had been the ingénue in the cosmetics business, always trailing behind Helena Rubinstein and Elizabeth Arden—and "the nail man," Charles Revson of Revlon. "It was the success of *Youth Dew* that rankled with Miss Arden," biographer Lindy Woodhouse wrote, "whereas it was the reinvention of Mrs. Lauder's persona as not being Jewish which infuriated Charles Revson." Also Jewish, "Revson once famously yelled, 'Her name's not Estée, it's *Esther!* Esther from Brooklyn.'"[10] Actually, it was Esther from Queens. If Estée wanted to pretend she wasn't Jewish, that was fine by

Florence, too. Besides, like most of Florence's friends, theirs was a truly symbiotic relationship. Florence was the Queen of le Tout-Riviera, and Estée wanted to join the club. Estée was the reigning queen of cosmetics, with tremendous connections in New York, and Florence wanted in.

Through Estée, Florence was honored at the first-ever private party at the New York Metropolitan Museum of Art, given by its museum director, Tom Hoving. During the week of Thanksgiving 1967, unusually dressed in white—yet sporting her dark sunglasses and usual array of nugget-like jewels—Florence was hosted by Mr. and Mrs. Joseph Lauder at the Met. Hoving was delighted. "We are both medievalists," he told *The New York Times*. "Whenever I saw her in the south of France, I'd invite her to visit the museum and she couldn't manage it, so this was one way of getting her here."[11]

Her thank-you note to Hoving was very warm, addressed to "Dearest Tom." She apologized for its tardiness, and yet rolled into one a thank-you for the Met party, a private tour of the Cloisters with Hoving as her tour guide, and Christmas wishes. After a lifetime vamping men, it is hardly surprising that her note should also be suggestive: "I have never had such a visit nor such a man of knowledge to go around with in my life—with my heartfelt thanks and gratitude for all that you are."[12] That March, Florence became an official benefactor. Their April correspondence was signed "love" by both, showing the deep—yet undoubtedly platonic—affection they each held for the other.[13] Or did it?

Hoving's no-holds-barred book, *Making the Mummies Dance*, about his ten years at the helm of the Met portrays him as a man on a mission to turn the Upper East Side museum from a dusty repository of art and artifacts into a dynamic, world-class, thrusting art world leader. He described himself as "part gunslinger, ward heeler, legal fixer, accomplice smuggler, anarchist, and toady." His approach for many was akin to a dictatorship of good taste, while for others it represented nothing more than a "vulgar circus." As for Florence, she is described by Hoving as "short, plump, with enormous lips slathered with ruby-red lipstick . . . and loaded down with what must have been, nestling in rock crystals of diamonds, a kilo of the darkest emeralds I have ever seen. . . . She looked like a mafia mistress."[14] Hoving's words were kind compared to former

Monuments Man and Met director James Rorimer's description of her. "She is disgusting, a spoiled, dissolute woman covered in emeralds who at all times of the day or night wears sunglasses with purple lenses and is so damned boring!" Rorimer exclaimed to Hoving, who was his special assistant at the time. "Oh those parties! One is expected to drink and drink and drink. Makes me sick!"[15] Perhaps Rorimer forgot that he, too, curried favor with Florence after the war to get his hands on the Gould medieval tapestries for the Met.

Hoving's book was published in 1993. After the Met benefited from its main gifts from Florence in her lifetime, Hoving shows himself up to be the ungentlemanly sort of parasite who frequently fed on Florence's overwhelming generosity. According to Hoving, like Rorimer before him and other museum directors elsewhere, he was merely acting out the part of "toady" described in his book, looking to improve the Met's offer.

Utterly unaware of what Hoving's feelings toward her were, Florence donated a Pierre Bonnard painting entitled *La Terrasse de Vernon* to the Met. As is frequently the case in valuable gifts, to maximize tax allowances the painting was deeded to the Met in various fractions of ownership until the museum owned the entire painting in September 1972.[16]

Still the relationship with the Met went back much further. In the same momentous year as the San Francisco earthquake, Frank Jay Gould wrote to then director Sir Casper Purdon Clarke that he would like to present to the Met photographs of his collection of "antique Roman and Greek glass, as well as some Egyptian antiques" with his compliments.[17] If Purdon Clarke had voiced an interest in the collection itself, Gould would most likely have given it to the Met.

Then there were those two tapestries that had been hidden in the vault of the American embassy in Paris just before the occupation. It took a great deal of time for the Met to negotiate their safe arrival— which was done with extreme care—and the first tapestry was shipped from Paris only in March 1946. *A Hawking Party* made in Arras sometime between 1420 and 1435 arrived at La Guardia Airport in New York along with *Judith with Head of Holofernes,* a Flemish tapestry from the mid-fifteenth century, after finally clearing customs that November. While each tapestry was insured for around $80,000, a separate Met valuation determined they were worth a combined $50,000.* Nonetheless, it was an incredibly generous gift, and one close to Frank's heart.

∽

While her art collection grew finer and more significant with each passing year, Florence strived to remain at the forefront among the world's elite. Age, rarely kind to women, was a sharply perceived enemy, always lurking in a mirror or reflected when passing a shop window. She lamented to her young friend Jean Chalon, "look what I have become." Her final fifteen years were spent giving parties, giving her time, giving to charity; giving, always giving. Years of holding a champagne glass aloft and eating rich food, the endless laughter and fun, the *nuits blanches,* or sleepless nights, were taking their final toll. She was dying of cancer. By 1982, she frequently used a wheelchair to get around. Travel became impossible, eating a burden.

Her final official lunch with friends at Le Patio began with an appetizer of foie gras, followed by tournedos of beef with capers, and plum mousse, served with an amusing Rothschild Bordeaux and Boldington champagne. Her champagne glass was filled with water while her friends enjoyed the wines; her plate of food remained practically untouched.

On the morning of February 18, 1983, Florence remarked to Madeleine Manigler, "I would have never believed it was so hard to die."[18] But die she did, later that day. She was the undisputed Queen of the Riviera. She was eighty-seven years old. Other Americans had come and gone, but only Florence had endured.

---

* Today both would be worth far in excess of the inflation calculator value of circa $500,000, due to their rarity and changes in the art market that have made artworks investment vehicles.

EPILOGUE

FLORENCE DECIDED LONG BEFORE HER DEATH THAT SHE WOULD lead the way, not follow, Anna Gould's example. Evidently, she had second thoughts about setting up a foundation in Frank's memory. Instead, she set up a foundation in her own name to promote Franco-American amity and understanding. All her possessions that were not bequeathed to trust funds for her close friends or those employees who had served her faithfully were to be sold at auction. The books and furniture were estimated to sell at Monte Carlo for $5 million, or just over double that value in 2016. The jewelry was exhibited privately before it was sold at Christie's in New York in 1984. Her art collection traveled to London to be put on show at the Royal Academy, prior to its auction in New York. In all, Florence's estate on her death was estimated to be worth some $123.8 million, or around $300 million now.

The Shah of Iran once said that only Florence's jewelry collection could rival his own. If the auction results are anything to go by, he was right. It sold for $8.1 million at Christie's in New York—the highest price achieved for a sole-owner jewel collection at that date. Today it would be worth closer to $182 million.

Her art collection of 180 artworks sold for $34 million ($76.4 million today). By our standards now, it was a paltry sum when one considers that the Van Gogh painting of *Dr. Gachet* sold only five years later to a Japanese businessman for $82.5 million. In part, it can be explained by the fact that in 1985 art was just becoming an investment vehicle—like gold or diamonds. After all, her Van Gogh *Landscape with Rising Sun* fetched the highest price to date for any Impressionist painting—$9.9 million. Only three of her other paintings sold for over a million dollars: the Degas *Three Dancers* ($1.1 million); Courbet's *Bouquet of Flowers in a Vase* ($1.21 million—a new high for a Courbet); and Monet's *Antibes Seen from the Salis Gardens* ($1.375 million).[1]

In part, however, the prices reflect the quality of some of the paintings. Many experts commented off the record that some of the artworks were disappointing, particularly when one considered the signature attached to them. On closer study, thirty-six of the fifty-six nineteenth- and twentieth-century paintings had Daniel Wildenstein as part of their provenance, giving pause for further thought, too. Then there's the fact that Wildenstein often acted as Florence's agent, even when his name does not appear on the provenance.

Others that do not bear a Wildenstein provenance have the dates of previous sales unstated, perhaps masking transactions that took place in the Nazi era, whether as forced sales or heavily discounted ones by a distressed owner. Three such examples were *Pivoines*; *Fleurs d'Été*; and *Nature Morte aux Quatre Pêches,* all by Henri Fantin-Latour. While many do not advertise the date of transfer of ownership, others bear the mark of families and art dealers who were looted during the war.

Names such as Weill, Bernstein, Bernheim, Bernheim-Jeune, and Cassirer tell their own tales of woe. Paintings bought through the large Paris art dealership Durand-Ruel may also be suspect, as the sales of Durand-Ruel are currently being evaluated by restitution experts.[2] Still others bear the clear signs of having been traded in the buoyant Paris art market of the occupation, like Toulouse-Lautrec's *L'Assomoir,* which has the sales mark of the notorious Galerie Charpentier in 1943. Then there are those, like *Madonna and Child Enthroned with Eight Male Saints*, described as belonging to the "Florence Gould Collection before 1932." Sotheby's acted entirely within the moral, ethical, and legal codes prevailing at the time of sale. The auction house relied heavily on information provided by Daniel Wildenstein. It is only since 1998 and the signing by forty-four countries of the Washington Principles regarding the restitution of Nazi looted art that public owners of paintings need to be concerned. In December 2016, the Holocaust Expropriated Art Restitution (HEAR) Act was passed in the United States, allowing civil claims for the recovery of Holocaust-era looted art. Any private owners of art from the Gould Collection—as well as any owners of looted art exhibited publicly in the United States—are now subject to the same laws.

The big question is, *Did Florence know* that some of her art might have had dubious origins? The even bigger question is, *Did she care?* Obviously, as a savvy buyer of art during the occupation, Florence was quite aware that much of the art appearing on the market was looted from less fortunate individuals who had their very lives ripped away from them. She even entertained one of Hitler's big art thieves, Erhard Goepel. So, yes to the first question. As for the second, Florence rarely showed empathy for those who were not in her vast circle of friends. Like most cunning people, too, she could reason away any wrongdoing, just as she had done during the occupation by helping both sides when it suited her.

∽

Despite any questionable ethics, Florence managed to successfully nail her legacy by always remaining a patron of the arts. Her lavish surroundings—be it in Paris or on the Riviera—were home to some of the greatest names in French literature—André Gide, André Malraux, Colette, and Jean Cocteau, to name names—as well as great living artists like Marie Laurencin, Georges Braque, and Henri Matisse. She supported the American Hospital in Paris, the American Library, also in Paris; and the Metropolitan Museum of Art in New York, which named four decorative arts galleries after her. She founded two literary prizes: the Max Jacob Prize for Poetry, after her friend and former lover who died at the hands of the occupiers at Drancy near Paris; and the Roger Nimier Prize for Literature, in honor of the right-wing writer beloved by Jean de Noël. Additionally, she funded the Engraving Prize and the Musical Composition Prize.[3] She was inducted into the Académie des Beaux-Arts in 1974. Yet neither she nor her foundation has ever given a cent to Jay Gould's Lyndhurst, Frank Gould's childhood family home.[4]

Her childhood was marred by one seismic and one biblical natural disaster. As a young woman, she like so many others, briefly became a nurse, during the First World War. These cataclysmic events helped fuel her insatiable desire for fun, and for creating a sort of Neverland for those who surrounded her. With Frank's money, she lived well, and the way she wanted—irrespective of the dangers and regardless of the cost. "She shone with equal luster at lunch when you sat down 6 or at a dinner for 24 or more," Peter C. Wilson, the former chairman of Sotheby's, recalled shortly before her death. "To both she brought her special quality of enjoyment. She was no lion hunter. Her guests were chosen for no other reason than that she wanted to see them and keep warm friendships."[5]

In another age, perhaps another lifetime, Florence would have sat upon a peacock-blue silk brocade sofa overstuffed with hummingbird feathers, attired seductively in the richest fashions, so that all could become captivated by her beauty, wit, and charm. She'd be sipping the finest drink of those times, delighting in an amuse-bouche of larks' tongues like a queen of old. Instead, she used her beauty to gain wealth beyond her own venal imagining, and with that wealth, the absolute power of a queen in the world of her own choosing. To be patronized by Florence, her authors and artists had to play by her rules or not at all. And play they did—in France.

While her foundation continues her wishes to promote Franco-American amity, it should be made clear that Florence never backed individual American artists, musicians, dancers, or writers during her lifetime. It is the foundation that has initiated and promoted any reciprocity for American artists. Though she lived most of her life in France, Florence is buried in America, in the Gould family crypt at Woodlawn Cemetery in New York. Why? Because that is where Jay Gould and Frank Gould—and all the Goulds of any repute—are buried. Above all else, Florence needed their cachet, even in death.

∽

The French have an expression that perfectly depicts the paradoxical—like Florence, with all her exquisite shining personality, hidden vulnerability, lust for wealth, and love of danger. Florence was *une originale*—unique, someone you could love and dislike in equal measure. Someone who could wound and control; then bestow tremendous favor upon those closest to her, and not even realize that she had done both in the blink of an eye. She was selfish, egotistical, generous, gorgeous, promiscuous, quick-tongued, and quick-witted. She was never dull, never boring—despite James Rorimer's harsh words. Above all, she moved with the times and, given the dangerous sweeps of history in which she lived at the height of society, she became—perhaps, despite herself—a dangerous woman.

AUTHOR'S NOTE AND ACKNOWLEDGMENTS

There are many unanswered questions about Florence's life, mostly because she decided from childhood that she would live a grand, worldly life with mirrors. The Florence Gould Foundation refused, despite my best efforts, to allow me access to their archives, their photographs (to which they hold the exclusive rights), and to letters that were clearly in their possession at the time the last biography of Florence was published in French in 1989. Indeed, they made it clear that they did not wish this book to be published. Similarly, many letters and documents that would have been useful were either destroyed during her lifetime or remain undocumented.

What is certain, however, is that Gandhi's words, "As in law or war, the deepest purse finally wins," applied to Florence, Frank, and many powerful, well-connected, or phenomenally wealthy people—then as now—who dare to play the odds and win, making the world a little more unjust daily. My path has crossed several talented "Florences" in my business life in hotel development and finance, as well as in investment banking, and they uniformly believe that laws they don't like are for other people. While I said in my previous book, *Hitler's Art Thief* (2015), that Florence was a Nazi, after having researched her as my primary subject, I must admit that this was an unfair remark. She, like most of her friends in the French Third Republic of the 1930s, was a capitalist, leaning heavily toward the right when it had gone out of fashion in a socialist state.

Both Christie's and Sotheby's did more than was required of them morally and legally at the time their auctions of Florence's collections were held. The laws governing Nazi looted art were different then, and since 1998 all major auction houses have set up art restitution departments headed by world-class experts to avoid the sale of and to report on Nazi looted art (and stolen art) being represented legitimately. Their investigations are ongoing. I believe that the HEAR Act in the United States makes ownership of any artwork with a Florence Gould provenance subject to closer scrutiny.

I have attempted to find the copyright holders of all images used, but with images from the Library of Congress it has not been possible, as the publishers no longer exist, and the photographers/owners are presumed dead or cannot otherwise be traced. If this book affects the copyright held by you, please contact my publisher, and it will be corrected in any future editions.

Finally, any errors in the telling of Florence's story are my own.

I am humbled by my husband's daily support for me while I was writing this book. Without Dr. Douglas Ronald, a gifted historian and writer, the germ of the idea for Florence Gould's biography would never have blossomed. He urged me to pitch it to my agent, Alexander C. Hoyt, who despite suffering from the "Florence Who?" syndrome, understood immediately why this story needed telling. When Alex Hoyt and I approached my editor, Charles Spicer at St. Martin's Press, with the idea for the biography, he was a bit skeptical at first, simply because of his understandable "Florence Who?" reaction. Fortunately, it didn't take very long for him to warm to the idea. Thank you, Charlie, and thanks to Alex for buying into what seemed like a silly idea. Others to acknowledge and thank for their help and goodwill are April Osborn at St. Martin's; Richard Aronowitz-Mercer at Sotheby's in London; interdisciplinary psychotherapist Alexander Balerdi; Matthew Balerdi, MBChB, MRCP; Marjorie Bliss; Jeff Bridger at the Library of Congress; Sir James Bulmer; Shep Burr; Kate Butterworth; Tom Campbell, Lizzie Fitzgerald, and

James Moske (The Metropolitan Museum of Art); Monica Dugot (Christie's Restitution in New York); Lynn Goldberg, Angela Baggetta, and Jeff Umbro at Goldberg McDuffie Communications; Pamela Head; Hugh Hildesley (Sotheby's in New York); Dotti Irving of Four Colman Getty; Richard and Susan Parker; Luc Requier (Archives Nationales de France); Alan Riding; Charlotte and Steve Sass; Amanda Vail; Vincent Virga; Bruce Weiner; and medical anthropologist Mara Weiner-Macario, MSc. Hons.

I owe a very special debt of thanks to Krystyn Hastings-Silver and Howard Zar at the Gould family estate in New York, Lyndhurst, for providing me with images of the family and the estate without charge. Similarly, I owe a special thanks to Floriane Malignon and the generosity of the Hyatt Regency Palais de la Méditerranée in Nice for giving me the photos of the hotel as Frank J. Gould and Florence originally developed it. Since writers must purchase licenses for photographs for the books they write, this is much appreciated.

Archives and libraries that I consulted are filled with banks of expert and willing people who also deserve acknowledgement. To the employees of the Archives Nationales de France at Pierrefitte, archives communales de Nice, archives municipales de Cannes, archives municipales d'Antibes, archives départementale des Alpes-Maritime, Bibliothèque nationale in Paris (Gallia online), the Préfecture de Police, Paris (archives de la Sûreté nationale), California State Archives (probate section), London Library, the Library of Congress, the National Archives in College Park, Maryland, and the Westchester Historical Society, thank you all. Websites that were extremely helpful include ancestry.com, chroniclingamerica.loc.gov, newspapers.com, oac.cdlib.org.

Above all, I hope that you, the reader, enjoyed the book.

SUSAN RONALD
Devon, England
February 2017

CAST OF CHARACTERS

Note: Dates of birth and death are given only for well-known individuals.

Florence Juliette Antoinette Lacaze Gould (1895–1983), society beauty, businesswoman, racketeer, Nazi collaborator, patron of the arts.

The Family

Bazille, Florence "Florinte" Rennesson (1837–1911), laundress grandmother of Florence. She gave birth to Berthe in 1869 and placed her in a convent. The father is unknown.

Castellane, Count Marie Ernest Paul Boniface "Boni" de (1867–1932), first husband of Anna Gould, noted as the leading Belle Epoque tastemaker. He married Anna for her money, and never hid the fact from the public. Florence befriended him in the 1930s.

Gould, Anna (1875–1961) was the second youngest of Jay and Helen Gould's children. She married Boni de Castellane against her family's wishes and after her divorce married Boni's cousin, Hélie de Talleyrand-Périgord, Duc de Sagan. She was Frank Jay Gould's closest family member.

Gould, Dorothy (1904–1969), twin daughter of Frank Jay Gould, sister of Helen, who believed her father was kept a virtual prisoner in his last years.

Gould, Edith Kelly, Frank Jay Gould's embittered second wife. After five years of unsuccessful litigation to overturn the French divorce decree, she finally married London director Albert de Courville.

Gould, Edwin (1866–1933), son of Jay and Helen Gould, was a railway official and investor, and had precious little to do with either sibling, Anna or Frank.

Gould, Frank Jay (1877–1956), Florence's multimillionaire second husband, son of railway robber baron Jay Gould. Frank exiled himself from the United States in 1913 when the first federal income taxes were collected, never returning to America. He was a canny investor, sportsman, and breeder of thoroughbred horses.

Gould, George Jay (1864–1923), railway executive and financier brother of the senior Gould children. He was the lead trustee of the family trust, engaged in a bitter feud with Frank Jay Gould from 1910 until his death due to Frank's marrying without the family's approval.

Gould, Helen (b. 1904), Frank and Helen Kelly Gould's twin daughter, sister of Dorothy.

Gould, Helen Day Miller (1838–1889), wife of Jay and mother of all the Jay Gould children.

Gould, Helen Kelly (1884–1952), first wife of Frank Jay Gould and mother of his two children. She gave birth to twin daughters, Helen and Dorothy, in 1904, divorcing Frank shortly after in 1906. She was married four times.

Gould, Howard (1871–1959) had little to do with his younger siblings once he left the family home. He married actress Katherine Clemmons in 1898, divorcing in 1909, naming "Buffalo Bill" Cody as the co-respondent.

Gould, Jay (1836–1892), father of Helen, Edwin, George, Anna, and Frank. American railway robber baron who left his fortune in trust for his children to avoid conflicts.

Heynemann, Henry Chittenden (1891–1974), San Francisco architect and first husband of Florence.

Lacaze, Berthe Josephine Rennesson Bazille (1869–1940), Florence and Isabelle's strong-willed mother. Florence looked after them both during their lifetimes.

Lacaze, Isabelle (1897–1956), younger sister of Florence. She never married and remained overshadowed by her sister throughout her life.

Lacaze, Maximin Victoire (1861–1911), father of Florence and Isabelle, husband of Berthe Lacaze. Newspaper editor at *Le Franco-Californien*.

Shepard, Helen Gould (1868–1938), philanthropist and eldest child of Jay and Helen Gould. She tried only to see the good in her tear-away siblings.

Talleyrand-Périgord, Hélène-Violette de (1915–2003), daughter of Anna Gould and Hélie de Talleyrand-Périgord, lover and later wife of Gaston Palewski.

Talleyrand-Périgord, Hélie de, Duc de Sagan (1859–1937), second husband of Anna Gould. After his death, Anna returned to Lyndhurst in New York in 1939.

The French

Arland, Marcel (1899–1986), friend of Florence who attended her Thursdays, novelist, literary critic, and journalist who directed the *Nouvelle Revue Française* from 1966 through 1977. He was elected to the French Academy in 1968.

Arletty (1898–1992), born Léonie Marie Julie Bathiat. She attended the same school as Florence in Paris, and was an actress, singer, and fashion model. Arletty had extremely poor taste in men, marrying the swindler Alexandre "Sasha" Stavisky, then living with Colonel Hans Jürgen Soehring at the Ritz during the war. She served eighteen months under house arrest after the war for *la collaboration horizontale*.

Barney, Natalie Clifford (1876–1972), American heiress, salonnière, playwright, poet, and novelist, held her salon at 20 rue Jacob for over sixty years. Her mother was artist Alice Pike Barney. Barney was openly lesbian, and had many overlapping love affairs. She attended Florence's Thursdays in the 1960s.

Baudoin, Edouard, business partner of the Goulds in Juan-les-Pins and Nice in casinos and hotels. Today, there is a boulevard named after him in Antibes.

Beaumont, Etienne de (1883–1956), French aristocrat, patron of the arts, librettist. Friend of Florence who was noted for the extravagant balls he gave to entertain his friends.

Bell, Marie (1900–1985), born Marie-Jeanne Ballon, was a French film actress and director. A friend of Florence's during the war, she was one of nine directors of the *Front National du Théâtre*. She wrote a letter of support for Florence to the DGER after the liberation.

Blanc, François (1806–1877), called the "Magician of Monte Carlo," was the first person to establish a casino and create what is today Monte Carlo. He was a founding director of Société des Bains de Mer (SBM), the Monégasque hotel and casino company.

Bousquet, Marie-Louise (1888–1975), salonnière whose Thursdays were a "renowned rallying point for persons of quality," was associated with *Harper's Bazaar* from 1937. She ran the gray mice network of high-class sex workers with Florence during the occupation of France. Her lover during that time was General Carl Albrecht Oberg, later a war criminal sentenced to death. She was made Paris editor of *Harper's Bazaar* in 1946.

Braque, Georges (1882–1963), a major French artist and sculptor known mostly for his Fauvist and Cubist periods. He was a friend of Florence's and attended her salon, yet she did not buy his art.

Céline (Dr. Louis Ferdinand Auguste Destouches) (1894–1961), right-wing French novelist, pamphleteer, and physician who refused to be "owned by a millionaire," Florence Gould. His 1932 novel, *Journey to the End of the Night*, was his most famous work. In 1944 he fled to Denmark, was tried in absentia in 1950 for collaboration with the Nazis, and was sentenced to one year's imprisonment and was declared a national disgrace. He was granted amnesty in 1951 and returned to France.

Chaigneau, Alfred, original owner of *Le Franco-Californien* newspaper in the nineteenth century who promoted Maximin Lacaze to the position of editor.

Chambrun, Josée de (1911–1992), only daughter of Pierre Laval and wife of René de Chambrun.

Chambrun, René de (1906–2002), great-great-grandson of Lafayette, son-in-law of Vichy Prime Minister Pierre Laval, and lawyer. He was legal counsel to Florence Gould, Pierre Laval, and Coco Chanel (against Wertheimer), among others. He practiced at the Paris Court of Appeals and was a member of the New York Bar.

Chanel, Gabrielle "Coco" (1883–1971), French fashion designer and business-woman. She was virulently anti-Semitic and during the war took Hans Gunther von Dincklage (a German spy) as her lover. She was a friend of Florence's and the fashion designer of her famous pajamas.

Chevalier, Maurice (1888–1972), French actor, cabaret singer, author, and entertainer. He knew Florence from their days at the Folies Bergère, and was very fond of her. In the 1960s he regularly attended her salon to meet publishers and writers, since he was writing his autobiography.

Cocteau, Jean (1889–1963), French writer, artist, designer, and filmmaker friend of Florence's from the 1920s. He was openly bisexual and his muse for over twenty-five years was actor Jean Marais.

Colette, Sidonie-Gabrielle (1873–1954), novelist and entertainer, nominated for the Nobel Prize in 1948. Bisexual friend of Florence's who notably attended her salons during the war and later demanded champagne and Camembert instead of biscuits and tea.

de Gaulle, Charles (1890–1970), French general and statesman. Leader of Free France (1940–1944) and founder of the French Fifth Republic in 1958.

Dequoy, Roger, faithful employee of the Wildensteins who took over their art-dealing operations in Paris during the occupation at the family's behest.

Drieu de la Rochelle, Pierre (1893–1945), right-wing novelist and writer who became the editor of the *Nouvelle Revue Française* during the occupation. He scorned Florence Gould and her Thursdays. Initially going into hiding at the liberation, he eventually committed suicide.

Du Pasquier, Pierre, French plenipotentiary minister to Monaco, friend of

Prince Louis II of Monaco, and owner of Du Pasquier & Co. of New Orleans, affiliated with the German-controlled Experta. He was involved with Florence and the Banque Charles scheme.

Faucigny-Lucinge, Prince Jean-Louis de (1904–1992), aristocrat, author, charitable patron, and giver of legendary parties. He decamped to London (marrying Baba d'Erlanger) and was part of de Gaulle's Free France in exile. He was also on the board of, and a shareholder in, SBM.

Fellowes, Daisy (1890–1962), celebrated beauty and socialite, raised by her aunt Winnaretta Singer, Princesse de Polignac. Her daughters were caught up in the purges after the liberation.

Gallauziaux, Mr., manager of the Goulds' French assets during the Second World War and beyond. He was deposed by the FBI and gave an unfavorable statement about Florence's involvement with Banque Charles.

Gallimard, Gaston (1881–1975), French publisher who founded the *Nouvelle Revue Française* in 1911 with Jean Schlumberger and André Gide. He and his authors were most favored by Florence's salon for fifty years, including during the occupation.

Georges, General Alphonse Joseph (1875–1951), commander-in-chief of French forces of the northeast, he wanted to move Allied forces into the Low Countries to defend against Hitler but was outvoted. He refused to have anything to do with Vichy, and fought alongside the Allies in North Africa. He believed Florence helped his family from being singled out by the Nazis.

Gide, André (1869–1951), French author and Nobel Laureate (1947). Gide attended Florence's Thursdays after the war, and, like Camus, did not want to see any more executions of collaborators.

Goustiaux, Auguste, purchaser of *Le Franco-Californien* from Alfred Chaigneau and family friend of the Lacazes.

Greffulhe, Élisabeth (1860–1952), French society beauty and renowned queen of the Faubourg St.-Germain salons. Florence eventually sang there.

Homo, Magdeleine, former award-winning ice skater and secretary to Florence Gould; then secretary to Frank Jay Gould until his death in 1956.

Jouhandeau, Marcel, (1888–1979), writer and high-school teacher who wrote *Le Peril Juif* (*The Jewish Peril*) in 1938. A friend of Jean Paulhan, Jouhandeau helped Florence run her Thursdays during and after the war until Jean de Noël took over.

Laurencin, Marie (1883–1956), French painter and printmaker associated with the Cubists and the Section d'Or. She was a frequent visitor to Florence's

Thursdays during and after the occupation, Florence's friend, and she painted Florence.

Manigler, Madeleine, Impressionist art expert, particularly knowledgeable about Monet. She worked for the Wildensteins and was a frequent companion of Florence Gould from the mid-1930s.

Melchior, Marie Charles Jean, Marquis de Polignac (1880–1950) French aristocrat, businessman, heir to the Pommery/Mumm champagne empire, and member of the International Olympic Committee in the 1930s. He was a lover and friend of Florence Gould.

Monnier, Adrienne (1892–1955), bookseller, writer, and publisher. Partner of Sylvia Beach.

Noailles, Marie-Laure de—(1902–1970), a descendant of the infamous Marquis de Sade, an artist and financier of films as well as a salonnière and a friend of Florence Gould's.

Palewski, Gaston (1901–1984), joined de Gaulle's Free French forces in London in 1940, and acted as his chef de cabinet, throughout the war. He met Nancy Mitford in London and was her lover for over twenty years, immortalized as Fabrice, Duc de Sauveterre, by her. He married Hélène-Violette de Talleyrand-Périgord (Florence's niece) and became very friendly with Florence Gould after the war.

Pétain, Maréchal Philippe (1856–1951), "Hero of Verdun" in the First World War; chief of state of Vichy France. He was found guilty of "state collaboration with Nazi Germany" but his sentence was commuted from death to life imprisonment.

Rochefoucauld, Armand de la (1870–1963) president of the Jockey Club in France (1919–1963) and also the Polo Club. A friend of both Frank and Florence Gould, he was also one of Florence's lovers.

Ruhl, Henri (1882–1955), an international hotelier of Swiss origin (becoming both a British and a French citizen) and widely regarded as a "personality" in his field.

Sella, Antoine (of Italian origin), owner and operator of the Hôtel du Cap from 1889 until his death. He famously kept the hotel open for the Murphys and their writer friends of the Lost Generation in the summer of 1923, giving birth to the French Riviera's summer season.

Singer, Winnaretta, Princesse de Polignac (1865–1943), daughter of Isaac Merritt Singer, inventor of the even-stitching sewing machine, salonnière most noted for her promotion of music. Among her protégés were Maurice Ravel, Claude Debussy, and Serge Diaghilev's Ballets Russes.

Sixte de Bourbon-Parma (1896–1986), born Hedwige de la Rochefoucauld, was the daughter of Armand de la Rochefoucauld, one of Florence's lovers, and Princess Louise Radziwill. Like her parents, she was a close friend of Florence. On her marriage to Prince Sixte de Bourbon-Parma in 1919, she became princesse Hedwige de Bourbon-Parma.

Stavisky, Alexandre (1886–1934), con man, swindler husband of Arletty, who created the greatest financial fraud of the French Third Republic. Florence and Frank Gould allowed him to gamble at their hotels, despite his having been banned from all casinos.

Tellier, Cécile, childhood friend of Florence and paid companion for Berthe Lacaze, and then after Berthe's death, for Frank Jay Gould.

Thomasson, Robert de, independent French journalist. His father was in the French military but retired at the time of the occupation. De Thomasson joined in the fight for liberation with the Maquis. He was a friend of Florence's before, during, and after the occupation.

Wildenstein, Daniel (1917–2001), art dealer and connoisseur, thoroughbred horse breeder, and third generation of the family to preside over Wildenstein & Co., one of the most successful art dealers ever. He was the personal art dealer to Florence Gould and adviser on her art estate.

The Germans

Abetz, Otto (1903–1958), Nazi spy in Paris in the 1930s for Ribbentrop who became German ambassador during the occupation. Florence knew him and was friendly with him from the 1930s on. In July 1949, he was sentenced by a French court to twenty years in prison for war crimes, particularly the deportation of Jews to death camps. He was released in April 1954 and died (along with his French wife, Suzanne) in an automobile accident in 1958.

Garthe, Arnold, aka "Colonel Patrick" (b. 1893, Port Elizabeth, South Africa), was head of the Abwehr in Paris until 1943 and was the lover of Marie-Louise Bousquet. In 1943, he was transferred to head up Abwehr operations in Lyon. He was tried at Nuremberg for war crimes.

Heller, Gerhard (1909–1982), German literary censor and later author. During the occupation of Paris, he was a great friend of Florence Gould and those who frequented her salon. His book *Un Allemand à Paris* portrays him as only concerned with saving French culture.

Jünger, Ernst (1895–1998), highly decorated German soldier and author who became a close personal friend of Florence and her set during the occupation. Florence financed the translation of his Paris diaries into French. They were part-time lovers during the war and remained friends for her entire life.

Klingeberg, Werner, director of the Deutsche Nachrichtenableitung, Paris (German Newspapers). An old friend of Melchior de Polignac, he was technical adviser to the 1936 and 1940 Olympic Games. Florence claimed he introduced her to Ludwig Vogel.

Knochen, Helmut (1910–2003), was the head of the security police in Paris during the occupation, and part-time lover of Florence Gould. He was found guilty of war crimes by both the British and the French courts, but was reprieved at the behest of Chancellor Konrad Adenauer after the war.

Medicus, General Franz (1890–1967), was in charge of operations based out of the Goulds' Maisons-Laffitte estate. After the war, he was taken to the U.S.A. as part of Operation Paperclip, designed to save the best German scientific brains.

Oberg, General Carl Albrecht (1897–1965), was also known as the "Butcher of Paris" and was sentenced to death by the French. He was well known to Florence Gould and helped her on many occasions. Both he and Helmut Knochen received a reprieve at the behest of Chancellor Konrad Adenauer.

Praeger-Gretsch, Willy, worked for Arnold Garthe and the Abwehr and introduced a spy into Florence Gould's home.

Steffens, Walter (1908–2006), was part of the Olympic gymnastics winning team in the 1936 Olympics. Arnold Garthe of the Abwehr thought that Steffens was incompetent and had him transferred.

Vogel, Carl Ludwig Adolf (b. 1909–1994), was an approved Nazi black marketeer, aeronautics businessman, and wartime lover of Florence Gould. Florence facilitated his inclusion in Operation Paperclip after the war so that he could immigrate to the United States. J. Edgar Hoover personally tried to keep Vogel out, but failed.

Warzinski, Hans Dietrich, Aryan manager of the Goulds' businesses, and key member of the team who helped Florence become involved with the Banque Charles scheme. He disappeared at the time of the liberation of Paris to Spain.

The Americans

Baker, Josephine (1906–1975), American-born cabaret singer and entertainer who became a star in Paris in the 1920s. Baker left Paris at the time of the occupation and worked for the Resistance throughout the war. She became a French citizen and received the Legion of Honor medal for her work.

Beach, Sylvia (1887–1962), publisher, writer, and founder of Shakespeare and Company in Paris promoting the works of the authors of the Lost Generation and in particular publishing James Joyce's *Ulysses*. An indefatigable patron and promoter of American and English literature in Paris, Beach was among the Americans rounded up and put into the camp at Vittel in 1942 after America entered the war. She never reopened Shakespeare and Company after the war ended.

Biddle, Francis B. (1886–1968), was a lawyer, judge, and attorney general of the United States. He was a primary judge for war crimes at Nuremberg, which more than likely affected his view of Florence's crimes.

Bullitt, William C. (1891–1967), first American ambassador to the Soviet Union, then ambassador to France. Bullitt rented his residence from the Goulds and became very friendly with Florence. He handed over the city of Paris to the Nazis *in loco* of the French government in exile. After the war, he retired to Neuilly to the home he had originally rented from the Goulds.

Cahill, John T. (1903–1966), joined Cotton & Franklin, the predecessor of the law firm Gordon, Cahill & Reindel. The son of an Irish-immigrant New York City police officer, Cahill took his law degree at Columbia University. In addition to the Goulds, he represented giant corporations like NBC, RCA, and W.R. Grace.

Daughters, Donald L. (d. 2006), was the officer serving in U.S. forces who wrote the most comprehensive and fair report of Florence's wartime activities.

Fitzgerald, F. Scott (1896–1940), novelist and friend of the Murphys, Hemingway, and the Goulds. He rewrote his great work *The Great Gatsby* based on the life he observed at Juan-les-Pins.

Fitzgerald, Zelda (1900–1948), novelist, dancer, friend of the Murphys, and wife of Scott Fitzgerald. Florence Gould adored her, but was forced to recognize that there was some sort of madness about Zelda. Frank Jay Gould ordered Florence not to entertain her anymore.

Hemingway, Ernest (1899–1961), newspaperman, novelist, and friend of the Murphys, Fitzgeralds, and Florence in the 1920s. He also supported Sylvia Beach for her many kindnesses.

Hoover, J. Edgar (1895–1972), director of the FBI and unrelenting opponent of Florence Gould and Ludwig Vogel.

Hoving, Tom (1931–2009), director of the Metropolitan Museum of Art and in his own words "toady" to Florence Gould.

Lauder, Estée (1906–2004), international cosmetics businesswoman and close personal friend of Florence Gould, who facilitated Florence's relationship with the Met.

Loeb, Charles G. (1885–1944), the Lacaze family lawyer and also Frank Jay Gould's lawyer through the early 1920s and 1930s before his return to New York.

Murphy, Gerald and Sara (Gerald, 1888–1964 and Sara Wiborg, 1883–1975), were expatriate Americans whose flare for living well attracted a number of writers of the Lost Generation as well as other friends, like Dorothy Parker and Cole Porter. They settled in the 1920s at Antibes–Juan-les-Pins.

Rorimer, James (1905–1966), was a World War II Monuments Man and director of the Metropolitan Museum of Art. He was the founding force behind the Cloisters, dedicated to the art and architecture of medieval Europe. He thought that Florence was a tremendous bore.

Smith, Ada "Bricktop" (1894–1984), American dancer, singer, and nightclub owner in Paris born to an Irish father and a black American mother. She continued to perform well into her eighties, but was best known as the doyenne of the café society of 1920s Paris.

Stein, Gertrude (1874–1946), novelist, poet, playwright, and art collector. She held her avant-garde salon on rue de Fleurus until the war, only a stone's throw from where Florence grew up in Paris.

Toklas, Alice B. (1877–1967), San Francisco–born member of the Paris avant-garde and life partner of Gertrude Stein.

Other Fellow Travelers

Benvenuti, Joseph (1898–1967), Florence's friend and pianist/violinist who acted as her go-between with Michel Szkolnikoff in 1944. He was born in Tunisia to Italian parents.

Chaplin, Sir Charles (1889–1977), KBE, entertainer, writer, director, and Hollywood film idol. Chaplin's first love was the sister of Frank Jay Gould's second wife, Edith Kelly. He had a brief affair with Florence, hoping to lure her to Hollywood.

Charles, Baron Johann, Nazi sympathizer and Swiss financier used by Aerobank and high-ranking Nazis to set up a bank in his name in Monaco. Florence was a director and investor.

Grosvenor, Hugh, Duke of Westminster, "Bendor" (1879–1953), 2nd Duke of Westminster and lover of Coco Chanel. His generosity and contacts not only launched Chanel as a couturier, but also more than likely saved her from prosecution for collaboration after the war.

Louis II, Prince of Monaco (1870–1949), was the Grimaldi ruler of Monaco during World War II, and grandfather of Rainier III. He allowed Monaco to be embroiled in the flight of Nazi capital at the end of the war by taking the advice of corrupt advisers.

Picasso, Pablo (1881–1973), painter, sculptor, and ceramicist who was very friendly with the Murphys in the 1920s. Picasso also rented La Vigie from the

Goulds after the war, and painted murals on their walls in thanks. Frank Jay Gould hated Picasso's art and had the walls whitewashed.

Roblot, Émile (1886–1963), corrupt Monégasque minister of state responsible for passing the laws that enabled Banque Charles to operate in Monaco.

Szkolnikoff, Michel (1895–1945), Russian businessman funded by the Nazis to help with the flight of Nazi capital and buy up luxury casinos and hotels. Florence was involved with his schemes regarding Monaco. He stole incriminating papers and was most likely murdered by his French pursuers.

Zaharoff, Sir Basil (1849–1936), a Greek-born arms dealer and industrialist who held a controlling interest in the hotel and casino company SBM of Monaco.

Zanini, Diego, Florence's butler before and during the war. He disappeared at the time of the liberation, but gave a glowing testimonial to OSS officers about both Florence and Ludwig Vogel.

GLOSSARY

AP	Associated Press
Action Française	the anti-Semitic league in France
arrondissement	city district of Paris
beau monde	beautiful people
boulets	manufactured balls of coal dust, straw, and peat
bouquinistes	booksellers, usually outdoor stalls lining the River Seine
cache-sexe	fig leaf used to hide sexual organs
Cagoule	an extreme right sect known for their hooded capes
cercles	private gambling clubs
Cercle Rive Gauche	Left Bank literary group sympathetic to the Third Reich
cocottes	darlings
collaboration horizontale	sleeping with the enemy
Comité France-Allemagne (CFA)	group founded in November 1935 by Otto Abetz as a propaganda tool
département	province
DNA (Deutsche Nachtrichtenabteilung)	German News Agency
Deuxième Bureau	Investigative intelligence service
Einsatzstab Reichsleiter Rosenberg	Art-looting arm of the Reich in France

en famille	together as a family
épureur	the judge in collaboration cases
ésprit parisien	Parisian mind or way of living
flâneur	a person who strolls aimlessly, an urban explorer of a literary penchant doing the opposite of nothing in search of a "gastronomy of the eye," according to Balzac
froussards	panic merchants
hivernants	snowbirds
hôtel particulier	a city mansion
IEQJ	Institut d'Études des Questions Juives—Institute for the Study of the Jewish Question
indignité nationale	1944 law enacted to stop vigilante reprisals against collaborators.
Kunstschutz	German Arts and Monuments Protection Office
le gratin	the upper crust
les enfers	private gambling clubs, or literally, hells
le Tout-Paris	the fashionable elite of Paris
Mairie	mayor's office or town hall
maisons de joie	brothels
mannequins habillés	scantily dressed models
maquisard	French commandos in the Free Zone
marriage blanc	an unconsummated marriage
Milice	French pro-Nazi paramilitary organization
nuits blanches	nights without sleep, partying
OSS	Office of Strategic Services
pays de cocagne	land of milk and honey
pickelhaube	German spiked helmet
poilus	common conscripts
rafles	lightning raids to round up Jews
Reichsjugendführung (RJF)	Reich Youth Directorate
salonnière	society hostess, usually with a special Coterie
Service de Renseignements	Intelligence Services
tableaux vivants	posing of live models as a painting
Tout Va	no limit gambling

NOTES

Abbreviations

ADAM	Archives des Alpes-Maritimes
ADVN	Archives de la ville de Nice
AMC	Archives municipales de Cannes
ANF	Archives nationales de France
BNF	Bibliothèque nationale de France
CDJC	Centre de Documentation Juive Contemporaine
FOLD3	Digital archive of NARA
JSTOR	Digital Scholarly Network for Articles and Books
MMA	Metropolitan Museum of Art (New York)
NARA	National Archives & Records Administration, College Park, Maryland, USA (renamed the National Archives since researching)
NYHS	New-York Historical Society
NYPL	New York Public Library
OED	Oxford English Dictionary
PP	Préfecture de Police

Note: All translations from French are the author's.

1. San Francisco

1 Simon Winchester, *A Crack in the Edge of the World: The Great American Earthquake of 1906* (London: Penguin Books, 2006), 215–216.

2 Ibid.

3 http://www.sfmuseum.net/1906/ew15.html.

4 Winchester, *A Crack in the Edge of the World*, 208.

5 Ibid., 209.

6 President Polk believed in the United States of America's "Manifest Destiny" to span the continent from coast to coast and took advantage of a number of border skirmishes with Mexico at the Rio Grande to fight for a third of Mexico's territory that forms much of modern-day Arizona, New Mexico, Utah, Nevada, and California. For a wonderful book on Polk and his ambitions, see Walter R. Borneman's *Polk: The Man Who Transformed the Presidency and America* (New York: Random House, 2008).

7 Gilles Cornut-Gentille and Philippe Michel-Thiriet, *Florence Gould: Une Américaine à Paris* (Paris: Mercure de France, 1989), 19.

8 Winchester, *A Crack in the Edge of the World*, 191.

9 Frank Soulé, *Annals of San Francisco: Containing a Summary of the History of California and a History of Its Great City* (Berlin: Jazzybee Verlag, 1855), p. 54.

10 http://www.oed.com.ezproxy2.londonlibrary.co.uk/view/Entry/177471 ?redirectedFrom=shanghaied#eid2317065.1.

11 Sarah Blaffer Hrdy, *Mothers and Others: The Evolutionary Origins of Mutual Understanding* (Cambridge, MA: Harvard University Press, 2011), 15.

12 https://www.newspapers.com/image/27523525/?terms=Franco-Californien, *San Francisco Chronicle*, July 13, 1893; http://cdnc.ucr.edu/cgi-bin/cdnc?a=d&d =SFC18981203.2.166, *San Francisco Call*, December 3, 1898; https://www.news papers.com/image/46547276/?terms=%22Goustiaux%22, *San Francisco Call*, October 14, 1901.

13 Dunbar H. Ogden, Douglas McDermott, and Robert Károly Sarlós, *Theatre West: Impact and Image* (Atlanta, GA: Rodopi, 1990), 20.

14 Cornut-Gentille and Michel-Thiriet, *Florence Gould*, 19.

15 https://www.newspapers.com/image/48768585/?terms=%22M%2BV%2 BLacaze%22, *San Francisco Call*, September 21, 1902.

16 https://www.newspapers.com/image/46551760/?terms=%22M.V.%2BLacaze%22, *San Francisco Call*, June 26, 1904.

17 http://www.sfmuseum.org/1906/sprr.html; https://www.newspapers.com/image /46518432/?terms=Bazille, *San Francisco Call*, February 3, 1905, 2.

18 Cornut-Gentille and Michel-Thiriet, *Florence Gould*, 24.

2. From Fire to Flood and Death

1 Gilles Cornut-Gentille and Philippe Michel-Thiriet, *Florence Gould: Une Américaine à Paris* (Paris: Mercure de France, 1989), 26.

2 Ibid., 27.

3 Ibid., 28–29.

4 Lacaze was listed as a "non-immigrant alien" on the ship's manifest in 1911 and in the 1900 census; however, he is also on the 1903 voting register in San Francisco as a naturalized American citizen. See entry M. V. Lacaze in ancestry.com. See too

http://search.ancestry.com/cgi-bin/sse.dll?_phsrc=nRx7&_phstart=successSourc
e&usePUBJs=true&gl=40&gss=angs-g&new=1&rank=1&msT=1&gsfn=Maxi
min%20V%20&gsfn_x=0&gsln=Lacaze&gsln_x=0&msypn__ftp=San%20Fran
cisco,%20San%20Francisco,%20California,%20USA&msypn=69183&msypn_
PInfo=8-%7C0%7C1652393%7C0%7C2%7C0%7C7%7C0%7C2599%7C69183%7C
0%7C0%7C&cp=0&catbucket=rstp&MSAV=0&so=2

5   www.newspapers.com, *San Francisco Call*, June 7, 1908.

6   Jeffrey H. Jackson, *Paris Under Water: How the City of Light Survived the Great
    Flood of 1910* (New York: Palgrave Macmillan, 2010), 9; cf. Harvey Levenstein,
    Selective Journeys: American Tourists in Paris from Jefferson to the Jazz Age (Chicago:
    University of Chicago Press, 1998), 88.

7   Ibid., 29.

8   Ibid., 34–35.

9   Ibid., 43. See also Auguste Pawlowski and Albert Radoux, *Les Crues de Paris:
    causes, méchanisme, histoire* (Paris: Berger-Levrault, 1910).

10 Ibid., 90.

11 Ibid., 74.

12 https://www.newspapers.com/image/82725022/?terms=M%2BV%2BLacaze, *San
    Francisco Call*, November 24, 1911, 4.

13 Cornut-Gentille and Michel-Thiriet, *Florence Gould*, 29.

14 Sylvia Kahan, *Music's Modern Muse: A Life of Winnaretta Singer, Princesse de
    Polignac* (Rochester, NY: University of Rochester Press, 2003), 100; cf. Barbara W.
    Tuchman, *The Proud Tower: A Portrait of the World Before the War, 1890–1914* (New
    York: Macmillan, 1966), 202.

15 http://interactive.ancestry.com/1174/USM1490_235-0394?pid=490830&backurl
    =http%3a%2f%2fsearch.ancestry.com%2f%2fcgi-bin%2fsse.dll%3findiv%3d1%26
    db%3dUSpassports%26h%3d490830%26tid%3d%26pid%3d%26usePUB%3dtrue
    %26rhSource%3d60525&treeid=&personid=&hintid=&usePUB=true, Charles
    Gerson Loeb's passport application dated January 13, 1915, made at the U.S. em-
    bassy in Paris.

16 Nancy L. Green, *The Other Americans in Paris: Businessmen, Countesses, Wayward
    Youth, 1880–1941* (Chicago: University of Chicago Press, Kindle Edition, 2014),
    1055–1068.

17 https://www.newspapers.com/image/82685583/?terms=M%2BV%2BLacaze, *San
    Francisco Call*, March 16, 1911, 8.

18 Email correspondence between the author and the California State Archives, re-
    garding the probate of Maximin Lacaze. The probate had been assumed as lost by
    the archives in the aftermath of the San Francisco earthquake, but as I pointed out
    to them, Lacaze did not die until five years later. It is probable that he had borrowed
    a great deal of money from his cousin Louis Lacaze to reestablish his business, and
    as Maximin had not yet repaid all of it, cousin Louis laid a legal claim to the estate.

3. *La Parisienne*

1 http://www.jstor.org/stable/42630841?seq=1&cid=pdf-reference#page_scan_tab
_contents, Anne Dymond, RACAR (Revue d'art Canadienne), Vol. 36, No. 2, 2011,
"Embodying the Nation: Art, Fashion, and Allegorical Women at the 1900 Exposition Universelle," 2–6.

2 Ibid., 7.

3 My thanks to Sir James Bulmer for sharing the private correspondence of Helena
Rubinstein from this period.

4 http://thesalonniere.com/salonnieres-in-history/Natalie Clifford Barney.

5 Edwin P. Hoyt, *The Goulds: A Social History* (New York: Weybright and Talley,
1969), 147–159.

6 Ibid., 210–211.

7 Ibid., 148.

8 Michael de Cossart, *The Food of Love: Princesse Edmond de Polignac (1865–1943)
and Her Salon* (London: Hamish Hamilton, 1978), 21–22.

9 Ibid., 89.

10 Ibid., 85.

11 Sylvia Kahan, *Music's Modern Muse: A Life of Winnaretta Singer, Princesse de
Polignac* (Rochester, NY: University of Rochester Press, 2003), 96.

4. War and the Boy Next Door

1 https://www.newspapers.com/image/80732331/?terms=%22Florence%
2BLacaze%22, *Oakland Tribune*, December 11, 1914, 18.

2 Gilles Cornut-Gentille and Philippe Michel-Thiriet, *Florence Gould: Une Américaine à Paris* (Paris: Mercure de France, 1989), 30.

3 http://interactive.ancestry.com/1174/USM1372_537-0564/1081863?backurl
=http://person.ancestry.com/tree/82308498/person/46462901543/facts/citation
/323180357152/edit/record#?imageId=USM1372_537-0564. The Ancestry file mis-
states Manfred H. Heynemann's given name as "Manford" based on the misread-
ing of his handwriting.

4 Cornut-Gentille and Michel-Thiriet, *Florence Gould*, 30–31; Charles Castle, *The
Folies-Bergère* (London: Methuen, 1982), 69–70.

5 Cornut-Gentille and Michel-Thiriet, *Florence Gould*, 31.

6 Barbara W. Tuchman, *The Proud Tower: A Portrait of the World Before the War:
1890–1914* (London: Hamish Hamilton, 1965), 459.

7 Harvey Levenstein, *Seductive Journey: American Tourists in France from Jefferson
to the Jazz Age* (Chicago: University of Chicago Press, 1998), 217.

8 Tuchman, *The Proud Tower*, 459, 461.

9 John Baxter, *Paris at the End of the World: The City of Light During the Great War,
1914–1918* (New York: Harper Perennial, 2014), 142.

10 https://www.newspapers.com/image/80732331/?terms=%22Florence%2BL
acaze%22, *Oakland Tribune*, December 11, 1914, 18.

11 The image of Florence portrayed here comes directly from a photograph reproduced in Cornut-Gentille and Michel-Thiriet's book, *Florence Gould*, which is in the Florence Gould Foundation's possession but was not made available to me.

12 Cornut-Gentille and Michel-Thiriet, *Florence Gould*, 31–32.

13 Ibid., 32–33, 36.

14 www.jstor.org/stable/1105586, Charles G. Loeb, *The Virginia Law Register, Virginia Law Review*, Vol. 18, No. 11, March 1913, 802.

15 Ibid.

16 Ibid., 35–36

17 Levenstein, *Seductive Journey*, 217.

5. Young Mrs. Heynemann

1 http://www.history.com/this-day-in-history/panama-canal-open-to-traffic.

2 https://www.newspapers.com/image/27553000/?terms=Florence%2BHeynemann, *San Francisco Chronicle*, November 10, 1914, 1.

3 https://www.newspapers.com/image/82092303/?terms=Florence%2BHeynemann, *Oakland Tribune*, November 19, 1914, 16.

4 Ibid.

5 https://www.newspapers.com/image/80732331/?terms=Florence%2BHeynemann, *Oakland Tribune*, December 11, 1914, 18.

6 https://www.newspapers.com/image/80757537/?terms=Henry%2BC.%2BHeynemann, *Oakland Tribune*, April 17, 1915, 9.

7 Gilles Cornut-Gentille and Philippe Michel-Thiriet, *Florence Gould: Une Américaine à Paris* (Paris: Mercure de France, 1989), 39–40. In verifying her statement to friends and her biographers, I wrote to the Conservatoire de Paris concerning its records of Florence's attendance. I was surprised, but not shocked, to learn that she had never attended the Conservatoire under the names Lacaze, Heynemann, or Gould, nor had she ever given them a penny in charitable contributions.

8 www.jstor.org/stable/1105586, Charles G. Loeb, *The Virginia Law Register, Virginia Law Review*, Vol. 18, No. 11, March 1913, 803.

9 www.oedonline.com "butterfly."

10 https://www.newspapers.com/image/27592141/?terms=Henry%2BC.%2BHeynemann, *San Francisco Chronicle*, August 12, 1916, 1. The italics are my own.

11 Ibid.

12 Cornut-Gentille and Michel-Thiriet, *Florence Gould*, 38. The biography wrongly states that the divorce occurred in 1917. The year of the divorce according to California state records was 1916.

6. Home Again, War, and Folies

1 Gilles Cornut-Gentille and Philippe Michel-Thiriet, *Florence Gould: Une Américaine à Paris* (Paris: Mercure de France, 1989), 40.

2 Sylvia Kahan, *Music's Modern Muse: A Life of Winnaretta Singer, Princesse de*

Polignac (Rochester, NY: University of Rochester Press, 2003), 193–194; cf. Winnaretta Singer de Polignac's letter to Marie Curie, July 30, 1915, BNF-Mss, MF2663:95.

3 Ibid., 194.

4 Cornut-Gentille and Michel-Thiriet, *Florence Gould*, 39.

5 Ernst Jünger, *Second Journal Parisien: Journal III, 1943–1945* (Paris: Christian Bourgois, 1980), 18.

6 I thank Dr. Matthew Balerdi for this insight.

7 John Baxter, *Paris at the End of the World: The City of Light During the Great War 1914–1918* (New York: Harper Perennial), 234.

8 Ibid., 152–153.

9 Ibid.,154–158.

10 https://www.newspapers.com/image/27444148/?terms=%22Frank%2BJ.%2BGould%22, *San Francisco Chronicle*, September 14, 1919, 3.

11 Cornut-Gentille and Michel-Thiriet, *Florence Gould*, 40.

12 Charles Castle, *The Folies-Bergère* (London: Methuen, 1982), 99.

13 Ibid., 105.

14 Ibid., 83–91.

15 Ibid., 108.

7. The Man They Call "Franck"

1 https://www.newspapers.com/image/32470762/?terms=%22Frank%2BJ.%2BGould%22, *Wall Street Journal*, July 28, 1911, 1. At the time Gould was president of the Old Dominion Iron and Nail Works of Virginia, and all the accused were indicted on the grounds of "restraint of trade."

2 https://www.newspapers.com/image/76003442/?terms=%22Frank%2BJ.%2BGould%22, *Washington Herald*, February 23, 1913, 27.

3 Edwin P. Hoyt, *The Goulds: A Social History* (New York: Weybright & Talley, 1969), 1–6.

4 Ibid., 19–21.

5 Ibid., 22–23.

6 Ibid., 26–45.

7 Author interview with Howard Zar at Lyndhurst, January 2016.

8 Hoyt, *The Goulds*, 131–132.

9 Ibid., 138–139.

10 Gilles Cornut-Gentille and Philippe Michel-Thiriet, *Florence Gould: Une Américaine à Paris* (Paris: Mercure de France, 1989), 62.

11 https://www.newspapers.com/image/20493262/?terms=%22Frank%2BJ%2BGould%22, *New York Times*, February 11, 1901, 5.

12 Ibid., 236.

13 https://www.newspapers.com/image/20424801/?terms=%22Frank%2BJ%2BGould%22, *New York Times*, January 27, 1909, 10.

14 https://www.newspapers.com/image/20315431/?terms=%22Frank%2BJ%2 BGould%22, *New York Times*, February 24, 1909, 16.

15 https://www.newspapers.com/image/31566463/?terms=%22Frank%2BJ.%2 BGould%22, *Washington Post*, November 3, 1910, 1.

16 https://books.google.com/books?id=9QfSAAAAMAAJ&pg=PA774&lpg =PA774&dq=history+of+le+robillard&source=bl&ots=I2bQNOtonh&sig =Cbfoy5tzFZ0cOH4_bOLiHE444H8&hl=en&sa=X&ved=0ahUKEwilp-CigsjO AhXMQyYKHZg7BFQQ6AEIQjAH#v=onepage&q=history%20of%20le%20 robillard&f=false, *The Fortnightly Review*, Vol. CVI, new series, July to December 1919, 773.

17 https://www.newspapers.com/image/31565143/?terms=%22Frank%2 BJ.%2BGould%22, *Washington Post*, October 11, 1910, 9; https://www.newspapers .com/image/80694239/?terms=%22Frank%2BJ.%2BGould%22, *Washington Post*, August 1, 1910, 8; https://www.newspapers.com/image/78323324/?terms=%22 Frank%2BJ.%2BGould%22, *Oregan Daily Journal*, October 2, 1910, 34; https://www. newspapers.com/image/28891190/?terms=%22Frank%2BJ.%2BGould%22, *Washington Post*, July 12, 1910, 9.

18 https://www.newspapers.com/image/20565651/?terms=%22Frank%2 BJ.%2BGould%22, *New York Times*, July 12, 1911; Hoyt, *The Goulds: A Social History*, 256.

19 Hoyt, *The Goulds: A Social History*, 282–283.

20 https://www.newspapers.com/image/80716023/?terms=%22Frank%2BJ.%2 BGould%22, *Washington Times*, December 18, 1918, 25.

21 https://www.newspapers.com/image/27444148/?terms=%22Frank%2BJ.%2 BGould%22, *San Francisco Chronicle*, September 14, 1919, 3.

22 William Wiser, *The Crazy Years: Paris in the Twenties* (London: Thames & Hudson, 1983), 15.

8. Taming All Those Monsters

1 Edwin P. Hoyt, *The Goulds: A Social History* (New York: Weybright & Talley, 1969), 279–281.

2 Ibid., 257–259.

3 http://www.williamwhitepapers.com/pr/AddictionTreatment&RecoveryInAmeri ca.pdf; catdir.loc.gov/catdir/samples/cam041/2002073459.pdf, Library of Congress "Treatment of Drinking Problems."

4 https://www.newspapers.com/image/50647527/?terms=%22Frank%2BJ.%2 BGould%22, *Evening World*, May 8, 1919, 1.

5 http://ezproxy.nypl.org/login?url=http://search.proquest.com/docview /103129428?accountid=35635, *New York Times*; https://www.newspapers.com /image/50647527/?terms=%22Frank%2BJ.%2BGould%22, *Evening World*, May 8, 1919, 1–2.

6 https://www.newspapers.com/image/79060531/?terms=%22Frank%2BJ.%2
   BGould%22, *Evening World,* May 3, 1921), 1.

7 http://ezproxy.nypl.org/login?url=http://search.proquest.com/docview/103
   129428?accountid=35635, *New York Times,* November 3, 1921, 5

8 https://www.newspapers.com/image/28930918/?terms=%22Frank%2BJ.%2
   BGould%22, *Washington Post,* January 21, 1921, 2; https://www.newspapers
   .com/image/35577856/?terms=%22Frank%2BJ.%2BGould%22, *Times Herald,* February 2, 1921, 13.

9 https://www.newspapers.com/image/26755054/?terms=%22Frank%2BJ.%2
   BGould%22, *New York Times,* May 26, 1921, 3.

10 https://www.newspapers.com/search/#query=%22Frank+J.+Gould%22&dr
   _year=1921-1927&offset=12&p_place=NY,CA,DC, *New-York Tribune,* August 20,
   1921, 5.

11 https://www.newspapers.com/image/100119106/?terms=%22Frank%2BJ.%2
   BGould%22, *New-York Tribune,* October 8, 1921, 7.

12 https://www.newspapers.com/image/31545981/?terms=%22Frank%2BJ.%2
   BGould%22, *Washington Post,* December 1, 1921, 16.

13 Library of Congress, *New York World-Telegram and Sun* Collection, March 13,
   1922 article. The photograph describing "Miss Edith Kelly who is said to have the
   highest kick in the world" was part of the article.

14 Gilles Cornut-Gentille and Philippe Michel-Thiriet, *Florence Gould: Une Américaine à Paris* (Paris: Mercure de France, 1989), 40–41.

15 Ibid.

16 Sylvia Kahan, *Music's Modern Muse: A Life of Winnaretta Singer, Princesse de
   Polignac* (Rochester, NY: University of Rochester Press, 2003), 107.

17 Ibid., 116, 200, 316.

18 Hoyt, *The Goulds: A Social History,* 251.

19 https://www.newspapers.com/image/34595017/?terms=%22Frank%2BJ.%2
   BGould%22, *Wall Street Journal,* October 25, 1923, 3.

20 https://www.newspapers.com/image/27597881/?terms=%22Frank%2BJ.%2
   BGould%22, *San Francisco Chronicle,* October 3, 1923, 2.

21 https://www.newspapers.com/image/157868976/?terms=%22Frank%2BJ.%2
   BGould%22, *Los Angeles Times,* March 24, 1924, 11.

9. Leaving the Perfumed Air of Bohemia

1 Amanda Vaill, *Everybody Was So Young: Gerald and Sara Murphy, A Lost Generation Love Story* (New York: Warner Books, 1999), 102–103.

2 Ibid., 103; cf. Jean Louis de Faucigny-Lucinge, *Un gentilhomme cosmopolite* (Paris:
   Perrin, 1990), 105.

3 Janet Flanner, *Paris Was Yesterday 1925–1939* (London: Virago Modern Classics,
   2003), 3.

4   Ibid., xiii.

5   Harvey Levenstein, *Seductive Journey: American Tourists in France from Jefferson to the Jazz Age* (Chicago: The University of Chicago Press, 1998), 213.

6   Ibid., 248.

7   Ibid., 198–199, for Twain quote; John Baxter, *We'll Always Have Paris: Sex and Love in the City of Light* (London: Doubleday, 2005), 85.

8   Ernest Hemingway, *On Paris*, (London: Hespersus, 2013), 3.

9   Levenstein, *Seductive Journey*, 212.

10 Gilles Cornut-Gentille and Philippe Michel-Thiriet, *Florence Gould: Une Américaine à Paris* (Paris: Mercure de France, 1989), 62; cf. Jean Chalon, *Florence et Louise les Magnifiques* (Paris: Le Rocher, 1987), 46.

10. Careless People

1   Mary Blume, *Côte d'Azur: Inventing the French Riviera* (London: Thames & Hudson, 1992), 30.

2   Ted Jones, *The French Riviera: A Literary Guide for Travellers* (London: Tauris Parke Paperbacks, 2007), 165–166.

3   Gilles Cornut-Gentille and Philippe Michel-Thiriet, *Florence Gould: Une Américaine à Paris* (Paris: Mercure de France, 1989), 67.

4   Ibid., 64–65.

5   AMC; Pierre Galante and Annie Michel Gall, *Les Années Américaines* (Paris: JC Lattès, 1985), 222. This book is an interesting account of Gerald Spalding's encounters with many of the rich and notable of the Riviera and has an especially accurate and fascinating chapter on his relationship with Frank Gould.

6   Harvey Levenstein, *Seductive Journey: American Tourists in France from Jefferson to the Jazz Age* (Chicago: The University of Chicago Press, 1998), 250–251.

7   Hal Vaughan, *Sleeping with the Enemy: Coco Chanel, Nazi Agent* (London: Chatto & Windus, 2011), 47. The remark was made by Lady Iya Abdy about Chanel only. The inference is from the author.

8   Amanda Vaill, *Everybody Was So Young: Gerald and Sara Murphy, A Lost Generation Love Story* (London: Warner Books, 1999), 101–102.

9   Michael Nelson, *Americans and the Making of the Riviera* (London: McFarland & Co., 2008), 83.

10 NYPL, *Chicago Tribune,* November 18, 1924, 1.

11 I thank Dr. Matthew Balerdi for this observation.

12 Jean Bresson, *La fabuleuse histoire de Cannes* (Monaco: Éditions du Rocher, 1981), 224–235.

13 http://www.post-gazette.com/movies/2013/05/10/The-Great-Gatsby-still-challenges-myth-of-American-Dream/stories/201305100196.

14 Xavier Giraud, *Les années Fitzgerald: La Côte d'Azur 1920–1930* (Paris: Éditions Assouline, 2002), 7.

15 Mark Braude, *Making Monte Carlo: A History of Speculation and Spectacle* (New York: Simon & Schuster, 2016), 150.

16 Cornut-Gentille and Michel-Thiriet, *Florence Gould*, 70; cf. Jules Roy, *Mémoires barbares* (Paris: Albin Michel, 1989), 32.

11. An Amusing Intermezzo for Millionaires

1 Mark Braude, *Making Monte Carlo: A History of Speculation and Spectacle* (New York: Simon & Schuster, 2016), 71.

2 Ibid., 11–18.

3 Ibid., 34–35.

4 Ibid., 42–50.

5 Ibid., 58–59.

6 https://www.library.ca.gov/crb/97/03/chapt2.html.

7 ADAM, rr127.1994.02, Jerôme Bracq, "La vie politique entre les deux guerres," 29–32. Baudoin was specifically targeted during the 1928 elections as part of the perceived corruption of the Guillaumont mayoralty.

8 Jean Bresson, *La fabuleuse histoire de Cannes* (Monaco: Éditions du Rocher, 1981), 219, 222.

9 AMC, loi du 1 janvier 1907 [law of January 1, 1907].

10 ADVN, folios 112, 116.

11 Amanda Vaill, *Everybody Was So Young: Gerald and Sara Murphy, A Lost Generation Love Story* (London: Warner Books, 1999), 121; cf. F. Scott Fitzgerald, *Tender Is the Night* (London: Penguin, 1934), 3. The passage differs slightly in the "final edited author's version" of 1939, where it appears on page 69.

12 There is a photograph of Florence from this period that I was unable to licence from the Florence Gould Foundation, but that was made available to Cornut-Gentille and Michel-Thiriet for their book, which depicts this precise image of her.

13 Frequent reference has been made to Florence "introducing" water-skiing to the Riviera. That was done in the years prior to 1923 by others. See Pierre Galante and Annie Michel Gall, *Les Années Américaines* (Paris: JC Lattès, 1985), 233.

14 Braude, *Making Monte Carlo*, 130; cf. *New York Times*, March 7, 1926.

15 Ibid., 131–137.

16 Ibid., 121–122.

17 Ibid., 134.

12. Taking Stock

1 Amanda Vaill, *Everybody Was So Young: Gerald and Sara Murphy, A Lost Generation Love Story* (London: Warner Books, 1999), 181–182.

2 Gilles Cornut-Gentille and Philippe Michel-Thiriet, *Florence Gould: Une Américaine à Paris* (Paris: Mercure de France, 1989), 66; see also Vaill, *Everybody Was So Young*, 181–182.

3　Vaill, *Everybody Was So Young*, 121; cf. F. Scott Fitzgerald, *Tender Is the Night* (London: Penguin, 1934), 174.

4　Cornut-Gentille and Michel-Thiriet, *Florence Gould*, 72.

5　AMC; Pierre Galante and Annie Michel Gall, *Les Années Américaines* (Paris: JC Lattès, 1985), 236.

6　https://www.newspapers.com/image/88697144/?terms=%22Frank%2BJ.%2BGould%22%2BAND%2B%22hotel%22, AP Newswire, February 11, 1926, 14.

7　Ibid.

8　AMC, Marcel Honoré Merle, "Le Rêve d'Auguste," in *Cannes Généalogie*, number 47, 4th trimester 2006, 23.

9　AMC, dossier 14M9, map of tennis courts; Galante and Gall, *Les Années Américaines*, 222.

10　Ibid., 246.

11　Ibid., 244.

12　AMC, *Le Littoral* newspapers, January 30, 1927, 1; February 3, 1929, 1; March 3, 1929, 1; May 5, 1929, 1. There are myriad other references in *Le Littoral* regarding the Goulds' attendance at charity balls.

13　AMC; Galante and Gall, *Les Années Américaines*, 244.

14　https://www.newspapers.com/image/103053544/?terms=%22Frank%2BJ.%2BGould%22, *Cincinnati Enquirer*, November 8, 1927, 24.

13. The Monégasque Feud Fit for a Prince

1　ADAM, recherchesregionales200_06Aletti.pdf, 2.

2　Edwin P. Hoyt, *The Goulds: A Social History* (New York, Weybright & Talley, 1969), 315.

3　AMC; Pierre Galante and Annie Michel Gall, *Les Années Américaines* (Paris: JC Lattès, 1985), 248.

4　Le Meurice privately printed a limited edition gray felt-bound book about the hotel and its history in 1988 to be given to serious buyers for the hotel. I was fortunate enough to be representing one such buyer and still have my copy.

5　ADAM, recherchesregionales200_06Aletti, 1–5.

6　Ibid., 3.

7　ADVN, dossier 1 I 2, petition (undated).

8　ADVN, dossier Frank Jay Gould. See also Mark Braude, *Making Monte Carlo: A History of Speculation and Spectacle* (New York: Simon & Schuster, 2016), 194.

9　Braude, *Making Monte Carlo*, 189.

10　Ibid., 191–194.

11　ADVN, dossier 1 I 8 Palais de la Méditerranée, interview with the mayor and letter from Baudoin dated January 28, 1928.

12　Ibid.

13　Ibid., poster.

14   Ibid., letter of April 19, 1928.

15   https://www.newspapers.com/image/74555973/?terms=%22Frank%2BJ.%2
     BGould%22, April 28, 1928.

16   https://www.newspapers.com/image/103041835/?terms=%22Frank%2BJ.%2
     BGould%22, *Cincinnati Enquirer*, Thursday, December 13, 1928, 5.

17   PP, dossier 88.926, letter dated June 27, 1950.

18   Braude, *Making Monte Carlo*, 197–198.

19   Janet Flanner, *Paris Was Yesterday: 1925–1939* (London: Virago Press, 2003), 73.

20   https://www.newspapers.com/image/18693938/?terms=%22Florence%2
     BLacaze%22, *Modesto News Herald*, December 27, 1928.

21   https://www.newspapers.com/image/103582774/?terms=%22Frank%2
     BJ.%2BGould%22, *Oakland Tribune*, December 29, 1929.

22   https://www.newspapers.com/image/89867520/?terms=%22Frank%2BJ.%2
     BGould%22, *Pittsburgh Post-Gazette*, February 12, 1930.

23   Ibid.

14. Hollywood Calling

1   Janet Flanner, *Paris Was Yesterday: 1925–1939*, (London: Virago Press, 2003,)
    80–82.

2   Carol Dyhouse, *Glamour: Women, History, Feminism* (London: Zed Books,
    2010), 29.

3   Again, these are my impressions from photographs made available to Cornut-
    Gentille and Michel-Thiriet by the Florence Gould Foundation, but not made
    available to me.

4   https://www.newspapers.com/image/138676706/?terms=%22Frank%2BJ.%2
    BGould%22, *St. Louis Post-Dispatch*, April 30, 1930.

5   https://www.newspapers.com/image/21926808/?terms=%22Frank%2BJ.%2
    BGould%22, *News-Palladium* (Benton Harbor, Michigan), April 1, 1931. Doumergue
    would be replaced in the May election by Aristide Briand.

6   Edwin Hoyt, *Sir Charlie* (London: Robert Hale, 1977), 114–116, 132.

7   Ibid., 137.

8   Ibid., 143.

9   https://www.newspapers.com/image/41327576/?terms=%22Frank%2BJ.%2
    BGould%22, *Valley Morning Star* (AP Newswire), September 9, 1931; https://www.
    newspapers.com/image/91751188/?terms=%22Florence%2BLacaze%22, *Valley
    Morning Star* (AP Newswire), *September* 12, 1931.

10 https://www.newspapers.com/image/146912855/?terms=%22Florence%2
    BLacaze%22, *Pittsburgh Press* (UPI Newswire) September 13, 1931.

11 Jean Chalon, *Florence et Louise les Magnifiques: Florence Jay-Gould et Louise de
    Vilmorin* (Paris: Éditions du Rocher, 1999), 45.

15. The Phoenix Rises

1   Gilles Cornut-Gentille and Philippe Michel-Thiriet, *Florence Gould: Une Améri-caine à Paris* (Paris: Mercure de France, 1989), 71.

2   Ibid. Garat's career was a complete failure. He was unhappily married six times, became a drug addict, was blinded in one eye by an angry croupier, and passed myriad bad checks. He died in 1959 in abject misery.

3   Interviews with several people at Sotheby's and Christie's.

4   Ibid., 73.

5   https://www.newspapers.com/image/49076344/?terms=%22Frank%2BJ.%2 BGould%22, *The Capital Times* (UPI Newswire—Madison, Wisconsin), June 13, 1930.

6   ADVN, dossier 1 I 8 Palais de la Méditerranée.

7   Ibid.

8   https://www.newspapers.com/image/154180387/?terms=%22Frank%2BJ.%2 BGould%22, *The Capital Times* (UPI Newswire—Madison, Wisconsin), November 12, 1930.

9   ADVN, dossier 1 I 8, *Le Reveil de la Montagne*, November 1932.

10 Ibid., Palais de la Méditerranée.

16. Scandal, America, and Separate Lives

1   The fallen government was that of Prime Minister Édouard Herriot on December 14, 1932, for the issue of war debts from Germany. On the issue of the budget, the governments of the following prime ministers fell: Augustin Paul-Boncour on January 28, 1933; Édouard Daladier on October 24, 1933; and Albert-Pierre Sarraut on November 23, 1933. Camille Chautemps achieved a working agreement on the budget—just—before falling over Stavisky on January 27, 1934, and Édouard Daladier fell almost immediately on February 7, 1934. Source: *Bulletin of International News*, Chatham House, London, vol. 10, no. 25 (June 7, 1934), 3–11.

2   Paul F. Jankowski, *Stavisky: A Confidence Man in the Republic of Virtue* (Ithaca, NY: Cornell University Press, 2002), 172.

3   Ibid., 40.

4   Ibid., 9.

5   Ibid., 73.

6   Ibid., 120.

7   Ibid., 102.

8   Ibid., 172–175.

9   Fenby, Jonathan, "The Republic of Broken Dreams," *History Today*, London, vol. 66, issue 11 (November 2016), 30.

10 NYPL, *New York Sun*, October 16, 1934, Arrivals section.

11   Robert A.M. Stern, Anne Walker, and Peter Pennoyer, *The Architecture of Delano and Aldrich* (New York: W.W. Norton & Co., 2003), 191.

12   Gilles Cornut-Gentille and Philippe Michel-Thiriet, *Florence Gould: Une Américaine à Paris* (Paris: Mercure de France, 1989), 74.

13   Laura Frankos, *The Broadway Musical Quiz Book* (New York: Applause Theatre and Cinema Books, 2010), 24.

14   Cornut-Gentille and Michel-Thiriet, *Florence Gould*, 75.

15   Ibid., 87.

16   NYHS, microfilm of *New York Sun*, October 16, 1934.

17   Ibid., 75–76.

17. Dark Horizons

1   JSTOR, Peter Jackson, "French Intelligence and Hitler's Rise to Power," *The History Journal*, vol. 41, no. 3 (September 1998), 798.

2   Ibid., 801.

3   Adolf Hitler, *Hitler's Secret Book* (New York: Grove Press, 1962), 129. This was a 1928 manuscript by Hitler but placed by Max Amman, Hitler's public relations genius, into a vault at the Nazi publishing house in Berlin with strict orders that it was never to be published. An American officer confiscated it in May 1945, and sent it back to the United States.

4   Barbara Lambauer, *Otto Abetz et les Français—ou l'envers de la Collaboration* (Paris: Fayard, 2001), 70–71.

5   Ibid., 73.

6   Ibid., 75.

7   Ibid., 86.

8   ANF, dossier 8AR/636.

9   Ibid., *Le Journal* article dated February 22, 1936.

10   ADVN, dossier 1 I 8, Sûreté Order dated December 20, 1935, concerning Palais de la Méditerranée, 2.

11   Ibid.

12   PP, dossier 77W22, 88926. The Sixième Bureau handles foreigners living or working in France.

13   ADVN, dossier 1 I 8.

14   Jack Colhoun, *Gangsterismo: The United States, Cuba and the Mafia, 1933 to 1966* (New York: O/R Books, 2013), Kindle Edition, location 272.

15   NARA, RG65, AHSCA (JFK Assassination Records) Files: FBI memo from LEGAT (JFK Assassination Records relating to foreign funds) to Hoover, October 11, 1955.

16   ADVN, dossier 1 I 8, enclosure 4 dated September 23, 1936.

17   Colhoun, *Gangsterismo*, location 388; cf. *A Tangled Web: CIA Complicity in International Drug Trafficking*, May 7, 1998, NARA: 8404–8405.

18 NYPL, *New York Times,* December 6, 1936.

19 Ibid.

20 Ibid., enclosure dated November 5, 1936, by the representative for the Municipal Casino, 4.

21 Gilles Cornut-Gentille and Philippe Michel-Thiriet, *Florence Gould: Une Américaine à Paris* (Paris: Mercure de France, 1989), 257.

22 Hal Vaughan, *Sleeping with the Enemy: Coco Chanel, Nazi Agent* (London: Chatto & Windus, 2011), 30–33.

23 Ibid., 79–80.

24 Paul F. Jankowski, *Stavisky: A Confidence Man in the Republic of Virtue* (Ithaca, NY: Cornell University Press, 2002), 261–263.

18. Fifth Columnists and Fellow Travelers

1   Jean Chalon, *Florence et Louise les Magnifiques: Florence Jay-Gould et Louise de Vilmorin* (Paris: Éditions du Rocher: 1999), 74.

2   Gilles Cornut-Gentille and Philippe Michel-Thiriet, *Florence Gould: Une Américaine à Paris* (Paris: Mercure de France, 1989), 78.

3   Noel Riley Fitch, *Sylvia Beach and the Lost Generation: A History of Literary Paris in the Twenties and Thirties* (New York: W. W. Norton & Co., 1969), 363.

4   Ibid., 361.

5   Ibid., 363.

6   Caroline Seebohm, *The Man Who Was Vogue: The Life and Times of Condé Nast* (New York: Viking Press, 1982), 137–138.

7   Riley Fitch, *Sylvia Beach and the Lost Generation,* 370–371.

8   Janet Flanner, *Paris Was Yesterday, 1925–1939* (London: Virago Press, 2003), 201.

9   Anne Sebba, *Les Parisiennes: How the Women of Paris Lived, Loved and Died in the 1940s* (London: Weidenfeld & Nicolson, 2016), 19.

10 Angie David, *Dominique Aury* (Paris: Éditions Léo Scheer, 2006), 149.

11 David Carroll, *French Literary Fascism: Nationalism, Anti-Semitism, and the Ideology of Culture* (Princeton, NJ: Princeton University Press, 1995), 114.

12 Susan Ronald, *Hitler's Art Thief: Hildebrand Gurlitt, the Nazis and the Looting of Europe's Treasures* (New York: St. Martin's Press, 2015), 161.

13 Kevin Desmond, *The Golden Age of Waterskiing* (St. Paul, MN: Motorbooks International, 2001), 56.

14 Stanislao G. Pugliese, *Carlo Rosselli: Socialist, Heretic, and Anti-Fascist Exile* (Boston, MA: Harvard University Press, 1999), 218–221; https://www.newspapers.com/image/146917075/?terms=%22Frank%2BJ.%2BGould%22, *Pittsburgh Press* (UPI Newswire), June 11, 1937.

15 Hal Vaughan, *Sleeping with the Enemy: Coco Chanel, Nazi Agent* (London: Chatto & Windus, 2011), 84, 89.

16 Barbara Lambauer, *Otto Abetz et les Français—ou l'envers de la Collaboration* (Paris: Fayard, 2001), 114–119.

17 Sebba, *Les Parisiennes*, 6.

18 Cornut-Gentille and Michel-Thiriet, *Florence Gould*, 81.

19. Fall of France

1 Gilles Cornut-Gentille and Philippe Michel-Thiriet, *Florence Gould: Une Américaine à Paris* (Paris: Mercure de France, 1989), 89–90; cf. Pierre Dux, *Vive le theatre!* (Paris: Stock, 1984), 97.

2 This is hearsay from the gossip columns of *La Littoral*.

3 Ibid., 90.

4 Susan Ronald, *Hitler's Art Thief: Hildebrand Gurlitt, the Nazis and the Looting of Europe's Treasures* (New York: St. Martin's Press, 2015), 213.

5 Tom Bower, *Nazi Gold* (New York: HarperCollins, 1997), 52.

6 Ronald, *Hitler's Art Thief*, 214.

7 Ibid., 215; cf. Lynn H. Nicholas, *The Rape of Europa: The Fate of Europe's Treasures in the Third Reich and the Second World War* (London: Macmillan, 1997), and William L. Shirer, *The Collapse of the Third Republic: An Inquiry into the Fall of France 1940*, (New York: Simon & Schuster, 1969), 914.

8 NARA, RG 84, 711.3, box 295, memo June 12, 1945.

9 NARA, Series 1, Section 1, File 65-HQ53642, "Florence Lacaze Gould alias Mrs. Frank Jay Gould, Treason Case," memo dated 10-4-46, hereinafter "Gould/OSS Testimony."

10 Cornut-Gentille and Michel-Thieriet, *Florence Gould*, 89–90.

11 NARA, "Gould/OSS Testimony," 6.

12 Nicholas, *The Rape of Europa*, 126.

13 Ibid.

14 Pierre Abramovici, *Un Rocher bien occupé: Monaco pendant la guerre 1939–1945* (Paris: Éditions du Seuil, 2001), 67.

15 Sylvia Kahan, *Music's Modern Muse: A Life of Winnaretta Singer, Princesse de Polignac* (Rochester, NY: University of Rochester Press, 2003), 340–341.

16 Hal Vaughan, *Sleeping with the Enemy: Coco Chanel, Nazi Agent* (London: Chatto & Windus, 2011), 106.

17 The saving of downed pilots was intimated rather than witnessed by Gehard Heller in his self-serving biography *Un Allemand à Paris*, (Paris: Éditions du Seuil, 1981), 63–64.

18 Ibid., 359–360.

19 NARA, RG 84, 711.3, box 3.

20 PP, dossier 77 W 22, file 88926, June 1943 memo.

21 NARA, "Gould/OSS Testimony," 6.

22 Alan Riding, *And the Show Went On: Cultural Life in Nazi-Occupied Paris* (London:

Duckworth Overlook, 2012), 264; cf. www.nizkor.org/ftp.cgi/imt/ftp.py?imt//nca
/nca-06/nca-06-3766-ps.

23 NARA, "Gould/OSS Testimony," 11.

24 Nicholas, *The Rape of Europa*, 138.

20. Ludwig

1 NARA, RG65, A1-136-Z, box 3, memo dated February 9, 1950, 2.

2 NARA, Series 1, Section 1, File 65-HQ53642, "Florence Lacaze Gould alias Mrs. Frank Jay Gould, Treason Case," hereinafter "Gould/OSS Testimony."

3 NARA, RG65, A-1-136-Z, box 9, biography of Ludwig Vogel prepared by the OSS July 20, 1945.

4 Ibid., affidavit dated June 30, 1947.

5 Ibid., photostat of Nazi Party membership card.

6 NARA, "Gould/OSS Testimony," Diego Zanini written statement.

7 NARA, RG65, A1-136-Z, box 3, Vogel interrogation October 21, 1944.

8 PP, dossier 77 W 22, file 88926, March 1945, 2.

9 Ibid.

21. The "Anything Goes" Occupation

1 Charles Glass, *Americans in Paris* (London: Harper Press, 2009), 37.

2 Ibid., 35.

3 O.H. Bullitt (ed.), *For the President, Personal and Secret* (London: Andre Deutsch, 1973), 484.

4 Alan Riding, *And the Show Went On: Cultural Life in Nazi-Occupied Paris* (London: Duckworth Overlook, 2012), 232.

5 Frederic Spotts, *The Shameful Peace: How French Artists and Intellectuals Survived the Nazi Occupation* (New Haven and London: Yale University Press, 2010), 159.

6 Riding, *And the Show Went On*, 71.

7 Ibid., 25; cf. André Gide, *Journals*, vol. 4. 1939–1949, translated by Justin O'Brien (Urbana, IL: University of Illinois Press, 2000).

8 Ibid., 208.

9 Ibid., 66.

10 Spotts, *The Shameful Peace*, 62–63.

11 Ibid., 64–65.

12 Gerard Heller, *Un Allemand à Paris* (Paris: Éditions du Seuil, 1981), 30.

13 Riding, *And the Show Went On*, 69.

14 NARA, Series 1, Section 1, File 65-HQ53642, "Florence Lacaze Gould alias Mrs. Frank Jay Gould, Treason Case," Donald L. Daughters's report.

15 Ibid.

16 Jean Chalon, *Florence et Louise les Magnifiques: Florence Jay-Gould et Louise de Vilmorin* (Paris: Éditions du Rocher, 1999), 75.

17   Ibid., appendix.

18   NARA, Series 1, Section 1, File 65-HQ53642, "Florence Lacaze Gould alias Mrs. Frank Jay Gould, Treason Case," Florence Gould statement, hereinafter "Gould/ OSS Testimony."

19   NARA, RG 238, NM66-52-D, CI-FIR/90. Garthe fired Steffens for incompetence.

20   NARA, "Gould/OSS Testimony," 8.

21   Ibid., 7.

22   NARA, RG65, A1-136-Z, box 3, memo dated January 7, 1949, attachment.

23   NARA, "Gould/OSS Testimony," 6.

24   NARA, RG65, A1-136-Z, box 3, report to Assistant Attorney General Caudle, September 17, 1945.

25   ANF, BB/30/1821, Rapport sur organisation du Marché-Noir en France par les allemands, attachments E, M. After the war, the official report, *La France au Pillage*, named "Captain" Ludwig Vogel as the day-to-day manager of Bosse's purchasing activities.

26   Robert O. Paxton. Olivier Corpet, and Claire Paulhan (eds.), *Collaboration and Resistance: French Literary Life under the Nazi Occupation* (New York: Five Ties, 2010), 85.

22. In the Garden of Earthly Delights

1   http://www.vanityfair.com/news/1998/03/wildenstein-art-collection-history.

2   NARA, RG65, A1-136-Z, box 3, Vogel interrogation October 21, 1944.

3   Cécile Desprairies, *Paris dans la collaboration* (Paris: Éditions du Seuil, 2008), 537.

4   NARA, Series 1, Section 1, File 65-HQ53642, "Florence Lacaze Gould alias Mrs. Frank Jay Gould, Treason Case," Donald L. Daughters's report.

5   Gilles Cornut-Gentille and Philippe Michel-Thiriet, *Florence Gould: Une Américaine à Paris* (Paris: Mercure de France, 1989), 96; cf. Dominique Aury, "Florence et les écrivains," preface to *Par le Don de Florence Gould* (Bibliothèque littéraire Jacques-Doucet, 1988), 7.

6   Gerard Heller, *Un Allemand à Paris* (Paris: Éditions du Seuil, 1981), 59.

7   Ibid., 62.

8   Cornut-Gentille and Michel-Thiriet, *Florence Gould*, 95; cf. unedited letter from Pierre Benoit to Florence Gould dated January 14, 1941.

9   Ibid., 98–99.

10   Ernst Jünger, *Premier Journal Parisien: Journal II, 1941–1943* (Paris: Christian Bourgois, 1980), 124–125.

11   Heller, *Un Allemand à Paris*, 163.

12   Gérard Loiseaux, *La Littérature de la défaite et de la collaboration* (Paris: Fayard, 1995), 515.

13   Alan Riding, *And the Show Went On: Cultural Life in Nazi-Occupied Paris* (London: Duckworth Overlook, 2012), 48.

14 Charles Glass, *Americans in Paris: Life and Death under the Nazi Occupation 1940–1944* (London: HarperPress, 2009), 233.

15 PP, 77 W 22, dossier 88926, exemption order for Florence Gould from the order concerning all Americans, signed by the "Police overseeing Foreign Residents."

16 NARA, Series 1, Section 1, File 65-HQ53642, "Florence Lacaze Gould alias Mrs. Frank Jay Gould, Treason Case," Florence Gould statement, hereinafter "Gould/OSS Testimony."

17 Heller, *Un Allemand à Paris*, 63–64.

18 NARA, "Gould/OSS Testimony."

23. The Occupation, 1942–1943

1 NARA, RG65, A1-136-Z, box 3.

2 Paul Léautaud, *Journal Littéraire*, vol. XV: *Novembre 1942–Juin 1944* (Paris: Mercure de France, 1963), 319.

3 Charles Glass, *Americans in Paris: Life and Death under the Nazi Occupation 1940–1944* (London: HarperPress, 2009), 231–234. It was the August 24, 1942, issue of *Life*.

4 NARA, Series 1, Section 1, File 65-HQ53642, "Florence Lacaze Gould alias Mrs. Frank Jay Gould, Treason Case," Florence Gould statement, hereinafter "Gould/OSS Testimony."

5 Glass, *Americans in Paris*, 240–241.

6 Ibid., 250.

7 Ibid., 254.

8 Léautaud, *Journal Littéraire*, vol. XV, 19.

9 PP, 77 W 22, dossier 88926, papers from 1940–44.

10 Ibid., June 1943 memo.

11 Edwin P. Hoyt, *The Goulds: A Social History* (New York: Weybright and Talley, 1969), 115.

12 CDJC, document LXXXIX-91.

13 M.R. Marcus and Robert O. Paxton, *Vichy France & the Jews* (New York: Basic Books, 1981), 317. See CDJC, L-35, too.

14 CDJC, V-64, Knochen to the MBF, January 28, 1941.

15 NARA, "Gould/OSS Testimony." Again, Florence fudges the dates, claiming it was later in the war, but this is the only reference to riding south with Garthe, so I presume she meant July 1943.

16 Pierre Giolitto, *Histoire de la Milice* (Paris: Éditions Perrin, 2002), 14.

17 Ibid., NARA, RG 65, A1-136-AR, box 3.

18 Ernst Jünger, *Premier Journal Parisien, Journal III, 1943–1945* (Paris: Christian Bourgois, 1980), 68–69.

19 Ibid., 71.

20 Ibid., 13–14.

21 Ibid., 269.

22 Léautaud, *Journal Littéraire*, vol. XV, 215.

23 Ibid., 526.

24 Ibid., 236, 306.

25 Ibid., 300–303.

26 Marcel Jouhandeau and Jean Paulhan, *Correspondance 1921–1968* (Paris: NRF, 2012), 22.

24. Florence the Banker

1   Susan Ronald, *Hitler's Art Thief: Hildebrand Gurlitt, the Nazis and the Looting of Europe's Treasures* (New York: St. Martin's Press, 2015), 179.

2   NARA, RG 65, 65-7267-68-1337, box 98.

3   NARA, RG 84, Safehaven on Interkommerz, box 45.

4   NARA, Series 1, Section 1, File 65-HQ53642, "Florence Lacaze Gould alias Mrs. Frank Jay Gould, Treason Case," Donald L. Daughters's report.

5   NARA, RG 263, [A]-44835 [CIA/EUR] to Chief EE and Chief SR.

6   NARA, RG 65, 65-7267-17-399, box 71.

7   NARA, RG 65, 65-7267-5-97x, box 67, NARA, RG 65, 65-7267-5-102x, box 67.

8   Pierre Abramovici, *Un Rocher bien occupé: Monaco pendant la guerre 1939–1945* (Paris: Éditions du Seuil, 2001), 56.

9   Fold3.com, NARA, M1933, RG 153, roll 0007, 14; NARA, RG 65, 65-7267-75-1635, box 95.

10 Annie Lacroix-Riz, *Industriels et banquiers français sous l'occupation* (Paris: Armand Colin, 2013), 436.

11 Pierre Abramovici, *Szkolnikoff: Hitler's Jewish Smuggler* (London: Pen & Sword, 2016), 31.

12 ANF, AJ/40-828a.

13 Abramovici, *Un Rocher bien occupé*, 152–154.

14 Ibid., 210–211.

15 ANF, Z6/NL/8950. This is a "Z" file restored to France by Russia after the breakup of the Soviet Union in 1990.

16 Gerald D. Feldman, *Austrian Banks in the Period of National Socialism* (New York: Cambridge University Press, 2015), 321–322.

17 Ibid., 212.

18 NARA, Series 1, Section 1, File 65-HQ53642, "Florence Lacaze Gould alias Mrs. Frank Jay Gould, Treason Case," Florence Gould statement, hereinafter "Gould/OSS Testimony."

19 Edwin P. Hoyt, *The Goulds: A Social History* (New York: Weybright & Talley, 1969), 315.

20 ANF, BB/30/1821, résumé grouped by company dated February 22, 1945.

21 PP, IEQJ, file 3E-C-VB, April 13, 1943.

22 Abramovici, *Un Rocher bien occupé*, 258. See also Abramovici, *Szkolnikoff*, 126.

23 NARA, "Gould/OSS Testimony."

24 Abramovici, *Un Rocher bien occupé*, 254–258; Abramovici, *Szkolnikoff*, 100. See also NARA, Berghaus Interrogation Reports, Exhibits 1–31.

25 Richard Breitman, et al., *U.S. Intelligence and the Nazis*, (Cambridge: Cambridge University Press, 2005), 192–193 cf. Conroy to Hoover, 10 May 1944, NARA, RG 65 65-7267-87-1890, box 99.

25. Liberation and Treason

1 Barbara Lambauer, *Otto Abetz et les Français—ou l'envers de la collaboration* (Paris: Fayard, 2001), 605–606.

2 Anne Sebba, *Les Parisiennes: How Women Lived, Loved and Died in the 1940s* (London: Weidenfeld & Nicolson, 2016), 219.

3 Marcel Léautaud, *Journal Littéraire*, vol. XV: *Novembre 1942–Juin 1944* (Paris: Mercure de France, 1963), 303.

4 Marcel Jouhandeau and Jean Paulhan, *Correspondance 1921–1968* (Paris: NRF, 2012), 525–526.

5 NARA, Series 1, Section 1, File 65-HQ53642, "Florence Lacaze Gould alias Mrs. Frank Jay Gould, Treason Case," Florence Gould statement, hereinafter "Gould/ OSS Testimony."

6 Ernst Jünger, *Premier Journal Parisien: Journal III, 1943–1945* (Paris: Christian Bourgois, 1980), 277–279.

7 Ibid., 295–296.

8 Ibid.

9 Antony Beevor and Artemis Cooper, *Paris After the Liberation 1945–1949* (London: Penguin Books, Kindle Edition, 2007), 85.

10 Jouhandeau and Paulhan, *Correspondance*, 559.

11 Sebba, *Les Parisiennes*, 231–233.

12 ANF, BB/30/1821, *La France au Pillage*, Rapport sur organisation du Marché-Noir en France par les allemands, 42.

13 NARA, RG 65, A1-136AR, box 3, Drohan memo dated January 3, 1956.

14 Ibid., letter from October 26, 1955.

15 NARA, "Gould/OSS Testimony," Donald Daughters' Report, appendix.

16 Ibid., interrogation of Ludwig Vogel by American Lt. Michaelis, October 21, 1944.

17 Ibid., PP 77W22 88924, October 7, 1944, note from Commandant Pallole, Directeur de la Sécurité Militaire.

18 NARA, RG84, 705.48 RET—711.3 GER, letter from Armour in Madrid to Secretary of State, April 17, 1945.

19 NYPL, *New York Times*, May 29, 1945, in-house microfilm.

20 ANF, BB/30/1821, cover Blanchet interrogation.

21 NARA, RG 84, 711.3-800.0, looted assets.

22 NARA, "Gould/OSS Testimony."

23 NARA, RG65-A1-136Z, box 3, letter from J. Edgar Hoover dated June 16, 1955, file 140-8299.

24 NARA, "Gould/OSS Testimony," November 2, 1944, Hoover to Agent Ayer re "Gould Treason."

25 NARA, RG65, A1-136Z, box 9, Vogel file, report dated 6-6-45.

26 Jouhandeau and Paulhan, *Correspondance*, 592–593, 597–598.

27 NARA, "Gould/OSS Testimony," Edward Kennedy AP article dated February 18, 1945.

28 Ibid.

29 Ibid.

30 Ibid., Donald L. Daughters's report dated April 5, 1945, Kennedy revealed as Source H and contains information not in the *Washington Star* article.

31 Ibid.

32 Ibid.

33 Ibid., letter from Theron Caudle to J. Edgar Hoover, November 2, 1945.

26. No Safe Havens

1 Marcel Jouhandeau and Jean Paulhan, *Correspondance 1921–1968* (Paris: NRF, 2012), 605.

2 Pierre Abramovici, *Un Rocher bien occupé: Monaco pendant la guerre 1939–1945* (Paris: Éditions du Seuil, 2001), 256. See also NARA, Berghaus Interrogation Reports, Exhibits 1–31.

3 ANF, AJ/40-828a. See also Hugh Brian Markus, *The History of the German Accounting Profession* (London: Taylor Francis, 1997), 9.

4 Pierre Abramovici, *Szkolnikoff: Hitler's Jewish Smuggler* (London: Pen & Sword, 2016), 120–121. Elizabeth Arden fared less well. Her sister, Gladys, was accused of espionage and sent to Ravensbruck initially, then joined the American prisoners at Vittel. See Lindy Woodhead, *War Paint: Elizabeth Arden & Helena Rubinstein, Their Lives, Their Times, Their Rivalry* (London: Virago Press, 2004).

5 Ibid., 147–149.

6 NARA, RG 84, file 851.6, box 260; RG 84, file 711.3, box 294, J. E. Charles and Co.; RG84, file 711.3, box 295, looted assets and Safehaven Monaco.

7 NARA, RG 65-A1-136Z, box 9, Ludwig Vogel file.

27. Paper Clips and Friends Cast Long Shadows

1 https://www.cia.gov/library/center-for-the-study-of-intelligence/csi-publications/csi-studies/studies/vol-58-no-3/operation-paperclip-the-secret-intelligence-program-to-bring-nazi-scientists-to-america.html.

2 NARA, RG 65-A1-136Z, box 9, Ludwig Vogel file.

3 Ibid., Wolfram Hirth affidavit.

4   NARA, RG 65-A1-136Z, box 3, Ludwig Vogel file, Hoover to Telford, January 7, 1949.

5   Ibid., Ludwig Vogel file 39–110, John D. Ryan Report, November 2, 1948.

6   Ibid., Ludwig Vogel file, 1948 affidavits.

7   ANF, AJ40-89/19.25, Ministère Public c/ x . . . pouvant être le personnel dirigeant de la Banque Charles de Monaco.

8   Jean Chalon, *Florence et Louise les Magnifiques: Florence Jay-Gould et Louise de Vilmorin* (Paris: Éditions du Rocher, 1999), 28–29

9   James Lord, *Six Exceptional Women* (New York: Farrar, Strauss, Giroux), 52–59.

10 Gilles Cornut-Gentille and Philippe Michel-Thiriet, *Florence Gould: Une Américaine à Paris* (Paris: Mercure de France, 1989), 163.

11 Ibid., 163–164. The date in the book is wrong, stating that the check was presented on February 27. I have corrected this to February 25, 1947, in accordance with the U.S. Supreme Court Ruling referenced below.

12 Martin J. Kelly, John T. Cahill, *U.S. Supreme Court Records and Briefs 1832–1978, Anne Vilbert De Sairigne, Petitioner, v. Frank Jay Gould. U.S. Supreme Court Transcript of Record with Supporting Pleadings* (Washington, D.C.: Gale, Making of Modern Law Print Edition, 1949), 3, hereinafter "Supreme Court Ruling."

13 Ibid., 3–9.

14 Ibid., Supreme Court Ruling, 2–6.

15 Ibid., Supreme Court Ruling, 3, 5.

16 NARA, Series 1, Section 1, File 65-HQ53642, "Florence Lacaze Gould alias Mrs. Frank Jay Gould, Treason Case," Florence Gould statement, hereinafter "Gould/OSS Testimony," letter dated April 25, 1945, 6.

17 Cornut-Gentille and Michel-Thiriet, *Florence Gould*, 164.

18 Lisa Hilton, *The Horror of Love* (London: Weidenfield & Nicolson, 2011), 171–172.

19 The private family Palewski files were requested at the ANF but not made available during my research period.

20 Hilton, *The Horror of Love*, 178.

21 JSTOR, Kenneth O'Reilly, *Illinois Historical Journal*, vol. 81, no. 1 (Spring, 1988), "Adlai E. Stevenson, McCarthyism, and the FBI," 45–60.

28. A Fortune to Give Away

1   Jean Chalon, *Florence et Louise les Magnifiques: Florence Jay-Gould et Louise de Vilmorin* (Paris: Éditions du Rocher, 1999), 29.

2   Paul Léautaud, *Journal Litteraire*, vol. XVII: *August 1946–August 1949* (Paris: Mercure de France, 1964), 256–257.

3   Gilles Cornut-Gentille and Philippe Michel-Thiriet, *Florence Gould: Une Américaine à Paris* (Paris: Mercure de France, 1989), 178.

4   https://www.newspapers.com/image/139840216/?terms=%22Frank%2BJ.%2BGould%22, *St. Louis Dispatch*, January 10, 1951.

5   Ibid., 167.

6   NARA, Series 1, Section 1, File 65-HQ53642, letter from Dorothy Gould Burns's lawyer.

7   Paul Léautaud and Jean Paulhan, *Correspondance 1921–1968* (Paris: NRF, Gallimard, 2012), 903, 904, 906–910.

8   I thank Dr. Matthew Balerdi for this tentative diagnosis.

9   Cornut-Gentille and Michel-Thiriet, *Florence Gould*, 168.

10   Ibid., 169.

11   NARA, Series 1, Section 1, File 65-HQ53642, Dorothy Gould Burns deposition to Russell Porter.

12   When I was in the hotel business beginning in 1974, I remarked to my boss one day that there was a preponderance of Swiss hoteliers, and I was told this adage for the first time. I soon learned that it was a commonly accepted fact in the industry that many "Swiss" (or German) hoteliers had been put into strategic positions at the close of the war.

13   NARA, Series 1, Section 1, File 65-HQ53642, March 6, 1958, letter.

14   NARA, Series 1, Section 1, File 65-HQ53642, Mattheson deposition, August 28, 1958.

15   NARA, A1-136AR, box 3, McCue report from Fock-Wulf, February 1956.

16   Ibid., Glenn W. Thompson report, October 4, 1955, witness statement of Elfriede Elsner Vogel Gassner.

17   http://tempsreel.nouvelobs.com/monde/20150805.OBS3750/quand-la-france -graciait-deux-ss-de-haut-rang.html.

18   Angie David, *Dominique Aury* (Paris: Éditions Léo Scheer, 2006), 156–157

19   Cornut-Gentille and Michel-Thiriet, *Florence Gould*, 224; cf. Maurice Chevalier, *Môme à cheveux blancs* (Paris: Presses de la Cité, 1969), 191–192

29. Queen of the Riviera

1   Gilles Cornut-Gentille and Philippe Michel-Thiriet, *Florence Gould: Une Américaine à Paris* (Paris: Mercure de France, 1989), 172–173.

2   ANF, 19940053/11, dossiers 82–87.

3   AMC, 7 W 120.

4   Cornut-Gentille and Michel-Thiriet, *Florence Gould*, 225.

5   Ibid., 179–180.

6   Magali Serre, *Les Wildenstein* (Paris: JC Lattès, 2013), 18–19.

7   Cornut-Gentille and Michel-Thiriet, *Florence Gould*, 188–189.

8   Ibid., 191–192.

9   Author interview with Howard Zar, director at Lyndhurst, January 2016.

10   Lindy Woodhouse, *War Paint: Elizabeth Arden and Helena Rubinstein, Their Lives, Their Times, Their Rivalry* (London: Virago Press, 2012), 349–350

11   MMA, Florence J. Gould file, *New York Times*, November 23, 1968.

12 MMA, ibid., letter dated Sunday [1967].
13 MMA, ibid., letters dated "Mercredi," received April 15, 1968, and April 9, 1968.
14 https://www.washingtonpost.com/archive/entertainment/books/1993/01/24/the
    -exhibitionist/be1d0618-e34a-43a2-b1a4-c8fcd7b5b877/?utm_term=.97d2f2ec
    fd3a; Thomas Hoving, *Making the Mummies Dance* (New York: Simon & Schuster,
    1993), 104.
15 Ibid., 105.
16 MMA, ibid., letter for deed of gift, dated September 25, 1972.
17 MMA, ibid., letter dated August 21, 1906.
18 Cornut-Gentille and Michel-Thiriet, *Florence Gould*, 258.

Epilogue
1 MMA, *New York Times,* "Gould Art Collection Brings Record Prices," April 26,
   1985.
2 http://lootedart.com/MFEU4A34776.
3 MMA, *New York Times,* "Florence Gould Dead—Benefactor of the Arts," March 2,
   1983.
4 Interview with Howard Zar at Lyndhurst, January 2016.
5 MMA, *New York Times,* "The Treasures of Mrs. Gould," June 22, 1984.

SELECTED BIBLIOGRAPHY

Archival Manuscripts
ANF:
AJ/40-828a
Z6/NL/8950
BB/30/1821
8AR/598
8AR/647
8AR/636
8AR/585
8AR/608
8AR/628
199/20627/18 (Files 82–87, French Foundations)
82/16321 (Ministry of the Interior, legal opinion)
La France au Pillage: Rapport d'activité du service français des investigations financières,
  supplément à l'actualité économique et financière de September 1946, Strictly Con-
  fidential.

ADAM:
rr127.1994.02
recherchesregionales200_06Aletti
rr73.1980.03
rr123.1993.02
rr123.1993.06
rr123.1993.04

rr124.1993.04
rr127.1993.04
rr128.1994.02—Szkolnikoff
rr146—negresco
rr163—journaux mondains
rr167—restaurants Zaharoff
rr171—vie culturelle nicoise
rr176—Palais Méditerrannée
rr184—Dalmas

ADVN:
1 I 2. (historic gambling clubs)
1 I 6. (historic gambling clubs)
I ii 8⁰ 1004
Dossier Frank Jay Gould
1 I 8. Palais de la Méditerranée

AMC:
Dossier "New Tennis Courts" 2.5.530
14M9
B257
B1059
Demeures anciens et beaux jardins, Commune de Cannes, no date.

CDJC:
LXXXIX-91
L-35
V-64

FOLD3 (online resource):
Dossier on General Oberg
Dossier on Col. Knochen
Dossier on Banque Charles

NARA:
RG 65, Series 1, Section 1, File 65-HQ53642
RG 65, A1-136-Z, box 3
RG65, A-1-136-Z, box 9
RG 65, A1-136-AR, box 3
RG 65, 65-7267-68-1337, box 98

RG 65, 65-7267-39-812, box 96
RG 65, 65-7267-17-399, box 71
RG 65, 65-7267-5-97x, box 67
RG 65, 65-7267-5-102x, box 67
RG 65, 65-7267-74-1519, box 95
RG 65 65-7267-87-1890, box 99
RG 84, box 45
RG 84, 711.3, box 3, 295
RG 131, box 174, file: Germany Rückwanderer Marks
RG 153, roll 2
RG 226, roll 4, Nuremberg Interrogation Records, Colonel Oberg and Helmut Knochen

<u>MMA:</u>
Florence and Frank Jay Gould files

<u>PP:</u>
Dossier 77 W 22, file 88926
Dossier IEQJ, file 3E-C-VB, April 13, 1943

Internet Primary Sources
www.newspapers.com: searches for Frank Jay Gould; Florence Lacaze Gould; *Le Franco-Californien*; Maximin Lacaze; Berthe Lacaze; Henry Heynemann; Manfred Heynemann.
http://interactive.ancestry.com/1174/USM1490_235-0394?pid=490830&backurl =http%3a%2f%2fsearch.ancestry.com%2f%2fcgi-bin%2fsse.dll%3findiv%3d1%26 db%3dUSpassports%26h%3d490830%26tid%3d%26pid%3d%26usePUB%3dtrue %26rhSource%3d60525&treeid=&personid=&hintid=&usePUB=true.
http://interactive.ancestry.com/1174/USM1372_537-0564/1081863?backurl=http:// person.ancestry.com/tree/82308498/person/46462901543/facts/citation/323180 357152/edit/record#?imageId=USM1372_537-0564.

Internet Secondary Sources
http://www.jstor.org.ezproxy2.londonlibrary.co.uk/stable/pdf/41298718.pdf?_ =1468943665649, "The Bergson Benda Affair."
http://www.jstor.org/stable/42630841?seq=1&cid=pdf-reference#page_scan_tab _contents, Anne Dymond, "Embodying the Nation: Art, Fashion, and Allegorical Women at the 1900 Exposition Universelle," *RACAR: revue d'art canadienne / Canadian Art Review*, vol. 36, no. 2 (2011), 1–14.
http://www.jstor.org/stable/3831896?seq=1#page_scan_tab_contents, Helen Southworth, "Correspondence in Two Cultures: The Social Ties Linking Colette and Virginia Woolf," *Journal of Modern Literature*, vol. 26, no. 2, Virginia Woolf and Others (Winter, 2003), 81–99.

www.jstor.org/stable/1105586, Charles G. Loeb, "The Virginia Law Register: International Marriages," *Virginia Law Review*, vol. 18, no. 11 (March 1913), 802.

http://www.jstor.org/stable/3657097, Elinor A. Accampo, "The Gendered Nature of Contraception in France: Neo-Malthusianism, 1900–1920," *Journal of Interdisciplinary History*, vol. 32, no. 2 (Autumn 2003), 235–262.

http://www.jstor.org/stable/41298985, Robert A. Nye, "Sexuality, Sex Difference and the Cult of Modern Love in the French Third Republic," *Historical Reflections*, Berghahn Books, vol. 20, no. 1 (Winter 1994), 57–76.

http://www.korsakoff_sfn_org.pdf, "S.S. Korsakoff's Psychic Disorder in Conjunction with Peripheral Neuritis," translated by Maurice Victor, M.D., and Paul A. Yakovlev, M.D.

http://www.sfmuseum.net/1906/ew15.html.

http://www.oed.com.ezproxy2.londonlibrary.co.uk/view/Entry/177471?redirected From=shanghaied#eid23170651.

https://books.google.com/books?id=9QfSAAAAMAAJ&pg=PA774&lpg=PA774&dq =history+of+le+robillard&source=bl&ots=I2bQNOtonh&sig=Cbfoy5tzFZ-0cOH4_bOLiHE444H8&hl=en&sa=X&ved=0ahUKEwilp-CigsjOAhXMQyYK HZg7BFQQ6AEIQjAH#v=onepage&q=history%20of%20le%20robillard&f =false, *The Fortnightly Review*, vol. CVI, new series July to December 1919, 773.

http://www.williamwhitepapers.com/pr/AddictionTreatment&RecoveryInAmerica .pdf; catdir.loc.gov/catdir/samples/cam041/2002073459.pdf, Library of Congress, "Treatment of Drinking Problems."

http://ezproxy.nypl.org/login?url=http://search.proquest.com/docview/103129428 ?accountid=35635, *New York Times*.

www.nizkor.org/ftp.cgi/imt/ftp.py?imt//nca/nca-06/nca-06-3766-ps.

Books

Abramovici, Pierre. *Un Rocher bien occupé: Monaco pendant la guerre 1939–1945*. Paris: Éditions Seuil, 2001.

———. *Szkolnikoff: Hitler's Jewish Smuggler*. London: Pen & Sword, 2016.

Baxter, John. *Chronicles of Old Paris: Exploring the Historic City of Light*. New York: Museyon Guides, 2011.

———. *Paris at the End of the World: The City of Light During the Great War 1914–1918*. New York: Harper Perennial, 2014.

———. *We'll Always Have Paris: Sex and Love in the City of Light*. New York: Doubleday, 2005.

Beevor, Antony, and Artemis Cooper. *Paris After the Liberation 1945–1949*. London: Penguin Books, Kindle Edition, 2007.

Benstock, Shari. *Women of the Left Bank: Paris, 1900–1940*. Austin: University of Texas Press, 1999.

Breitman, Richard, Norman J. W. Goda, Timothy Naftali, and Robert Wolfe. *U.S. Intelligence and the Nazis*. New York: Cambridge University Press, 2005.

Castle, Charles. *The Folies-Bergère*. London: Methuen, 1982.

Colhoun, Jack. *Gangsterismo: The United States, Cuba and the Mafia 1933–.1966*, New York: O/R Books, Kindle Edition, 2013.

Cornut-Gentille, Gilles, and Philippe Michel-Thiriet. *Florence Gould: Une Américaine à Paris*. Paris: Mercure de France, 1989.

de Cossart, Michael. *The Food of Love: Princesse Edmond de Polignac (1865–1943) and Her Salon*. London: Hamish Hamilton, 1978.

David, Angie. *Dominique Aury*. Paris: Éditions Léo Scheer, 2006.

Duff Cooper, Alfred. *The Duff Cooper Diaries 1915–1951*. London: Weidenfeld & Nicolson, 2005.

Dyhouse, Carol. *Glamour*. London: Zed Books, 2010.

Eismann, Gael. *Hôtel Majestic: Ordre et sécurité en France occupée (1940–44)*. Paris: Tallandier, 2010.

Feliciano, Hector. *The Lost Museum*. New York: Basic Books, 1997.

Ferro, Alfred. *Historical Dictionary of Paris*. Historical Dictionaries of Cities, No. 4. Lanham Md., and London: Scarecrow Press, 1998.

Flanner, Janet. *Men & Monuments: Profiles of Picasso, Matisse, Braque & Malraux*. London: Da Capo, 1990.

———. *Paris Was Yesterday 1925–1939*, London: Virago Press, 2003.

———.———. Irving Drutman, ed. *Janet Flanner's World: Uncollected Writings, 1932–1975*. New York: Harcourt Brace Jovanovich, 1979.

———. William Shawn, ed. *Paris Journal 1944–1955*. New York: Harcourt Brace Jovanovich, 1965.

———. William Shawn, ed. *Paris Journal 1965–1970*. New York: Harcourt Brace Jovanovich, 1971.

Gallant, Mavis. *Paris Notebooks*. London: Bloomsbury, 1988.

Gallant, Pierre, and Annie Michelle Gall. *Les Années Américaines: La vie de château sur la Côte d'Azur 1918–1940*. Paris: JC Lattès, 1985.

Giolitto, Pierre. *Histoire de la Milice*. Paris: Éditions Perrin, 2002.

Glass, Charles. *Americans in Pairs*. London: Harper Press, 2009.

Gordon, Bertram M., ed. *Historical Dictionary of World War II France: The Occupation, Vichy and the Resistance, 1938–1946*. Westport, CT: Greenwood Press, 1998.

Green, Nancy L. *The Other Americans in Paris: Businessmen, Countesses, Wayward Youth, 1880–1941*. Chicago: University of Chicago Press, 2014.

Guehenno, Jean. *Journal des années noires (1940–1944)*. 10th ed. Paris: Éditions Gallimard, 1947.

Guillet, Jean-Luc. *American's Riviera: Les années folles*. Paris: Equinox, 2005.

Herbert, David. *Second Son*. London: Peter Owen, 1972.

Hilton, Lisa. *The Horror of Love*. London: Weidenfeld & Nicolson, 2011.

Hitler, Adolf. *Hitler's Secret Book*. New York: Grove Press, 1962.

Hoving, Thomas. *Making the Mummies Dance*. New York: Simon & Schuster, 1993.

Hoyt, Edwin P. *The Goulds: A Social History*. New York: Weybright and Talley, 1969.

Hughes, Alex, and Keith Reader, eds. *Encyclopaedie of French Culture*. London: Routledge, 1998.

Hutton, Patrick H., ed.-in-chief. *Historical Dictionary of the Third French Republic 1870–1940*, vols. 1–.2, London: Greenwood Press, 1986.

Israel, Lee. *Estée Lauder: Beyond the Magic*. New York: Macmillan, 1985.

Jackson, Jeffrey H. *Paris Under Water*. New York: Palgrave Macmillan, 2010.

Jankowski, Paul F. *Stavisky: A Confidence Man in the Republic of Virtue*. New York: Cornell University Press, 2002.

Kahan, Sylvia. *Music's Modern Muse*. Rochester, NY: University of Rochester Press, 2003.

Kitson, Simon. *The Hunt for Nazi Spies*. Chicago: University of Chicago Press, 2008.

Léautaud, Paul. *Journal Littéraire*, vols. 14–15. Paris: Mercure de France, 1963.

———. *Journal Littéraire*, vols. 16–17. Paris: Mercure de France, 1964.

Levenstein, Harvey. *Seductive Journey: American Tourists in France from Jefferson to the Jazz Age*. Chicago: University of Chicago Press, 1998.

Lord, James. *Six Exceptional Women*. New York: Farrar Straus & Giroux, 1994.

Laub, Thomas J. *After the Fall: German Policy in Occupied France 1940–1944*. Oxford: Oxford University Press, 2010.

Markus, Hugh Brian. *The History of the German Accounting Profession*. London: Taylor Francis, 1997.

Marrus, M.R., and Robert O. Paxton. *Vichy France and the Jews*. New York: Basic Books, 1981.

Nelson, Michael. *Americans and the Making of the Riviera*. London: McFarland & Co., 2008.

Ogden, Dunbar H., Douglas McDermott, and Robert Károly Sarlós. *Theatre West: Impact and Image*. Atlanta, GA: Rodopi, 1990.

Paxton, Robert O., Olivier Corpet, and Claire Paulhan. *Collaboration and Resistance: French Literary Life under the Nazi Occupation*. New York: Five Ties, 2009.

Peyrefitte, Roger. *Propos Sécrets*. Paris: Albin Michel, 1977.

Riding, Alan. *And the Show Went On: Cultural Life in Nazi Occupied Paris*. London: Duckworth Overlook, 2012.

Ronald, Susan. *Hitler's Art Thief: Hildebrand Gurlitt, the Nazis and the Looting of Europe's Treasures*. New York, St. Martin's Press, 2015.

Rosbottom, Ronald. *When Paris Went Dark: The City of Light Under German Occupation, 1940–44*. London: John Murray, 2015.

Schwartz, David G. *Roll the Bones: The History of Gambling*. Casino ed.. Las Vegas: Winchester Books, Kindle Edition, 2013.

Sebba, Anne. *Les Parisiennes: How the Women of Paris Lived, Loved and Died in the 1940s*. London: Weidenfeld & Nicolson, 2016.

Serre, Magali. *Les Wildenstein*. Paris, JC Lattès, 2013.

Vaughan, Hal. *Sleeping with the Enemy: Coco Chanel, Nazi Agent*. London: Chatto & Windus, 2011.

Wiser, William. *The Crazy Years: Paris in the Twenties*. London: Thames & Hudson, 1983.

INDEX

Abetz, Otto, 178–81, 193, 200–1, 202, 210, 222–3, 225, 240, 331
Abetz, Suzanne, 178, 200
the Abwehr (Nazi intelligence), 200, 266, 270, 331, 332
Académie des Beaux-Arts, 308, 317
Académie Française, 191, 308
Action Française, 95, 172, 191, 196, 337
Adenauer, Konrad, 304, 332
Aerobank, 254–9, 280, 292, 303, 334
the *Affaire*, 22–3, 23*n*, 38, 95–6, 187
Aiken, Charles, 7
Aitken, Max, Lord Beaverbrook, 127
Albert, Prince of Monaco, 128
Alcott, Louisa May, 108
Aldrich, Chester Holmes, 174
Aletti, Joseph, 140–2, 145, 147, 160
Alexandre, Serge. *See* Stavisky, Alexandre "Sasha"
Alice, Princess of Monaco, 28–9, 29*n*
Un Allemand à Paris (Heller), 223, 331
Alphand, Hervé, 197, 208
Ambassadeurs Casino, Cannes, 123–5, 136, 170
American Express, 49, 250
American Hospital, Paris, 192, 239, 317
American Lawn Tennis Association, 135
American Library, Paris, 192, 238, 317
American Volunteer Corps, 63
Amphiction (racehorse), 79
Annals of San Francisco, 10
Antibes Seen from the Salis Gardens, 316
anti-Semitism
  the *Affaire*'s contribution to, 22–3, 23*n*
  in France, 22–4, 23*n*, 95, 110, 172, 187, 194–6, 199–201, 220, 222, 235, 243
  in Monaco, 144
  during occupation, 217, 221, 230–2, 235, 243, 250
Apollinaire, Guillaume, 20
Arden, Elizabeth, 152, 153, 311, 360*n*4
Ardenti, Regina, 132
Arland, Marcel, 235, 262, 327
Arletty (Léonie Marie Julie Bathiat), 66, 126, 161, 191–2, 208, 235–6
  Nazi collaboration by, 240, 264–5, 289–90, 327
  Stavisky Affair and, 166–7, 169–73, 187–8, 327, 331

Arnaud, Marcela, 214, 217, 226
Astor, Caroline, 73
Auden, W. H., 193
Aureglia, Louis, 257
Aurore newspaper, 23
Aury, Dominique, 194, 305

Bagnoles Hôtel and Casino du Lac,
   France, 139, 160, 170, 198
La Baïonnette, 62
Baker, Josephine (Freda Josephine
   McDonald), 102, 177, 220, 332
Ballon, Marie-Jeanne. *See* Bell, Marie
Balzac, Honoré de, 17
Bank of International Settlement,
   Switzerland, 172
Banque Charles scheme, 290
   Florence's participation in, 249–60,
   265–6, 267–8, 270–5, 280–3,
   287–8, 292, 293, 295, 300–1, 329,
   332, 334, 335
Banque de France, 179, 208
Barnard, George G., 72
Barnes, Maynard, 227
Barney, Alice Pike, 31, 327
Barney, Natalie Clifford, 30–2, 34,
   59, 327
Barthou, Louis, 144
Bathiat, Léonie Marie Julie. *See* Arletty
Battisti, Amleto, 184–5
Baudoin, Edouard, 122–3, 125, 140–1,
   145–7, 164–5, 183–5, 327
Bazille, Florence "Florinte" Rennesson,
   9, 12–13, 14–20, 325
   death/estate of, 21–2, 25–6, 40–1,
   53–4
Bazille, Jean, 9, 12*n*
Beach, Sylvester, 63, 83
Beach, Sylvia, 63, 83, 101, 192–3, 240,
   240*n*, 330, 332–3
Beaumont, Count Étienne de, 101, 110,
   187, 327
The Beautiful and the Damned
   (Fitzgerald), 85
Beauvoir, Simone de, 232

Bedaux, Charles, 239–40
Bedaux, Fern, 240
Bedaux, Philip, 239
Beer Hall Putsch, 172
Belbeuf, Marquise de "Missy," 35, 65
Bellanger, Jacques, 289–90
Bell, Marie, 161, 233, 235–6, 244, 262,
   270, 273, 327
Bénazet, Jacques, 118–19
Bennet, James Henry, 108
Bennett, James Gordon, Jr., 108
Benoist-Méchin, Jacques, 200
Benoit, Pierre, 116, 130, 181, 191–2, 201,
   233, 235, 307
Benvenuti, Joseph, 266–7, 270, 275, 334
Bérénice (Brasillach), 220
Beresford, Helen Vivien Gould, 91
Beresford, John Graham Hope de la
   Poer, 5th Baron Decies, 91
Berghaus, Bernhard, 259, 300
Bernheim-Jeune, Gaston, 210, 310
Bernheim-Jeune, Josse, 210
Bernstein, Marcel, 310
Biddle, Francis B., 252, 259, 333
Blanc, Camille, 128–9
Blanc, François, 118–20, 122, 128, 137,
   143, 149, 327
Blanc, Louis, 118–19
Blum, Léon, 194, 197, 222
Blumner, Lester, 268
Blum, René, 194
Bluysen, Auguste, 139
Bohemian Club, San Francisco, 11
Bolshevik Revolution of 1917, 63,
   109, 281
Bonaparte, Napoléon, I, 311
Bonaparte, Napoléon, III, 17, 124
Bonnard, Pierre, 149, 220, 310, 313
Bosch, Hieronymus, 235
Bosse, Colonel, 216, 217, 229, 240
Bouquet of Flowers in a Vase, 316
Bousquet, Marie-Louise, 200, 223,
   225–6, 227, 232–5, 246, 279, 289,
   327, 331
Boussac, Marcel, 253

Brancovan, Princesse de, 95–6
Braque, Georges, 38, 101, 236, 279, 310, 317, 327
Brasillach, Robert, 169, 196, 200, 220, 222, 264, 279–80
Briand, Aristide, 156
Brougham, Lord Henry, 107, 137
Bryant, Louise, 206
The Buccaneers (Wharton), 32
Bullard, Eugene, 63
Bullitt, William C., 206–7, 219–20, 227, 297, 333
Bunau-Varilla, Philippe, 144
Bunjes, Hermann, 211
Burke, Albert, 134–6
Burke, Billie, 75
Burke, Tom, 134

Café de Paris, Monte Carlo, 120
Caffery, Jefferson, 269, 282
Cagoule sect, France, 198, 337
Cahill, John T., 259–60, 274, 291, 299, 301, 302, 333
Calais-Méditerranée Express, 122
Callas, Maria, 1
Camus, Albert, 280, 329
Cannes Film Festival, 296
Cannes, France, 135, 296
    casinos in, 123–5, 136, 137, 170
Capote, Truman, 31
Carbone, Paul, 253
Carleton Hotel, Cannes, 135
Carlton Casino, Cannes, 124
Carmen, 7
Caruso, Enrico, 7
Casasus, Don Joaquin de, 80
Casasus, Mario, 80–1
Casino de Juan-les-Pins, 122, 136, 165
Casino de la Jetée, Nice, 124, 132
Casino de la Variétés, Nice, 143
Casino de Paris, Monte Carlo, 149
Casino Ruhl, Nice, 124
casinos, 117
    Gould's, 118–29, 130–9, 140–51, 160, 163–7, 182–6, 252–3

    money laundered via, 123–4, 167, 185
    regulation of, 123–4, 145–7, 164, 182–6
Casteja, Emmeline de, 264
Castellane, Count Marie Paul Ernest Boniface "Boni" de, 32–3, 75, 91, 134, 135, 232, 325
Catherine the Great (of Russia), 311
Catholic Sisters of Charity, 20
Caudle, Theron L., 274
Céline (Louis Ferdinand Auguste Destouches), 232, 233, 264, 328
Cercle Rive Gauche, 200, 337
cercles (private gambling clubs), 124, 337
CFA. See Comité France-Allemagne
Chaigneau, Alfred, 11–12, 328, 329
Chalon, Jean, 314
Chambrun, Aldebert de, 239
Chambrun, Clara de, 238
Chambrun, Josée de, 161, 192, 283, 289, 328
Chambrun, René de, 161, 181, 187, 192, 201, 231, 236, 238–9, 243, 289, 328
Chanel, Gabrielle "Coco," 60, 96, 109–11, 126, 170, 186–7, 193, 199–200, 208, 240, 264, 301, 328, 334
Chaplin, Sir Charles, 65, 78, 130, 133, 135, 154–8, 159, 334
Chaplin, Stanley, 154, 156
Chapouilly, Edouard-Charles, 189
Charles, Baron Johann, 255–7, 259, 267, 300, 334
Charles III, Prince of Monaco, 120, 120n
Chase National Bank, 250–2, 259–60, 274
Cheri (Colette), 115
Chevalier, Maurice, 64–6, 93, 137, 161, 225, 297, 306, 328
Chiappe, Jean, 172
Chicago Tribune, 112, 150

Chronique d'une passion (Jouhandeau), 279

Churchill, Lady Randolph (Jennie Jerome), 29, 108

Churchill, Sir Winston, 29, 108, 187, 206, 213, 264, 301

City Lights, 156

Clarke, Sir Casper Purdon, 313

Clemenceau, Georges, 22–3

Clemmons, Katherine, 76, 326

Cluny Museum, Paris, 210–11

Cocteau, Jean, 35, 100, 116, 153, 161, 208, 221–2, 224, 246, 288, 317, 328

Cold War, 283, 295, 297, 302, 305

Colette, Sidonie-Gabrielle, 29, 35, 35*n*, 64–5, 101, 115, 187, 209, 236, 317, 328

Combat, 280

Combourg (racehorse), 79

Comité France-Allemagne (CFA), 178, 181, 201, 337

communism, 168–9, 202, 221, 222, 293–5, 302

Connolly, Cyril, 115, 118

Conservatoire de Paris, 54, 59

Cornuché, Eugène, 113

Coubertin, Pierre de, 181

Coughlin, Charles, 251

Courbet (painter), 316

Coward, Noël, 174

Le Crapouillot, 224

Crédit Municipale, Bayonne, 169–72

Crocker, Charles, 13

Crowder, Henry, 102

CSAR (Comité Sécret d'Action Révolutionnaire), 198

Cunard, Nancy, 102

Curie, Marie, 60–1

Czechoslovakia's invasion, 202

Daily Telegraph (London), 21

Daladier, Edouard, 168–9, 222

Dalbane, Marthe, 144

Dalbouse, Jacques, 182–3

Dali, Salvador, 297, 310

Dante (Alighieri), 108

Darracq, François, 142–3, 145

Daughters, Donald L., 273, 286–7, 302, 333

Daval, Pierre Auguste, 119–20

Davenport, Mrs. George, 174

David-Weill, David, 210

D-Day, WW II, 257–8, 261–75

Debrec, Edouard, 11

Debussy, Claude, 35, 330

Degas (painter), 309, 316

de Gaulle, Charles, 209, 264, 280, 289, 293, 328, 329, 330

de Haas, Irmela, 303

Delano, William Adams, 174

de Lesseps, Ferdinand, 50

Delpierre, Alfred, 129

de Montherlant, Henry, 200

de Noël, Jean, 288, 308, 317, 329

Dequenne, Geo, 97

Dequoy, Roger, 230–1, 238, 269, 328

Derval, Paul, 66

de Sairigné, Anne Marie Vilbert, 260, 270, 290–2

Descazes, Isabelle-Blanche Singer, 60, 153

Descazes, Jacques, 60

Deslys, Gaby, 27, 42

Destouches, Louis. *See* Céline

Deutsche Bank, 88

Deutsche Waren Treuhand-Aktiengesellschaft, 253, 281

DeVoe, Bessie, 78

de Wolfe, Elsie, 201

DGER (Direction Générale des Études et Recherches), France, 228, 268–70, 273, 275, 281–2, 287–8, 293, 327

Diaghilev, Serge, 35, 37–8, 103, 110, 114, 330

Dialogues upon Republican and Monarchial Government (Brougham), 107

Dierks, Barry, 308

The Divine Comedy (Dante), 108

Dmitri, Grand Duke of Russia, 96, 109, 136

Dr. Gachet, 315

Donovan, William, 287

Dostoyevsky, Fyodor, 119

Doumergue, Gaston, 155

Dreiser, Theodore, 140

Drew, Daniel, 72

Dreyfus, Alfred, 22–3, 23*n*, 38, 95–6, 187

Drieu de la Rochelle, Pierre, 181, 200, 222, 224, 232, 264, 280, 328

Dubuffet, Jean, 236, 310

Ducros, Georges, 197

Dudley, Katherine, 240

Dumas, Alexandre, 139

Duncan, Isadora, 31, 96, 108–9, 131

Du Pasquier, Pierre, 253–6, 258–9, 281, 287, 328–9

Durand-Ruel art dealership, 316

Dux, Pierre, 203

earthquake of 1906, San Francisco, 3–7, 12–13, 14

L'Echo du Pacifique, 11

L'Éclaireur de Nice, 183

Les Éditions de Minuit, 223, 264

Edward VIII, King of United Kingdom, 161, 240

Eichmann, Adolf, 302

Einstein, Albert, 156

Eisenhower, Dwight D., 295

Emery, Audrey, 136

Epting, Karl, 223

Erie Railroad, 72–3

ERR (German), 210–11

Evening World, 90

Expatriation Act of 1907, U.S., 24–5

Experta, 239, 253, 281

Exposition Universelle of 1900, 27

Fabre-Luce, Alfred, 294

Fairbanks, Douglas, 137, 155

Fantin-Latour, Henri, 316

Faucigny-Lucinge, Prince Jean-Louis de, 101, 129, 209, 294, 329

Fayard, Jean, 232

FBI

  Rückwanderer Mark Scheme and, 250–1

  war crime investigation by, 216, 259, 269–75, 285–7, 294–5, 300–4, 329

Fellowes, Daisy, 153, 264, 329

Ferdinand, Archduke Franz, 41

Le Figaro, 118, 181

"Final Solution" (Nazi), 196

Fitzgerald, F. Scott, 85, 101, 102, 106, 114–15, 117, 125, 130–2, 192, 333

Fitzgerald, Zelda, 114, 125, 130–2, 135, 333

Flanner, Janet, 102

Fleming, Julia, 78

Fleurs d'Été, 316

Les fleurs de tarbes (Paulhan), 192

flood of 1910, Paris, 18–21

Focke-Wulf, 215–16, 258, 266, 269, 303

Folies Bergère, Paris, 27, 35, 42, 59, 64–6, 93, 103, 161

Foreign Legion, 63

Foujita (painter), 83

"Four Hundred" list, 73, 73*n*, 87, 111

Fournier, Pierre, 234

France. *See also* occupation of France; Riviera, French

  American immigrants to, 100–5

  anti-Semitism in, 22–4, 23*n*, 95, 110, 172, 187, 194–6, 199–201, 220, 222, 235, 243

  Battle of, 205, 219

  Dreyfus scandal in, 22–3, 23*n*, 38, 95–6, 187

  internal unrest in, 168–73

  Jewish immigrants to, 195–6, 195*n*

  occupation, WW II, of, 23*n*, 205–18, 219–29, 230–7, 238–47, 248–60, 261–4

  Panama Canal scandal in, 187, 187*n*

  Stavisky scandal in, 166–7, 168–73, 177, 187–8, 327, 331

  voting rights in, 194, 194*n*, 293

France (*continued*)
  war crime investigation by, 228,
    268–70, 273, 275, 281–2, 287–8,
    293, 327
  in WW I, 37, 39, 43–9
France, Anatole, 22, 43
Francezon, Mr., 213, 216
Franco-American Committee for the
    War Blind, 61
Le Franco-Californien, 10–13, 326,
    328, 329
Franco-Prussian War (1870–71),
    22–3, 34
French, Stewart, 287

Gabin, Jean, 66
Galerie Charpentier, Paris, 225, 269,
    310, 316
Gallauziaux, Mr., 292, 329
Galliard, Miss (Nazi spy), 227
Gallia Tennis Courts, Cannes, 135
Gallimard, Gaston, 222–3, 329
Galtier-Boissière, Jean, 221, 224
Gandhi, Mahatma, 178
Garat, Henri, 159–60
Garat, Joseph, 171–2
Garnier, Charles, 17
Garthe, Arnold, "Colonel Patrick,"
    225–7, 237, 243, 282, 331, 332
Le Gaulois, 95
Gausebeck, August T., 249–59, 267
Gauthier-Villars, Henry "Willy," 35, 65
Gehlen, Reinhard, 284
General Committee for Polish
    Relief, 61
Un gentilhomme cosmopolite
    (Faucigny-Lucinge), 101
Georges, Alphonse Joseph, 214, 250,
    273, 287, 329
Germany. *See also* Nazi Party; World
    War II
  denazification program in, 305
  in WW I, 37, 39, 43–9
Gestapo, 209, 217, 228, 244, 264, 266,
    274

Gibbons, Helen Davenport, 20
Gide, André, 192, 221, 308, 317, 329
Gigi (Colette), 29
Giustizia e Libertà, 198
Goddard, Paulette, 157–8
Goepel, Erhard, 245
Goering, Franz, 300–1
Gold, Nathan, 69
Gold Rush, U.S., 7–8
Göring Corporation, 215–16, 258
Göring, Hermann, 210–11, 225, 228–9,
    249, 251, 255, 258–9, 289, 301
Gorlitius Matinus, 196
Gould, Anna (Frank's sister), 74*n*,
    134, 135, 165*n*, 174, 232, 294,
    311, 315
  salon by, 32–3
  siblings' relations with, 74–6, 87–8,
    90–1, 325
Gould, Dorothy (Frank's daughter), 77,
    121, 165, 298–302, 325, 326
Gould, Edith Kingdon (George's
    1st wife), 76, 87, 97
Gould, Edith Maud Kelly (Frank's
    2nd wife), 64, 68, 78–83, 87–8,
    90–1, 93–4, 96–9, 100, 132, 157,
    325, 334
Gould, Edwin (Frank's brother), 73–4,
    74*n*, 87–8, 325
Gould, Florence Juliette Antoinette
    Lacaze, 325
  Allied Forces support by, 203–4,
    207–9, 228, 244, 273–4
  art collection of, 39, 149, 206–7,
    210–12, 227–8, 231, 245, 252,
    268–9, 297, 309–11, 313–14,
    315–17
  banking scheme collusion by,
    249–60, 265–6, 267–8, 270–5,
    280–3, 287–8, 292, 295, 300–1,
    329, 332, 334, 335
  birth/childhood of, 3–13, 14–21
  casino/hotel operations by, 118–29,
    130–9, 140–51, 160, 163–7, 182–6,
    252–3

Chaplin's relationship with, 155–8, 159

charitable giving by, 137–8, 148, 192, 292, 296, 308, 312–14

death of, 4, 314, 318

in earthquake of 1906, 3–7, 12–13, 14

in flood of 1910, 18–21

Gould's courtship of, 64, 67, 75, 80, 81–2, 87–98

Gould's death and, 298–302

Gould's marriage to, 97–9, 132–6, 155–8, 159–60, 176–7, 217, 266, 270, 272, 274, 290–3, 326

gray mice network of, 225, 227, 234, 241, 248, 252, 289, 327

health of, 138, 314

Heynemann's marriage to, 40–9, 50–7, 77, 97–8, 112, 150, 326

inheritances of, 21–6, 29, 40–9, 53–4, 341n18

legacy of, 315–19

in Legion of Honor, 308

Manigler's relationship with, 161–3

nationality of, 4, 24–5, 40–1, 47–9, 124, 165, 340n4

Nazi ties to, 176, 178–82, 210–12, 213, 217–18, 224–6, 228–9, 231–2, 236–7, 238, 241, 243–4, 249–60, 262–75, 280–3, 287–8, 292, 295

opera singing by, 15, 17, 27, 29–30, 36, 41, 46, 54, 59, 64, 96–7, 237

Paris relocation by, 12–13, 14–17, 58

Riviera residency by, 105, 106–17, 118–29, 130–9, 140–51, 207, 288, 308–14

salon hosted by, 233–6, 244–7, 288–9, 296–7, 306, 308, 317, 327–31

salons coveted by, 30–6, 64

San Francisco residency of, 3–13, 49, 50–7, 75

as showgirl, 64–7

treason investigation of, 267–75, 280–3, 287–8, 292, 295, 300–1, 333

Vogel's relationship with, 213, 217, 226, 228–9, 231–2, 236–7, 238, 241, 243–4, 248–9, 263–5, 285–6, 295, 304

as WW I nurse, 61–2

as WW II nurse, 204, 207, 274

Gould, Frank Jay (Florence's 2nd husband)

alcohol use by, 77, 79–80, 89–90, 95, 97, 99, 100, 100n

banking scheme and, 255–6, 260, 275, 290

casino/hotel operations by, 118–29, 130–9, 140–51, 160, 163–7, 182–6, 252–3

charitable giving by, 77n, 137–8, 298, 313–14

death of, 298–303

de Sairigné's relationship with, 260, 270, 290–2

Edith Kelly's marriage to, 64, 68, 78–83, 87–8, 90–1, 93–4, 96–9, 100, 132, 157, 325, 334

Florence's courtship by, 64, 67, 75, 80, 81–2, 87–98

Florence's marriage to, 97–9, 132–6, 155–8, 159–60, 176–7, 217, 266, 270, 272, 274, 290–3, 326

health of, 100, 111–12, 121, 138–9, 184, 198–9, 203, 217, 231, 266, 268, 331

Helen Kelly's marriage to, 33, 77–8, 326

Riviera residency by, 105, 106–17, 118–29, 130–9, 140–51, 207, 228, 231, 241

sibling relations/feuds with, 68–76, 87–92, 97–8, 326

taxes paid by, 68, 77, 99, 122, 147, 164, 175–6, 204–5, 301–2, 326

Gould, George Jay (Frank's brother), 13, 69, 74–6, 74n

siblings' relations with, 32–3, 87–92, 97–8, 326

Gould, Guinevere Jeanne Sinclair
   (George's 2nd wife), 76, 87, 91,
   97–8
Gould, Helen (Frank's daughter), 77,
   121, 257, 298–300, 325, 326
Gould, Helen Day Miller (Frank's
   mother), 73, 326
Gould, Helen Kelly (Frank's 1st wife),
   33, 77–8, 326
Gould, Howard (Frank's brother), 69,
   74–6, 74n, 78, 326
Gould, Jason "Jay" (Frank's father), 13,
   77, 90, 92, 123, 286
   background of, 69–73
   death/estate of, 74–5, 326
   Jewish ties to, 242
Gould, John Burr (Frank's
   grandfather), 69
Gouldsboro, New York, 70
Goustiaux, Auguste, 11, 329
Grace, Princess of Monaco, 4, 29n,
   309
Grady, Michael, 6
Granville, France, 163, 170, 199
gray mice prostitute network, 225, 227,
   234, 241, 248, 252, 289, 327
Great Depression, 153–7, 160–1, 165,
   172, 214
The Great Gatsby (Fitzgerald), 106,
   114–15, 117, 333
Greffulhe, Élisabeth, 37–8, 95–6, 101,
   329
Grew, Joseph, 282
Grimaldi dynasty, 120, 123–4, 128–9
Le Gringoire, 283
Grom, Hans, 300–1
Grosvenor, Hugh, Duke of
   Westminster ("Bendor"), 110, 187,
   264, 301, 334
Grynszpan, Herschel, 200
Guéhenno, Jean, 229
Guevara, Alvaro, 153
Guilbert, Yvette, 42
Guillaumont, Charles, 122–3
Guinness, Meraud, 153

Guisan, Henri, 214, 250–1, 256, 257
Guisan, Jean, 210, 214, 217, 227, 250–2,
   257, 258, 281
Guitry, Sacha, 236
Gurlitt, Cornelius, 196
Gurlitt, Hildebrand, 196, 245

Haberstock, Karl, 231
Hahn, Reynaldo, 35, 96
Hamburg-Amerika Line, 250
d'Harcourt, Antoinette, 208
Hargreaves, Henry, 48
Hari, Mata, 31
Harper's Bazaar, 223, 289, 327
Harriman, Edward, 13, 32, 76, 89n
Harriman, Oliver, 32
Harte, Bret, 11
Haussmann, Georges-Eugène, 17–18
A Hawking Party, 313–14
Heald, Henry T., 298
Hearst, William Randolph, 134
Heine, Marie Alice, 28–9, 29n
Heinz, F. Augustus, 88
Heller, Gerhard, 223–4, 232–5, 237,
   245, 262–3, 279, 331
Hemingway, Ernest, 37, 50, 62, 83, 101,
   102, 104, 114, 125, 192–3, 333
Hemingway, Hadley, 114, 125
Henri-Haye, Gaston, 201, 242
Hermann, Madame Kurt, 310
Hess, Rudolf, 180
Heynemann, Alice M. Hotchkiss, 40,
   42, 44–5, 47, 52, 54, 57
Heynemann, Henry Chittenden, 39
   Florence's marriage to, 40–9, 50–7,
   77, 97–8, 112, 150, 326
Heynemann, James, 40–2
Heynemann, Manfred H., 40, 41
Himmler, Heinrich, 242, 255
Hirth, Wolfram, 285–6
Hitler, Adolf, 161, 172, 231, 256, 317,
   352n3. See also Nazi Party
   assassination attempt on, 263
Hitler Youth, 180
Hogan, Hugh, 52

the Holocaust, 303, 317
Holocaust Expropriated Art
  Restitution (HEAR) Act (2016),
  317
Homo, Magdeleine, 161, 177, 203, 228,
  273–4, 290, 298–9, 302, 311, 329
Hoover, Edgar J., 251, 259, 269, 271,
  274, 283, 285–7, 294–5, 300–4,
  332, 333
Hopkins, Mark, 13
Horscher, Mr. (restaurateur), 238, 267
Hôtel Alba, Juan-les-Pins, 136, 298
Hôtel Bristol, Paris, 211, 217–18, 219,
  224, 228, 231–3, 236–7, 247
Hôtel du Cap, Antibes, 111, 113–14,
  116, 124–5, 141, 330
Hôtel/Casino Castellamare Nice,
  145–6
Hôtel des Deux Plages, Juan-les-Pins,
  136
Hôtel Impérial, Menton, 141
Hôtel Majestic, Nice, 141
Hôtel Le Meurice, Paris, 247, 308
Hôtel Negresco, Nice, 142–3
Hôtel de Paris, Monte Carlo, 120,
  136, 143
Hôtel Provençal, Juan-les-Pins, 123,
  125, 136, 160
Hôtel Ruhl, Nice, 140, 142
Hoving, Tom, 312–13, 333
Howard, Kathleen, 103
*How I Won and Lost Anna Gould's
  Millions* (Castellane), 134
Hughes, Langston, 102
Hugo, Victor, 19, 194
Huisman, Philippe, 309
L'Humanité, 43
Huntington, Collis P., 13

IEQJ (Nazi Jewish affairs bureau), 210,
  230, 242, 244, 338
L'Illustration, 62, 126
Interkommerz, 250–1, 258
Internal Revenue Service (IRS), 99,
  204, 301–2

Iribe, Paul, 187
Italy, in WW II, 241–3, 254

Jackson, Sumner, 239
Jacob, Max, 194, 317
Jamet, Annie, 200
Jannis, Elsie, 92
Japan, in WW II, 231
Jaspar, Marcel-Henri, 197
Jaurès, Jean, 43
Jay Gould and Co., 70
Jazz at Juan Festival, 126
Jefferson, Thomas, 107
Jerome, Jennie. *See* Churchill, Lady
  Randolph
Jerrold, Laurence, 21
Je suis partout, 196, 222, 280
The Jews (Peyrefitte), 307
J. Henry Schroder company, 250
Josephine, Empress of France, 311
Jouhandeau, Élise, 235–6
Jouhandeau, Marcel, 223, 233–6, 246,
  262, 264, 270–1, 277, 279–80, 288,
  297, 308, 329
Le Journal, 169, 181
Jouvenel, Bertrand de, 115
Jouvenel, Henri de, 115
Joyce, James, 101, 192, 332
Joyce, Peggy Hopkins, 155
Juan-les-Pins, France, 113–17, 207, 231,
  241, 288
  casinos/hotels in, 122–7, 129, 136,
  160, 165, 170, 297–8
Judith with Head of Holofernes, 313–14
Jünger, Ernst, 61, 233–4, 237, 238,
  244–5, 263–4, 279, 305, 309, 331

Kahnweiler, Daniel, 230
Kann, Alphonse, 210, 230
Keeley Institute, U.S., 89
Kelly, Grace, 4, 29n
Kelly, Hetty, 78
Kelly, Martin J., 290–1
Kennedy, Edward, 271–3
Kennedy, Joseph, 137, 271

Kirtland, Bessie (aka Odette Tyler), 76
Klingeberg, Werner, 214, 226–7, 282, 332
Knickerbocker Panic of 1907, 88
Knochen, Helmut, 217, 242–3, 248, 253–4, 265, 282, 304–5, 332
Königlichen National-Galerie, Berlin, 39
Korsakoff Syndrome, 100, 100n, 231
Krausen, Captain, 226
Kremling, George, 226–7
Kriegsgefahr ultimatum, 43
Kropf, Emil, 215
Krupp, Gustav, 249
Kuhn, Loeb & Co., 89
Kunstschutz (Nazi arts office), 209, 211, 223, 338

Lacaze, Berthe Josephine Rennesson Bazille (Florence's mother), 52, 95, 97, 132, 162, 326, 331
background of, 8–9
death of, 203
inheritance to, 21–6, 29, 40–9, 53–4, 341n18
marriage of, 8–13, 16–17, 21–6
Paris relocation by, 12–13, 14–17
Lacaze, Isabelle (Florence's sister), 9–10, 12–13, 14–26, 29, 40, 42, 97, 132, 177, 203, 228, 252, 258, 288, 299, 326, 341n18
Lacaze, Louis, 21–2
Lacaze, Maximin Victoire (Florence's father), 340n4
background of, 7–8, 112
death/estate of, 21–6, 40–1, 52–3, 341n18
as Le Franco-Californien editor, 10–13, 326, 328
marriage of, 8–13, 16–17
The Lancet, 108
Landscape with Rising Sun, 316
Langstaff, B. Meredith, 287
Lansky, Meyer, 185
Lanvin, Jeanne, 199

L'Assomoir, 316
Lauder, Estée, 311–12, 333
Lauder, Joseph, 312
Laurencin, Marie, 200, 236, 238, 247, 279, 288–9, 317, 329–30
Laurent, Vianay, 106
Laval, Pierre, 206, 231, 236, 239, 243, 283, 289n, 328
Law, George, 72
Lawrence, D. H., 35, 115, 138
Leahy, William, 209, 227–8
Lean, David, 296
Léautaud, Paul, 133, 236, 238, 245–7, 262, 264, 279, 288, 297
Lecesne, Guillaume, 257
Lee, David, 71–2
Legion of Honor, France, 64, 148, 156, 182, 308, 332
Leiris, Louise, 230
Lenglen, Suzanne, 125, 135
Léon, René, 129, 143–5, 148–51, 154, 163–4
Lépine, Louis, 19
Les lettres françaises, 279–80
Les Lettres portugaises de Marianna Alcoforado, 310–11
Leupp, Charles, 70–2
Lewis, Lady Orr, 308
Little Women (Alcott), 108
Loeb, Charles G., 22–6, 29, 40–1, 46–8, 80, 83, 97, 333
London Treaty of 1943, 268
Lorroy, France, 18
Louis II, Prince of Monaco, 128, 163–5, 253–4, 281, 287, 329, 334
Luce, Henry, 239
Luchaire, Jean, 200
Luciano, Lucky, 185
Ludwig of Hessen-Homburg, 119
Luftwaffe (Nazi air force), 209, 216, 249, 255, 258–9
Lupin, Arsène, 169

MacCausland, Mabel, 78
Machiavelli, Niccolò, 87

La Machine de Marly et le Barrage, 310

MacLeish, Archibald, 116

Madonna and Child Enthroned with Eight Male Saints, 316

Maison, Leon, 52

Making the Mummies Dance (Hoving), 312

M-Aktion operation, 211

Malraux, André, 317

Manet (painter), 310

Manigler, Madeleine, 161–3, 174, 176–7, 231, 238, 311, 314, 329–30

Mansfield, Katherine, 138

the Maquis (anti-Nazi force), 270, 290, 331

Marais, Jean, 208, 328

Maria, Doña, 127

Mari, Alexandre, 145–7

Marie-Antoinette, Queen of France, 34, 265

Marlborough, Duke of, 28, 61

Marshall, John W., 8

Martinez Casino, Cannes, 124

Marx, Harpo, 125, 133, 155

Masson, André, 239

Matheson, William L., 301–2

Matisse, Henri, 101, 108, 115, 209, 220, 288, 310–11, 317

Mauriac, François, 280

Maurras, Charles, 191, 196, 200

Max Jacob Prize for Poetry, 317

Maxwell, Elsa, 144, 153, 156, 288

McCarthy, Joe, 295, 305

McCoy, H. M., 287

McCue, James T., 303

McDonald, Freda Josephine. *See* Baker, Josephine

Mead, Mrs. William Rutherford, 174

Médecin, Jean, 182, 186

Medicus, Franz, 210, 282, 284, 332

Mein Kampf (Hitler), 179, 352n3

Melchior, Marie Charles Jean, Marquis de Polignac, 159, 174, 178, 181–2, 201, 226, 330, 332

Mendes-France, Pierre, 304

Metropolitan Museum of Art, New York City, 312–14, 317, 333, 334

Mexican-American War (1846–48), 8, 340n6

Meyer, Arthur, 95–6

Mikhailovich, Grand Duke Michel, 109

the Milice (French pro-Nazi force), 243–4, 257, 264, 338

Miller, Arthur, 14

Mr. and Mrs. Haddock Abroad (Stewart), 111

Mistinguett, 65–6, 93, 159, 225

Mitford, Nancy, 195, 293, 330

Modern Times, 158

the Mogador, Paris, 93

Monaco, 127–9. *See also* Banque Charles scheme; Monte Carlo gambling's origins in, 119–20

Le Monégasque, 144

Monet, Claude, 162, 228, 316

money laundering
via casinos, 123–4, 167, 182, 185
via Nazi banking scheme, 249–60, 265–6, 267–8, 270–5, 280–3, 287–8, 290, 292, 293, 295, 300–1, 329, 332, 333, 334, 335

Monnier, Adrienne, 101, 192, 330

Monte Carlo. *See also* Banque Charles scheme
casinos/hotels in, 120, 124, 127–9, 136, 143–5, 148–51, 154, 163–4, 166, 173, 182–6, 252–4, 258–9, 267, 275, 327, 329, 335
founding of, 120

Montenach, Baron Jean de, 257

Montesquiou d'Artagnan, Pierre de, 79

Montesquiou, Robert de, 33

Monuments Men, WW II, 305, 313, 334

Moore, Grace, 130

Moreau-Vauthier, Paul, 27

Morgan, Anne, 192

Morgan, J. Pierpont, 28, 48–9, 76, 192

Morgenthau, Henry, 251, 258, 271–2

Moss, L. Harold, 302
Moulin Rouge, Paris, 42, 59, 103, 159
Mousley, Harry, 78
Mühlmann, Kajetan, 245
Mullan, George V., 94
Munich Agreement (1938), 200
Municipal Casino, Nice, 124, 143, 184,
    186, 198
MUNIMIM (Nazi department), 229,
    265
Munson, William H., 287
Murger, Henri, 11
Murphy, Gerald, 102, 105, 114, 116–17,
    125, 130–3, 330, 333, 334
Murphy, Sara, 102, 105, 110, 114,
    116–17, 125, 130–2, 330, 333, 334
Musée d'Orsay, Paris, 308
Mussolini, Benito, 156, 254

NASA, 284
Nast, Condé, 193
Nature Morte aux Quatre Pêches, 316
Nazi Party (NSDAP), 195. See also
    occupation of France; World War II
  Abwehr of, 200
  Austria-Germany unification by, 199
  banking schemes by, 249–60, 265–6,
    267–8, 270–5, 280–3, 287–8, 290,
    292, 293, 295, 300–1, 329, 332, 333,
    334, 335
  Battle of France by, 205, 219
  Battle of Stalingrad by, 241, 243
  Czechoslovakia's invasion by, 202
  escape, postwar, of, 267, 281–2, 302
  "Final Solution" of, 196
  Florence's ties to, 176, 178–82,
    210–12, 213, 217–18, 224–6,
    228–9, 231–2, 236–7, 238, 241,
    243–4, 249–60, 262–75, 280–3,
    287–8, 292, 295
  France's cultural campaign by,
    178–82, 199–201, 235
  France's occupation by, 23n, 205–75,
    280–3, 287–8, 289, 290, 292, 293,
    295, 300–1, 304, 305, 310, 313,

316–17, 327, 329, 331, 332, 333,
    334, 335
  Kristallnacht by, 200
  Poland's invasion by, 202
  Rhineland's occupation by, 193
  Vogel's membership in, 216, 285
Needles and Pins, 94
Negri, Pola, 136
Neosalvarsan, 99, 99n, 138
Neutrality Act, U.S., 251
New Yorker, 102
New York Herald, 93, 108, 175
New York Overseas Corporation, 250
New York Sun, 173, 176
New York Times, 78, 79, 91, 267,
    275, 312
New York University, 77, 308
  Frank's donations to, 77n, 298
New York World, 94
Neyer, Christian, 303
Nice, France, 124, 129, 132, 137–9,
    140–3, 145–8, 149–51, 160, 164–7,
    170, 173, 182–6, 198
Nicholas II, Czar of Russia, 109
Nijinsky, Vaslav, 38, 65, 103
Nixon, Richard, 295
Noailles, Marie-Laure de, 200, 208,
    225, 330
Notre Temps, 200
Nouvelle Revue Française (NRF), 192,
    202, 222–3, 327, 328, 329
Nuremberg Laws of 1935 (Nazi), 196
Nuremberg Trials, 303, 331, 333

Oakland Tribune, 51–2
Oberg, Carl Albrecht ("Butcher of
    Paris"), 217, 241–2, 253, 304–5,
    327, 332
occupation of France, 23n
  American roundup during, 238–40
  art thefts during, 205–12, 217–18,
    223, 227–8, 230–1, 237, 245,
    268–9, 305, 310, 313, 316–17, 334
  black market in, 226, 228–9, 245–7,
    265, 268, 332

cultural activities during, 220–2, 225, 232–6, 244–7

D-Day in, 257–8, 261–75

gray mice prostitute network in, 225, 227, 234, 241, 248, 252, 289, 327

Jewish oppression under, 221–2, 225, 230–2, 239, 241–2, 244, 250, 268–9

the Milice support of, 243–4, 257, 264, 338

Nazi banking scheme during, 249–60, 265–6, 267–8, 270–5, 280–3, 287–8, 290, 292, 293, 295, 300–1, 329, 332, 333, 334, 335

prisoner releases during, 236, 239

the Resistance during, 214, 239, 244, 262, 270, 273–4, 290, 304, 331, 332

Vichy government during, 209, 219, 222, 225, 227, 231, 236, 238–9, 241–4, 261

Odewald, Walter, 241–3, 282

Olympic Games/Committee, 181, 214, 226, 330, 332

On the Marble Cliffs (Jünger), 234, 244

Operation Paperclip (U.S.), 284–5, 332

Operation Safehaven (U.S.), 258, 282–3, 305

Operation Sea Lion (Nazi), 234

Organisation Todt (Nazi), 216–17, 221, 273

Organisation Otto (Nazi), 216, 228–9

Orloff, Count, 311

Orwell, George, 193

OSS, (Office of Strategic Services), U.S., 212, 212n, 216, 228, 244, 247, 274, 282–3, 287, 293, 338

Paderewski, Ignace, 61

Palais de la Méditerranée, Nice, 141–3, 145–8, 149–51, 160, 164–7, 173, 182–6, 198

Palewski, Gaston, 293–4, 311, 326, 330

Panama Canal, 50

scandal, 187, 187n

Paquin, Jeanne, 27–8, 110

Paris. See also France; occupation of France

cultural salons of, 30–6, 59, 64, 220–1, 225, 233–6, 244–7, 288–9, 296–7, 306, 308, 317, 327, 330

flood of 1910 in, 18–21

modernization of, 17–18

occupation, WW II, of, 23n, 205–75, 280–3, 287–8, 289, 290, 292, 293, 295, 300–1, 304, 305, 310, 313, 316–17, 327, 329, 331, 332, 333, 334, 335

WW I's impact on, 41–4, 58–67, 82–3

La Parisienne, 27–8

Paris-Soir, 169

Paris with the Lid Lifted (Reynolds), 104

Parker, Dorothy, 102, 114, 334

Passos, John Dos, 62, 101, 111

Patou, Jean, 59

Paulhan, Jean, 192–3, 194, 222–3, 235, 245–7, 262, 264, 270, 273, 279–80, 305, 308, 329

Pearl Harbor attack, 231

Pêches, 310

Pellier, Lazare, 299

Le Peril Juif (The Jewish Peril) (Jouhandeau), 235, 329

Perkins, Maxwell, 114

Pétain, Maréchal Philippe, 137, 204, 206, 209, 219, 231, 236, 239, 244, 261, 289n, 330

Peter, Marcel, 282

Le Petit Parisien, 282

Peyrefitte, Roger, 307

Le Phare, 11

Picasso, Olga, 114, 125

Picasso, Pablo, 38, 83, 101, 114–15, 125, 132–3, 209, 220, 334–5

Pichot, Henri, 180

Pickford, Mary, 137, 155

Pivoines, 316

Plard, Henri, 305

Platzek, M. Warley, 91
Poincaré, Raymond, 61
Poiret, Paul, 59, 66, 110
The Poisoned Paradise (Service), 128
Poland's invasion, 202, 245
Polignac, Edmond, Prince de, 34, 96, 214
Polignac, Henri de, 60
Polignac, Melchior de. *See* Melchior, Marie Charles Jean, Marquis de Polignac
Polignac Prize, 35
Polignac, Winnaretta de. *See* Singer, Winnaretta, Princesse de Polignac
Polignac, Yolande, Duchesse de, 34
Porter, Cole, 102, 105, 113, 219, 334
Porter, Russell, 300
Praeger-Gretsch, Willy, 227, 282, 332
Pratt, Zadoc, 70–2
Prin, Alice "Kiki," 116
Prohibition (U.S.), 102, 115, 147, 151, 151*n*
Prophylactic Institute, Paris, 137–8, 233, 266
Propos Secrets (Peyrefitte), 307
Proust, Marcel, 22, 35, 58, 59, 96, 100, 101
Pugnaire, Marc, 299
Pulitzer, Joseph, 73, 90, 94
The Pursuit of Love (Mitford), 293

Radziwill, Léon, 129, 143–4
Radziwill, Princess Louise, 331
Rainier III, Prince of Monaco, 29*n*, 120*n*, 128, 309, 334
Rarig, Frederick, 252, 259
Ravel, Maurice, 35, 330
Ray, Man, 116
Red Cross, 20
Reed, Anna, 32
Reichsbank (German), 222, 243, 250, 254–6, 287, 300
Reichswerke Hermann Göring, 255
Renoir (painter), 228, 309

the *Résistance*, French, 214, 239, 244, 262, 273–4, 304, 332
via the Maquis, 270, 290, 331
Retour de l'U.R.S.S. (Gide), 221
Revson, Charles, 311
Reynolds, Bruce, 104
Ribbentrop, Joachim von, 178´–80, 200, 215, 255, 261, 331
Ritz, César, 141
Ritz, Leone, 80, 308
Riviera, French, 105–6. *See also* Cannes, France; Juan-les-Pins, France; Monaco; Monte Carlo; Nice, France
as cultural hub, 107–17
Robert C. Mayer & Co., 249–50
Roberts, Quincey, 292
Roblot, Émile, 254, 256, 257, 281, 287, 335
Rochefoucauld, Armand de la, 125, 131, 159, 174, 330, 331
Rockefeller, John D., 88
Rodin, Auguste, 82
Roger, Gustavus, 93
Roger Nimier Prize for Literature, 317
Roissard de Bellet, Baron, 137
Rombaldi, T., 242
Roosevelt, Eleanor, 248
Roosevelt, Franklin D., 161, 206, 219–20, 295
Rorimer, James, 313, 319, 334
Rosenberg, Paul, 210, 230
Rosselli, Carlo, 198
Rosselli, Nello, 198
Rothschild, Baron Edouard de, 79, 131, 153, 208, 210, 211–12, 230
Rothschild, Baron Maurice de, 161, 230
Rozan Chocolats, 210, 226
Rubinstein, Helena, 29–30, 153, 192, 281, 311
Rückwanderer Mark Scheme, 250–2
Ruhl, Henri, 113, 123, 124, 140, 142, 143, 145, 259, 275, 330

salons, 30
  Anna Gould's, 32–3
  Barney's, 31–2, 34, 59, 327
  Florence's, 233–6, 244–7, 288–9, 296–7, 306, 308, 317
  Florence's performances at, 64
  during occupation, 220–1, 225
  Polignoc's, 33–6, 330
Salvarsan, 99n, 138
San Francisco, 6n, 11
  earthquake of 1906, 3–7, 12–13, 14
  Florence's residence in, 3–13, 49, 50–7, 75
San Francisco Call, 12, 21
San Francisco Chronicle, 11, 51, 55–6, 82, 98
Sappho (poet), 31
Sartre, Jean-Paul, 62, 221, 232
Saturday Evening Post, 103
Saurès, André, 191
SBM casino company (Société des Bains de Mer), 127–9, 143–5, 148–51, 154, 163–4, 166, 173, 182–6, 252–4, 258–9, 267, 275, 327, 329, 335
  founding of, 119–20
Scènes de la vie bohème (Murger), 11
Scey-Montbéliard, Prince Louis de, 34
Schacht, Hjalmar, 249–50
Schaeffer, Karl, 208, 243, 255, 258, 287
Schellenberg, Walter, 254–6, 301
Schempp, Reinhold, 214
Schiller, Friedrich, 205
Schlesser, Emma, 217
Schloss, Adolphe, 230
Schlumberger, Jean, 192, 329
Schrader, Gerhard, 284
Seine River, France, 14, 18–21
Seligman, Jesse, 242
Seligmann, François-Gérard, 210
Sella, Antoine, 116, 125, 330
Seneca (philosopher), 89
A Sentimental Journey Through France and Italy (Sterne), 107
Sert, José Maria, 101, 110

Sert, Marie "Misia," 110–11
Service, Robert, 128
Shakespeare and Company, Paris, 101, 192–3, 240n, 332–3
Shakespeare, William, 159
Shepard, Finley J., 77
Shepard, Helen Gould (Frank's sister), 73–6, 74n, 87, 92, 242, 326
Sherman Anti-Trust Law, U.S., 68
Shirer, William, 150–1
Simenon, Georges, 169
Simpson, Mrs. Wallis, 161, 196, 199, 240
Singer, Isaac Merritt, 28, 28n, 34, 330
Singer, Isabella Eugénie Boyer, 34
Singer, Paris, 96
Singer, Winnaretta, Princesse de Polignac, 33–6, 60–1, 95–6, 101, 153, 199, 209, 225, 247, 264, 329, 330
Singh, Maharajah Bhupinder, 109
Sisley, Alfred, 310
Sixte de Bourbon-Parma, Prince, 331
Sixte de Bourbon-Parma, Princesse Hedwige, 204, 263, 273, 287, 330–1
Smith, Ada "Bricktop," 102, 334
Smollett, Tobias, 107
Snow, Carmel, 289
Société du Palais de la Méditerranée, 183
Société Fermière du Palais de la Méditerranée, 182–4, 186
Société Immobilière du Palais Vénitien, 182–3
Société Nationale des Constructions Aéronautiques du Sud-Quest (SNCASO), 213, 216, 258
Soehring, Hans Jürgen, 240, 289, 327
"Sonia" (Frank mistress), 80
Sotheby's, 316, 318
Soviet Union, 37–8, 43
  Battle of Stalingrad by, 241, 243
  Bolshevik Revolution in, 63, 109, 281
  Cold War by, 283, 295, 297, 302, 305

Spain, 193
Nazi flight to, 267, 281–2
Les Spélugues, Monaco, 120
Spender, Stephen, 193
SR (French intelligence service), 179
Stalin, Joseph, 215
Standard Oil, 215–16
Stanford, Leland, 13
Stavisky, Alexandre "Sasha," 126,
166–7, 168–73, 177, 187–8, 327, 331
Steffens, Walter, 227–8, 282, 332
Stein, Gertrude, 15, 24, 30, 31, 63, 101,
220, 334
Stein, Leo, 15
Sterne, Laurence, 107–8
Stevenson, Adlai E., 295
Stevenson, Robert Louis, 35
Stewart, Donald Ogden, 111
Storm of Steel (Jünger), 234
Stravinsky, Igor, 35, 38, 103, 110
Strughold, Hurbertus, 284
Sunset magazine, 7
Sutter, John, 8
Swanson, Gloria, 137
syphilis, 99, 99n, 100, 138
Szkolnikoff, Michel, 253–4, 256–9,
266–8, 273, 275, 281–3, 334, 335

Tagliaferro, Magda, 64, 95
Talleyrand-Périgord, Hélène-Violette
de, 294, 311, 326, 330
Talleyrand-Périgord, Hélie de, Duc de
Sagan, 32–3, 87, 325, 326
Tartière, Drue (Drue Leyton), 240
Taylor, George H., 92, 148–9
Teal, Margaret, 78
Tellier, Cécile, 15–16, 31, 41–2, 48, 64,
132, 162, 203, 228, 299, 302, 311,
331
Le Témoin, 187
The Tempest (Shakespeare), 159
Tender Is the Night (Fitzgerald), 115,
125
La Terrasse de Vernon, 313
Theroux, Alexander, 27

Thibergian Group, 257
Thoeny, Richard F., 287
Thomas, Henri, 305
Thomasson, Robert de, 159, 181, 239,
244, 262, 273, 279, 331
Thorez, Maurice, 168–9
Three Dancers, 309, 316
Thyssen, Fritz, 249
Time magazine, 239
To Have or Have Not (Hemingway), 193
Toklas, Alice B., 24, 101, 220, 334
Toronto Star Weekly, 104
Toulouse-Lautrec (painter), 316
Towarnicki, Frédéric de, 305
Trafficante, Santo, 185
Travels Through France and Italy
(Smollett), 107
Treaty of Guadelupe Hidalgo (1848), 8
Treaty of Versailles (1918), 83, 193, 223
Treville, René de, 262
Truman, Harry S., 295
Twain, Mark, 3, 9, 103

Union of French Women, 20
United Kingdom, 202, 205, 234
United States (U.S.). See also FBI; OSS
earthquake of 1906 in, 3–7, 12–13, 14
Gold Rush in, 7–8
Nazis' emigration to, 214–15, 216,
284–7, 294–5, 303–4, 332
WW II entry by, 231
WW I troops from, 63

Val-de-Grâce Hospital, Paris, 204, 207
Valentino, Rudolph, 125, 133, 135
Vallat, Xavier, 244
Valmy, duc de, 120
Valois & Loeb, 22
Vanderbilt, Alice, 73
Vanderbilt, Consuelo, 28, 61
Vanderbilt, Cornelius, 71, 72–3
Vanderbilt, William, 28, 79
Van Gogh, Vincent, 245, 309, 315–16
Vaudable, Octave, 238
Vernes, Arthur, 137–8, 233, 246, 299

Vichy, France, 170, 207–8
  as occupied government seat, 209,
    219, 222, 225, 227, 231, 236, 238–9,
    241–4, 261
Victoria, Queen of United Kingdom, 119
La Vie Parisienne, 62
Vionovitch (Nazi soldier), 207, 226
On vit mal (Life is Hard) (Guéhenno),
  229
Viviani, René, 43, 82
Vivien, Renée, 31–2
Vogel, Carl Ludwig Adolf, 290
  black market activities of, 228–9,
    265, 268, 332
  Florence's relationship with, 213–14,
    216–17, 226, 228–9, 231–2, 236–7,
    238, 241, 243–4, 248–9, 256, 258,
    263–70, 274
  Nazi Party membership by, 216, 285
  U.S. emigration by, 214–15, 216,
    284–7, 294–5, 303–4, 332
  war crime investigation of, 267–9,
    273, 280, 283, 285–7, 333, 335
  as X-2 agent, 269–70, 274, 285
Vogel, Elfriede K. Elsner, 216, 304
Vogel, Renate, 216, 304
Vogue, 193, 305
Volstead Act, U.S., 102, 151n
vom Rath, Ernst, 200
von Behr, Kurt, 210–11
von Blomberg, Werner, 215
von Braun, Wernher, 284
von Choltitz, Dieter, 216
von Derwies, Paul, 109
von Dincklage, Hans Gunther "Spatz,"
  200, 240, 328
von Metternich, Count, 211, 223
von Schirach, Baldur, 180
Vue de l'atélier, 310
Vues sur l'Europe (Saurès), 191

Wagner-Rogers Bill, U.S. (1939), 251
Walker, Lola, 173
Wall Street Crash of 1929, 148–9, 151,
  152–4

The Wall Street Journal, 91, 128
Walsin-Esterhazy, Ferdinand, 23
Ward, Justine B., 174
Warzinski, Hans Dietrich, 238, 248,
  256, 267, 280, 292, 300, 332
Washington, George, 230
Washington Post, 91
Washington Principles, 316–17
Washington Times, 81
Wertheimer, Pierre, 186–7
Westminster Kennel Club, 78
Weygand, Maxime, 189
Wharton, Edith, 24, 32, 62–3, 108
Whistler, James McNeill, 31
Wiborg, Mary Hoyt, 110
Wildenstein, Daniel, 161–2, 230–1, 237,
  245, 269, 297, 309–10, 316, 328,
  330, 331
Wildenstein, Félix, 174
Wildenstein, Georges, 174, 309
Wildenstein, Nathan, 174, 297
Wildenstein, Sylvia, 310
Wilde, Oscar, 31
Wilder, Billy, 296
Wilhelm II, Kaiser of Germany,
  37, 39
Willard, Marian, 192
Wills, Helen, 135
Wilson, Peter C., 318
Wilson, Woodrow, 83
Windsor, Duke and Duchess of, 161,
  196, 199, 240
Wiper Times, 224
women's voting rights, 194, 194n, 293
Woodhouse, Lindy, 311
The World, 73
World War I (WW I) (1914–18), 58–9n,
  58–67, 61–2, 82–3
  Armistice Day in, 241
  outbreak of, 39, 41–9
World War II (WW II) (1939–45)
  African campaign in, 241, 243, 250
  Battle of France in, 205, 219
  Battle of Stalingrad in, 241, 243
  casualties in, 205

World War II (*continued*)
  D-Day in, 257–8, 261–75
  France's occupation in, 23*n*, 205–75,
    280–3, 287–8, 289, 290, 292, 293,
    295, 300–1, 304, 305, 310, 313,
    316–17, 327, 329, 331, 332, 333,
    334, 335
  lead-up to, 178–82, 191, 193–202
  U.S.'s entry into, 231
  war crime investigations post-,
    264–75, 280–3, 285–90, 293–5,
    300–1, 302–5
Worth, Gaston, 28, 32

X-2 unit, U.S., 269–70, 274, 285

Yesenin, Sergei, 96

Zaharoff, Zacharias Basileios "Sir
    Basil," 127–9, 335
Zanini, Diego, 216–17, 270, 273,
    335
Ziegfeld, Florenz, 65, 66, 175
Zographos, Nico, 149–50, 164,
    170, 186
Zola, Émile, 23, 104
Zweig, Stefan, 43